The strategic management of, and innovation with, information technology resources remains a key and sometimes vexed issue - the more so when aspects of these critical resources are outsourced. A key to success includes careful husbanding of inter-organisational relationships and an understanding of the added complexities of the digital age. *The Routledge Companion to Managing Digital Outsourcing* deals head-on with these issues. Written in a theoretically sound but clearly accessible manner, the book is an essential read for deep thinking practitioners and Master's level students alike.

Bob Galliers, The University Distinguished Professor Emeritus
and former Provost, Bentley University, USA

Essential reading for business executives motivated to build sustainable digital partnerships over time and better their sourcing outcomes.

Eric van Heck, Professor of Information Management and Markets,
Erasmus University Rotterdam, Netherlands.

This volume offers a wonderful compendium of chapters on outsourcing that range from traditional topics such as offshore outsourcing and contractual/compliance issues to a treasure trove of forward-looking topics including the influence of new business models and technology on the outsourcing partnerships, socially-responsible outsourcing, governing multi-vendor IT outsourcing relationships and cloud computing services, blockchains, and the Internet of Things. The chapters provide insights on governing complex client/vendor relationships under turbulence. While theoretically grounded to appeal to the academic and master student audience, business practitioners too can benefit from understandable discussions of important emerging outsourcing issues and rich case studies.

Carol S. Saunders PhD, Professor Emeritus,
University of Central Florida, USA

THE ROUTLEDGE COMPANION TO MANAGING DIGITAL OUTSOURCING

This unique comprehensive collection presents the latest multi-disciplinary research in strategic digital outsourcing and digital business strategy, providing a management decision-making framework for successful long-term relationships and collaboration based on trust and governance.

- **Part 1: Innovation in Business Models and Digital Outsourcing** takes an internal company perspective on strategic digital outsourcing, and the importance of trust in outsourcing relationships.
- **Part 2: Inter-Organizational Relations and Transfer** explores topics underpinning service recipients and service suppliers' relationships including governance, knowledge transfer and legal aspects.
- **Part 3: From On-Site to Cloud** discusses the challenges presented by moving to a Cloud environment, including risks and controls.
- **Part 4: Developments to Come** explores emerging technologies and their impact on digital outsourcing such as blockchain and the Internet of Things.

In a fiercely competitive market, companies must transform their business models and embrace new approaches. This companion provides a comprehensive management overview of strategic digital outsourcing and is an invaluable resource for researchers and advanced students in business and strategic information management, as well as a timely resource for systems professionals.

Erik Beulen is a full professor at Tilburg University and the Academic Director for the executive MSc Information Management and core faculty for the executive MSc IT-audit at TIAS School for Business and Society at Tilburg University – the Netherlands. He created and lectures Managing Disruptive Technology at Manchester Business School (MBS) - in-class as well as online lectures. He is also an academic supervisor/coach of the Global MBS Live Business Projects.

Additionally, Erik has 25 years of international industry and consulting experience. Starting his career in global infrastructure & application outsourcing at Atos, he then moved to Accenture and spent five years within global application outsourcing, performing international business development roles and global delivery management roles. He led global contracting engagements and advised CXOs in developing and implementing their global (technology) strategy as well as leading engagements for global corporate clients with global delivery centers in China, India, Brazil and the US. He joined KPMG, followed by the Boston Consulting Group and Alvarez & Marsal, advising global clients and working from many client locations including Indonesia, Russia, Thailand, Switzerland, UK and US. His consulting engagements include digital transformations, benchmarks and audits.

Since January 2020 he has been the chairman of XBRL the Netherlands (https://nl.xbrl. org) and since 2017 has been a board member of Sourcing Nederland which is an association to develop & share learnings in partnering/outsourcing (https://sourcingnederland.nl).

Pieter M. Ribbers graduated in Economics from Tilburg University in 1971, specializing in supply chain management and in 1980 obtained his doctorate cum laude. His career began as assistant professor at the Limburg School of Economics in Hasselt, Belgium, where he was appointed Full Professor of Organization and Information Systems and Chairman of the Department of Business Administration. In 1986 he was appointed as full professor of Information Management at the school of Economics and Management of Tilburg University where he was responsible for the development of research and education in this new and emerging field. He served the university as Chairman of the Department of Information Management and Accountancy and as Dean of the School of Economics. His teaching and research interests in the impact of IS/IT on business organizations led to him joining Washington University in St. Louis, USA as Affiliate Professor at the School of Technology and Information Management from 1995–1999.

ROUTLEDGE COMPANIONS IN BUSINESS, MANAGEMENT AND ACCOUNTING

Routledge Companions in Business, Management and Accounting are prestige reference works providing an overview of a whole subject area or sub-discipline. These books survey the state of the discipline including emerging and cutting-edge areas. Providing a comprehensive, up to date, definitive work of reference, Routledge Companions can be cited as an authoritative source on the subject.

A key aspect of these Routledge Companions is their international scope and relevance. Edited by an array of highly regarded scholars, these volumes also benefit from teams of contributors which reflect an international range of perspectives.

Individually, Routledge Companions in Business, Management and Accounting provide an impactful one-stop-shop resource for each theme covered. Collectively, they represent a comprehensive learning and research resource for researchers, postgraduate students and practitioners.

Published titles in this

THE ROUTLEDGE COMPANION TO ACCOUNTING HISTORY, 2ND EDITION
Edited by John Richard Edwards and Stephen Walker

THE ROUTLEDGE COMPANION TO MANAGING DIGITAL OUTSOURCING
Edited by Erik Beulen and Pieter M. Ribbers

THE ROUTLEDGE COMPANION TO HAPPINESS AT WORK
Edited by Joan Marques

THE ROUTLEDGE COMPANION TO ANTHROPOLOGY AND BUSINESS
Edited by Raza Mir and Anne-Laure Fayard

For more information about this series, please visit: www.routledge.com/Routledge-Companions-in-Business-Management-and-Accounting/book-series/RCBMA

THE ROUTLEDGE COMPANION TO MANAGING DIGITAL OUTSOURCING

Edited by
Erik Beulen and Pieter M. Ribbers

LONDON AND NEW YORK

First published 2020
by Routledge
4 Park Square, Milton Park, Abingdon, Oxon OX14 4RN
605 Third Avenue, New York, NY 10017

First issued in paperback 2023

Routledge is an imprint of the Taylor & Francis Group, an informa business

© 2020 selection and editorial matter, Erik Beulen and Pieter M. Ribbers;
individual chapters, the contributors

Publisher's Note
The publisher has gone to great lengths to ensure the quality of this
reprint but points out that some imperfections in the original copies
may be apparent.

British Library Cataloguing-in-Publication Data
A catalogue record for this book is available from the British Library

Library of Congress Cataloging-in-Publication Data
A catalog record has been requested for this book

ISBN-13: 978-1-138-48937-0 (hbk)
ISBN-13: 978-1-03-265257-3 (pbk)
ISBN-13: 978-1-351-03778-5 (ebk)

DOI: 10.4324/9781351037785

Typeset in Bembo
by codeMantra

CONTENTS

Contents

CONTRIBUTORS

Ron Babin teaches IT Management in graduate and executive programs at Ryerson University, with an emphasis on outsourcing and digital transformation. His background as a consulting partner at KPMG and at Accenture provides a practical perspective on emerging technology management issues, such as disruptive innovation in outsourcing.

Marcel Baron, Senior Managing Consultant, digital strategy & iX, IBM Global Services.

Robert J. Benson has served as Professor, Researcher, author and consultant in the strategic management of information technology. Currently, he is focusing on authorship and consulting. He has worked and taught/lectured in companies and government agencies in 20 countries and in over 100 companies and organizations. He has been a senior executive in computing and a part-time professor of information management at Washington University, USA, and professor of information systems at Tilburg University, the Netherlands, where he taught at TIAS for 35 years. He has co-authored four books on IT management, most recently *Trust and Partnership: Strategic IT Management for Turbulent Times* (together with P. Ribbers), Wiley, 2014. Previously, he co-authored *Information Economics* (Prentice-Hall, 1988), *Information Strategy and Economics* Prentice-Hall 1989), and *From Business Strategy to IT Action*, Wiley 2004, and has written many book chapters and articles.

Dissa R. Chandra is a Lecturer in Department of Industrial Engineering, Bandung Institute of Technology (ITB), Indonesia. Her research focus is on the implementation and management of information systems in industrial context.

Arjan Eriks is a Managing Director at Schuberg Philis.

Juan Manuel Gonzalez Muñoz, MSc, is Partner and Practice Lead of the Sourcing/Cloud Advisory practice of Quint Iberia. He advises key clients of Quint all over the world on technology strategy, strategic sourcing and Cloud.

Petter Gottschalk is a Norwegian Professor of IT Strategy employed at the BI Norwegian Business School at its Institute for Leadership and Organizational Management. He is educated Diplom-Kaufmann from Berlin Institute of Technology, Master of Science from Dartmouth College and Massachusetts Institute of Technology and Doctor of Business Administration from Henley Management College and Brunel University.

Steven De Haes, PhD, is Dean of Antwerp Management School and Professor Information Systems Management at the University of Antwerp – Faculty of Business and Economics. He is actively engaged in research and teaching in the domains of IT Governance and Management, IT Strategy and Alignment, IT Value and Performance Management, IT Assurance and Audit, and Information Risk and Security.

André Halckenhaeusser is a PhD Student with the Chair of General Management and Information Systems at the University of Mannheim. His research focuses on competition within digital platform ecosystems as well as on Cloud computing.

Armin Heinzl is a Full Professor and Chairperson in General Management and Information Systems at the University of Mannheim. His research focuses on Cloud Computing, Healthcare IT and platform ecosystems.

Jos van Hillegersberg is a Full Professor in business information systems and the Chairman of the program committee of the Dutch research institute for advanced logistics. His research and projects deal with innovation of supply chains, collaborative businesses and industrial networks using ICT.

Dr. Christopher P. Holland is Professor of Information Management and Director of Decision Sciences at Loughborough University. He is a visiting professor at Münster University and works closely with the European Centre for Information Systems (ERCIS). His research interests are digital strategy, business models and online consumer behavior.

Tim Huygh is a PhD Candidate and Visiting Lecturer at the Department of Management Information Systems in the Faculty of Business and Economics of the University of Antwerp in Belgium. He (co-)authored several books, journal articles and conference proceedings.

Dr. Marijn Janssen is a Full Professor in ICT & Governance of Delft University of Technology. He was nominated in 2018 by Apolitical as one of the 100 most influential people in the Digital Government worldwide (https://apolitical.co/lists/digital-government-world100). For more information, see www.tbm.tudelft.nl/marijnj.

Antje Susanne Koch is employed as IT Project Lead at AXA (DE). In parallel, she is pursuing a PhD at Tilburg University, the Netherlands. She graduated with an Information Management Diploma from Reutlingen University (DE) and an EMBA from Duke University, USA, and Frankfurter University (DE).

Julia Kotlarsky is a Professor of Technology and Global Sourcing at the University of Auckland, New Zealand. Her research and consultancy work revolve around sourcing and innovation of knowledge-intensive business services. Her book *The Handbook of Global Outsourcing and Offshoring* is widely used by practitioners and academics. She is a co-founder of the annual Global Sourcing Workshop (www.globalsourcing.org.uk).

Oliver Krancher is an associate professor at IT University of Copenhagen. His research revolves around learning processes in the development, use and management of IT. He has published in journals such as the *Journal of Management Information Systems* and the *Journal of the Association for Information Systems*.

André Mertel is Managing Director of EWERK Group. He led a large number of complex and business-critical IT transformations, especially in finance industry and energy sector. He is trusted advisor, very knowledgably person for his mandates, and specializes in advising IT strategy and organizational development.

Mathew Mertens is a Technology Advisor at KPMG Belgium. As a key member of both the "IT Strategy and Management" and the "IT Audit" competence groups, Mathew is experienced in assessing and optimizing Enterprise Governance of IT, IT Strategy, IT Risk and Controls.

Dr. Brian Nicholson is Professor of Information Systems at the University of Manchester. His teaching, research and consultancy projects are in the broad area of global outsourcing of software and other business processes. Current research projects are within the Socially Responsible Outsourcing Unit and others focusing on a socio-technical view of ICT for development.

Albert Plugge is a senior research fellow at the Information and Communication Technology Section, Faculty of Technology, Policy and Management, Delft University of Technology, The Netherlands. He lectures on information systems, information technology and supply chain management.

Kiron Ravindran is an Assistant Professor of Information Systems and Technology at IE Business School. His research interests span IT Outsourcing, Contracting, Organizational Networks and Technology-Enabled Innovation. He has published in top academic journals in Information Systems. He has developed and teaches a course on a step-by-step approach to digital transformation.

Dr. Pieter M. Ribbers, emeritus professor at Tilburg University, held the chair of Information Management at the School of Economics and Management. He has served as dean, head of department, academic director of executive programs in Information Management; author and consultant for almost 30 years; and (co-)authored several books and a large number of journal publications.

Anne-Françoise Rutkowski is full professor in Management of Information at Tilburg University, the Netherlands. Her research interests and publications bridged IS and human sciences in addressing topics such as decision making, emotion, processes of attention, overload/underload, as well as socially responsible use of IT. Applications of her work are found mostly in the context of high reliability organization. Results of her research have been published in journals such as *IEEE Computer, Decision Support System* and *MIS Quarterly.* Recently, she co-authored a book entitled *Cognitive and Emotional Overload: The Dark Side of Information Technology* (with Carol Saunders, Routledge, 2018).

Bill Schiano is Professor of Computer Information Systems at Bentley University and a former Director of Bentley's Master of Science in Information Technology program. He has written numerous journal articles and Harvard Business School cases, and co-authored *Teaching with Cases: A Practical Guide.*

Hans Solli-Sæther is a professor at the Department of International Business in Norwegian University of Science and Technology. His research interests include the intersection of strategy, organization and project management with a particular emphasis on topics of outsourcing and offshoring.

Jan Teckemeyer is an Associate Director in Management Consulting Practice at UBS. Before joining UBS, he was Senior Consultant in Deloitte China and Senior Business Consultant in BearingPoint. Jan graduated with MSc in Strategy and International Business from Aston Business School, UK and holds a BA degree from Hamburg School of Business Administration.

Kai Spohrer is an assistant professor in information systems with the University of Mannheim. His research focuses on collaboration and coordination in developing and using information systems. He is the director of content and media of the AIS Special Interest Group in Advances in Sourcing.

Dr. Kees Stuurman is full professor of Regulation of Information Technology at the Tilburg Law School and Legal Director with Considerati, a consultancy for the digital world. He also acts as an independent consultant. Kees has practiced law for over 30 years.

Eddy H.J. Vaassen is a full professor at Tilburg University.

Alex van den Bergh, MSc, is partner and practice lead of the Sourcing/Cloud Advisory practice of Quint Wellington Redwood. He advises key clients of Quint all over the world and is a regular speaker on international conferences on the subject of strategic sourcing and Cloud.

Dr. Ir. Marlies van Steenbergen is principal consultant enterprise architecture at Sogeti Netherlands and professor of Digital Smart Services at Utrecht University of Applied Sciences. She is a frequent lecturer and publisher in both academic and professional outlets and has co-authored several books.

Dr. Erik Wende is co-founder and managing partner of EWERK Group as well as active researcher of strategic information management and digital business at universities of Leipzig and Zurich. Erik is an innovative person and impulse giver. He empowers his clients on their digital journey.

DIGITAL OUTSOURCING

Preface

Objective

Traditional outsourcing was a matter of make-or-buy decisions, based on cost analysis. It concerned a limited number of specific goods and services. Companies engaging in such transactions experienced little interdependence, while their main motive was cost efficiency. Strategic outsourcing changed this picture. The motives, the relationships between the participants and the contract periods do not resemble those of traditional sourcing. The focus of strategic outsourcing is on long-term motives such as gaining access to important resources and capabilities that are better supplied by external parties than developed internally.[1] It is geared toward long-term relationships, collaborative moves in a shared competitive environment. Strategic outsourcing is defined as the way organizations obtain products and services in exchange for returns while considering the long-term impact on the context, scope and external relationships[2] and supplier ecosystems.[3]

Strategic IT outsourcing decisions are an integral part of the longer-term Information Systems strategy and subsequently of the business strategy. For long the relation between the "business strategy" and the "IS/IT strategy" has been difficult. These two areas do not have a good history of mutual understanding. A recent development in this domain is the rise of the "Digital Business Strategy,"[4] to be defined as an "organizational strategy formulated and executed by leveraging digital resources to create differential value."[5] The digital strategy causes a further integration of business and IT. IT potentially impacts all primary and supporting business processes putting more pressure on the business/IT relationship. Digital strategies take strategic outsourcing one step further by enabling the development of innovative business models. How this development impacts the governance and management of IS/IT sourcing decisions is the question that is addressed in this study.

Much recent attention has focused on digital transformations and innovations accelerated by e.g. data mining and Cloud computing but these are a subset of IT-outsourcing relevant aspects. The book takes a broader definition of IT outsourcing to incorporate these trends in a business and management context, including the digital business strategy. The aim is to present the many complex and interrelated issues associated with strategic and digital outsourcing of information systems. This study includes the latest research on digital outsourcing, providing a valuable source of reference to scholars on what is known about digital outsourcing and where further developments are likely to occur. For MBA and Information Systems students taking a course in strategic information management or a similar subject, the book offers a rich source of material on many of the key issues that business and information systems management executives are facing when deciding how and where to source their information services. However, the 19 chapters in this book are not only valuable to academics but also relevant for professionals who are working or intending to work on the area of Information Systems Management:

- Chief Information Officers (CIOs), Chief Financial Officers (CFOs), other senior managers and directors seeking to understand the business and technological issues involved in decisions about digital outsourcing.
- Information systems managers who are developing and implementing digital outsourcing strategies.
- Consultants who seek support and a source of information for the digital outsourcing solutions they suggest to their clients.

Rationale

Fierce competition, ranging from platform companies such as Uber and AirBNB to mature tech companies such as Accenture, Amazon, Facebook, IBM, Google, Oracle and Microsoft entering traditional markets, challenges Chief Executive Officers on their companies' capabilities to transform their business models. CIOs orchestrate the implementation of transformation strategies with help from external IT vendors. However, while digital outsourcing has been for decades on the agenda of CIOs, the current market conditions require a different collaboration with external vendors. Partnerships have to be established and managed. This will result in further growth of the market. In addition to the business challenges, there are regulation and compliancy requirements which increase the challenges CIOs have to deal with.

Content and organization

The book is structured in four parts. Part 1 "Innovation in business models and digital outsourcing" starts the discussion from an internal company perspective and positions the digital outsourcing discussion in a strategic context of understanding the impact of turbulent environment and the requirements of trust on the creation of digital outsourcing relationships (Chapter 1) followed by explanation on changing business models (Chapter 2). The need to be pro-active, and to react to unexpected developments impact the internal structure of the firm (through its enterprise architecture (Chapter 3)). Being agile and applying DevOps in combination with new technologies are necessary requirements to react fast enough in a turbulent environment (Chapter 4) as also the external structure in the supply chain (Chapter 5). The search for efficient capabilities and competences stimulates offshoring (Chapter 6); however, impact sourcing is an emerging requirement (Chapter 7). Part 1 concludes with two case studies. The first is the story of a century-old insurance company and its endeavor to be ambidextrous by developing a digital strategy while managing the going concern (Chapter 8). The second is the case of a retail bank addressing the question whether outsourcing can improve competitive advantage (Chapter 9).

Part 2 "Inter-organizational relations and transfer" moves the discussion to topics that pertain to the relation between services recipient and services supplier. The portfolio of different IT services, needed to enable digital strategies, requires multiple outsourcing, which involves a number of different providers. Adequate governance is a prerequisite for effective coordination of the different providers and for alignment of the service delivery between service providers and recipients. The problem of governing and orchestrating multiple vendors is addressed in Chapter 10. Chapter 11 discusses the problem of knowledge transfer in the transition phase and its implications for digital strategy and agility. The success of these transitions heavily depends on human interaction. Chapter 12 explains KAIWA, a method to facilitate adequate communication between the parties involved. Part 2 ends with a discussion on legal and contractual implications that govern the relationship (Chapter 13).

Part 3 "From on-site to Cloud" provides a discussion on issues that pertain to moving from an on-site to a Cloud environment. Chapter 14 opens with a chapter that describes the transition to mission critical Cloud. Chapter 15 focuses on SaaS-centric platforms, i.e. platforms that provide marketplaces to execute and trade SaaS solutions, and examines which factors help them to attract and retain participants. Cloud computing entails specific risks. Chapter 16 looks at governance of Cloud computing, in particular at risks and mitigating controls. Finally, Chapter 17 raises the issue that adopting a Cloud computing strategy typically involves a one-way migration of IT skills and capabilities out of the organization. This chapter describes, based on a survey, what happens when organizations wish to put an end to such engagements.

In Part 4 "Developments to come" two technological developments and their effect on digital outsourcing are discussed. Chapter 18 analyzes blockchain and other distributed ledgers; Chapter 19 focuses on the Internet of Things.

We will summarize the individual chapters in the introduction to the relevant parts, and hence they are not discussed here.

Erik Beulen
Pieter M. Ribbers

Notes

1 Erik Beulen, Pieter Ribbers and Jan Roos: *Managing IT Outsourcing.* Second edition, Routledge, 2011.
2 Su, N., N. Levina and J. W. Ross: The Long-Tail Strategy of IT Outsourcing. *MIT Sloan Management Review,* 57 (2) (2016) 81.
3 Van der Zee, H and P. van Wijngaarden: *Strategic Sourcing and Partnerships: Challenging Scenarios for IT Alliances in the Network Era.* Addison Wesley Longman, 1999.
4 Joe Peppard and John Ward: *The Strategic Management of Information Systems – Building a Digital Strategy.* Wiley 2016.
5 Anandhi Bharadwai, Omar El Sawy, Paul A. Pavlou, and N. Venkatraman: Digital Business Strategy: Towards a Next Generation of Insights. *MIS Quarterly,* 37(2), (June 2013) 471.

PART 1

Innovation in business models and digital outsourcing

In Chapter 1, Benson and Ribbers turn to the topic of managing outsourcing in turbulent times, and the impact of trust and partnership. Outsourcing relations are becoming increasingly complex and uncertain. Change requires to adapt the sourcing arrangements, uncertainty makes them difficult to predict, which complicates timely adaption. An important question addressed in this chapter is how to shape complex (out)sourcing relationships between services supplier and services recipient. These relationships are shaped to last for a longer term; consequently, it becomes an increasingly pressing question how to deal with uncertainty in the relationship. Related to this, how trust impacts these relationships is a central topic of this chapter.

In Chapter 2, Chris Holland sets the strategic context for (out)sourcing. The strategic role of technology and digital strategies is exemplified by the emergence of new types of business models such as Elimica, Li & Fung, Uber, Didi, Airbnb, Expedia, and Strava. These recent developments raise important questions regarding the way that IT is conceptualized and related to business constructs such as strategy and outsourcing. Does its strategic importance mean that it needs to be controlled closely and "owned" by the business? Or is it possible to outsource technology and treat it as an input function, rather like a raw material or component supplier to a manufacturing business? A different model is to think of relationships between a company and its technology providers as partnerships – these relationships are much more dynamic and can change in response to competitive pressures, new strategic intent, and business performance.

Flexibility in sourcing is an extremely important aspect of modern enterprises, as it determines how fast an enterprise can implement new business models and new manners of collaboration with others. Hence, as Van Steenbergen argues in Chapter 3, this flexibility must be designed into the structure of the enterprise. Enterprise architecture is the discipline that concerns itself with designing the overall structure of the enterprise. Digital sourcing in today's world puts specific requirements on enterprise architecture. Above all, it asks for the ability to quickly respond to changes in the environment, it requires to be able to start and end collaborations with other parties quickly.

In Chapter 4, Schiano extends the discussion to agility. Digital business is enlacing information technology and the IT organization in most or even all of companies' products and services. This has put enormous pressure on traditional approaches in all aspects of IT to transform, and particularly to become more agile. Although the struggle within development organizations is the best-known aspect, the changes have extended beyond development. DevOps is the most famous of these extensions, but the need for agility spans the entire product lifecycle and value chain. Given that most IT organizations spend the majority of their budget outside the organization, sourcing faces particular pressure. This chapter explores how organizations are adapting to these pressures and becoming more agile to meet digital business needs.

Chapter 5, by Van Hillegersberg and Chandra, focuses on inter-organizational relations and their impact on IT sourcing. Supply chains and business networks are dynamic, and subject to forces of disintegration and re-integration. Agility is required to provide value to the end customer. Agility and responsiveness require effective and efficient collaboration between organizations in the network. This can only be realized with properly designed and well-governed IT and information systems. This can be viewed as a new type of alignment – the alignment between inter-organizational services, processes, and governance and the IT and systems that support it. The chapter discusses inter-organizational governance as the interplay between technology and governance and an important part of sustainable collaboration.

In Chapter 6, Solli-Saether and Gottschalk discuss offshore outsourcing. Offshore outsourcing (or short "offshoring") may be defined as the transfer of the responsibility for delivering IT services to one or more providers who deliver these services from a continent different from where the recipient operates[1]. Based on the stages-of-growth model for outsourcing, offshoring, and back-sourcing, the authors suggest a framework to analyze and predict organizational change associated with offshoring. Using the costs, resources, and partnership parameters of the framework, benchmarks applicable to each stage are applied in two business examples. The lessons learned from the experiences of these two examples are useful in analyzing stages, dominant problems at each stage, evolutionary path, and the economies of outsourcing. The findings indicate that companies face different issues, expectations, and benefits, depending on their maturity.

Chapter 7, by Babin and Nicholson, focuses on Socially Responsible Outsourcing (SRO). The practice of offshoring relies on moving work to low-cost locations; it has contributed to a robust outsourcing industry in regions such as India, Africa, China, and south-east Asia. These regions also contain some of the highest populations of poverty. This chapter discusses research on this topic from the last decade in three parts. Part 1 describes the authors' initial 2008–2009 research of the background for Corporate Social Responsibility (CSR) in outsourcing, with an identification of the need for industry standards. Part 2 describes the Rockefeller Foundation's uptake of CSR in outsourcing starting in 2011 and provides an assessment of SRO today. Part 3 describes 2018 plans for the global industry standards for SRO, now referred to as Impact Sourcing. These standards are being defined by an industry consortium called the Global Impact Sourcing Coalition (GISC).

Part 1 closes with two case studies dealing with the critical issues of digital outsourcing. Chapter 8, by Koch, Ribbers, and Rutkowski, focuses on Ambidexterity as it is being developed at AXA Konzern AG. Ambidexterity is defined as the ability to combine two opposing components and to simultaneously manage the exploration of new possibilities as well as the exploitation of old certainties, by introducing Bimodal IT. Bimodal IT illustrates the IT function decomposition into the traditional mode (focusing on stability) and the agile mode (centering on speed and experimentation). The chapter presents the result of an explorative case study conducted at AXA Konzern AG. Particularly, it investigates AXA Konzern AG's exploitative and explorative initiatives which should support its future development in order to overcome disruptive innovations. This chapter outlines, based on a concrete example, the impact of ambidexterity, IT ambidexterity and bimodal IT on business, IT and sourcing strategies.

Kotlarsky and Teckemeyer, in Chapter 9, analyze the possible impact of IT outsourcing on core competences in the banking industry. Today, banks operate in highly competitive and turbulent environment. One of the ways to reduce costs, improve operational efficiencies, and extend offering of online services is considered to be through outsourcing. However, before embarking on an outsourcing journey, it is important to understand whether a high degree of outsourcing means that a bank loses its core competences in banking and therefore only acts as a manager of different external service providers. To address this challenge, this research study aims to assess suitability of value-creating activities of a direct bank to outsourcing, and the implication of outsourcing to bank's competitive advantage.

1

STRATEGIC SOURCING IN TURBULENT TIMES

The impact of trust and partnership[2]

Robert J. Benson and Pieter M. Ribbers

1.1 Introduction

Outsourcing relations are becoming increasingly complex and uncertain. Complex IT-business relationships can typically be defined as multi-site, multi-vendor, internal and external IT – service provisioning relationships. Complexity of a system is basically about the number of elements that form the system and the type of their relations. A sourcing arrangement can be a very complex system dependent on the number of parties that are involved and the type of relationships with them. Change and uncertainty make a system even more complex. Change requires to adapt the sourcing arrangements, uncertainty makes them difficult to predict, which complicates timely adaption.

An important question addressed in this chapter is how to shape complex (out)sourcing relationships between services supplier and services recipient. These relationships are shaped to last for a longer term; consequently, it becomes an increasingly pressing question how to deal with uncertainty in the relationship. Related to this, how trust impacts these relationships is a central topic of this chapter. The structure of the chapter is as follows:

* Section 1.2 sets the context for strategic sourcing. Given the definition of strategic sourcing, we consider sourcing as a service relationship, how digital strategy results in best of breed sourcing, and the necessity of integration. We finalize this section with a discussion of the economic and behavioral contributions to the (out)sourcing discussion and suggest the nature of changes facing managers responsible for sourcing.
* Section 1.3 analyzes the concept of trust. How to define trust, what are its characteristics, and how does it improve business performance? Can trust be built, especially in outsourcing relationships?
* Section 1.4 discusses turbulence, and its organizational impact. The section ends with a discussion on strategic sourcing in the context of turbulence and trust.
* Section 1.5 focuses on how to shape the relationship between service provider and service recipient and discusses the dilemma between contracts and relational management.
* Section 1.6 concludes the discussion by focusing on the significant differences between organizations involved in ICT sourcing, and the implications for executives and managers responsible for the sourcing relationships.

1.2 Strategic sourcing

1.2.1 Strategic sourcing defined

"Sourcing" as a concept originated with the supply-chain and procurement part of the enterprise. The idea is to regularize and manage how an organization acquires the materials it uses in its business. Most often this is in the acquisition of raw or manufactured materials used in the enterprise's products and services.

"Strategic" sourcing in this context refers to the methods with which the enterprise selects and manages its internal or external suppliers. The emphasis here is on establishing long-term relationships between buyer and seller; the term "strategic" suggests the choices made in crafting those relationships would reflect the buyer's business strategies. For example, an enterprise dependent on high-speed response to its own customers' requirements would likely seek out suppliers – its sourcers – capable of meeting those high-speed needs. As a current example, the aircraft manufacturing enterprise, particularly the duopoly of Boeing and Airbus, continues to spend substantial time and resources on crafting the permanent supplier relationships consistent with their needs in supplying their aircraft manufacturing activities.[3]

"Strategic" in this example means two complementary things. First, the aircraft manufactures require a stable and permanent relationship with their suppliers. For example, Spirit Aerosystems has manufactured the major components of the Boeing 737 for nearly 30 years. Second, the manufacturers require their suppliers to support their basic business strategies. For example, Spirit actively works with and supports Boeing strategies for manufacturing and marketing its airplanes, particularly associated with quality, timing, cost, and the management of the overall supply chain.[4]

There are, of course, plenty of books and articles on business strategic sourcing. One interesting whitepaper, *The Strategic Sourcing Lifecycle*, describes at length the process of successfully creating the strategic relationship between buyer and seller in sourcing engagements [1].

"Strategic" also has two different though complementary contexts based on the business situation. In one case where sourcing supplies essential business infrastructure, permanence and reliability and stability over a very long period of time, having a strategic partnerships is essential. However, as described in the following sections, business and technical turbulence adds requirements for flexibility and change in business infrastructure, termed "dynamic capability." In the second case where sourcing contributes directly toward the enterprise's products and services, a more dynamic and time-focused orientation applies, as these products and services will change rapidly in response to industry, market, and customer demands. Both contexts are "strategic" in their own terms.

In effect, the concept of strategic sourcing moves the relationship between buyer and seller from a simple transactional view to a long-term relationship view. This introduces important relationship issues such as trust and partnership between buyer and seller. While this definition of strategic sourcing is based on business supply chain examples, the same characteristics apply when the sourcing involves ICT.

1.2.2 Sourcing information services

As originally developed, ICT sourcing focused on providing fundamental ICT infrastructure such as networks and the operational functions of data centers, and typically was a relationship between one buyer (the ICT organization) and one seller (a large provider such

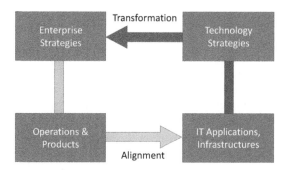

Figure 1.1 Enterprise and technology strategies

as IBM or DXC). But for many enterprises, this relationship also became integral to their products and services, for example in internet-based businesses and in businesses where ICT is the primary service delivery, and customer interface, for example in industries such as financial services.

It is helpful to examine the relationship of the business part of the enterprise and of ICT. Figure 1.1[5] shows how the enterprise strategies flow into ICT infrastructure and applications support, which then flow back as part of technology strategies into change in strategies and operations. Strategic ICT sourcing can be a great contributor, both from the infrastructure and stability perspective – that is, alignment – and from the transformation perspective, providing new transformative operational methods and enterprise strategies. ICT technology strategies also generate innovations to business processes and products/services. Figure 1.1 applies to any enterprise whether or not sourcing is involved. Strategic ICT sourcing creates the strategic relationship, the strategic sourcing of ICT, both for infrastructure and for product/services and competitive strategy support.

Issues about strategic sourcing as mentioned in the whitepaper cited above, and considered in great detail in books and publications, for example from the Supply Chain Institute (one of many important sources about strategic sourcing apply fully in ICT sourcing) [2]. However, differences between business sourcing and ICT sourcing can be blurred. For example, in enterprises that rely on sourced product delivery to their customers such as using Amazon to distribute products, the line between operational sourcing (the delivery) and ICT sourcing (the systems that support customers ordering and scheduling) is blurred, but both can certainly be strategic. For this reason, it can be instructive to consider how business supply-chain sourcing has evolved and is managed.

1.2.3 Demand and supply in strategic ICT sourcing

The business and ICT relationship is described in "supply" and "demand" terms. The supply side reflects back on the basic notion of sourcing ICT – in other words, arranging for and agreeing on the supply relationship with ICT providers. Here though is a critical characteristic. From the perspective of the enterprise and its business units, all ICT sources are sourcers. In other words, if a business unit depends on the corporate ICT department, it is in effect agreeing to obtaining those services from another organizational unit in the enterprise. Whether this unit is inside the corporation or outside does not change the basic dynamic.

By the same token, a business unit's "demand" for ICT services is just that – a decision on what is required for their successful ICT supply. This is in the context of general supply issues – stability, cost, and so forth – but is most certainly also a strategic reflection. The ICT supplier whether inside or out simply has to be consistent with the overall business strategy requirements for the enterprise. Just like the aircraft example cited earlier, the strategic ICT sourcing demand calls for elements of the infrastructure stability, reliability, and cost characteristics, and also the requirements for dynamic capabilities and product and service strategies required for the business. This is true for all parts of ICT supply – internal or sourced. From the ICT governance perspective, these sourcing factors are central to managing the relationship among the various ICT sourcers and the various enterprise business units.

1.2.4 Strategic ICT sourcing and ICT capability

ICT[6] outsourcing can be a critical part of the overall structure the enterprise uses to provide its ICT services throughout the organization and to its customers and suppliers. In very broad terms, strategic IT sourcing is a fundamental business infrastructure strategic characteristic – an infrastructure basic to the organization itself. We describe this infrastructure as the organization's "ICT Capability," defined as the organization-wide capability that depends on the competencies of both enterprise and ICT functions."[7] This is represented in Figure 1.2[8] as a set of relationships within the organization between business units and ICT providers. Strategic ICT sourcing consequently includes one or more of the seven basic capabilities: planning, development, Information Management, service optimization, operational excellence, sourcing itself, and cost/performance management. In this context, strategic ICT sourcing is much more than simply buying/selling ICT services, it is creating long-term relationships and trust capable of providing the rich set of ICT capabilities described here.

Figure 1.2 describes the business side as potentially multiple units. Often these include a corporate set of "back office" business units (e.g., human resources, finance, marketing) and individual business units (with their specific products and services which also include the associated relationships with industries and customers). Figure 1.2 also shows an example of four sets of ICT providers, providing ICT services to the business units. For a particular enterprise, these can include (1) a corporate ICT organization, (2) individual (separate) business unit organizations, (3) externally sourced ICT providers (best example is network and communications, which almost all enterprises would acquire from external enterprises), and (4) what we call "DIY" or do-it-yourself sources where individuals provide ICT support through their individual effects.

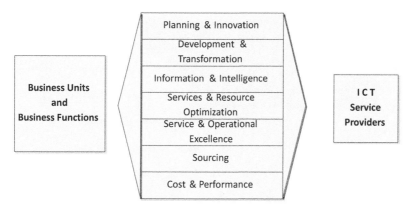

Figure 1.2   Business and ICT relationships

To summarize, strategic ICT sourcing involves the full set of ICT relationships from the business perspective, the demand side, which defines the requirements for and the performance required for the ICT services to be provided by one or more of the service providers. Strategic ICT sourcing consequently also involves the capabilities of ICT service providers to respond to the demand requirements, across the many ICT capabilities required, for the long term and within the context of a trusting and partnership relationship. While the original development of ICT sourcing most often involved just one buyer, typically the corporate ICT organization, and one provider, typically a large ICT enterprise such as IBM or EDS. In today's situation, as Figure 1.2 implies, strategic ICT sourcing can involve multiple providers, working with multiple business units. It has moved from a one-to-one relationship to an *N* to *M* set of relationships.

1.2.5 IT's contribution to business performance

To understand the value of the IT function to the organization and the consequential interactions between business functions and the IT function, we distinguish six service levels of IT to the business [3].

The first is *Service Delivery*. The focus is on operations and infrastructure; the service is reliable and dependable. The IT organization must ensure that basic IT services are delivered against agreed-upon service levels and at agreed costs. At this level, the business views the contribution of the IT function as one that provides agreed upon support for the technology infrastructure that has been deployed.

The second is *Software Configuration and Development*. The IT organization must demonstrate the ability to develop, acquire, and implement technology solutions that satisfy the business process and informational needs. The organization has technical and organizational measures in place to ensure a secure operation. It is at this level that management typically recognizes the critical nature of IT in providing and contributing to successful business operations. The third level of service concerns *Project Development and Benefit Realization*. This area addresses the quality, predictability, and timeliness associated with the deployment of projects. The IT function here expands its impact and contributes to the optimization of business benefits from investments that have a high information technology content.

As Figure 1.3[9] shows, these first levels of service are foundational and represent basic performance levels that the IT organization must master to create and grow trust. If these are not realized the business cannot develop, or at least will be hampered in its development.

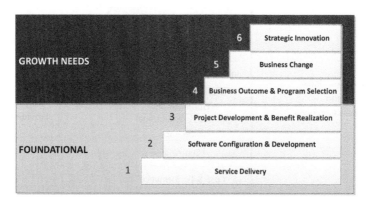

Figure 1.3 Six levels of service

Thus, being able to perform successfully within each of these areas is crucial for any organization, even when the IT function is in a supporting (not strategic) role.

The fourth level of service concerns *Business Outcome and Program Realization*. IT management are active participants and decision makers in the planning and selection of business projects or programs. The IT organization must demonstrate its ability to work closely with the business partners. IT technology trends are not only actively monitored by the IT organization but form an input for business strategic planning, including decisions concerning the strategic sourcing of IT.

The fifth level is *Business Change*. This level refers to the ability to implement business strategy by investing in programs with high levels of IT content. These investments require significant change plans because of their effects on markets, products, structures, processes, procedures, and IT. Plans are thoroughly integrated business and IT change plans.

The sixth level is *Strategic Innovation*, where an organization develops unique uses of IT that form the basis for a radical and sustainable change in its business model. IT has become a driver of innovation. Business strategy development is the result of co-creation. The business vision affects IT solutions, and new IT solutions affect the business vision. On this level, the Digital Business Strategy is created.

The latter three levels of service, concerning the so-called growth needs, need not be addressed to the same extent by every organization. The role of the IT service provider depends on the role that information technology plays in the industry and within the particular firm. If that role is already a strategic one, then indeed these growth needs are present and need to be fulfilled. If that role is limited to back-office, factory-type function, it is unlikely that growth needs will be actively pursued. Consequently, it is not necessary for every organization to develop the responsibility areas in the same way.

The relationship between the IT service provider and the IT service recipient differs with delivering so-called foundational services or growth services. For growth-type services, the IT function moves from a support function to a business partner, critical to the organization's future. It has to mirror business change competences for IT-induced business change.

Of course, successful delivery and implementation of IT services does not depend on the service supplier (internal or external) alone. The business organization should have specific IT competences in this respect. The support role interactions between business and IT are operational/tactical concerned with service delivery to users. Business functions are expected to define their *service requirements*. These have to be met by the IT function's service delivery apparatus. At the next level, business functions need to define their *Information and Process Requirements*, which are the input for *Software Configuration and Development*. For the level of *Project Development and Benefit Realization* closer collaboration between business and IT is critical, where the focus for the business is on *benefit realization*. On this level, it is a primary business responsibility to ensure adequate conditions (like sufficient user/organizational acceptance and training) for optimal implementation and utilization of installed systems.

Being successful with IT on the higher growth levels of IT use (*Business Outcomes and Program Selection, Business Change,* and eventually *Strategic Innovation*) depends as much from the business as from the IT service provider. The capabilities to identify, select, deploy, and implement new IT-based solutions, which are in line with the business strategy, need to exist in the business functions themselves.

These levels are characterized by intense business – IT collaboration. Our prior discussion on the effects of trust is very relevant at this level (in particular *openness-based trust, caring-based trust,* and *reliability-based trust*). Especially relevant is the remark made that for trust to exist at growth levels, it first has to be earned at foundational levels. If the company is not happy with IT's performance and contribution, there will be no room for IT to participate in strategic discussions; the relation with the external services supplier will probably be discontinued.

Uncertainty and change impact IT at each of the levels of service. As for the three foundational levels, uncertainty affects directly the volumes, the required quality, and types of services. Changes in business volume impact the volume of required services and thus the available capacity in terms of machine capacity, bandwidth, staff, and response times. Sudden changes in service requirements (i.e, by changing laws or regulations) require timely software adaptations. Timely communication between the IT service provider (outsourced or in-house) enabling the service provider to make the necessary adjustments is mandatory for a smooth continuity of service delivery. In this respect, the technology of Cloud solutions (e.g., Infrastructure as a Service, Platform as a Service, Software as a Service) offers opportunities of increased agility. It is supposed to allow organizations to get their application up and running faster, and it enables IT organizations to more rapidly adjust resources to meet fluctuating and unpredictable demands [4]. Agile software development approaches, like scrum and devops, are used to speed up software delivery.

As for the so-called growth areas, the question is how a company should timely include developments that trigger a more fundamental change into its strategic business and IT management. It needs strategies and plans to run its current operations and reach its objectives, in combination with reacting to new, unexpected events. Concurrent exploitation of existing resources and capabilities and exploring and taking advantage of or reacting to initially not foreseen opportunities require combining two fundamentally different management styles. Exploitation goes together with routinization, control, mechanistic structures; exploration is associated with flexibility, autonomy, organic structures. The combination of these two fundamentally different sets, of skills, processes, management styles, etc., is known as ambidexterity [5,6,7]. IT ambidexterity is the joint consideration of IT exploration (related to new IT resources and practices) and IT exploitation (related to current resources and practices) [8]. In this respect, Gartner introduced the term bimodal IT: "the practice of managing two separate but coherent styles of work: one focused on predictability, the other on exploration" [9].

1.2.6 *Sourcing as a service relationship*

Strategic ICT sourcing is an integral part of the development of the organization's ICT supply strategy. The actual decision-making about sourcing may vary – in the business units, perhaps some corporate units (for example, marketing), or the corporate ICT organization itself, could find sourcing an attractive way of providing the ICT services required. A current example of the latter is the Cloud phenomenon, both as a platform for SaaS and as a prime component of data storage, management, and security strategies. In some respects, the existence of an outside source for ICT, from the perspective of the organization and of the organization's ICT leadership, is simply an alternative to the in-house provisioning of the same capabilities. Except of course it means that the company does not require the expertise involved.

Figure 1.4[10] shows the five types of ICT services that represent what ICT provides the business:

*   Application and Information Services – providing and supporting the applications and information processing capabilities, including internet capabilities.

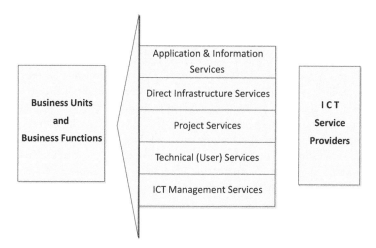

Figure 1.4 Services from IT to the business

- Direct Infrastructure Services – for example, e-mail, network support, hardware and software support, server administration, technical internet support.
- Project Services – the development of applications and ICT capabilities.
- User Services – for example, the help desk.
- IT Management Services – for example, training, ICT budgeting, enterprise architecture.

In effect, strategic ICT sourcing – represented by the various service-level agreements that identify what is to be provided – address some or all of these elements [3]. The recent Ward and Pepper book on ICT management highlights the main drivers for entering into strategic sourcing, namely (1) improving how ICT is done, (2) providing better business impact (value), and (3) exploiting commercial ICT (selling ICT to customers) [10]. These, however, are the exact drivers any ICT leadership pursues, whether or not sourcing is the desired method for producing and provisioning them in the organization. In effect, the question becomes: "can we do it better" with outside providers? This begs the question of what "better" is, which we will discuss later. But simply, it's cheaper, faster, and more reliable and flexible.

However, within the set of ICT sources, a mixture of local services and externally provided services exists. For example, the same example of network and communications providers often works for the corporate ICT unit, which then provides organization-specific ICT services to the business areas.

This entire fabric represented by Figure 1.3 is the context within which "strategic ICT sourcing" occurs for the organization as a whole and for the individual business units within the enterprise. The point to this is to see this fabric in strategic terms – that the enterprise depends on the providers of ICT services to be successful, to be strategic, in the providing of ICT services. This requires at least these seven capabilities.

But this illustrates the underlying requirement, the development of trust – in effect a full partnership in providing the required services to the enterprise. This trust/partnership covers all the aspects, but in particular the idea of longevity and permanence and stability. If the enterprise is strategically dependent on the relationship, it must be one that persists and responds to all issues, for example, turbulence and change in the environment.

1.2.7 *Digital Strategy and best of breed sourcing*

Digital Strategy reflects the enterprises strategic direction for acquiring and deploying ICT. Certainly, over the past 20 years this has become a pressing concern for many companies, particularly those engaged in an industry where ICT is pervasive. As one set of researchers put it: "To succeed today, companies need a unique value proposition that incorporates digital technologies in a way that is difficult for competitors to replicate" [11]. The key question here is how strategic ICT sourcing plays a role in achieving this. As noted in the above, certainly trust and partnership is a key element in achieving this, and therefore becomes a core aspect of the ICT sourcing relationships. As another set of researchers put it: "How can we use technology as a strategic asset to enable new competencies or maintain a competitive advantage?" [12].

This is more than just a better mousetrap strategy.

> Accordingly, we argue that the time is right to rethink the role of IT strategy, from that of a functional-level strategy – aligned but essentially always subordinate to business strategy – to one that reflects a fusion between IT strategy and business strategy. This fusion is herein termed digital business strategy.
>
> *[13]*

At times the issue of ICT strategy confuses the supply-side issues (the ways in which ICT is delivered to the enterprise) with the demand-side issues (the ways in which ICT is used and applied in the enterprise) [10]. Both are considered in the ICT strategy – but, most importantly, thus affect the strategic ICT sourcing relationship. The sourcing provider has to be capable of support both – excellence in ICT supply and effectiveness in meeting ICT demands. From the strategy perspective, going back to Figure 1.1, this also means effectiveness in building the relationships of "alignment" and "transformation" between ICT and business.

This changes the nature of "best of breed" sourcing. This concept grew out of the last part of the 1990s as a way to describe a sourcing provider capable of both efficiency (cost) and excellent performance (in traditional ICT supply terms.) Now, as Digital ICT Strategy becomes more critical, the sourcing relationship needs to be capable of alignment (which is, in effect, the "best of breed" ideas) with the capabilities for business transformation through ICT's application.

A good summary is: "In a digital world, the focus of ICT is shifting from backend operations to driving business growth." This chapter suggests aspects of the resulting ICT strategy as adopting (what they call) a more liquid workforce, capable of content change, migrating to as-a-service commercial model, with levels of variability to ICT sourcing, and finding the right balance of local and global sourcing [14].

1.2.8 *Integration*

This carries forward on the ideas presented about, that is, the emergence of Digital Strategy as a Fusion of demand (use of ICT to transform the business) and supply (the expansion of opportunities such as Cloud, SaaS, Infrastructure as a service), and so forth. The issue is that the lines are increasingly blurring between supply and demand. ICT is no longer something to be "aligned" with the business – rather ICT is a major force transforming the business in fundamental ways.

A recent MIT study on Digital Strategy opened with this statement: "maturing digital businesses are focused on integrating digital technologies, such as social, mobile, analytics and Cloud, in the service of transforming how their businesses work. Less-mature digital businesses are focused on solving discrete business problems with individual digital technologies" [15].

Both cases described here illustrate the profound role strategic ICT sourcing can play, by providing the business and technology resources to achieve this integration and achievement of Digital Strategy. But the first case – integrating technologies in transforming how businesses work – is the primary effect of integrating ICT sourcing. In effect, this is managing the complete set of technology and sources for the transforming benefit to the enterprise.

Also just like the traditional strategic sourcing in an organization's supply chain, the relationship between buyer and seller, between enterprise and ICT, has to be managed, and managed consistent with the notions of strategic sourcing. That is, with the elements of permanence, stability, cost, and partnership that one must find in any sourcing partnership. To accomplish this, of course, raises the issue of trust, which is the single most important characteristic of the overall strategic ICT sourcing relationships.

Management includes accountability. Figure 1.5 shows an idealized version of where accountabilities rest. The center reflects the basic ICT management activities: development, operations, and business/user services. The business units (including corporate) rely on the ICT management activity to deliver according to their requirements (that is, ICT demand). ICT management then provides those ICT services by relying on one or more service providers – some internal to the corporation, some external. For example, the system development providers may be in the internal ICT organization, while the technical network management and provision can be external.

1.2.8.1 Why outsource: economic and social perspectives

Establishing the boundaries of a firm encompasses strategic decisions. Whether resources, competences, and capabilities should be kept and developed in-house or procured in the market has a major impact on how an organization will thrive. Explanations of how and on

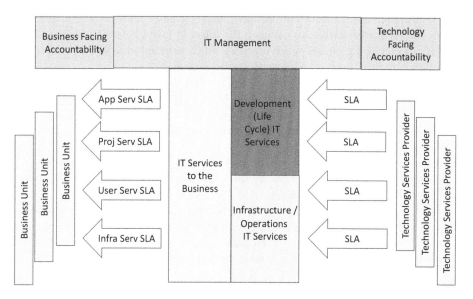

Figure 1.5 Sourcing accountability and responsibility

what grounds these decisions are made have been developed in economics, management, and behavioral theory.

The classical analysis comes from economics with transaction costs economics. Transactions are the exchanges of goods and services between economic actors inside or outside the organization [16]. When sourcing the inputs for its final products and services, a firm has the fundamental choice between developing and producing these in-house – thus within the boundaries of the firm – or procuring them from outside the firm – in the market. This dichotomy between hierarchy and market is typical for the traditional economic analysis. A firm is supposed to choose the most rational (efficient) alternative by minimizing the sum of production cost and transaction cost. The latter encompasses the cost of ensuring that the necessary services and products can either be produced or made available by procuring them. Transaction cost of in-house production encompasses, e.g., internal planning and coordination cost; transaction cost of procuring in the market comprises, e.g., search cost (i.e, for a reliable supplier) and contracting cost.

The type and context of transactions determines the transaction cost and thus influences whether a transaction will be carried out in the market or in a hierarchy. In general, in-house transaction costs are supposed to be lower than external transaction costs. However, exchange hazards may necessitate complex and thus costly contracts, which may stimulate managers to choose for vertical integration. The following characteristics of transactions are particularly relevant [17]:

Asset specificity: the asset specificity of a transaction refers to the degree to which it is supported by assets that are specific to this transaction alone, and which cannot be used otherwise or elsewhere without incurring a significant reduction of value [18]. Transactions, involving highly asset-specific resources, involve long processes of development and adjustment for the supplier to meet the needs of the buyer. Such processes are favored by the continuity of relationships found in a hierarchy. Also, since there are few alternative buyers or suppliers of such highly specific products and services, both parties are vulnerable [17].

Product complexity: it [19] plays a role in choosing between hierarchy and market. In the case of simple and standardized products, buyers need to know little but their price. They likely prefer markets to compare the offers of many potential suppliers. Buyers selecting complex products or services need much more information. The extra information exchange involved increases the transaction costs.

Uncertainty: it, for example in technology and in markets, requires parties to adapt to unforeseeable changes. When fast complex technological and/or organizational adaptations are required, governance through markets lacks coordinating capabilities. Contracts may contain clauses and procedures to facilitate negotiations that are deemed necessary to respond to changes [20].

Difficulty to measure performance: when performance is hard to measure, parties may develop opportunistic behavior, e.g., by spending fewer or more resources or delivering lower quality than initially agreed.

Frequency: setting up specialized governance structures, such as those that organizations employ for their transactions, involves high expenditures. These costs are only recovered if the transaction volume or frequency of transactions is high enough. Consequently, low frequencies point to market procurement [18].

As said, the above factors increase the cost of transactions, and in particular the contracting cost. Asset specificity, product complexity, uncertainty, and difficulty to measure performance result in more complex contracts, which demand more resources to develop. The combination of these factors makes contracting even more problematic [20] and consequently favors in-house production.

However, as information technology drives down search and coordination costs, IT is hypothesized to stimulate outsourcing. With information technologies like the internet, interoperable ERP systems, electronic market places, etc., products and services can be procured from low-cost areas, with extremely efficient logistical coordination. IT thus enables efficient external procurement.

A rival theory in economics is offered by the Resource-Based View (RBV) [21]. According to this theory, an organization has a collection of resources that generate rents. Some of these resources are critical for its competitive position and some are necessary but not critical. Critical resources are those that are VRIN – valuable, rare, imperfectly imitable, and not substitutable. Of course, resources alone will not help the firm much further. Competencies and capabilities to deploy the resources toward the strategic and operational objectives of the firm have to be developed and maintained. According to this view, resources and their adjacent competencies and capabilities that are VRIN will be kept in-house, while others may be sourced externally. Related theory to the RBV is the Resource Dependency Theory (RDT), a social theory, which theorizes about resources, which are outsourced, as they are not VRIN, but nevertheless are critical for the company's operations [22]. These resources create critical dependencies for which organizations need to develop strategies to mitigate the risks.

1.2.9 A relational perspective

As a reaction to this narrow perspective of the original markets and hierarchies framework, increased emphasis is placed on intermediate organizational forms, where independent organizations engage in longer-term relationships [17]. On one hand, these relationships bear the characteristics of markets: the participants are independent, transactions are governed by contracts in which prices have been agreed, and the participants have the possibility to put an end to the relationship. On the other hand, however, these relationships also bear the characteristics of hierarchies. The participants are tied together by legal contracts for a longer period. Multiple coordination mechanisms are applied to improve the efficiency and effectiveness of their transactions. In addition, critical and confidential information is shared, participants engage in collaborative processes, and coordination occurs through mutual adjustment. The emerging organizational form is called the network organization, made up of more or less equal members who have formal and informal relationships with one another. *Inter-company networks* (or simply *networks*) are complex arrays of relationships between companies, which establish these relationships by interacting with each other [23]. The basis of these relationships is trust. The companies' interactions imply making investments in order to build their mutual relationships, thus consolidating the network; caring for the company's relationships becomes a management priority. Competing is a matter of positioning one's company in the network rather than of attacking the environment.

Inter-organizational relationships may be of three types: operational, tactical, and strategic. Typical for tactical and strategic types of relationships is an increased commitment to each other. The relation on an operational level exists for the duration of a single order; on a tactical level, it may have the scope of a year or longer (e.g., needing sharing of planning information and assuring the position as service provider for that same period). Managers or entrepreneurs can also use networks to move their companies into stronger competitive positions. That is why these are called *strategic* networks: long-term, purposeful arrangements among distinct but related profit-oriented organizations that allow their participants to gain or sustain competitive advantages over their competitors outside the network [23]. The participating companies remain independent in that they do not depend on each other completely, but their relationships are essential to their competitive position. Networks are a mode of organization that is based strictly neither on the price mechanism nor on hierarchical decision-making, but on coordination through adaptation. However, realizing the benefits from such a partnership is contingent upon mutual trust and organizational complementarity in such things as decision-making processes, control systems, organizational culture, etc. [24]. Partnerships require relational governance: practice-based measures to promote a desired collaborative behavior [3].

1.2.10 Wrapping up Section 1.2: consequences for management

Increased competition forces companies to fundamentally rethink their position in their markets. Traditionally, they carried out all the necessary activities for the production and delivery of their products themselves, unless some were procured from external suppliers for specific reasons. But companies think differently nowadays. They feel there is no reason to do something themselves unless they are really good at it. And they therefore ask themselves which of their competences are unique and of core importance, which of their resources and functional capabilities really add value – and, consequently, which might more efficiently be procured externally. Because of this change in their point of view, outsourcing and insourcing movements are expected to cause fundamental changes in the way companies are configured. Uniqueness and value-adding competences are the business drivers of future-oriented companies [25].

Concentrating on core business has become a trend in many industries. This means that those activities that are not core to the business are outsourced to specialized suppliers. For future-oriented companies, decisions on how to acquire the basic products and services to meet their customer's needs have come to be of strategic importance. They define the company's position in its competitive environment. The long-term relationships with suppliers are therefore included in the company's strategic planning processes. Traditional sourcing was a matter of make-or-buy decisions, typically based on cost analysis and focused on limited numbers of specific goods and services delivered for a limited number of times or over a limited period. Companies engaging in such transactions experienced little interdependence and their main motive was cost efficiency. Many such sourcing decisions are still taken, of course, on a day-to-day basis all over the world. Strategic sourcing, however, is completely different. The dependence between participants, their motives, the contract periods, and many other characteristics are unlike those of traditional sourcing [26]. Strategic sourcing concentrates on long-term motives such as making one's organization more agile or gaining access to important resources that are better supplied by external parties than developed internally. It therefore focuses on long-term relationships: the participants collaboratively plan their moves in what becomes a common competitive environment. They are therefore much more dependent on one another. The decisions to be made concern the company's strategic planning horizons.

As a result of these developments, traditional value chains are becoming unbundled. On the one hand, many support activities and some primary activities (logistics, operations) are being outsourced – even some parts of the company's infrastructure (accounting, financial services, and human resources). On the other hand, the outsourced activities have to be procured from one or more external suppliers, a process that rebundles them in another way. Clearly, this process causes the relationships between businesses to become increasingly complex. The popular term used in business literature for these new ways of doing business is the "business model." Business models may be defined as descriptive representations of an enterprise's planned activities (also called "business processes") [17].

Managers are confronted with complex, multifaceted decisions in this respect. Various organizational theories provide explanations and support. In Part 1, we provide a brief overview. Several approaches are discussed in the economics and organization literature. The most important of these for our purpose are the theory of transaction costs economics, the resource-based view, and the resource dependency theory. As supplier-buyer relationships in IT sourcing involve long-term relationships, the relational view offers a complementary perspective: economics and behavioral theories go hand in hand for explaining and creating effective long-term relationships between IT services suppliers and IT service recipients.

Managers are also confronted with the problems inherent in acquiring and managing complex relationships and activities. In the past, these problems have focused on the contractual aspects in a relatively stable circumstance. Today, with the technology dynamics and the much broader scope of the activities, not limited to simply ICT technologies, managers must command a broad range of aspects of the relationship between the acquirer and the supplier. Much of this is suggested above, and Part 1 offers several mental models/frameworks to assist the manager in successfully dealing with these new aspects.

ICT Services focuses on the actual activities expected to be provided, covering the full range of ICT activities including planning, project development, operations, security, user services, and ICT management services. *ICT Capability* expands each services area by specifying the components of an ICT service, including innovation, business transformation, information/intelligence/analytics, operational excellence, and resource management and costs. This broadening of ICT outsourcing, considering services and its myriad components, materially changes the *Bes of Breed* concept, moving into the domain of business performance and competitiveness.

As Section 1.2 demonstrates, it is not enough to simply think of ICT sourcing as providing technology, in this larger view ICT sourcing brings with its relationships and partnerships to move the business forward in its competitive environment. Accordingly, this requires managing the partnership which requires a view of integration that is new. The partnership itself moves the business closer to the digital Fusion, the integration of the ICT demand and ICT supply activities.

In effect, while previous views of sourcing management may have considered the problems as a form of procurement, current requirements bring the full set of management issues inherent in partnerships between companies and their ICT activities. Managers involved in Sourcing (and this chapter) thus must consider issues such as Trust (Section 1.3), Turbulence and Uncertainty (Section 1.4), and Governance (Section 1.5).

1.3 The impact of trust

1.3.1 Trust defined

Trust plays a pivotal role in business and sustainable interpersonal relationships. Trust is essential in nearly all circumstances where human beings and/or organizations are dependent on each other. High interdependence requires increased trust. Mutual trust is a precondition for inter-organizational cooperation. Especially collaboration in the primary activities of the value chain requires sharing confidential planning information. Trust is a pre-requisite for sharing. Also, collaboration between firms in product development constitutes a key strategic activity and will not happen without mutual trust. In the absence of trust, any collaboration is hindered. The collaboration includes shielding important information and setting up controls and procedures to protect the interests of the parties. In essence, trust is an important coordination mechanism [27].

In the business, trust can be defined as the expectation that the other (person or organization) will behave in a mutually acceptable and predictable manner. This includes the expectation that neither party will take advantage of the other's vulnerabilities [28]. In a business environment[11] characterized by turbulence and complexity, sustainable joint competitive success is widely perceived as being dependent on the existence of trust between the parties commonly engaged in business. Handling turbulence requires swift and pro-active actions, which can only be developed if there is close to blind faith in the other. Equally, when facing complex managerial problems (e.g., in business and IT), no one has, nor can have, a full view on the situation at hand and potential future developments/scenarios. As a result, the views and opinions of those implicated in the problem situation should be trusted. Simon and March labeled the situation that occurs under these circumstances as "uncertainty absorption" [29].

Trust is a concept with many dimensions. Trust is based on the expectation that the parties concerned are competent, open, caring, and reliable [30]. In the case of inter-organizational trust, e.g., between a supplier and a client, trust encompasses also contractual trust [28]. *Competence-based* trust refers to the skills and capabilities of the other person or organization in a specific domain, service, or product: is the other capable of doing what he/she says he/she will do? It is based on the perception that one can rely on activities, deliverables, and processes performed by the other.

Openness-based trust is founded on perceived honest, morally sound behavior by parties. Openness impacts the willingness to share information, insights, and knowledge. *Caring-based* trust refers to the belief that the other party will support the other's interests. This goes beyond the basic expectation that the other will refrain from opportunistic behavior by taking unfair advantage; the other party is also expected to be concerned that the other party's interests will not be damaged [30].

Reliability-based trust refers to the expected consistency in behavior based on experience with and commitments and promises made by the business partner. Personal, not just organizational, integrity and reliability are foundations for reliability trust within and between organizations [31]. However, the company culture of parties also contributes to this foundation. Finally, *contractual trust* refers to the question of whether the other party will carry out the contractual agreements [28]. The applicable jurisdiction is also important as this impacts the enforceability of the contractual commitments.

These trust dimensions also suggest a hierarchy [28]. Advanced levels of trust depend first and foremost on the existence of competence-based trust and, in inter-organizational settings, also on contractual trust. If one of the parties proves not to be able to do and deliver what was promised or does not live up to one's contractual obligations, there is no basis for advanced levels of trust. However, next to competence, openness/ transparency (demonstrating moral responsibility and positive intentions) is necessary for the other party to accept a potentially vulnerable position [31].

For true business-IT partnerships, business trust in IT requires a foundation of proven competency and openness. When occurring on an operational management level, the system availability competency and responsiveness to incidents as agreed is the dominant trust dimension. Similar for the tactical and strategic managerial levels, where the freedom for IT to act as a credible partner depends upon the ability to deliver the services. On higher strata, the additional dimensions of trust, including caring and reliability, become more important. Next to organizational trust, person-based trust is a foundation for a true business–IT partnership. These conditions also apply to the business, seen from the perspective of IT, as trust is a relational concept. For the business–IT relationship to function well, it is pivotal that trust is reciprocal.

1.3.2 Trust improves business performance

There is a general belief that trust improves business performance. Let us understand the how. First, trust reduces the coordination costs, as it is a coordination mechanism in and of itself. Trust reduces the need for extensive procedures and protocols, for negotiations to reach a mutually supported solution for specific problems as well as a reduced need to strictly monitor behavior and its outcomes during the collaboration. Also, under conditions of change, all possible future contingencies need not be anticipated, because one can rely on fair and balanced adjustments and judgment when necessary. Second, trust is expected to contribute to joint innovation and learning. Under conditions of trust, unconstrained information and knowledge sharing are possible, as the other(s) are not expected to use it for their own benefit at the expense of the one from whom the party received this information. No opportunistic behavior!

1.3.3 Can trust be built?

According to a well-known saying, unfortunately trust comes by foot and leaves by horse. Establishing trust takes time and is based on past experience of trustworthy behavior. Apparently, losing trust goes faster. Although there is considerable disagreement among theorists whether trust can be built actively, it is, however, believed that an organization can adopt and manage practices to promote and establish trust between parties.

The different dimensions of trust can be improved by a set of interdependent and mutually enforcing governance and policies. First, proven competency through past performance is a key condition for business and IT functions to gradually develop and establish reciprocal trust. The credibility of the other, in this respect, improves with competent behavior through the course of time; it will be built by demonstrated capability in the past to solve problems, by interpersonal skills, and by consistent professionalism [31]. Also, processes are important in enabling to build trust as they contribute to the performance and competencies of parties.

Performance relates not only to competent execution of responsibilities, but also to the ability to collaborate in open, caring, and reliable ways. This implies that, on one hand, both IT and business functions should be able to apply the right tools, dashboards, and techniques to ensure the business gets the services that it needs. However, this is not enough. A good functioning of the informal organization, through socializing and team development, has proven to be a prerequisite for a seamless collaboration.

Related to the latter is a second policy: open communication about goals, commitments, and intentions. Communication has to take place regularly and planned for each level and must be embedded in organizational processes and procedures.

Third, various organizational measures can help overcome the barriers of differentiation and different mental models. They include promoting working in (joint) teams, encouraging collective training and learning experiences, job rotation, co-location, etc. [32]. IT staff should develop a competent understanding of the (client) business side of IT, while business managers should understand how IT brings value to the business. The effects of (absence of) physical proximity should be well understood. For instance, having IT expertise concentrated in a shared service center or distant service supplier is an impediment for effective communication and does not contribute to the establishment of trust. However, technology such as video conferencing and collaboration tools contribute to bridging the gap.

Finally, measuring is important. Organizations promoting trust should actively measure and monitor objectively the level of existing trust. Several consulting companies, such as Gartner, offer tools with which such measurements can be facilitated. These tools generally resemble balanced scorecards. An alternative formal tool is the Organizational Trust Index (OTI) developed by researchers at the University of Colorado [33]. It is based on the trust dimensions discussed above and assists managers in determining the level of existing trust in their organizations. Organization can use the outcomes to implement additional measures such as boot camp sessions and/or replacing staff members.

1.3.4 Trust in outsourcing relations

In general, from a trust perspective, outsourcing forms a bigger challenge than in-house production and delivery. Companies have their own P&L statements and are driven by them. Opportunistic behavior lurks behind every potential outsourcing agreement. Not everyone is equally honest. Some people try to exploit situations to their own advantage. Not everybody does, of course, and not all of the time. But the problem is that some people do some of the time, and when you do business, it is difficult to distinguish between the honest and the dishonest. As a result, most transactions involve numerous inspections, controls, certifications, and the like, even if the partner involved is considered perfectly trustworthy. Once the contract has been signed, the recipient must ensure that the tasks he/she is paying for are carried out in his best interests. The service supplier, however, has a major information advantage, so his actions are difficult to assess from the recipient side. Service suppliers may boost their own profits, for example, by spending less time or utilizing fewer resources than agreed. Monitoring is one way of countering this risk, but it is costly since one must set performance standards and measure the actual work performed or have it audited by an independent authority. Another method to combat this problem is to align the supplier's interests with those of the outsourcing company by introducing positive enforcement measures such as incentive schemes, for example [34].

The occurrence of opportunism will therefore increase costs. This is especially important when there are few potential trading partners. These partners will care less about their reputations, as there are few alternatives to which their clients may turn to if they are not satisfied. The fact is that outsourcing companies can never fully and accurately judge the quality of their potential suppliers, nor their true intentions. Therefore, it is important that they mitigate the risks involved in the selection stage by gathering as much independent information about their potential suppliers as possible. Sources for such information include market research and current and former clients, who are familiar with the supplier's track record, and sometimes independent authorities or institutes, which may carry out benchmarking activities. Opportunism may also explain the rise of certification procedures in the past decade or two, such as the ISO certification process.

A targeted policy aimed at promoting confidence in an outsourcing relationship comprises several components. Of primary importance is a mutually agreed method of transparent conflict resolution, whereby both parties view the decision process to be fair and just. This type of atmosphere supports feelings of fair treatment. Communication is a key in building trust, as two-way communication has been widely identified as a major contributing factor in trusting relationships. For example, service providers must provide clear and understandable reports on the services they have delivered; service recipients should give clear feedback on their supplier's performance. Essentially, this is a matter of communication hygiene, and it applies to the parties' formal communication protocols. With respect to informal communication, trust may be generated through consultation prior to more formal discussion formats. In addition to trust between organizations and groups, trust must be established between individuals. Both provider and recipient must get a feel for which personal profiles best fit the management of their relationship, and staff in both organizations need to take the time to get to know each other. Trust also plays a role in reporting. Reports should concern not only the services delivered but the degree of trust between partners as well. It goes without saying that these measures also apply when IT services delivery is the responsibility of an internal department; however, as said before, outsourcing makes it more difficult.

1.3.5 Wrapping up Section 1.3: consequences for management

Managing IT outsourcing partnerships is not a matter of the "hard side" only. Much attention must be paid to the soft side, especially trust, which is of essential importance. It is our opinion that trust is a factor that must be governed, managed, and monitored. A lack of trust, for example by opportunistic behavior, results in an accelerated failure time [35]. We defined several dimensions of trust. Trust is based on the expectation that the party concerned is competent, open, caring, and reliable. All these dimensions require attention if the partnership is to be a success. The major difficulties with trust are that it takes time to generate and that it is hard to measure. To give it time to grow, providers and recipients must begin by clearly expressing to one another that they will put effort into it. Then trust-building is on the program explicitly [25]. To work actively at building trust, several policies in combination can be applied.

A first step toward building trust is to make sure that agreements are closely observed by both sides. The service supplier delivers as promised: services are on time, of the right quality and quantity, and at the agreed price. The service recipient makes sure that the necessary, agreed upon resources are available and that invoices are paid. This is the foundation, without which a trustful relationship cannot be built.

The next important factor is being open in one's communication. Service suppliers must provide clear and understandable reports, in business terms, on the services they have delivered; service recipients should give clear feedback on their supplier's performance [36]. There should be no hidden agendas. Essentially this is a matter of communication hygiene and applies especially to the parties' formal communication. With respect to their informal communication, much trust may be generated by consultation: before any formal communication takes place, the parties discuss matters informally [25].

Third, it is important to realize that trust between organizations and groups is important but not enough. For collaboration efforts to work, personal trust is needed too [37]. Both provider and recipient must get a feel for which personal profiles best fit the management of their partnership. Key people on both sides must take time to get to know each other. This applies in particular also to offshore outsourcing. Sports and cultural outings are excellent opportunities to do so.

Finally, IT outsourcing partnerships involve much reporting. These reports should concern not only the services delivered but also the degree of trust between the partners. We mentioned earlier Organizational Trust Index (OTI) but also several consulting companies, such as Equa Terra and Gartner, offer tools with which such measurement can be facilitated. Once the degree of trust between the partners has been measured, the results must be used to increase it further. To this end, boot camp sessions can be effective, but it may also be necessary to replace some of the team members.

1.4 Change and uncertainty: turbulence

1.4.1 Turbulence defined

Under conditions of relative certainty in major parts of its environment, an organization can, for the most part, initiate its own agenda of change [32]. Under stable conditions, when launching new products or entering new markets, an organization would make incremental, planned modifications to its organization, strategy, and technology support. Strategies and operational planning methodologies would focus on change management, based upon those assumptions that the organization could anticipate, plan for, and methodically integrate any change into its existing structure. Businesses used to have annual strategic planning sessions to plan for incremental changes for the next year, and every two to five years, they developed (or updated) a long-range plan. This was an effective approach in relatively stable market conditions.

How different is a dynamic environment? It changes frequently, if not continuously, in an unpredictable way. The turn of this century coincides with an increasingly turbulent and competitive business landscape, in which the intensity, unpredictability, and diversity of change accelerates to create a condition of constant flux [38]. D'Aveni describes the current business environment as "hypercompetitive," characterized by D'Aveni and Gunther [39].

Figure 1.4[12] shows the five types of ICT services that represent what ICT provides the business:

* Time and cost compression in product-life and design cycles.
* Accelerating technological advancements.
* Fickle customer loyalty.
* Unexpected entry by new competitors and repositioning of incumbents.
* Redefinition of industry and organizational boundaries.
* Lingering economic growth.

The new contextual environment requires reassessment of potential markets, customers, and competitors. What is the optimal focus for making these reassessments and for developing new plans? Under highly unpredictable and ambiguous conditions, there is little time to reassess and replan. Unexpected changes occur continuously. In this context, elongated strategic planning processes and cycles have all the benefit of a séance. The organization must be able to adapt per direct to changing conditions.

Change per se does not cause many problems, provided that organizations have the capability to change and prepare for it in time. In line with Ansoff [38], we shall refer to the degree of changeability of environmental challenges as the "level of environmental turbulence." The level of turbulence is determined by a combination of the above listed factors. High levels of turbulence are characterized by highly uncertain and unexpected events.

Figure 1.6[13] depicts the effect of uncertainty on planning. The figure applies to any (functional) area for which planning takes place. So, it may represent a situation, e.g., in production, supply chain management as in IT. It also applies to all three planning levels: the

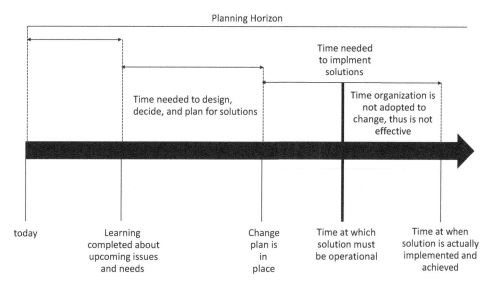

Figure 1.6 Uncertainty and planning

strategic, tactical planning, and operational level. The figure shows a decision maker, who finds out "today" that in the foreseeable future the current activities will be affected by a change in environmental conditions. The decision maker can be the corporate management team, a CxO, or a departmental manager. Examples of changes in conditions are an important client who will discontinue a contract, a supplier of a critical raw material will be out of business, a sudden turndown of the economy; an important legal change, the IT services supplier who stops supporting one of the key systems, etc. As a consequence, existing plans and operations need to be adapted or reconsidered in response to the new situation at hand. The dotted line shows when the solution will be needed. In this example, the solution is achieved much later than when it is actually needed.

The actual time available for developing a solution comprises of the time that elapses between when management learns about the "issue" and the moment that a solution is available and implemented: the available "reaction time."

1.4.2 *Organizational impact of turbulence*

How to deal with change has always been an important issue for organizations. Change requires an organization to be adaptable and responsive. Conditions of stability do not impose an acute level of responsiveness on an organization – even a blind squirrel can find an acorn if given enough time and an absence of predators. Enterprises that principally operate in stable conditions (e.g., markets, products, customers) are typically designed to promote efficiency, control, and predictability of behavior/outcomes. However, different levels of change require different levels of responsiveness. When change is reasonably predictable, the organization must have the capabilities to timely adjust its structures, processes, and systems. However, when confronted with change that is unfamiliar (e.g., scale, range, depth, speed, etc.), this type of flexibility may not be sufficient. Under these conditions, organizations need the capability to "sense and respond" [40], to timely detect potentially important developments and respond to them by adjusting its ways of working beyond its normal level of flexibility. As Steve Haeckel denotes, organizations must have the capability to "know earlier" and "react faster." In other words, they need to be agile.

Business-related turbulence is not the only type of turbulence affecting IT. Irrespective of business-related turbulence, the IT function can experience turbulence because of (sudden) changes in the available technology and in the supply market of IT services. These may affect the mere service provisioning by the IT department, but they may also directly or indirectly affect the business. New technologies and practices are being introduced with an increasing frequency it seems, such as mobile infrastructures and applications, social media, Cloud computing, and Bring Your Own Device (BYOD). New, easy-to-use applications, mashups, are downloadable from the internet and challenging the position of the traditional IT department.

1.4.3 *The impact of uncertainty and change on (out)sourcing*

Traditional analyses of outsourcing, which focus on choices of either markets or hierarchies, give little guidance for sourcing decisions under different environmental contexts. According to Transaction Cost Economics, uncertainty in business and/or technological conditions causes complex contracts and consequently leads to higher contracting costs. As such, uncertainty favors internal integration of activities. It is however clear that frequent changes, e.g., in markets, regulations, or technology, make it impossible for any organization to have all potential resources, competencies, and capabilities to sustain its market position [41]. Thus, outsourcing comes to the table as a viable alternative. However, the same argument applies to external suppliers: they are equally not able to react instantly to these changes. That is why solutions to handle problems and opportunities caused by environmental turbulence are sought in so-called intermediate organizational forms like alliances and partnerships. Trusted, long-term alliances create a safe environment to share (strategic and otherwise critical) planning information and commit resources that enable the future service delivery.

Intermediate organizational forms should create conditions of stability of internal integration, combined with the flexibility of the market. This is supported by management and economic literature. For example, Jay Galbraith, in his information processing view on organizations, discusses how an organization can change the environment, and manage its dependence to others by developing a variety of cooperative strategies [42]. The observation that change and uncertainty leads to intermediate organizational forms is also supported by Folta [43]. In later publications, additional advantages of intermediate organizational forms have been recognized.[14] Examples are accessing resources faster than internal development [44], creating a way to access complementary resources from other organizations [45], exposing a firm to new ideas, and learning about the level of technology held by competitors [46]. In line with the foregoing, a recent study by Irge Sener based on 16 interviews with top managers concluded that managers perceiving environmental dynamism and complexity tend to form strategic alliances [47].

To conclude, this analysis adds an argument to the traditional (IT-) outsourcing discussion. Transaction Cost Economics explains outsourcing from an efficiency perspective: the rational manager should seek to minimize the sum of production and coordination (transaction) costs [48] of his organization. Production costs comprise of the costs of all primary processes that are necessary to produce and distribute the goods and services eventually delivered to a client or customer. Coordination costs include the transaction costs necessary to coordinate the activities of staff and equipment that perform the primary processes [49]. The resource-based view explains the outsourcing phenomenon from a (business) strategic angle. Resources, competences, and capabilities that are VRIN should be kept internally in order to fence them off from competition. Resources, that are non-VRIN are potential candidates for outsourcing but from a resource dependency perspective the manager should watch out not to become too dependent from a critical and thus powerful supplier. The "uncertainty" perspective, adding to the strategic perspective, looks at outsourcing from the point of view of creating a flexible, responsive organization. By creating a network organization with a selected number of alliances and partnerships, the managers establish a structure that allows them to be responsive to changing information systems requirements caused by business and/or information technology changes.

1.4.4 Wrapping up Section 1.4: consequences for management

Today's business is very dynamic. Nowadays, flexibility is needed to keep up with market dynamics. These, in turn, influence IT services delivery and IT strategies. Uncertainty makes it difficult to define information needs and information systems requirements far in advance; in other words, this leads to "incomplete contracts," which favors keeping activities in-house. Integrating these activities in the "demanding" organizations is however not an option either. As a result, organizations are "moving to the middle" [50], finding solutions where IT services are neither developed and managed internally, nor are the result of open market transactions. Outsourcing IT services are developed and delivered in the context of long-term relationships with several IT services suppliers.

Business and IT developments together trigger business dynamics and uncertainty. Organizations are on the move and many companies join networks [51]. When companies merge or when they are bought, their information systems must be coupled and realigned with those of their new colleagues. Divestments, however, require that they be disentangled. Such changes usually come unexpectedly, with very little time between the announcement and their becoming effective. Therefore, it is wise for service recipients to organize their IT services such that their constituent parts can be disconnected easily from one another or integrated with those of other companies.

In addition to mergers and takeovers, the convergence of IT and telecommunication, and the increasing availability of bandwidth, the growing insights from data continue to reduce the transaction and coordination costs associated with old-economy business operations. This enables companies to transform their value chains and focus on core competences. Thus, new technologies gradually converge with newly developed business models [53]: digital transformations [52].

Companies that can handle these dynamics well are more successful than those that cannot. Doing so, however, creates major demands on their IT services. Reacting to changes in the services requested is pivotal, with respect to both the quantity of these services and their nature. On the basis of their IT strategies, companies may decide to change from one information services platform to another [25]. This is not a one-off task, these developments are expected to continue, strategic sourcing instead of isolated make-or-buy decisions. Therefore, not only would the output side of many companies change, but also their input (purchasing) side will change. The focus is on standardization while enabling flexibility, with the aim to realize connectivity and advantages of scale. Due to the growing need for flexibility, with respect to both the volume and the nature of the services involved, outsourcing is expected to grow in the next decade. As a result, the outsourcing landscape is changing. We mention three developments that we feel play an important role in the sense that they significantly influence outsourcing relationships and their management: (1) commoditization, (2) business process outsourcing, and (3) Cloud computing [25].

Commoditization takes place in two main areas: applications and infrastructure services. Standardizing applications makes it easier for companies to communicate and collaborate with each other, especially important in the context of a network organization. Commercial Off-The-Shelf (COTS) solutions are the preferred option and their customization is kept to a minimum. This facilitates the exchange of information between parties. Such collaborative relationships require that the connected organizations communicate adequately across their supply chains. Infrastructure services themselves are also being commoditized. Unit prices are common practice for both desktop and ERP seat [25].

Business Process Outsourcing (BPO) began slowly in the 1980s and matured in the 1990s. It regards the delegation of an entire business process to a third-party provider, including its underpinning supporting services [53]. Essentially, it may be considered an extension of IT outsourcing: the provider not only delivers IT services but uses those business/support services to carry out one or more of the recipient's entire business processes, such as HR, customer care, payroll, or claim handling for insurance companies. Generally, the business processes concerned are so-called IT-centered services. Nowadays, many industries outsource part of their (customer-facing) processes. A lot of consumers in B2C (and employees) often do not even realize that the company they are dealing with is not the same that handles their claims, mortgages, phone connections, or pay-roll sheet [54]. BPO also includes core processes. In these relationships, processes are provided to multiple services recipients on a therefore by default less customized basis and more closely interwoven with the primary processes of the service recipient. These collaborative patterns may be characterized as partnerships and result in increasingly tight collaborative connections. Business processes are becoming increasingly "digitized," and as such are a core part of a firm's digital transformation strategies. As a consequence, BPO is increasingly about technology, and much less to remove back-office staff from the payroll.

Cloud computing has managerial and economic consequences that make it highly attractive for business users. The main drivers for the adoption of Cloud computing today are the business need for growth and flexibility (in terms of new products and services, globalization, and opening new markets) and technological innovation (introducing new technologies and standardization) [55]. The concept is founded on sharing the capacity of available resources, or even going a step further and opening their infrastructure to other companies [56]. Clouds are large pools of easily usable and accessible virtualized resources, such as hardware, development platforms, or services/software. These resources can be dynamically reconfigured to adjust to a viable load (scale), allowing optimum resource utilization [57]. Next to virtualization, the primary mechanisms for Cloud computing are standardization and automation. While companies face problems with their traditional IT caused by increasing demand for IT and unpredictable load peaks, the advantages of Cloud computing are attractive. They include no, or strongly reduced upfront costs, scalability, no need to worry about maintenance and upgrades, pay per use and the same services available all over the world. It goes without saying that trust is very important in Cloud computing, as it involves letting go of the dedicated environment used for one client only (public Cloud). This worries auditors who must assess the way in which companies have organized their IT services [58]. Alternatively, Cloud service providers can offer dedicated environments (private Clouds). Also, the Cloud market is maturing, security and compliance concerns continue to require attention but to a far less extent than five years ago.

1.5 Governing complex client/vendor relationships under turbulence

1.5.1 Success factors for complex information technology outsourcing relations

Outsourcing IT creates relationships between the service recipient and service providers. Making these relationships work is a critical condition for effective outsourcing. Already in 1995, McFarlan and Nolan recognized the problems created by a rapid-changing environment and suggested clients and their suppliers to form strategic partnership alliances [59]. Outsourcing relations differ with respect to their complexity and therefore the management attention they need. Complex IT outsourcing relations obviously must be much more closely monitored than small IT projects. Also, there is a relationship between the services needed and the sourcing types chosen, on the one hand, and the level of experience required for the relationship's management, on the other [60]. Generally, the higher the degree of client-supplier interdependence and the more complex the IT services involved, the higher the level of experience needed [61].

For successful outsourcing partnership relationships, it is critical that strategies, tactics, and operations of service recipients and service suppliers are well aligned. Alignment requires governance, to be defined as conditions that must ensure that the right decisions are being made and executed [62].

As part of a research program at Tilburg University, 14 case studies of European multinational companies with global or pan-European operations[15] were analyzed in order to understand what contributes to the success of, in particular, complex IT outsourcing relationships. Complex IT business-IT relationships can typically be defined as multi-site, multi-vendor, and combined internal and external IT service provisioning relationships. The underlying (internal) contracts and Service Level Agreements include service delivery commitments. They often concern significant contract value of over 20 million USD. The services in the investigated IT outsourcing relationships include a very broad scope of IT services. The service recipients in these cases operate in different sectors. The total contract values vary from 0.4 million USD to an annual contract value of 550 million USD. The IT supplier in all cases is Atos and its predecessors. Atos presents itself as a leader in digital transformation with circa 100,000 employees in 73 countries and pro forma annual revenue of circa €13 billion. Serving a global client base, the Group provides infrastructure and data management services, including Cloud services and digital workplace services, business and platform solutions, big data, and cybersecurity products and services, as well as transactional services through its subsidiary Worldline. Atos is positioned as a European or global leader in most of those activities [63].

To determine whether an IT outsourcing case was successful, we applied ten measures of success. The measures included both hard and soft criteria. Hard criteria included (1) realization of goals, (2) realization of service levels, (3) expansion of the scope of the contract, (4) absence of escalation of conflicts, and (5) contract renewal. Soft criteria included (1) customer satisfaction, (2) active communication, (3) involvement, (4) culture fit, and (5) trust. At least eight of the ten criteria for success were met by the investigated cases. Also, at the end of the (initial) contract period, all investigated contracts were renewed except for two of the investigated cases, which were not renewed for reasons related to external market conditions. In addition to the case studies, senior experts with more than five years of experience in IT outsourcing from leading consulting organizations were interviewed. From these cases and expert interviews, three factors appear to be critical for a successful IT outsourcing relationship: (1) a clear strategic positioning, (2) formal organizational arrangements that allow for adequate collaboration, and (3) the presence of trust.

1.5.1.1 *Clear strategic positioning*

The business needs a clear vision on what it wants to accomplish with IT. Business strategies and IT strategies are closely related, and need to be integrated to enable digital transformation. Shaping the business and IT strategies is a matter of co-creation between business and IT and is an integral responsibility of the senior management team.

In the case of outsourcing of IT, the need for clear strategic positioning of both the service recipient and the IT services suppliers is unanimously supported by all case study companies and experts. The client organizations should have a clear view with respect to their use of IT, IT services, and role these play in their company. Clear IT strategies show service suppliers the direction in which their clients intend to move. Formulating this strategy remains the responsibility of the client organization, and, as such, is never a candidate for outsourcing. The contribution of the business, and in particular that of the CEO, is indispensable. Also, senior managers should be highly involved in developing the IT strategy. The pressure to do so grows as IT services and business processes are becoming increasingly interdependent and intertwined. In the case of outsourcing parts of the IT operations, if the company cannot provide unambiguous requirements and/or has no clear IT strategy, many service suppliers will react to a request for proposal with a no-bid response. On the other side, service suppliers, both internal and external, must be able to show their clients and potential clients what IT services they can deliver and how. This is detailed in service catalogues and account plans. This includes their plans for the future, which form the basis of any business-IT partnership.

1.5.1.2 *Formal organizational arrangements*

Formal organizational arrangements and governance for managing and monitoring the IT (out)sourcing relationship are essential. These include structural provisions to support communication and collaboration between the service recipient and service suppliers, such as the organization and location of the IS/IT functions, outlining clearly defined roles and responsibilities, and the diversity of IT/business committees needed to support the IT (out) sourcing relationship [62].

Structural provisions are necessary on both sides of the relationship. Client organizations must adequately structure their Information Management function, which represents their demand management, service delivery, and contract management and constitutes the interface between the business processes and the IT suppliers. The role of the Chief Information Officer (CIO) and the Information Managers is key in this regard. They are ultimately responsible for the company's IT strategy and the optimal use of the IT services delivered.

Information Managers typically report to the CIO; their main responsibility is to ensure that the information needs of the business are met by the IT services provided. They form the link between the divisions/business units/departments and their service suppliers. Keeping internal and external IT service providers on track is a challenging task and requires significant coordination, alignment, and consultation, especially with regard to the delivery of diverse IT services by multiple service suppliers. Under conditions of change and turbulence, Information Managers have to contribute to the flexibility of services provided. The organizational embedding of Information Managers has to be adapted, so that hierarchically they report to business managers, while reporting functionally to the CIO [25]. By being embedded in and maintaining close relationships with the business, they can react quickly and ensure adequate and up-to-date service delivery. However, success depends on communication skills and collaboration of the staff directly involved.

These formal arrangements are present in all of the cases investigated in the study. Each outsourcing company had a well-developed Information Management function in place to represent company interests in the relationship with the service suppliers. In all cases, these Information Management functions are independent of the internal IT department to avoid conflicts of interests. When economically feasible, the Information Management function is set up per division/business unit.

The IT services suppliers, be it an internal department or external suppliers, have to carefully structure Contract and Account Management (CAM), which operates as the counterpart of the Information Management function of the client organization. It is important that service recipients and service suppliers can contact each other easily. Account management is about maintaining and building one's relationship with the client. The service providers must build a network of relationships within the recipient's organization as well as staying ahead of the developments in their industry [64]. The service suppliers' contract managers represent an additional major contact for the recipient next to their dedicated account managers.

Contract management involves optimizing the contractual agreements between supplier and client. It also requires managing the IT professionals who execute the work and the resources/assets such as infrastructure and networks, as well as taking care of the administrative aspects of the relationship, including (service level) reporting. As a result, service suppliers have to make allowances for substantial costs involved in contract management [65]. These findings are supported by all our interviews. With respect to structuring CAM, all the experts interviewed agreed: "The structure of the CAM must mirror the structure of the outsourcing company." In all of the cases studied except for one, there is a mirrored structure with a consensus that this contributes to successfully managing IT outsourcing partnerships. In the exception case study the CAM part of a larger CAM organization, which was responsible for a large number of complex IT outsourcing partnership contracts. This resulted in a relative limited attention from the CAM for this IT outsourcing partnership. This negatively impacted the relationship. As the responsible manager from the client said,

> The responsibilities for the CAM and the service delivery are embedded in one role. This results in possible conflicts of interest. The contract manager is responsible for customer satisfaction, and the service delivery manager [for] utilizing the service delivery capabilities.

Another important point of attention for CAM is the continuity of personnel in CAM positions. Changeover results in discontinuity in the management of the partnership, endangers the continuity of service delivery, and jeopardizes trusts.

Organizational and governance arrangements also include a diversity of business/IT committees and coordinating roles to support communication and collaboration between service recipient and suppliers at different levels. It is essential that senior managers of both suppliers and the recipient can easily contact one another. This does not only relate to the CIO, also the recipient's business managers must have an easy access to the suppliers' senior managers. As such, these organizational arrangements facilitate active participation, alignment, and cooperation between stakeholders, a strategic dialogue, and shared learnings [62].

Planned and regular communication between the client organization and the IT suppliers is essential in establishing flexible partnership relationships [66]. The communication structure of most of the investigated case studies is quite similar and organized on three management levels. There is a steering committee at the strategic level, which includes senior management and IT management for the service recipient, and senior management and account management for the IT service provider. Meetings typically take place once or twice a year. At a tactical level, there is a need for a monthly service review meeting to monitor overall ongoing performance and to anticipate the service recipient's future requirements/demand. Here, service supplier's performance is discussed on the basis of regular reporting and relate to service-level management processes. At the operational level, daily discussions with the Information Managers concerning operational issues are taking place.

The case study companies with an adequate communication structure show a similarly clear and layered arrangement between the service recipient and service suppliers. At each level, the authorizations and topics to be discussed are detailed and described in the outsourcing contracts. Typically, the contracts include a separate governance schedule.

A key element in communication between service suppliers and recipient is reporting. In order to track service delivery, the IT suppliers must report on a regular basis regarding the IT services delivered to the service recipient and the service level at which they were delivered [65,67]. For most of the outsourcing contracts studied, this required monthly reporting [68]. In five of the investigated case studies, inadequate reporting hindered the IT outsourcing relationship. Most of the problems were related to a too technically oriented reporting as opposed to reporting on more business-related items by metrics such as balanced scorecards and dashboards.

1.5.1.3 Trust

As said before, and as a key theme of this chapter, managing the business–IT relationship is not a matter of the "hard side" only. Much attention must be paid to the "soft side," especially trust between the service recipient and their suppliers is of utmost importance. Such trust has to be created and maintained at all organizational levels as between the involved individuals. Open formal and informal communication through the structures discussed above are instrumental to this.

A purposeful organizational policy, which contributes to the creation of mutual trust, is establishing relational mechanisms at all levels [62]. The objective of relational mechanisms is to facilitate open two-way communication, active collaboration, alignment, and knowledge sharing. This may be achieved by measures like physically locating business and IT staff close to each other, cross-training about the value adding role of IT in the business and informal meetings between business and IT management. Of course, this will challenge the "comfort zone" of all concerned. All these measures can only be effective if and only if they are actively endorsed by the senior management teams of both the client and the suppliers. They need to set the example. Again, the case of outsourcing is no different, only more difficult. Both service recipient and external service providers have to actively assess how and what relational mechanisms can improve the collaboration on both organizational levels and the personal level.

While these measures are worth pursuing under all circumstances, they are especially required under dynamic environmental conditions, which impose flexible adaptation by both recipient and suppliers. Trust provides the glue for a flexible relationship between the organizations concerned, allowing them to sustain the relationship over the strategic planning horizon [69].

1.5.2 Contracts and relational management

Managing this relationship is inherently problematic and characterized by a tension between control and trust. Service recipients and service providers are not only contractually but also socially related to each other. These two types of relationships also represent two streams in research.

The outsourcing contracts play an important role during the period that the outsourcing relationship is in effect [70]. They constitute the foundation for transferring responsibility. Contracts include the agreements that form the basis for executing the IT service. Typical components are the general conditions, agreements concerning the scope, the service levels, and costs associated with the specific services to be provided [71]. In addition, contracts will include agreements concerning Intellectual Property Rights (IPR), which are important when licenses are transferred from the outsourcing organization, and software is developed by the IT supplier on behalf of the outsourcing organization during the course of the contract. Especially in the case of a Digital Business Strategy, which encompasses business process outsourcing, this is an important issue [70]. The IPR in principle belongs to the outsourcing organization. However, BPO makes it essential for IT suppliers to acquire the IPR, while in the case of transfer to another IT supplier, the outsourcing organization must be able to continue to use the software licenses whose IPR remains with the "old" supplier [71].

As Lacity and Hirschheim formulated: "If a company decides to outsource, the contract is the only mechanism to ensure that expectations are realized" [72]. However, as the saying goes "it needs two to tango." The outsourcing reality must be seen as a success by both the outsourcing organization and the IT services supplier. Consequently, the basic premise must be that the service supplier and the outsourcing are always ready to help one another and are willing to cooperate at all levels to make the relationship a success. Facing uncertainty and change, parties that wish to enter into an agreement together are not able to predict all the future situations that may occur as a result of the transaction they want to conclude. As a consequence, they are not able to describe all possible future scenarios as part of the contracts they negotiate. This does not concern questions of uncertainty in relation to the contracting parties involved, but uncertainties concerning the transaction itself.

In this context, the outsourcing literature has studied the Incomplete Contract Theory developed by Nam et al. [73]. Attempts to include all possible future scenarios into an outsourcing contract require intense efforts from both the outsourcing organization and the IT services suppliers, and may well be an impossible task. When preparing IT outsourcing contracts, the question is to what extent both parties are prepared to attempt to be complete. The degree to which this is possible for IT outsourcing contracts depends on characteristics of the transaction involved: asset specificity, uncertainty and measurement, and frequency of the transaction [74]. Moreover, in many outsourcing situations, the opportunity to include details into the contract is very limited. This is related to the time pressures that often exist to come to an agreement and the costs associated with the preparation of the outsourcing contract. Management may deem it essential for certain services to be quickly available [70].

Contracts form a safety net upon which the parties eventually may rely. Especially under uncertain and changing conditions, the future IT services needs of the outsourcing organizations are elements that cannot be defined when a contract is signed. Consequently, parties need to agree on procedures for dealing with changes that are not covered by the contract. These procedures need to enable a rapid resolution of the problem at hand, which saves costs and ensures that any damage to the image of both the services supplier and recipient is avoided or minimized [70]. In short, the right governance must ensure that parties are willing and able to collaborate in a positive way. This type of governance is called "relational governance."

Social intervention plays a role in compensating the efficiency and technical limits of formal contracts. Relational governance comprises a social component by emphasizing trust and commitment. Relational governance refers to unwritten enforcement of obligations, promises, and expectations through social processes [75]. These processes promote a flexible behavior to adapt to unforeseen events, solidarity, and open information exchange. Key characteristics of relational governance are expected and accepted behavior, harmonious conflict resolution, and mutual dependence. Empirical research shows that relational governance is associated with trust, which improves performance in inter-organizational exchanges.

Do these two types of governance form substitutes or are they complements [20]? The opinion of being substitutes is found in expressions like "trust is good, but control is better" and "trust in the relationship avoids complex contracts." Recent research has clearly shown that whether to craft formal contracts or to apply a more socially oriented relational governance in outsourcing is not a matter of either/or. Both are recognized to be complements to each other, as was empirically shown [20,75,76]. Greater levels of relational norms were employed as contracts became increasingly customized; also, more complex contracts were developed with greater levels of relational governance. Clearly stated contractual terms and processes, and the presence of accepted and expected relational norms together provide confidence and trust to organizations to cooperate. This conclusion is in line with earlier related research on governance of information systems in general. For example, in their study on IT governance under environmental dynamism, Peterson et al. studied nine case studies of large organizations in different industries, located in Europe and the USA [77]. The results of this study show that, regardless of the level of environmental dynamism, effective IT governance processes are characterized by both application of formal methods and approaches for control and rational decision-making together with relational governance in which coalition building, trust, conflict resolution, and strategic experimentation are regarded as pivotal.

1.5.3 *Wrapping up Section 1.5: consequences for management*

Managing complex IT outsourcing partnerships is not an easy task. Both the outsourcing company and the IT suppliers must do their utmost to turn their collaboration into a sustained success [78]. The case studies we investigated and the interviews we[16] conducted with experts in the field showed that having the best people available is not sufficient to manage complex IT outsourcing partnerships successfully.

IT outsourcing governance requires substantial senior management attention. Three areas appear to be critical for a successful partnership.

1   Clear strategic positioning. The business needs a clear vision as to what it wants, this vision should be clearly communicated to the supplier(s). The same applies to the suppliers: without their clear positioning the (potential) recipients do not know who to approach.
2   Formal organizational arrangements. They include structural provisions that enable communication and collaboration at all levels. The case study companies with an adequate communication structure show unanimously a clear layered arrangement between provider and recipient.
3   Trust. Managing and enhancing trustful relations, on a personal and organizational level, is of highest importance. A purposeful organizational policy, which contributes to creating and maintaining trust, is establishing relational mechanisms at all levels. These are actively stimulated by senior management: again, "the tone at the top" shows the way.

Senior management (eventually the CEO) are responsible for designing and monitoring their organization. The above three areas delineate three clear areas of management responsibility for ensuring effective IT sourcing relationships.

Relationships with their reciprocal responsibilities are laid down in contracts. However, as we have discussed, specifying all requirements and obligations in advance is impossible, especially under conditions of change and uncertainty. That is where "relational governance" comes in: unwritten enforcement of obligations through social processes, which promotes a flexible behavior to adapt to unforeseen events, solidarity and open information exchange. There is a complementary relationship between formal contracts and relational governance: both are needed to shape an effective outsourcing relationship and are a prerequisite for trust.

1.6 Conclusion

1.6.1 Introduction

What does all this mean to the executive running the business and the manager responsible for developing and managing sourcing relationships? By reviewing this chapter, the reader can conclude that we suggest executives/managers stand back from the specifics of the sourcing agreement and think through three fundamental issues.

First: Expectation – what does the business acquiring the services and the organization providing them actually expect from the agreement, from their particular perspectives? Expectations certainly include the business outcomes expected (separately for each) but perhaps more importantly for a successful sourcing agreement, their expectations about the business, and technical roles to be played by *each* organization. These expectations form the foundation for the relationship – whether they are achieved is critical, and whether they are actually well defined and agreed to is even more important.

Second: Governance – how are these expectations, especially about roles and responsibilities, communicated with clarity and specificity among all participants in the agreement? Contracts are important but person-to person communications and relationships are important as well. Given the role of turbulence, change, and uncertainty in all aspects of the sourcing relationship which work to change the context and requirements, this ongoing problem requires continual attention throughout the life of the agreement. Governance on both sides of the agreement needs to be continuously focused on this issue.

Third: Performance: – what exactly are the specific success variables in the agreement? This goes to outcome expectations of course, but what exactly has to go well to make the agreements successful for all participants. This also goes to the requirements for on-going day-to-day management responsibilities and the clarity of communications on their performance among the participants in the agreement.

To be sure, this chapter provides many mental models and frameworks to assist the executive and manager to think through these three issues.

1.6.2 Fitting the agreement to the specific circumstances

While the above statements are perhaps obvious, what may not be so clear is that "one size does not fit all." Every business circumstance is unique, and every technology supplier has unique characteristics and capabilities. This is obvious. But what isn't so obvious is that the set of expectations and roles/relationships are, because of the uniqueness of both parties, especially unique to the agreement.

Considering all of the aspects discussed in previous parts of this chapter, two characteristics of an outsourcing agreement stand out in terms of differentiating each situation uniquely.

1.6.2.1 Degree of ICT and business integration (Fusion)

As mentioned at the beginning of the chapter, outsourcing originated with simple technology-focused services, for example, communications networks, application development, and data centers. Recently, the idea of "Fusion" has evolved [79], where ICT and business are combined to create a single joint operation, often in back-office business areas. For example, a supplier may provide complete payroll or accounting or even marketing services where the ICT component is imbedded in the service itself. The acquiring company purchases payroll services without its bundled ICT component.

This has rapidly evolved into more strategic relationships, where the parties jointly provide a product or service to end customers. In some senses, traditional supply chain relationships bundle the actual components involved with the ICT needed to plan, produce, and deliver them. As a recent research note put it:

> During the last decade, the business infrastructure has become digital with increased interconnections among products, processes, and services. Across many firms spanning different industries and sectors, digital technologies (viewed as combinations of information, computing, communication, and connectivity technologies) are fundamentally transforming business strategies, business processes, firm capabilities, products and services, and key interfirm relationships in extended business networks.
>
> *[80]*

Figure 1.7 shows this Fusion dimension as the "Degree of ICT and Business Integration" (Fusion). For any given sourcing relationship, this can vary from none (for example, a simple acquisition of network services) to complete (for example, acquiring payroll services). While these are relatively operational examples, Fusion works even more powerfully in products, services, and competitive strategies.

The question presented here, to differentiate sourcing agreements, to what extent ICT and Business Integration – Fusion – is expected and to be managed. The answer addresses the three issues mentioned above: the expectations of *each* of the participants, roles, and responsibilities, and the significant success variables.

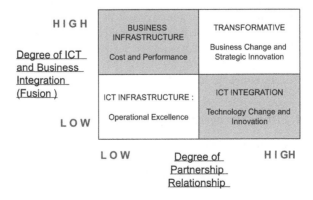

Figure 1.7 Partnership and Fusion in sourcing

1.6.2.2 Degree of partnership relationship

We devoted many pages in our previous book to the idea of partnership between its business and ICT areas [3]. For example, we cited Eisner: "Partnerships encourage a set of characteristics – trust, teamwork, a regard for someone else, and continuing checks and balances – that run counter to the factors that (contribute) to … messes" [81]. His key expressions here are trust and teamwork to which we added "common goals and mutual commitment" [3].

This is *partnership*, two or more enterprises coming together to (seamlessly and jointly) produce products, services, competitive initiatives, and goals common to all the participants. This idea suffuses much of current outsourcing – often more than just outsourcing, but the creation of group effort combining ICT with business. Often, this partnership is limited to technology areas, creating joint ways of providing ICT infrastructure to businesses.

1.6.3 Implications for ICT management

Specifying, understanding, and managing the implications of the various kinds of outsourcing arrangements puts a great challenge on what had been a typical technology service-oriented CIO management role. Gartner recently observed:

> 84% of CIOs from top digital performers have reimagined their role and have responsibility for areas of the business outside of traditional IT, the most common being innovation and transformation. These CIOs are also expanding their success criteria from IT delivery objectives to more broadly business-based measures.
>
> *[82]*

In admittedly simplistic terms, the first part of this observation likely describes circumstances for a company in the *Business Infrastructure* quadrant; the second the Transformative quadrant. The other two much more are ICT intensive: the ICT Integration quadrant requiring more outside management capabilities as well. In the ICT Infrastructure quadrant, more traditional ICT and sourcing management skills are required (and necessary in the other quadrants as well). Of course, the degree to which this observation applies to a given situation largely depends on the nature of the sourcing arrangement, with variables such as those considered in Figure X above. The issues for business management also change from merely a consumer of ICT services to, in many cases, active participants in the planning and management of outsourcing arrangements.

Again, things are different in every circumstance. As we observed above, "one size does not fit all."

1.6.4 Implications of multi-party arrangements: an integration responsibility

Throughout this chapter, the discussion can be read as though all sourcing is a two-party process: the purchaser (typically the business or its ICT management) and the supplier. In reality, many, perhaps most sourcing arrangements, involve multiple parties. In the past, this put an integration management responsibility largely on the CIO or the business purchasing group. An analogy perhaps is the general supply chain function in manufacturing firms, something that is intensely multi-party with considerable integration issues.[17]

Who is responsible for the integration and governance of the overall arrangement? As suggested above, it may be the CIO with advanced responsibilities, or perhaps this itself is something that is outsourced. The nature of this does differ in the different kinds of agreement: managing the ICT INFRASTRUCTURE agreement with multiple parties is clearly different from managing multiple parties in the TRANSFORMATIVE area. Nevertheless, this is an important issue and has to be addressed.

1.6.5 *The outsourcing relationship: combining Fusion and partnership*

To give a simple example of possible implications of the issues described in the chapter and summarized here, we offer this example table. It is not intended to be prescriptive, but rather to encourage discussion of the issues.

Every sourcing arrangement has elements of both Fusion and Partnership, though to a very different degree. Figure X shows the potential characteristics in each domain. Figure Y is shown here as simplistic example to demonstrate how various sourcing arrangements can differ from company to company (Table 1.1).

Table 1.1 Quadrants in transformation and Fusion

Quadrant	Quadrant characteristics	Example expectations from the business and ICT provider	Example governance: roles and responsibilities	Example performance: example success variables
ICT infrastructure	Low Fusion Low partnership (e.g., supplier)	Well-defined services and costs meeting ICT requirements	Monitoring ICT cost and performance Monitoring to performance Typically, ICT-targeted SLA	Operational excellence Cost and performance Flexibility in ICT terms
Business infrastructure	High business/ ICT Fusion Low partnership	Supply business capability: well-defined business services and costs meeting functional business needs	Business function planning and execution Typically, business-targeted SLA	Business functionality Flexibility in business terms
ICT integration	Low business/ ICT Fusion High partnership	ICT services meeting current and future ICT requirements, with access to innovation and advanced capabilities Pro-active change management	Seamless governance and decision-making Access to technology developments and innovations	Flexibility Timely change management
Transformative	High business/ ICT Fusion High partnership	Bundled business activities, seamlessly combining ICT and business capability from all parties	Establishing roles and responsibilities among the partied; overall providing direction and guidance, for each part, specific roles	Flexibility Clear, common goals Innovation

1.6.6 Summing up: conclusion

There is some irony here. While discussing each quadrant as though they are relatively the same size and timing – such minor issues as timing (speed to establish, execute, revise as circumstances change), length of term, intellectual property, and so forth – many complex variables are vastly different from agreement to agreement. (In some ways, there is a hint of agile here; as one moves more strategic, or more Fusion, the more traditional decision processes may not be so appropriate.) The irony is that so much is relatively old (for example, ICT Infrastructure), but overall the sourcing landscape is now so dynamic and multifaceted, it's all new.

But overall, the key point in our summary is this: executives and managers engaged in sourcing agreements should understand what the issues are – not a generic set of issues applicable to all, but rather the specific issues applicable to their own situation. Define them, and then execute.

Notes

1 E. Carmel: *Global Software Teams, Collaboration across Borders and Time Zones*, Prentice Hall, 1999.
2 This research was done as part of a research program at Tilburg University. For a complete report on the analysis and validation of conclusions, we refer to R.J. Benson, Pieter M. Ribbers and Ronald Blitstein: *Trust and Partnership – Strategic IT Management for Turbulent Times*, Wiley, 2014; for a complete report on the validation of conclusions on governance of complex IT outsourcing partnership, we refer to E. Beulen, P. Ribbers: "Governance of Complex IT Outsourcing Partnerships" in L.S. Rivard and B. Aubert (eds.), *Information Technology Outsourcing*, M.E. Sharpe, 2008. More extensive analyses are provided in E. Beulen, P. Ribbers, and J. Roos, *Managing IT Outsourcing*, 2nd ed. Routledge, 2011.
3 See, for example, Aircraft news, 2018, about the supply chain issues in aircraft manufacturing dealing with the specific Boeing and Airbus strategies in reducing cost, increasing quality reflected in reliability in the manufacturing process, and increasing throughput.
4 See, as example of the interconnection/dependence of supply chain participants: https://www.cmtc.com/blog/4-must-know-aerospace-supply-chain-management-issues.
5 This figure originated in Benson and Parker, "Introduction to Enterprise-wide Information Management," IBM, 1985, now adapted from Benson, Ribbers, and Weinstein, *Trust and Partnership*, Wiley 2014, page 5.
6 ICT: Information Communications and Technology. We'll use this acronym throughout this chapter.
7 ICT Capability is a central theme of Benson, Ribbers, and Blitstein, op. cit.
8 Adapted from Benson et al., op. cit., page 10.
9 Figure 1.3 is adapted from Benson et al., op. cit., page 40.
10 Figure 1.4 is adapted from Benson et al., op. cit., page 175.
11 See discussion on Incomplete Contract Theory in: Goo, J., Rajiv, K., Rao, H.R., Nam, K.: The Role of Service Level Agreements in Relational Management of Information Technology Outsourcing. *MIS Quarterly* 33 (1), pp. 119–145, March 2009; and in Beulen, E., Ribbers, P.: *IT Outsourcing Contracts: Practical Implications of Incomplete Contract Theory*. HICSS, 2003.
12 Figure 1.4 is adapted from Benson et al., op. cit., page 175.
13 Adapted from Benson et al., op. cit., page 68.
14 See for a discussion on this David R. King: Implications of uncertainty on firm outsourcing decisions. *Human 1.*
15 This research was done as a part of a research program at Tilburg University. This summary is based on Benson et al. For a complete report on the validation of the conclusions, we refer to Beulen, E., Ribbers P.: Governance of Complex Outsourcing Partnerships. In: L S. Rivard, B. Aubert (eds.), *Information Technology Outsourcing*. M. E. Sharpe, 2008. More extensive analyses are provided in Beulen, E., Ribbers, P., Roos. J.: *Managing IT Outsourcing*, 2nd ed., Routledge, 2011.
16 "We" refers here to E. Beulen and P. Ribbers.
17 One has only to look at the aircraft industry as an example, with Boeing and Airbus both struggling to effectively deal with an enormous supply chain. ICT-related situations are not so enormous, but can show similar dynamics.

References

1. Lamoureux, M.G.: The Strategic Sourcing Life Cycle – A Brief Introduction. *Coupa Software*, 2018. http://get.coupa.com/rs/950-OLU-185/images/20180205-CSO_Whitepaper_LifeCycle.pdf

2. Engel, R.J.: Strategic Sourcing: A Step-By-Step Practical Model. 89th Annual International Supply Management Conference, April 2004. https://www.instituteforsupplymanagement.org/files/pubs/proceedings/fbengel.pdf

3. Benson, R.J., Ribbers, P.M. with Blitstein, R.B.: *Trust and Partnership – Strategic IT Management for Turbulent Times*. Wiley, Hoboken, NJ, 2014.

4. Knorr, E.: What Is Cloud Computing? Everything You Need to Know Now. *InfoWorld* – From IDG, 31 May 2018. https://www.infoworld.com/author/Eric-Knorr/

5. See for this analysis: Koch, A., Ribbers, P.M., Rutkowski, A.F.: Ambidexterity at Axa Concern. Chapter 8.

6. Gibson, C.B., Birkinshaw, J.: The Antecedents, Consequences and Mediating Role of Organizational Ambidexterity. *Academy of Management Journal* 47 (2), pp. 209–226, 2004.

7. March, J.: Exploration and Exploitation in Organizational Learning. *Organization Science* 2 (1), pp. 71–87, 1991.

8. Lee, O.-K., Sambamurthy, V., Lim, K.H., Wei, K.K.: How Does IT Ambidexterity Impact Organizational Agility? *Information Systems Research* 26 (2), pp. 398–417, 2015.

9. Gartner: From the Gartner IT Glossary: What Is Bimodal? 31 August 2017. https://research.gartner.com/definition-whatis-bimodal?resId=3216217&srcId=1-8163325102

10. Peppard, J., Ward, J.: *The Strategic Management of Information Systems – Building a Digital Strategy*. Wiley, Hoboken, NJ, 2016.

11. Ross, J.W., Beath, C.M., Sebastian, I.M.: How to Develop a Great Digital Strategy. *MIT Sloan Management Review* 58 (2), pp. 7–9, 2017.

12. Mithas, S., Lucas, H.C.: What Is Your Digital Business Strategy? *IT Professional IEEE Computer Society* 12 (6), pp. 4–6, 2010.

13. Bharadwaj, A., El Sawy, O.A., Pavlou, P.A., Venkatraman, N.V.: Digital Business Strategy: Toward a Next Generation of Insights. *MIS Quarterly* 37 (2), pp. 471–482, 2013.

14. https://cio-wiki.org/?page=it-sourcing.

15. Kane, G.C., Palmer, D., Phillips, A.N., Kiron, D., Buckley, N.: Strategy, Not Technology, Drives Digital Transformation – Becoming a Digital Mature Enterprise. *MITSloan Management Review* 2015, https://sloanreview.mit.edu/projects/strategy-drives-digital-transformation

16. Williamson, O.E.: Organizational Innovation: The Transaction Cost Approach. In: Ronen, J. (ed.) *Entrepreneurship*. Lexington Books, Lexington, MA, 1983.

17. Papazoglou, M.P., Ribbers, P.M.: *E-Business – Organizational and Technical Foundations*. Wiley, Hoboken, NJ, 2006.

18. Douma, S., Schreuder, H.: *Economic Approaches to Organizations*. Prentice Hall, Upper Saddle River, NJ, 1998.

19. Williamson, O.E.: Comparative Economics Organization: The Analysis of Discrete Structural Alternatives. *Administrative Science Quarterly* 36, pp. 219–244, 1991.

20. Poppo, L., Zenger, T.: Do Formal Contracts and Relational Governance Function as Substitutes or Complements? *Strategic Management Journal* 23, pp. 707–725, 2002.

21. Barney, J.B.: Firm Resources and Sustained Competitive Advantage. *Journal of Management* 17, pp. 19–120, 1991.

22. Pfeffer, J., Salancik, G.R.: *The External Control of Organizations: A Resource Dependence Perspective*. Harper and Row, New York, NY, 1978.

23. Jarillo, J.C.: On Strategic Networks. *Strategic Management Journal* 9, pp. 31–41, 1988.

24. Dyer, J.D., Singh, H.: The Relational View: Cooperative Strategy and Sources of Interorganizational Competitive Advantage. *Academy of Management Review* 23, pp. 660–679, 1998.

25. Beulen, E., Ribbers, P., Roos, J.: *Managing IT Outsourcing*. 2nd ed. Routledge, London, 2011.

26. Sucky, E.: A Model for Dynamic Strategic Vendor Selection. *Computers and Operations Research* 34 (12), pp. 3638–3651, 2007.

27. Lane, C.: Introduction: Theories and Issues in the Study of Trust. In: Lane, R., Bachman R. (eds): *Trust within and between Organizations*. Oxford University Press, Oxford, 1998.

28. Sako, M.: Does Trust Improve Business Performance? In: Lane, R., Bachman R. (eds): *Trust within and between Organizations*. Oxford University Press, Oxford, 1998.

29. March, J.G., Simon, H.A.: *Organizations*. Wiley, Hoboken, NJ, 1958.
30. Mishra, A.K.: Organizational Responses to Crises: The Centrality of Trust. In: Kramer, R.M., Tyler, T. (eds): *Trust in Organizations*. Sage, Beverly Hills, CA, 1996.
31. Blomqvist, K., Stahle, P.: *Building Organizational Trust*. In: Proceedings of 16th Annual IMP Conference, Bath, London, 2000.
32. Parker-Priebe, M.: *Theory and Practice of Business-IT Organizational Interdependencies*. PhD Thesis Tilburg University, MM Parker, New York, NY, 1999.
33. Shockley-Zalabak, P., Ellis, K., Cesaria, R.: *Measuring Organizational Trust: A Diagnostic Survey and International Indicator*. International Association of Business Communicators, San Francisco, VA, 2000.
34. Baron, R.A.: *Behavior in Organizations*. Pearson, London, 1999.
35. Goo, J., Kishore, R., Nam, R., Rao, H., Song, Y.: An Investigation of Factors that Influence the Duration of IT Outsourcing Relationships. *Decisions Support Systems* 42 (4), pp. 2107–2125, 2007.
36. Langfield-Smith, K., Smith, D.: Management Control Systems and Trust in Outsourcing Relationships. *Management Accounting Research* 14 (3), pp. 281–297, 2003.
37. Fukuyama, F.: *Trust*. Hamish Hamilton, London, 1995.
38. Ansoff, I.: *Corporate Strategy*. Penguin Business Books, London, 1987.
39. D'Aveni, R.A., Gunther, R.: *Hypercompetition: Managing the Dynamics of Strategic Maneuvering*. The Free Press, New York, NY, 1994.
40. Haeckel, S.: *Adaptive Enterprise—Creating and Leading Sense-and-Respond Organizations*. Harvard Business School Press, Boston, MA, 1999.
41. Teece, D.: *Managing Intellectual Capital: Organizational, Strategic, and Policy Dimensions*. Oxford University Press, Oxford, 2000.
42. Galbraith, J.R.: *Organization Design*. Addison Wesley Publishing Company, Boston, MA, 1977.
43. Folta, T.: Governance and Uncertainty: The Tradeoff between Administrative Control and Commitment. *Strategic Management Journal* 19, pp. 1007–1028, 1998.
44. Kogut, B.: Joint Ventures and the Option to Expand and Acquire. *Management Science* 37, pp. 19–33, 1991.
45. Dyer, J., Kale, P., Singh, H.: How to Make Strategic Alliances Work. *Sloan Management Review* 42, pp. 37–43, 2001.
46. Leonard-Barton, D.: *Wellsprings of Knowledge: Building and Sustaining the Sources of Innovation*. Harvard Business School Press, Boston, MA, 1995.
47. Sener, I.: Strategic Responses of Top Managers to Environmental Uncertainty. *Procedia – Social and Behavioral Sciences* 58, pp. 169–177, 2012.
48. Malone, T.W., Yates, J., Benjamin, R.I.: Electronic Markets and Electronic Hierarchies. *Communications of the ACM* 30, pp. 484–496, 1987.
49. Williamson, O.E.: *Markets and Hierarchies*. Free Press, New York, NY, 1975.
50. Clemons, E.K., Sashidhar, P.R., Row, M.C.: The Impact of Information Technology on the Organization of Economic Activity: The "Move the Middle Hypothesis". *Journal of Management Information Systems* 10, pp. 9–35, 1993.
51. Kanter, R.: Collaborative Advantage: The Art of Alliances. *Harvard Business Review*, July/August, 1994.
52. Andriole, S.J.: Five Myths about Digital Transformation. *MIT Sloan Management Review* 58 (3), pp. 20–22, 2017.
53. Gewald, H., Dibbern, J.: Risks and Benefits of Business Process Outsourcing: A Study of Transaction Services in the German Banking Industry. *Information and Management* 46, pp. 249–251, 2009.
54. Holderman, R.-J.: 5 Success Factors for Business Process Outsourcing. BPM Leader – Independent Community for Business Process Management Professionals. BPMleader.com 10 July 2018.
55. Zerbe, S.: *Guiding Digital Champions – Cloud Transformation*. Presentation at the SEA Seminar at TUM School of Management, Munchen, 24 April 2018.
56. Cusamano, M.: Cloud Computing and SaaS as New Computing Platforms. *Communications of the Association for Computing Machinery* 53, pp. 27–29, 2010.
57. Vaquero, L., Caceres, J., Linder, M., Rodero-Merino, L.: A Break in the Clouds: Towards a Cloud Definition. *ACM SIGCOMM Computer Communication Review* 39, pp. 50–55, 2009.
58. Weinhardt, C., Anandasivam, A., Blau, B., Borissov, N., Meinl, T., Michalk, W., Stosser, J.: Cloud Computing. *Wirtschaftsinformatik* 51 (5), pp. 453–462, 2009.

59. McFarlan, F.W., Nolan, R.: How to Manage an IT Outsourcing Alliance. *MIT Sloan Management Review* 36, pp. 9–23, 1995.
60. Curry, W., Willcocks, L.: Analyzing for Types of IT Outsourcing Decisions in the Context of Scale, Client/Server Interdependency and Risk Mitigation. *Information Systems Journal* 8 (2), pp. 119–143, 1998.
61. Willcocks, L., Choi, C.: Co-Operative Partnerships and 'Total' IT-Outsourcing: From Contractual Obligation to Strategic Alliance? *European Management Journal* 13 (1), pp. 67–78, 1995.
62. Van Grembergen, W., De Haes, S.: *Implementing Information Technology Governance – Models, Practices, and Cases.* IGI Publishing, Hershey, PA, 2008.
63. ATOS Registration Document, 2017. Downloaded 3 June, 2018.
64. Verra, G.: *International Account Management.* Kluwer, Deventer, 2003.
65. Cullen, S., Willcocks, L.: *Intelligent IT Outsourcing: Eight Building Blocks to Success.* Butterworth-Heineman, Oxford, 2003.
66. Lee, J.N., Kim, Y.G. Effect of Partnership Quality on IS Outsourcing Success: Conceptual Framework and Empirical Validation. *Journal of Management Information Systems* 15 (4), pp. 29–61, 1999.
67. Palvia, P.: A Dialectic View on Information Systems Outsourcing: Pros and Cons. *Information and Management* 29 (5), pp. 265–275, 1995.
68. Wallace, W. Reporting Practices: Potential Lessons from Cendant Corporation. *European Management Journal* 18 (3), pp. 328–333, 2000.
69. Sabherwal, K. The Role of Trust in Outsourced IS Development Projects. *Communications of the Association for Computing Machinery* 42 (2), pp. 80–86, 1999.
70. Beulen, E., Ribbers, P.: *IT Outsourcing Contracts: Practical Implications of the Incomplete Contract Theory.* Proceedings of the 36th Hawaii International Conference on Systems Sciences, Hawaii, 2003.
71. Wheeler-Carmichael, G.: With this Contract I Thee Wed: A Look at the Legal Process Involved in IT Outsourcing. *Montgomery Research Europe*, ISSN 1476-2064, 2002.
72. Lacity, M., Hirschheim, R.: *Beyond the Information Systems Outsourcing Bandwagon.* Wiley, Hoboken, NJ, 1995.
73. Nam, K., Rajagopalan, S., Rao, H.: A Two Level Investigation of Information Systems Outsourcing. *Communication of the ACM* 39, pp. 36–44, 1996.
74. Aubert, B.S., Rivard, S.P.: A Transaction Cost Approach to Outsourcing Behavior: Some Empirical Evidence. *Information & Management* 30, pp. 51–64, 1996.
75. Goo, J., Rajiv, K., Rao, H.R., Nam, K.: The Role of Service Level Agreements in Relational Management of Information Technology Outsourcing. *MIS Quarterly* 33 (1), p. 119, 2009.
76. Qi, C., Patrick, Y.K. C.: Relationship, Contract and IT Outsourcing Success: Evidence from Two Descriptive Case Studies. *Decision Support Systems* 53, pp. 859–869, 2012.
77. Peterson, R.R., Parker, M.M., Ribbers, P.M.: Information Technology Governance Processes under Environmental Dynamism: Competing Theories of Decision Making and Knowledge Sharing. Twenty-Third International Conference on Information Systems, 2002.
78. Beulen, E., Ribbers, P.: Governance of Complex IT Outsourcing Partnerships. In: Rivard, S., Aubert, B.A. (eds): *Information Technology Outsourcing.* M.E. Sharpe, Armonk, NY, 2008.
79. Hinnsen, P.: *Business/IT Fusion: How to Move Beyond Alignment and Transform IT in Your Organization.* Mach Media NV/SA, Gent, 2009.
80. Bharadwai, A., et al.: Digital Business Strategy: Toward a Next Generation of Insights. *MIS Quarterly* 37 (2), pp. 483–509, 2013.
81. Eisner, M.D., Cohen, A.: *Working Together: Why Great Partnerships Succeed.* Harper Collins, New York, NY, 2010.
82. Gartner: Redefine IT's Business Value – CIOs Must Change How They Communicate IT Value in the Digital Era, 2019. gartner.com.

2

INFLUENCE OF NEW BUSINESS MODELS AND TECHNOLOGY ON TECHNOLOGY STRATEGY AND PARTNERSHIPS

Christopher P. Holland

2.1 Introduction

The relationship between Information Technology (IT) and business strategy has evolved, as technology has become more embedded in organizational processes and strategies. In the 1980s and 1990s, research articles and business publications emphasized the importance of IT and strategy alignment [1,2], while companies wrestled with the implementation of Enterprise Resource Planning (ERP) and supply chain management systems [3]. In the late 1990s, the emergence of e-commerce in both business and consumer markets opened up a whole new set of opportunities and challenges and saw the emergence of the early retail technology giants such as eBay and Amazon. Academic researchers and business commentators quickly realized that IT was not simply a supporting function but had the potential to generate competitive advantage and also to create new types of organizations and markets, which simply didn't or couldn't exist without digital technology. Leaving aside the debate on whether or not IT can create competitive advantage [4,5], its central role in the design, operation and growth of modern business organizations and market networks cannot be disputed [6].

The strategic role of technology is exemplified by the emergence of new types of business models across sectors, for example Elimica and Li & Fung in supply chain management, Uber and Didi in transportation, Airbnb and Expedia in travel and hotels, and Strava in social media sports. In these examples of business model innovation, technology is not simply a supporting function but instead is the genesis of the business model and vital to its continuing operations and evolution, i.e. technology is an integral component of key activities such as customer acquisition and retention strategies and the delivery of the product or service. The software encapsulates the algorithms that act as recommendation agents and manage the social media feedback process, which enables the development of trust between participants. The technology also plays a crucial role in the organization and management of supply capacity, e.g. rooms or drivers, and in the development of social capital that binds these enterprises together and makes them accessible and usable to both customers and workers alike. These recent developments raise important questions regarding the way that IT is conceptualized and related to business constructs such as strategy and outsourcing. One way of incorporating technology into business thinking is through the idea of business models [7–10].

Theoreticians have recognized that new developments in business models and technology require a new outlook on how to conceptualize business and technology as separate entities, and in their inter-dependency with each other. For example, in a review of Information Systems (IS) strategy models, three distinct groups of models were identified: (1) IS strategy as a support function; (2) IS strategy as a plan for the IS function itself and (3) IS strategy as a shared view of the broader role of IS within the organization [11]. In a similar vein, but focused on digital business strategy, a transition from IS is a supporting function to a fusion of IT and business, where IT and business are equal in importance [12], i.e. neither is subservient to the other but instead are related to each other in a recursive manner. In this view, IT plays a crucial role in all aspects of the supply chain, including business-to-business supply management innovations, and in retail customer-facing activities. The business model concept takes this a stage further by placing technology as an integral component together with business constructs that form an overall logic, or model of how a business works, which can be used as a strategy blueprint, and in the Internet era, for raising funds for new ideas and ventures.

The question remains though of how to manage IT? Does its strategic importance mean that it needs to be controlled closely and 'owned' by the business? Or is it possible to outsource technology and treat it as an input function, rather like a raw material or component supplier to a manufacturing business? A different model is to think of relationships between a company and its technology providers as partnerships, the implication being that these relationships are much more dynamic and can change in response to competitive pressures, new strategic intent and business performance.

One way of exploring this problem is to examine new business models where technology appears, prima facie, to play such a crucial role in the success of companies such as Airbnb or Uber and many other innovative companies that are often called 'industry disruptors'. By gaining a better understanding of the avant-garde of the digital revolution, it should be possible to develop more general insights and ideas into the relationships between technology and business, and the appropriate types of relationships with technology vendors and consultants. In the next section, a brief review of historical themes that preceded business model concepts is presented. This is relevant to the discussion of business models because many of the concepts from earlier academic and business discussion underpin the development of the business model framework. The ideas are therefore still valid and apply to some extent equally well to today's IT management issues.

2.2 Historical themes

2.2.1 IT and management

A comment about the general nature of IT and its relationship with management is a logical place to start and it may also partly explain the complexity and inherent difficulty of managing IT resources and the roles of information and communication in management. Fundamentally, management is the coordination of economic activity and the only way to coordinate activities of any kind is through the sharing, i.e. communication, of meaningful information [13]. The key phrase here is the communication of information, rather than the processing of information, or storage. Computers on their own would therefore have relatively little impact on management – it is only when they are connected together in networks, that computers create IT systems that process, store and communicate information, and therefore influence management in a direct and fundamental manner, by changing the coordination of activities. IT systems and management are therefore closely bound up with each other because changes to networked IT systems inevitably lead to new forms of decision-making and organizational change [13]. Other technologies, e.g. production technologies, or developments in materials, do not have this direct relationship with management.

2.2.2 The productivity paradox

Despite huge investments into new IT systems in the 1980s, there was not an accompanying significant growth in productivity. The term 'productivity paradox' was coined to capture the situation where productivity gains were only marginal and not as high as expected in the US economy [14]. Several explanations have been suggested, and perhaps the most relevant one to this discussion related to business models is the idea that most companies only changed their technology and did not attempt to significantly improve on their existing business model or create brand new ones, which led to the philosophy of Business Process Reengineering (BPR) [15] that was arguably the precursor to business model redesign.

Another explanation is that IT was viewed as a capital resource, and the emphasis was therefore on the efficient management of the technology itself to reduce IT costs, and less effort was spent on its creative potential. In this environment, it was quite natural to treat IT as an input into an organization's activities, together with raw materials, staff, components, energy and so on. It was therefore a logical strategy to outsource IT systems to specialist providers.

2.2.3 Outsourcing

Some commentators might argue that the use of shared mainframe systems in the 1970s was the first example of outsourcing but the distinction is that companies bought computing power from mainframe suppliers and never directly owned and controlled it. It's not possible to 'outsource' something that is not currently owned and managed within the enterprise, though there are clearly parallels between buying mainframe computing power on a 'per use' basis and today's Cloud computing services.

The business practice of IToutsourcing first came to prominence in the 1980s, mainly in large organizations. Outsourcing part or all of a company's IT systems was seen as a way of gaining control over an expensive and fast-changing capital infrastructure [16]. The idea was taken further still by increasing the scope of the outsourcing to include business processes. This was a natural development because the IT systems defined and contained the business processes. Indeed, it was actually quite hard to separate processes from systems, as had been discovered in much earlier research [13] and the technology of enterprise systems explicitly linked common databases with functional areas of a business and software configuration was linked directly to business process design [17].

To many CEOs grappling with new technology such as Enterprise Resource Planning (ERP) systems and Personal Computers (PCs) for all administrative workers and managers, IT was a necessary evil. Companies could not survive without these new systems because the core business processes of large organizations were being automated: sales order processing, production, warehousing, finance and marketing. In addition, the first developments of e-commerce were happening in the form of Electronic Data Interchange (EDI) with the potential of integrated supply chains. Waves of new technology including ERP systems, EDI, PCs and smart software to manage the supply chain were introduced in order to achieve an organization-wide view of information and performance across all functional areas of the business and increased integration along the supply chain. In addition, large companies also had the problems of managing legacy systems in parallel with new developments.

2.2.4 Information Technology and competitive advantage?

The sheer scale of investments into IT systems in the 1980s and 1990s meant that IT costs came under increased scrutiny and questions about its economic and strategic benefits were naturally raised. Two statistics stand out from this era. In the US economy in the 1980s, firms spent a trillion dollars on IT yet failed to realize significant economic productivity. In the 1990s, IT investment accounted for almost half of most firms' capital expenditures [16]. It is then not surprising that the value of IT outsourcing grew rapidly in the 1980s and 1990s in response to clear and difficult challenges.

Although there were isolated, almost storied examples of IT and competitive advantage in the 1980s and 1990s such as American Airlines and Baxter Travenol Healthcare [18,19], these were very much the exception rather than the rule. Most managers were much more concerned with the successful implementation of new technology, IT cost justification in terms of administrative and headcount savings and figuring out ways of keeping it running in an orderly and cost-effective manner, i.e. maintenance, technical support and software package updates. The argument put forward by Carr in his controversial book *IT Doesn't Matter* argued persuasively that managers should focus on IT cost management and risk reduction of IT projects, and stop seeking out mythical competitive advantage [20]. Carr's arguments strongly support the ethos of outsourcing of IT systems.

In summary, outsourcing seemed to be a good solution to managing complex and costly IT systems that required teams of specialized staff to operate them and offered operational performance benefits only. The outsourcing companies could manage IT systems more effectively by exploiting their economies of scale and also economies of scope because they were able to employ staff with a broad range of technology skills that led to synergistic benefits, not least, in terms of integrating separate systems and technologies together. But there were also significant problems starting to emerge in two distinct areas. First, what if the outsourcing arrangements soured or went wrong? Who was to blame, and what were the consequences?

In the case of Sainsbury's, which entered into a multi-billion dollar outsourcing deal with Accenture in 2000, the decision was reversed before the end of the contract because of poor logistics performance and resulted in a significant write-down of IT assets [21,22]. Other companies that struggled with moving beyond complex legacy systems include Sears. When Sears merged with Kmart, Kmart had multiple systems for each logistics area, inventory (3), logistics (5), supply chain management (5) and merchandise planning systems (4). Sears had a similarly complex set of legacy systems. In the article titled 'Code Blue', the sheer complexity of Kmart's IT systems is shown in an inventory of its base systems for different functional areas. It had technology partnerships with i2, IBM, GEIS, PriceWaterhouseCoopers, Manugistics, JDA, NCR Corp., NCR and others [23]. In this type of situation, it would be extremely difficult to think about new business models based on a blank sheet of paper with this huge inertia from legacy systems. Over the period 2006–2016, Sears lost 96% of its market capitalization. Of course, its legacy systems were not the only explanation for its dismal performance but they played a vital role in hampering their ability to adapt to the growth of the Internet as a sales and search channel, and also made it extremely difficult to integrate the two companies onto a common technology platform.

The point here is that IT can be a remarkable tool to create new business models, re-engineer existing ones, but as the technology changes, as new business models emerge, those companies that mismanage their IT systems and are unable to adapt and change their business models can fail spectacularly. Conversely, IT coupled with novel business models can create enormous value.

The second issue with outsourcing is: how should a company react when the technology landscape changes dramatically? If it has outsourced its IT capabilities, this could place it in a disadvantaged position because it no longer owns or controls its own staff and systems. One way of thinking about this problem is to group technologies into stable and emerging technology. The rate of change in a technology is of crucial importance in determining how a company should choose to manage a particular technology, in particular how it works with technology companies and these issues are discussed in the next section.

2.2.5 *Change and stability*

Several important themes emerge from this initial exploration of IT and business change. IT has evolved very quickly over the past 40 years and continues to change rapidly. While some aspects of IT appear to have 'settled down', i.e. become relatively stable and homogenous, other aspects of technology continue to raise many unknown threats and opportunities, e.g. the Internet of Things and cognitive computing. In the product lifecycle of technology, there is constant change and adaptation in the initial and growth stages, followed by a period of relative stability in the maturity phase. The introduction of a new technology may then stimulate the move towards a period of further change.

For example, large corporations first implemented ERP systems in the late 1980s, in order to impose a set of standards and disciplines on business processes, often on an international scale. The ERP systems continued to develop enhanced functionality and new capabilities, and new versions of the software were released on a regular basis but the core concept and capabilities of an ERP system settled down, and the market matured, evidenced by the emergence of simpler, cut-down versions of the software, that were simpler to manage and implement, and were priced more attractively for smaller businesses.

Of course, the large vendors SAP and Oracle continued to develop new software functionality, but the main developments were in areas that were arguably unrelated to the original concept of an enterprise system, e.g. data analytics and supply chain management systems. The core ERP systems themselves could be accurately described as a stable technology. The next main technology change was not to do with the software itself, but how it was managed and delivered. Cloud computing services made it possible to deliver the software remotely, which reduced the IT infrastructure requirements for the business, and also made it possible to introduce new pricing mechanisms, e.g. on a per transaction basis with very little or no upfront capital cost to the ERP project.

ERP development is a classic example of a new technology that was widely adopted, settled into a period of stability and maturity, and then underwent a further transformation through the introduction of another technology, Cloud computing. Similar observations can be made regarding the development of trading networks based on EDI where the technology matured and was then superseded very quickly by Internet standards.

A lot of the core IT infrastructure such as networks, operating systems, data storage, processors and transaction software systems are in a mature stage of development. The new technologies outlined in Table 2.1 are still in a state of flux, and it is difficult to predict even their technical trajectory let alone their likely business importance. Managing stable and emerging technologies presents very different sets of problems that require different skills sets, staff, strategic objectives and philosophies. Companies therefore need to distinguish between stable technologies and new technologies.

Looking forward, two themes emerge that will arguably have the most influence on how firms approach the management of IT systems. The first is that over the next five to ten years, a new wave of IT is apparent. This is termed 'new emerging technology'. The second is the business phenomenon of novel business models that have disrupted whole industries, on a global scale. It is argued that these two phenomena should be viewed together and that it is necessary to develop technology partnerships to compete successfully and exploit new technologies in a rapidly changing business landscape.

2.3 Review of emerging technology and new business models

2.3.1 Emerging technology

Emerging technology is not a single new development or innovation but rather a wave of inter-related technologies that together create a new technology landscape where there are arguably very few significant technology barriers to the development of new business models. In the same way that ERP and supply chain systems emerged in the 1980s and early 1990s and transformed organization design and business processes, the Internet and e-commerce started to revolutionize retailing in the late 1990s and social media that only appeared in the 2000s has redefined the dynamics and rules of communication, the current wave of emerging technologies is reshaping the business models of individual companies that are in turn disrupting whole industries. This idea is perhaps best explained by Marc Andreessen, who has been at the forefront of technology and business throughout his career. He describes the current position as 'software is eating the world' [24]. An overview of the emerging technology is given in Table 2.1.

The technologies outlined in Table 2.1 act in tandem with each other and it is their collective impact that matters. The combination of the individual technologies leads to a rich and diverse set of outcomes, not least the initiation of many new start-ups, some of which will blossom into successful companies. Uber, the poster child of new business models, uses a combination of the ubiquity of mobile phones, a smart app to connect customers with drivers, social media systems to review both drivers and customers, automated billing and payment systems that give surety of payment for the driver and security for the customer, and a technology platform that once it has started benefits from network economics [25], which makes it more attractive to customers and therefore increases the incentive for new drivers to join, which in turn increases customer service and stimulates further demand. Data analytics of the sea of data generated from this business are then used to further refine new customer acquisition strategies, shape incentives for customers and drivers, and are used to design dynamic pricing strategies.

In some ways, there is nothing new in the pattern of technology innovation here. Technology innovation has always worked in this manner, where a set of seemingly diverse and unrelated developments come together in a coherent manner to create a new product or service. For example, the PC revolution that started in the 1980s depended crucially on the widespread availability of general purpose computing chips, memory chips, hard disk drives for data storage and useful business software. In turn, the PC paved the way for the e-commerce revolution when the Internet became usable to the general

Table 2.1 Definition of the main categories of new emerging technology

Technology	Technology implications and business consequences
Mobile connectivity from Wi-Fi and mobile networks	Pervasive and low-cost, high-bandwidth connectivity between individuals, business organizations, market networks and government, and also between physical entities that form the Internet of Things (IOT)
Internet of Things	Connection between all types of physical devices such as clothes, household appliances, industrial infrastructure, buildings, public lighting systems, security devices and transport, which generates large volumes of new forms of data that can potentially be used in creative and novel ways to improve existing services and develop ones
Software development platforms	Ease of software development, and opening up of software development opportunities to non-experts
Cloud computing	Cheap and flexible data storage, access to low-cost processing power by anyone, removal of high initial capital costs to new technology projects, access to high-quality systems on a per transaction basis, simplification of technology maintenance by separating technology infrastructure from software services
Encryption standards	Secure communication is open to everyone, including individuals and new entrants as well as large corporations and government organizations
Virtual currencies	Bitcoin and similar developments simplify the payment systems for business models that require complex interactions between groups of individuals and organizations that often require high volumes of low value payments
Platforms for everything	Critical mass can be achieved in almost any market in a very short space of time, e.g. markets for software developers, trading platforms, online music and films, knowledge exchange in specialized fields, social media communication and government services
Virtual reality	Rich, interactive interfaces that are necessary for complex and services that require an immersive and realistic virtual experience, e.g. online gaming and remote surgery
Artificial intelligence	Smart interfaces between man and machine to enhance everyday services and enable non-technical individuals to access complex services without understanding the intricacies of how systems work
Big data and analytics	Application of analytical techniques and often large amounts of processing power to uncover and make sense of all types of data
Machine learning	Automation of analytics and pattern finding
3D printing	Distributed manufacturing and production management based on additive 3D printing and manufacturing technology

public through the availability of easy-to-use World-Wide-Web interfaces such as Mosaic and Internet Explorer.

To explore how the technologies shown in Table 2.1 create new possibilities and underpin novel business models, three case vignettes are presented in Table 2.2. The purpose is to illustrate the characteristics and operations of a range of business models, and to explore the role of technology and how it relates to activities, or business processes such as new customer acquisition, and growth. A lifecycle framework of business models is used starting with technology, the launch of the company with a product offer, the acquisition and retention of customers, the growth strategy and then an overview of the business model.

Table 2.2 New business models and the role of new, emerging technology

	Big data technologies	Launch and product offer	Customer acquisition and retention	Growth strategy	Business model
Sharing economy: Didi	Relatively simple mobile app that relied on high penetration of mobile phones. Technology partnership with Tencent proved vital for both technology infrastructure and digital payments.	The company offered its app to taxi drivers (yellow cabs in China), who far outnumber private vehicles, and targeted young drivers who already had mobile phones and were more likely to share the app with friends and colleagues. The launch city was Shenzhen because of its lower regulatory hurdles.	Heavy use of promotional codes and discounts to increase the customer database, in severe competition, in particular with Uber.	Geographic expansion across China, where each market is local to a city and through acquisition in the USA via a shareholding in Lyft.	Build market power through the simultaneous recruitment of taxi drivers (followed by other categories of drivers, i.e. limousines, private cars and buses), and customers on a city-by-city basis. Estimated penetration of app with taxi drivers is 80%, which is strong evidence of benefitting from network economics, where the growth in customers and taxi capacity have a positive influence on each other, and then build significant barriers to entry for new startups.

| Digital intermediary and comparison tool: Expedia | The company launched from within Microsoft and was designed to showcase the innovative use of technology for the travel industry. The partnership with Microsoft gave it access to technology expertise and seed-corn funding. | The original concept of Expedia was a technology start-up for the travel industry. The product offer is very simple and compelling: to offer price and product comparisons across a wide choice of airlines, hotels, car hire, ancillary travel services and holiday packages to consumers through an advanced search platform. The principal customer benefit is an easy to use, fast search process, across a large number of providers. Expedia's product offers have since expanded to include technology platforms that its travel partners use to manage their own businesses, e.g. the packaging and presentation of hotel information directly to customers through a hotel's own websites and also through intermediaries. | The venture capital funding that made the company more independent from Microsoft was spent largely on promotions and marketing activity to grow the customer base to a critical mass that would enable it to generate transaction fees from airlines and hotels, and also to make it more attractive for new travel companies so they use its platform as a distribution channel. | Expedia has grown to be one of the world's largest travel intermediaries through a comparison of organic growth that has benefited from network economics and also from a significant number of acquisitions of related travel platforms. | There is no single 'business model' that encapsulates the company's activities. The original concept was to showcase the use of technology in the travel industry, and this resulted in the digital intermediary concept, where Expedia is an intermediary or travel agent (Ye et al. 2017). Based on its spate of acquisitions and the push towards the vertical integration of technology into travel provider's IT infrastructure, the company also resembles a technology solutions provider, where it sells travel software to hotels, airlines, car hire and other travel companies. |

(Continued)

	Big data technologies	Launch and product offer	Customer acquisition and retention	Growth strategy	Business model
Social media: strava	The founders already had experience of running technology companies, and Strava is fundamentally a specialist social network, which is targeted at athletes. The company manages its own software development, which is important because almost all product innovations rely on new Strava software developments and partnerships with other technology companies such as smartphone platforms, specialist GPS device and camera manufacturers.	Strava is a social network for athletes that has two main benefits: (1) motivate athletes to train better through competition with themselves over time and with other athletes; (2) entertain athletes and encourage them to continue with their activities. In cycling, separate riders can compete against each other for specific sections of rides termed 'segments', which enable direct comparability. The company launched into a single sports sector, cycling, in order to build a critical mass of riders. Cycling and running account for 90% of the users, with 26 other sports accounting for the remaining 10%.	Around 80% of new customers initially sign on through a mobile app, and many of these then switch to specific GPS cycling devices to track their rides. Customers sign up to a free app and are then encouraged to become 'active', i.e. to post details of their rides and also to follow other riders, and to be followed, so that they are more likely to continue to use the service. The product innovation strategy is to incrementally improve it, e.g. better personalization, security, ride features, live segments.	The company enjoyed six years of organic growth through word of mouth, starting with elite cyclists and then broadening its appeal to a larger cycling audience and then to the running community. Cycling 'influencers' are targeted, and the company focuses on around 12 cities worldwide for most of its growth. Smartphone penetration provides the crucial technology infrastructure to sign new customers via apps. The sales funnel is very simple: free users, active users who upload rides, premium users. Active users and social connectivity are two crucial components that determine the conversion level from free to premium user.	The free signup of new athletes encourages use of the application and is an opportunity to showcase the benefits of the social network. In addition, free users generate valuable data for other users, e.g. times, distances, routes and comments, as well as introducing their friends. There is an opportunity to cross-sell GPS tracking devices and a spinoff service, Strava Metro, exploits the athletes' big data from GPS tracking for city and town planning, where cycle and walkways are important elements of urban design and planning.

2.4 Discussion

Each of the companies in Table 2.2 is an example of a type of new business model, broadly categorized by sharing economy, digital intermediary and comparison tool, behavioural ecosystems and social media. Other categories of business model include trading platforms (eBay, Taobao, Amazon), streaming services (Netflix, Spotify) and Business-to-Business (B2B) focused platforms (Elimica, Covisint, Li & Fung). In addition, there is extensive use of apps for simple e-service applications that connect business organizations directly with consumers, i.e. with no wider networking with other consumers or links to multiple businesses. For example, airline apps for online ticketing, boarding, flight information and payment, and mobile phone apps for online top-ups of pre-paid phones and account management.

It is argued that each of the companies in Table 2.2 is representative in a broad sense of its group, and the use of these individual companies as examples therefore has implications for new business models and the associated use of technology in general. The other categories of business models could be used to extend the argument.

Didi is an example of the sharing economy, which includes Airbnb, Uber, Lyft and many other smaller examples. The term sharing economy, or collaborative consumption, is applied to a whole category of new types of business, which are based on the novel use of technology to enable new forms of coordination that make it economically possible to share resources, whether this is to share cars, lawn mowers, spare rooms or whatever. These services tend to emphasize the peer-to-peer nature of the sharing, though the extent of the influence of the technology platform over the providers is clearly open to debate, e.g. see the recent discussion about whether Uber drivers are private providers of 'spare' driving capacity, or are employees. However, the crucial point with respect to new types of business models is that technology is at the centre of the sharing economy business models, and these new businesses epitomize the effects of Information Systems to reduce coordination costs and match providers and users of a range of services that would otherwise not even be aware of each other. In a sense, the structures in these business models were predicted by the electronic markets hypothesis [26], though the resulting networks of organizations and individuals are perhaps better described as market networks that incorporate businesses and consumers rather than electronic markets. The business models described in Table 2.1, together with business-to-business examples of Elimica, Covisint and Li & Fung, align more closely with the theories of smart market networks [6, 27] and mixed mode network structures [28], and move to the middle [29] theories.

The fact that technology is at the heart of the business model is also true for the digital intermediaries such as Expedia, moneysavingexpert, ctrip and hotels.com, and also for the social media companies such as Strava.com. This is important because it raises important questions about the conceptualization and understanding of IT and business. An impact-theoretic approach [29, 30], where IT is viewed as an external factor impacting on a company's strategy, organization and operations is clearly inadequate [31] and a more nuanced approach is required that captures the interactions between managerial actions, technology and business constructs, and the relationships between them. The work of Chen and others [11] also seems to fall short because their most advanced model describes IS strategy as the shared view of its broad role within the organization. The positioning of IT and business as separate and equal is perhaps closer to what is required [12] but even this approach may be insufficient to capture what is happening with the rapid changes in business models.

The new business models have several things in common with each other, and the examples in Table 2.2 are used to illustrate the points.

2.4.1 Information-centric businesses

They are all information-centric businesses, which make them technology-centric businesses. What I mean by information-centric is that the strategic logic and operations of the business model are defined and managed in terms of the capture, storage, processing and sharing of information between the social and business networks of customers, individual providers, business organizations and the digital platforms themselves. Although it is possible to separate technology from the strategy, in practice it makes much more sense to consider them together in a holistic manner.

Consider the problem of allocating a driver to a Didi customer. The request is captured via a mobile app, which then goes to a central server that relays back relevant drivers within a geographic proximity of the customer, together with driver ratings and feedback. In parallel, the customer information is sent to drivers who are also able to see information about the customer. On the basis of this exchange of information, a matching process takes place and the driver is directed to the customer's location. The whole process is defined in terms of information and the associated use of technology and it is much easier to define, model, comprehend and change, if one considers technology and business simultaneously.

2.4.2 Technology-induced disruption

Technology-induced business disruption creates opportunities for new companies to enter a market. The general explanation for this phenomenon is that existing companies have vested interests in maintaining the status quo and are therefore unlikely to destroy themselves by building a competing organization. They also have extensive investments into their current business models, including legacy information systems, relationships with trading partners, as well as operations and cultures that are designed around their current way of doing business. All of these elements are difficult to change individually, and to change them all requires a herculean effort. Perhaps the best example of a company that epitomizes these issues is that of Kmart.

2.4.3 Business model launch patterns

The launch and growth of these new businesses required a combination of innovative technology coupled with novel marketing strategies to reach a critical mass of users, and then to exploit network effects accompanied by a period of continuous improvements. A significant part of Expedia's initial funding was spent on promotional activity to build up the customer base, which then enabled Expedia to attract more airline companies onto the platform. Once a critical mass of customers and airlines was reached, the platform benefited from network effects, which allowed it to grow organically through word of mouth with consumers, and the larger customer base made it an important distribution channel for airlines, so they were encouraged to remain on the platform. Strava focused all of its initial marketing efforts on a single sector, cycling, and targeted its offer on elite cyclists, in order to build a critical mass and not dilute its resources. Once users started to sign onto the service, the appeal was widened to a broader range of cyclists and then to runners and other sports.

2.4.4 Network scale versus market share

The scale of the network is important to create value for different members of the technology platform, whether these are airline companies on Expedia, taxi drivers on Didi or cyclists on Strava. Taking an extreme example of Ford in the 1920s, which was a highly vertically integrated business, the benefits from its size were economies of scale in production, distribution and marketing. There were also significant economies of scope with the introduction of new models. Of course, Ford now works with many more suppliers and is less vertically integrated, but it still enjoys significant economies of scale and scope in its operations. These same benefits also apply to today's largest retailers such as Walmart and Tesco. However, the definition of scale is different in a network economy and network scale features in many new business models.

In the Strava example, scale still matters but it is very different because it is not concerned with ownership of assets but rather control over information. The key variable for a sports social network that matters most to potential new customers is the number of active athletes in their chosen sport in their geographic location. A large number of riders in San Francisco are of little or no value to a potential customer in Chicago or London. The network economics are important because they determine the nature of competition, in particular the ability to acquire and retain customers [25]. For many new business models, the size and growth of the technology platform are the key measures of success, which ultimately determine long-term survival and profitability.

The measurement of network size needs to be carefully defined because the market definition needs to incorporate (a) sector, (b) type of athlete (elite, club runner, jogger, event participant) and (c) geographic location. This also means that marketing efforts need to take these factors into account, which is why marketing that is focused on specific cities is important, and the network influencers are important targets to 'seed' the network. This measurement of network size has parallels with the measurement of market share at a local level, e.g. to measure the market share of a bank in the 1980s before the Internet, then this could be done nationally, within a geographic region (e.g. US State or city), or by individual branch.

2.4.5 The technology encapsulates the definition and operations of the business model

The role of technology in all of these business models is to define and encapsulate the business model, which comprises a range of inter-related business processes that connect individuals and organizations. It is not accurate to think of IT as a separate entity, or artefact. It is rather the ether in which the business model exists. The definition of the individual business processes and the relationships between them are captured as information templates that are then instantiated through digital technology.

An important implication of technology encapsulation of business processes is that changes to any business process or relationship between them, whether this is the product offer, the nature of the customer acquisition process, pricing algorithms or the relationship with external partners to stimulate growth, all require concomitant changes to the technology. The business processes and technology are inseparable. By separating them, the essence and characteristics of the business model are lost.

The business model can be described in terms of an information template, without reference to technology, but it can only operate with digital technology. This is similar to the production component of an ERP system, which can be described in terms of materials requirements planning algorithms and an information specification, but it can only be implemented, at least on any kind of scale, using databases, software and networked systems.

A further implication of the tight coupling between technology and the business model is that any type of innovation or improvement to a business model – whether this is to develop easier-to-use software, build new product attributes through new software features – improved data analytics to offer new services or enhance existing ones, new ways of communicating with other customers or managing the review process on social media, all require associated technology changes. An example of how changes to the product offer are reflected through changes in technology and business process is the development of the Strava product offer.

Strava uses segments to compare an athlete with other athletes over the same section of a cycling route or running course. This is fine for elite athletes, who tended to be early adopters of the service, because they are at or near the top of the list. But for a club athlete, or social runner, it is not so encouraging to be scored as being in the top 5,000 of other athletes who have already completed a popular segment. No matter how hard a social runner competes, they are never, ever going to get anywhere near to the top of a complete list of other cyclists or runners for a particular segment, which goes against the raison d'etre of the company, which is to encourage and entertain athletes.

For this reason, the company introduced a filtering process so that individuals can compare themselves against similar athletes. A runner can compare themselves to runners in the same age bracket, weight, level of training, type of bike, gender or whatever, and the inducement of competition can then become an encouraging factor rather than a demotivating one. This filtering process depends entirely on software enhancements, as do almost all new features. In fact, the analysis and interpretation of the data is now such an important facet of Strava, that the company features Strava labs in its marketing, to showcase the power of data from a large community of athletes, e.g. see the global heat map example (https://labs.strava.com/heatmap/).

2.4.6 All companies are or will become technology companies

To an extent, all companies are technology companies. The idea is an extension of one proposed by David Pottruck, former CEO of Schwab.com. Schwab.com was a leader in online trading during the dot com boom, and technology was at the heart of its operations. Pottruck stated that every single employee should be a part-time technologist. This was regardless of their functional title or position.

In the current environment, this idea has become more important as technology is more embedded in the fabric of organizations and market networks. This means that outsourcing of technology and technology staff needs to be approached with extreme care because a company's management team risks abdicating responsibility for technology management and therefore surrendering part of its business. Of course, the new sharing economy companies such as Uber and Airbnb, and the technology giants Taobao, Amazon and Google, may be extreme cases, but the logic still holds for all types of companies. Perhaps the term 'outsourcing' is simply too problematic and rather than thinking of technology as something that can be separated out from the business, managers should think in terms of partnerships where the focus of attention is on managing the technology in the context of the business model.

2.4.7 Business models must evolve and adapt

There is a risk when managers start to talk about their organizations as a 'business model' because the logic of the model becomes so enticing and attractive that it become difficult to challenge or question it. That is, managers become so wrapped up in their current success that they fail to recognize or anticipate changes to their market, technology and competition. For an external change to register an impact on an organization, its management must go through a series of hurdles: anticipate or recognize the change, understand it, work out its consequences and then make an appropriate reaction. In the case of TESCO, it appeared to have an unassailable position as the UK's leading grocery firm because of its scale, its novel use of customer loyalty card data, its control over building lands for new stores, and the strong financial position gained from positive cash flow because customers paid immediately and suppliers were paid months later. The culmination of TESCO's business model logic was to build enormous stores with space for electrical goods and clothes, as well as a huge range of food items.

Several changes occurred together that had a competitive impact. The online channel grew in importance and customers started to order bulky items online and then started to shop for other food items as more of a leisure activity or last minute chore. This made visits to a large out of store shop much less attractive and convenience stores grew in importance. Value or discount retailers came to the fore, especially Aldi and Lidl, challenging the price advantage of TESCO by focusing on a smaller range of goods and lower levels of customer service. The sale of electrical items through physical retail stores was decimated by the onslaught of online competition. In a relatively short period of time, the large mega-stores became white elephants, and the company scrambled to figure out how to utilize the unwanted and unneeded space.

Vitality insurance is an excellent example of an existing and established company that has transformed its business model from a traditional insurer to a behavioural ecosystem where the customer is at the centre of the ecosystem [32] and Vitality's business role changes to being a pro-active provider of health and fitness feedback that is designed to motivate the customer to make healthier choices that will logically lead to a reduction in medical expenses and insurance premiums.

Static business models have a natural lifetime and do not last forever. By formulating business model logic, it sometimes becomes difficult to question, let alone change and adapt an existing business model, vide Tesco. Self-awareness and self-criticism should be built into the culture of the company, even if it cannot be specified in the governance. Technology partners can play a crucial role here because of their external focus, with the caveat that they are not already embroiled in existing IT infrastructures.

A related issue is that a single business model often oversimplifies a company's strategy and how it is changing to survive and grow. Managers should therefore think in terms of multiple business models and be clear about whether they can operate separately, or need to work in conjunction with each other. This may reflect distinctive lines of business, i.e. separate products, or it may reflect different aspects of a market in which the company has several roles. For example, in the mobile phone market, the shift towards bundled products that combine fast home Internet connection, mobile phones and entertainment packages means that companies such as Telefonica, T-Mobile and Vodafone must also have business models that define them as entertainment companies in addition to their positions as telecommunications businesses.

The example of telecommunications companies becoming entertainment companies is a good illustration of the more general phenomenon of strategic transitions between eras that are defined by technological change. The car industry came out of the horse-and-carriage business, and both are perhaps better described as transportation businesses. The technologies in Table 2.1 are at the heart of Ford's stated strategy to become an operating system for transportation, which is an even more general business model that gives them freedom to innovate far beyond the confines of a traditional automotive company and to take advantage of revolutionary technology that is disrupting consumer behaviour and expectations towards mobility and transportation.

2.5 Implications for technology strategy and partnerships

Commentators tend to focus on what is new, i.e. the technology in Table 2.1, and largely ignore mature and stable technology that exists within established legacy businesses. The term 'legacy business model' is used to describe established business models, often with significant assets and legacy information systems, which may have significant market share and be financially successful. For example, retail banks, chemical companies, traditional car manufacturing and high-street grocery firms operate legacy business models that utilize a large amount of stable technology such as enterprise systems, e-commerce standards, simple tracking technology using barcodes and management reporting based on 'little' data. In addition, they will be exploiting new forms of technology that are changing more rapidly but overall legacy business models utilize a large amount of legacy technology, and this should be managed quite differently from the new and rapidly changing technology. Likewise, new forms of business models are built mainly around new technology, and will also use stable technology though with a much greater focus on business innovation and novel technology. The dilemma for legacy business models has been discussed widely in the business literature [33]. The debate here therefore focuses on the implications of stable and fast-changing technology on technology strategy and partnerships.

2.5.1 *Proposed model and managerial implications for technology strategy and outsourcing*

For stable technologies the emphasis should be on risk reduction, cost efficiencies and high quality of service delivery. More traditional outsourcing arrangements may work in this context with the caveat that the company should retain enough intelligence and capability to monitor the performance of contracts and be aware of any new developments that may create new types of change, e.g. the shift to Cloud computing for ERP and CRM systems. For new and emerging technologies, the emphasis should be on experimentation, flexibility, multiple partnerships with external companies, relatively small teams of exceptional staff and of course a willingness to accept failure and move on quickly.

The influence of stable and new/emerging technology on technology strategy and partnerships is shown in Figure 2.1. New/emerging technology is linked to innovative business models, and legacy systems management are linked to legacy business models. Note that in practice legacy business models will also try and incorporate new forms of technology, and that innovative business models will also incorporate elements of stable technologies such as enterprise systems. A good way of conceptualizing this mix of technologies, and the need for multiple technology strategies, is to think of a company as having multiple business models.

For legacy companies, this often leads to tensions and conflicts between different areas of the business, because the new business model is seen as cannibalizing or stealing customers from the legacy business model, vide online sales for high-street retailers, and novel forms of lending versus established lending models for legacy banks. However, the main use of the diagram is to illustrate the clear need to develop specific technology strategy and partnerships for each category of technology.

New and innovative business models illustrate the need for flexibility and speed, and legacy business models emphasize the need for stability, risk reduction and careful technology cost management. The tension between new and legacy business models is therefore not only in the design of the business model, but in the approach to the management of technology, which creates challenges for established companies wishing to transform themselves, e.g. Ford moving from a manufacturer of cars to a transport operating system, and for new business modes such as Uber and Strava, that some of their technology should be treated as routine and managed accordingly.

Innovative Business Model Characteristics

- Launch business model and test initial assumptions
- Experiment with market offer
- Quickly evolve business processes and operate a continuous 'Beta' model organization
- Rapid customer growth that exploits the technology to achieve
  - Network economics
  - Economies of scale
- Close monitoring of competitor innovations
- 'Lead where possible but be prepared to be a close follower of innovative strategies

Legacy Business Model Characteristics

- Manage cost structure closely
- Business model change is gradual and incremental
- Business processes are stable and embodied in the legacy systems
- Relationships with all economic partners, including technology companies, tend to be long-term and relatively stable
- The strategic role of the technology is to defend market position
- Monitor competitors' use of technology and maintain parity only, i.e. do not aim to lead or innovate unnecessarily
- Return on capital and maintenance of market position are the most important business performance indicators
- Protect market share through advertising and establishing channels to market

Technology Strategy for New/Emerging and Rapidly Changing Technologies

- Fast adoption and possible ownership of new technologies
- Experimentation with new systems linked to business model change
- Combination of close partnering and in-house development
- Scale successful technology to support rapid growth in customer base
- Design technology to facilitate and capture network economies
- Build in-house technical expertise as a central function and supported by distributed technology ambassadors in functional units

Legacy Systems Management

- Manage existing technology assets with a focus on reducing costs
- Maintain staff experience, either in-house or through outsourcing arrangements to maintain legacy systems
- Reduce risks in current and new technology projects
- Outsource the management of established and stable technologies, including the management processes around them
- Focus on lifetime technology costs
- Stability and reliability of systems are the most important performance factor
- Enhancement of legacy systems is kept to a minimum and only done to support essential changes to the business model

Technology enables innovation and new business models

Business model places new demands on the technology

Legacy systems support the legacy business model but constrain innovation

Changes to the business model stretch legacy systems and risk increasing the complexity of systems

Figure 2.1   Coherence of new/emerging technology, innovative business models, and legacy business models

2.6 Conclusion

If the ideas in this chapter are developed to their natural conclusion, one reaches the view that the value of modern company is represented by the nexus of its intellectual property, information assets, technology capabilities and partnerships (Jensen and Meckling 1976). Partnerships with external technology companies must therefore be highly collaborative and capable of mutual adaptation and change, especially in the context of new/emerging technology (Whitley and Willcocks 2011).

Of course, physical assets still matter to many organizations, but when comparing Airbnb with Hilton, Strava with a sportswear company or a bank with a peer-to-peer lending company, the traditional financial measures of success, i.e. the size of balance sheets, profit and loss accounts, are no longer sufficient. To capture the value that is generated by a new business model such as Uber, Strava or Amazon, it is necessary to evaluate them in terms of a range of variables, many of them non-financial, for example information assets, technology, social capital, network links and analytical capabilities.

In this context of (1) new/emerging and therefore rapidly changing technology, and (2) stable and mature technology, companies must develop strategies that can cope with both of these modes of technology strategy, and these are outlined in Figure 2.1. This is difficult to achieve because the skill sets and philosophy of close cost control, risk reduction and consolidation of legacy systems are in sharp contrast to those required for experimentation, rapid and continuous change, with close iterations between the evolving business model and the new technology.

For new and innovative business models, companies must develop and retain staff with high levels of technology skills and capabilities and be able to integrate this expertise with entrepreneurial managers in order to build and grow novel business models. For legacy businesses, it is likely that they will need a combination of skills to maintain and carefully adapt legacy systems, and simultaneously manage new technologies in order to build new business models or transform legacy business models into completely different enterprises. One size of technology strategy and partnership certainly does not fit all types of business model and technology.

Acknowledgement

This paper is an output of the Technology and Next Generation Insurance Services (TECHNGI) investigating the opportunities and challenges for the UK insurance industry arising from new AI and data technologies. TECHNGI is funded by Innovate UK and the Economic and Social Science Research Council (grant reference ES/S010416/1) as part of the £20 million Next Generation Services Research Challenge www.ukri.org/innovation/industrial-strategy-challenge-fund/next-generation-services/.

Notes

1. Afuah, A., Tucci, C.: *Internet business models and strategies*. McGraw-Hill, New York (2001).
2. Andreessen, M.: Why software is eating the world. *The Wall Street Journal*. 20: p. C2 (2011).
3. Baden-Fuller, C., Morgan, M.: Business models as models. *Long Range Planning*. 43 (2): pp. 156–171 (2010).
4. Bhagwatwar, A., Hackney, R., Desouza, K.: Considerations for information systems "back-sourcing": a framework for knowledge re-integration. *Information Systems Management*. 28 (2): pp. 165–173 (2011).
5. Bharadwaj, A., El Sawy, O., Pavlou, P., Venkatraman, N.: Digital business strategy: toward a next generation of insights. *MIS Quarterly*. 37: pp. 471–482 (2013).

6. Broadbent, M., Weill, P.: Improving business and information strategy alignment: learning from the banking industry. *IBM Systems Journal.* 32 (1): pp. 162–179 (1983).

7. Brynjolfsson, E.; The productivity paradox of information technology. *Communications of the ACM.* 36 (12): pp. 66–77 (1993).

8. Carr, D., Cone, E.: Code Blue, Case 005. Dissection. *Baseline*, pp. 30–46 (2001).

9. Carr, N.: IT doesn't matter. *Harvard Business Review.* 81 (5), pp. 41–49 (2003).

10. Chen, D., Mocker, M., Preston, D., Teubner, A.: Information systems strategy: reconceptualization, measurement, and implications. *MIS Quarterly.* 34 (2): pp. 233–259 (2010).

11. Chesbrough, H.: Business model innovation: opportunities and barriers. *Long Range Planning.* 43 (2): pp. 354–363 (2010).

12. Christensen, C.: *The innovator's dilemma: when new technologies cause great firms to fail.* Harvard Business Review Press, Boston, MA (2013).

13. Clemons, E., Reddi, S., Row, M.: The impact of information technology on the organization of economic activity: the "move to the middle" hypothesis. *Journal of Management Information Systems.* 10 (2): pp. 9–35 (1993).

14. Eisenmann, T., Parker, G., Van Alstyne Marshall, W.: Strategies for two-sided markets. *Harvard Business Review.* 84 (10): p. 92 (2006).

15. Hammer, M., Champy, J.: *Reengineering the corporation: a manifesto for business revolution.* Harper Business, London (1993).

16. Heck, E. van, Vervest, P.: Smart business networks: how the network wins. *Communications of the ACM.* 50 (6): pp. 28–37 (2007).

17. Henderson, J., Venkatraman, H.: Strategic alignment: leveraging information technology for transforming organizations. *IBM Systems Journal.* 32 (1): pp. 472–484 (1983).

18. Holland, C., Lockett, A.: Mixed mode network structures: the strategic use of electronic communication by organizations. *Organization Science.* 8 (5): pp. 475–488 (1997).

19. Holland, C., Light, B., Gibson, N.: A critical success factors model for Enterprise Resource Planning. In proceedings of *The 7th European Conference on Information Systems*, Copenhagen, Denmark, pp. 273–287 (1999).

20. Jensen, M., Meckling, W.: Theory of the firm: Managerial behavior, agency costs and ownership structure. *Journal of Financial Economics.* 3 (4): pp. 305–360 (1976).

21. Johnston, H., Vitale M.: Creating competitive advantage with interorganizational information systems. *MIS Quarterly.* 12: pp. 153–165 (1988).

22. Keen, P.: *Shaping the future: business design through information technology.* Harvard Business School Press, Boston, MA (1991).

23. Kelly, S., Holland, C., Light, B.: Enterprise resource planning: a business approach to systems development. *AMCIS Proceedings.* p. 271 (1999).

24. Kiesler, S.: The hidden messages in computer networks. *Harvard Business Review.* 64 (1): pp. 46–60 (1986).

25. Malone, T., Yates, J., Benjamin R.: The logic of electronic markets. *Harvard Business Review.* 67 (3): pp. 166–172 (1989).

26. Orlikowski, W.: The duality of technology: rethinking the concept of technology in organizations. *Organization Science.* 3: pp. 398–427 (1992).

27. Porter, M., Millar V.: How information gives you competitive advantage. *Harvard Business Review.* 63: pp. 149–160 (1985).

28. Shaw, D., Snowdon, B., Holland, C., Kawalek, P., Warboys, B.: The viable systems model applied to a smart network: the case of the UK electricity market. *Journal of Information Technology.* 19 (4): pp. 270–280 (2004).

29. Short J., Venkatraman N.: Beyond business process redesign: redefining Baxter's business network. *Sloan Management Review.* 34 (1): p. 7 (1992).

30. Tapscott D.: Rethinking strategy in a networked world (or why Michael Porter is wrong about the Internet). *Strategy + Business.* 24: pp. 34–41 (2001).

31. Whisler, T.: *Impact of computers on organizations.* Praeger Publishers, New York (1970).

32. Whitley, E., Willcocks, L.: Achieving step-change in outsourcing maturity: toward collaborative innovation. *MIS Quarterly Executive.* 10 (3): pp. 95–109 (2010).

33. Willcocks, L.: The next step for the CEO: moving IT-enabled services outsourcing to the strategic agenda. *Strategic Outsourcing: An International Journal.* 3 (1): pp. 62–66 (2010).

3

ENTERPRISE ARCHITECTURE

Marlies van Steenbergen

3.1 Introduction

To keep up with the rapid changes happening in technology, markets and society, enterprises must be flexible and adaptive. This flexibility must be designed into the structure of the enterprise. In accordance with The Open Group, we consider an enterprise any organization of people, processes and means that share a common goal [1]. Thus, an enterprise can be a company or institution, but it can also be part of a company or a network of cooperating parties. An enterprise is a complex system, acting in a complex environment with many types of stakeholders such as customers, shareholders, partners, suppliers, jobseekers and regulators.

Enterprise architecture is the discipline that concerns itself with designing the structure of the enterprise. The aim of enterprise architecture is to translate the ambitions and strategy of an enterprise into guidelines on how to structure the necessary processes, information systems and technology, to enable the continued realization of the strategy. It takes a holistic view of the enterprise, looking for a seamless integration of products and services, processes, information flows and technology.

A widely adopted definition of architecture is the ISO/IEC 42010:2007 definition, which defines architecture as "the fundamental organization of a system embodied in its components, their relationships to each other and the environment, and the principles guiding its design and evolution." This definition indicates that enterprise architecture is about components, relationships and principles. In the case of enterprise architecture, the system is the entire enterprise. The components, an enterprise is made up of, are of various types, such as organizational components (departments, roles), processes, data and information, and technology (software, hardware). In this definition, enterprise architecture is regarded as an artifact, i.e. the models and principles defining the enterprise. When we talk about the development and application of the models and principles, we speak of enterprise architecture management.

3.1.1 Enterprise architecture artifacts

An enterprise architecture consists of a descriptive part, depicting the various components and how they relate to each other and the environment, as well as a normative part, the principles guiding the design and evolution of the enterprise structure. The descriptive part is represented in the form of models. These models can be of various levels of detail and they can focus on different parts of the enterprise. It is common to find a high-level enterprise-wide model spanning the entire enterprise, complemented with more detailed models of narrower scope, for instance a business domain (the production function) or an aspect (data). Models are time-bound in the sense that they depict a situation at a certain timespan in the past, present (current architecture) and/or future (target architecture). The normative part is expressed in the form of statements that constrain the available choices for the target models. These statements, too, can differ in level of detail and scope. High-level principles express what is to be achieved, specific rules express how things are to be achieved. The level of detail greatly impacts the level of freedom left to the designer.

Principles and target models represent choices in how an enterprise expects to best be able to achieve its ambitions and goals. These choices are not the same for all enterprises, for what constitutes a good choice depends on the situation. Both the ambitions of an enterprise and the context it finds itself in impact the content of the enterprise architecture. An enterprise in a dynamic environment requires different architectural choices than an enterprise in a stable environment. Also, an enterprise focused on customer intimacy requires different architectural choices than an enterprise focused on operational excellence. The enterprise architect faces the challenge to balance all factors and translate them into a solution that best meets the entirety of different stakeholder concerns and contextual constraints. In doing so, the architect balances requirements such as reliability, flexibility and efficiency.

3.1.2 *Enterprise architecture management*

An enterprise architecture must be designed, maintained and applied. This is the responsibility of the enterprise architecture management function. The enterprise architecture management function takes the business strategy of the enterprise as its starting point and translates it into principles and models that fit this strategy, taking stakeholders and context into account. This implies that changes in the strategy may lead to changes in the enterprise architecture. Though the other way around is also possible: an enterprise architecture may also enable and stimulate changes in strategy [2]. The choices made in the enterprise architecture define the strategic room for maneuver. Investment in the enterprise architecture is an investment in the future ability to grasp opportunities and respond to social and market trends. Besides designing and maintaining the enterprise architecture models and principles, the enterprise architecture management function entails applying these models and principles in the development processes [3]. This is closely related to the governance processes of the organization. Decisions relating to the structuring of the enterprise's processes, information and technology are constantly made at the strategic, tactical or operational level. At each of these levels, it is important to ensure that no decisions are made that are contrary to the enterprise architecture. This means that decision-makers must have access to the architectural norms. This access must be organized, either by providing a role for architects in the decision-making process or by providing architectural knowledge to the decision-makers. What choices are made in this regard depends on the complexity of the situation.

Enterprise architecture management is essential to the execution of business strategy and as such it is a core competence of the enterprise. We use competence here in the sense of the ability to successfully perform certain actions and achieve certain results [4]. Examples of competences are business strategy, systems and process innovation, managing change and applications development. This is not to be confused with the concept of capability. When enterprises turn competences into business value, we speak of a capability. A capability is the ability to achieve sustained superior performance and business value. An example of a capability is the IS capability, which is the ability of an organization to deliver business value from investments in IS/IT continuously. Competences emerge out of the integration and co-ordination of resources. A resource is a means an enterprise has at its disposal. Resources can be tangible or intangible. Examples of resources are buildings, computers, skills, knowledge, processes, brands and customer relationships.

Summarizing, the aim of enterprise architecture is to provide structure to an enterprise that fits its strategic ambitions. It does so from a holistic perspective, aiming for the seamless connection of products and services, processes, information flows and technology. The topic of enterprise architecture concerns both the enterprise architecture artifacts, to be distinguished in models and principles, and the enterprise architecture management function of developing and applying the enterprise architecture artifacts.

3.3 Architecture frameworks

Over the decades, the views on position and goal of enterprise architecture have evolved. In the 1980s, architecture was regarded as part of information planning. An information plan often had a scope of up to five years. The architecture had the form of a blueprint, was all-compassing and based on the idea that the world is malleable. In the 90s, IT architecture is no longer considered part of an information plan, but as a set of principles and models that exist in their own right and must be maintained. The aim of the IT architecture was mainly standardization in IT. Attempts were made to address organizations' wishes for more rapid change, but that appeared difficult. Around 2000 realization dawns that architecture should be not only about IT, but also about processes and products and services: business architecture is born [5]. Models are made distinguishing front, mid and back office, and customers, channels and products, organizations move from product-oriented to process-oriented, etc. Gradually, it becomes clear that business and IT architectures should be integrated in an enterprise architecture covering all aspects of the organization: products/services, processes, organizational structure, information flows, applications, middleware, hardware and network technology must be considered together. One cannot be seen separate from the other.

Over the decades, various architecture frameworks have been developed to guide the development and application of enterprise architecture [6]. These frameworks support the architects in doing their job. They provide structure as well as a common language between architects. Architecture frameworks differ in focus and in their perception of architecture, but most frameworks have in common that they make the connection between strategy and solutions and distinguish various perspectives. Most frameworks distinguish in some way or another between the perspectives of business, information systems and technical infrastructure. Dependent on the focus of the framework, attention may be paid to the architecture artifacts, the architecture processes and/or the organization of the architecture management function.

One of the first architecture frameworks was the Zachmann Framework [7]. The Zachmann Framework focuses on the enterprise architecture artifacts. It provides a logical structure for classifying and organizing the descriptive representations of an enterprise, covering the entire set of descriptions necessary to describe an enterprise, or any other system. The Zachmann Framework is a two-dimensional matrix. The horizontal axis is based on the interrogatives What, How, When, Who, Where and Why. The vertical axis is based on the transformation from an abstract idea into instantiation: Identification, Definition,

Representation, Specification, Configuration and Instantiation, which represents the perspectives of different stakeholders. This provides a matrix in which the 30 cells represent the classification of the framework. The framework purports to be normalized, complete and stable. The normalized primitives (the cells) can be combined into composites needed to "build" a working enterprise. The framework enables focusing on one component, without losing track of the complete picture and the context in which the component exists. The Zachmann Framework is considered by many the mother of all EA classifying frameworks. Besides the Zachmann Framework, various other similar frameworks have been developed, sometimes for specific domains. In practice today, Zachmann is more of a reference framework than an integrated framework that is implemented.

In the early 90s, TOGAF™, which stands for The Open Group Architecture Framework, was launched. TOGAF is developed and maintained by The Open Group Architecture Forum [8]. The first version of TOGAF was developed in 1995. The core of TOGAF is the Architecture Development Method (ADM), which describes the various phases in architecture development. It starts with a preliminary phase, in which the foundation is laid by tuning the framework to the organization and defining the foundational principles for architecture. After this groundwork, a cycle of eight phases is executed for each change initiative, the first phase being the definition of an architecture vision and the last phase the execution of architecture change management. TOGAF distinguishes four types of architecture as part of an enterprise architecture: business architecture, data architecture and application architecture (together referred to as Information Systems Architecture in the ADM) and technology architecture. The ADM cycle can be applied at various levels, such as the enterprise level, domain level or program level. It always starts with a need for a (business) change. Besides the ADM, TOGAF provides a lot of practices for enterprise architects to use, including guidelines and techniques to support the application of the ADM, the Architecture Content Framework that provides a detailed model of architectural work products, the Enterprise Continuum that provides a model for structuring a virtual repository and classification of architecture and solution artifacts, the TOGAF reference models: Technical Reference Model and Integrated Information Infrastructure Model, and the Architecture Capability Framework to help establish an architecture practice within an enterprise. TOGAF is an extensive framework with many useful practices from which an enterprise must make its own selection. The ADM provides a clear structure to the architectural processes.

ArchiMate is a modeling language. It was developed between 2002 and 2004 for architecture modeling and aims to contain all concepts that are relevant to describe an enterprise architecture [9]. The core concepts of the language are classified into aspects and layers. A concept may be labeled an active structure element (e.g. business actors or application components), a behavior element (e.g. business process or application function) or a passive structure element (e.g. business object or data object). A concept also belongs to one of three layers: business layer (e.g. business actors or business processes), application layer (e.g. application components or data objects) and technology layer (e.g. infrastructure function or node). The most recent version saw an extension of two additional layers: strategy and physical. Besides the core concepts, ArchiMate distinguishes concepts related to motivation, such as driver, goals and principle, and to migration, such as plateau and deliverable. A very important concept in ArchiMate is the service. The service is the externally visible behavior of a system. It is also the glue between the layers. Thus, the infrastructure layer is accessed by the application layer via infrastructure services. Similarly, the business layer can use the functions of the application layer via application services. The business layer delivers its services to the environment via business services. In 2008, ArchiMate was transferred to

The Open Group. ArchiMate is an architect's tool. It is very useful for accurate modeling as well as for communication among architects and designers. It is less suitable as a means of communication toward management. ArchiMate is supported by many modeling tools, including freeware.

In the 80s and 90s, the primary focus of most architecture frameworks was on the architecture artifacts. As a reaction to this, in 2002 Dynamic Architecture (DYA) was launched [10]. DYA focuses on the architecture process and on how to effectively apply architecture to realize strategic goals. It distinguishes four main processes: strategic dialogue, architecture services, development with architecture and development without architecture. The leading principles of DYA are a just enough, just in time approach, i.e. only developing architectural artifacts where and when there is a need, and the embedding of architecture in the change processes of the enterprise. DYA contains various instruments, such as the project-start architecture, an architecture artifact that tunes the enterprise architecture to the specific context of a project.

In more recent years, new frameworks were introduced, such as General Enterprise Architecting (GEA) [11] and Risk- and Cost-Driven Architecture (RCDA) [12].

Architecture frameworks are designed from the perspective of the architect. However, architecture is not a goal, but a means to achieve the business goals. To this end, architecture must be embedded in the change processes of the organization. These change processes recently underwent considerable changes with the rise of Agile development. With Agile, the focus shifted from central governance to autonomous development teams, with little or no room for architecture. Many of the premises of the existing architecture frameworks were no longer valid and architects struggled to establish new ways of working, adapting to the new development paradigms. Gradually, however, a new way of collaboration between architects and agile teams is emerging.

One Agile development framework that positions architecture within Agile development is SAFe®. SAFe® stands for Scaled Agile Framework [13]. It is developed and maintained by Scaled Agile, Inc. It is a scalable and configurable framework based on Lean-Agile principles and values. It helps organizations "deliver new products, services, and solutions in the shortest sustainable lead time, with the best possible quality and value... It provides guidance for the roles, responsibilities, artifacts, and activities necessary to achieve better business outcomes" ([14], p. 1). SAFe combines Agile, Lean product development and systems thinking. It is used to synchronize Agile teams. It distinguishes various configurations ranging from Essential SAFe containing the basic building blocks and most critical elements, to Full SAFe that is used to build large solutions and contains the levels of team, program, large solution and portfolio. One of the framework's fundamental principles is to decentralize decision-making. Arguments for this are among others that decentralized decision-making reduces delays and improves quality of decision where local knowledge is involved. This is not to say that central decisions are not necessary at all. However, they are far less frequent and limited to strategic decisions, i.e. decisions that have far-reaching impact and are outside the scope or knowledge of the teams. Examples of such decisions are decisions about product strategy or the standards to be used.

SAFe aims to break the functional silos by creating teams of Agile teams in the form of an Agile Release Train (ART). An ART is a networked organizational structure that is self-organizing and self-managing. In the ART teams, key stakeholders and other resources work toward an important ongoing solution mission. They share a single vision, roadmap and program backlog. ARTs deliver features (user functionality) and enablers (technical infrastructure).

The ART is positioned at program level. At this level, the role of the system architect is recognized. The system architect defines the overall architecture for a system, helps define nonfunctional requirements, determines the major elements and subsystems, and identifies the interfaces and collaborations among them. Above the program level, SAFe distinguishes two other potential levels: large solution and portfolio. The large solution configuration is meant for complex solutions spanning more than one ART. At this level, the solution architect is the one that defines a common technical and architectural vision for the larger solution. The portfolio configuration aligns portfolio execution, organizing development around one or more value streams. At this level, the enterprise architect works across value streams and programs to provide strategic technical direction and often acts as the epic owner for enabler epics.

In SAFe, architecture is not regarded as something that must be defined centrally in a top-down fashion. Instead, there is a need to balance emergent design and intentional architecture. Emergent design allows designers to respond to immediate user needs, intentional architecture takes care of matters that are beyond the scope of the team and provides guidance for inter-team design and implementation synchronization. Intentional architecture constrains emergent design, but only to the extent necessary, leaving enough room for maneuver for the teams. Emergent design corrects and feeds intentional architecture. Emergent design and intentional architecture together build the Architectural Runway, the technical foundation for future creation of business value. This only works if there is true collaboration between teams, architects and product management.

SAFe has a very different approach to enterprise architecture than TOGAF, giving it a more supportive role instead of a controlling role as is the case in TOGAF.

3.4 Thinking in services

An increasingly important concept within architecture is the concept of service. A service is a discrete unit of functionality that is well-defined, self-contained and remotely accessible, and does not depend on the context or state of other services. Services are defined by their interface, abstracting away the underlying implementation, which makes it easier to change the implementation of a service without disabling its use. The collaboration of services is often done by an orchestration function. Services can be internal to the enterprise or external. External services may reside in the Cloud. A service registry enables the publication and retrieval of available services. The concept of service can be applied at various levels, ranging from business services such as on-line payment services to application services such as financial administration to infrastructure services such as storage space. A Service-Oriented Architecture (SOA) consists of services that jointly achieve specific results [15].

A recent further development on the service-oriented architecture is the microservices architecture [16]. A microservices architecture structures an application as a collection of loosely coupled microservices. Microservices are services organized around business capabilities that can be independently developed and are independently deployable and scalable. Scalability is achieved by running multiple instances of a microservice. There are various infrastructural solutions for this, such as containers or serverless deployment. Microservices can be implemented using different programming languages, databases, hardware and software environment per microservice, depending on what best fits the specific microservice.

SOA, and its successor microservices architecture, has gained great popularity over the years because of its modular approach which provides the potential for flexibility. Therefore, it is very suitable to enable a sourcing strategy.

3.5 Enterprise architecture and digital sourcing

Digital sourcing is about the ability to flexibly combine digital capabilities provided by different parties, in offering propositions to the market. These digital capabilities, offered as services, can be of very different types, varying from managed applications in the Cloud (SaaS), providing scalability, to the delivery of back-office business services, such as salary administration, providing efficiency, to the provisioning of new customer interaction, by data-analytics, gamification and/or chatbots, providing better service to customers, and everything in-between. Enterprises must decide on their position concerning digital sourcing: where do they stand on outsourcing, co-sourcing and insourcing? This is a strategic decision. It relates to the prime value proposition of the enterprise: what unique value does the enterprise offer to the market? And what is needed to deliver this value in terms of competences and capabilities? A complicating factor is that it is increasingly hard for enterprises to define this value on their own. Instead, consumers determine value to an increasing extent [17]. The better the enterprise architecture enables flexible coupling and decoupling of capabilities, the better the enterprise can switch between capabilities and make just-enough, just-in-time use of capabilities offered in the market.

Flexibility in sourcing is an extremely important aspect of modern enterprises, as it determines how fast an enterprise can implement new business models and new manners of collaboration with others. Over the years, the role and conduct of enterprises in the market has changed. Several large companies that traditionally dominated a substantial part of the market got into trouble. Nokia, for instance, dominated a large part of the mobile phone market, but did not realize fast enough that their customers started to rate design above functionality and price. And it lost market share to Apple [17]. We also see that the average lifespan of companies is steadily decreasing [18]. Enterprises that try to do it all on their own are being replaced by enterprises that are open to cooperation with other enterprises [19]. Or enterprises that provide others the platform to cooperate, as is done by the new platform organizations.

The digital business strategies that are the result of rapid technological innovation lead to new value creation models. Pagani distinguishes three types of value networks [19].

The closely vertically integrated model is the classic value chain model. It is designed to centralize organizational intelligence. It is characterized by the presence of a (limited) number of giant components that are strongly connected in a sequential value chain. The driver behind this model is the need to achieve independence and achieve control over the entire value chain.

The loosely coupled coalition model emerged as a response to increasing market complexity because of incremental innovation. Instead of a singular value chain, a value network emerges with various kinds of partnerships between the different parties in the network. Usually some firms achieve more prominence and power by occupying a central position in the value network structure. They use their prominence to grasp a leadership role in pulling together resources. In other words, they take charge of network orchestration. This results in a value chain that is more disintegrated and open. The ability to connect effectively with others becomes a core competence.

The multisided platforms are the result of the emergence of cross-boundary industry disruptions. In contrast to the previous two models, the multisided platform is non-linear. In the multisided platform model, a company brings together two or more distinct groups of participants (sides) that need each other in some way. A multisided platform company builds an infrastructure (platform) that creates value by reducing distribution, transaction and search costs generated when these groups interact with one another. Well-known examples of multisided platform companies are eBay, Visa and Booking.com to name but a few. Multisided platforms can have two, three, four or more sides. The more the sides, the higher the degree of complexity and the greater the challenge of balancing the interests of all sides. The choice of which side to sponsor or not is a fundamental strategic choice. Multisided platforms strive for network effects. Network effect means that the value of a service increases as more consumers use it or more suppliers augment it. In a world of digital and connected services, network effects are the key differentiator and driver of value creation. The multisided platform model may very well penetrate all industries in the near future. And with the multisided platform model new characteristics become important, such as openness, transparency and modularity.

Pagani argues that to survive in an increasingly uncertain and complex environment, organizations must transform their organizational intelligence into a new relational intelligence, enacting an open communication process with their stakeholders. For architecture, this implies a focus on enabling open communication and ensuring a modular structure.

Various factors play a role in catering for the flexible coupling and decoupling of resources or services. One determining factor is the granularity of the components on which the enterprise architecture is built. It is more difficult to outsource only part of a component than it is to outsource an entire component. For instance, if an enterprise has implemented an integrated ERP suite that supports sales, delivery, inventory management, payments and financial administration, it may be hard to outsource just the payments part.

Another factor is the ease with which a component can be extracted from its environment, i.e. how entangled it is with other components. Entanglement can occur horizontally and vertically. Horizontal entanglement means that components of similar nature are entangled. For instance, if the way a process is executed depends on the way another process is executed, or if the working of an application depends on the working of another application. Vertical entanglement means that components of different nature are entangled. For instance, the way a process is executed depends on the way a supporting application is designed. A component that communicates with other components by way of well-defined services can be outsourced easier.

Also relevant is the extent of standardization, especially the standardization of communication. Usually, an outsourced component does not function in isolation but exchanges information with other components. Broadly accepted communication standards enable such exchanges. A component that communicates by means of a widely recognized standard is easier to outsource than a component that communicates in an organization-specific manner. This holds not only for standardization of technical protocols, but, maybe even more importantly, also for semantic standardization. Within an ecosystem of collaborating parties, it is essential for smooth collaboration that participants understand each other. That is why many industry sectors develop common vocabularies, for instance in the water sector (Aquo), the building sector (building information modeling) and the care sector (HL7). Using such standards enables communication in precisely defined terms, making it easier to exchange information without misunderstandings or the need for complex translations, and thus to collaborate.

As technology becomes an important driver, the architecture must be able to absorb new relevant technologies [20]. Thus, the architecture must contain provisions to connect to new digital resources and services. Many organizations have been standardizing on technology for efficiency reasons. For core systems, this may still be a prudent way to go. For continuous delivery of digital services, however, organizations must be able to make use of the newest digital resources, either as a service or as a technology. Adherence to strict standardization rules is not advisable. However, though standardization on technology may hamper innovation, standardization on interfaces stimulates it. Standardization on interfaces enables enterprises to use each other's services. It stimulates collaboration and interaction. It enables rapid innovation by combining existing building blocks in new ways. While standardization on technology is driven by efficiency, standardization on interfaces is driven by value delivery: it enables seamless interaction of capabilities from different sources to combinedly offer value that none of the collaborating parties could have offered on its own. Thus, a collaboration between Spotify and Uber enables Uber users waiting for their ride to personalize the music during their ride by selecting, via the Uber app, a Spotify playlist to be played during their ride.

Thus, we see that the enterprise architecture enables digital sourcing by (1) incorporating the right form of standardization, (2) defining the right granularity of components and (3) employing a form of service-oriented architecture. However, there is more to the picture. There are a couple of trends that further impact the enterprise architecture management function. These are discussed in the next three paragraphs.

3.5.1 *Acting in an unpredictable context*

Enterprise architecture looks at the bigger picture. It takes a holistic view of the enterprise—not only in terms of taking into account various facets of the enterprise, but also in terms of looking further ahead than the here and now. It is the aim of enterprise architecture to also cater for the future needs of the enterprise. This poses an increasingly hard challenge, as the future seems increasingly hard to predict. It is hard to capture beforehand all possible issues in a predefined set of detailed rules—especially where interaction with customers and partners is concerned.

Recently, awareness has grown that enterprises may need to differentiate between architecture regimes to cater for bimodal or multi-modal IT. Ross et al. argue that enterprises must distinguish between their operational backbone and their digital services backbone [21]. *The operational backbone* provides the resources for operational excellence. They define an operational backbone as the set of business and technology capabilities that ensure the efficiency, scalability, reliability, quality and predictability of core operations. Common elements of an operational backbone are master data management providing a single source of truth for key data that is to be shared throughout the enterprise (e.g. customer, order and product data), seamless and transparent transaction processing and standardized back-office shared services. This description of operational backbone is reminiscent of the concept of systems of record introduced by Gartner in their pace-layered applications model [22]. The important difference between the two concepts is the fact that Ross et al. are looking at it from a business perspective, i.e. sets of capabilities, whereas Gartner refers to applications. *The digital services backbone* facilitates rapid innovation and responsiveness to new market opportunities. Ross et al. define a digital services backbone as the set of business and technology capabilities that enable rapid development and implementation of digital innovations. Common characteristics of a digital services backbone are digital components including both technical services, like biometrics, and business services, like customer alerts, platform as a service—a technology hosting environment where the company can store and access large numbers of loosely connected microservices, repositories for collecting massive amounts of public (e.g. from social media), purchased, and/or sensor data, analytics engines for converting the above data into meaningful insights and connections to data and processes residing in the operational backbone. This is reminiscent of the systems of innovation layer in Gartners pace-layered model—with again the distinction that the digital services backbone is viewed from a business perspective as a set of capabilities. Ross et al. argue that while the technological differences between the two backbones are likely to diminish with time, the need for their differing organizational characteristics will likely remain.

The implication for architecture is that it must enable the enterprise to quickly adjust to external developments and experimental results while at the same time maintaining robustness where necessary. One way to accommodate both these requirements is to vary the level at which architectural normative statements are made, i.e. the principle part of the enterprise architecture. In [23], it is argued that, just as is the case with regulations, architecture principles can be placed on a continuum from very abstract to very detailed (see for the distinction between rules and principles in the regulatory compliance context [24,25,26]). Principles are more abstract, expressing what is to be achieved and leaving room for interpretation. Rules are more concrete, expressing how things are to be done and leaving little room for interpretation. Rules are very useful in stable environments with a need for consistency and coherence—as may be the case in an operational backbone. Principles are more suitable in a dynamic environment, with a need for variation in responses, as in the digital services backbone. This is supported by the so-called knowledge-based view of the firm discussed by Grant [27]. Grant distinguishes four mechanisms for integrating knowledge: rules and directives, sequencing, routines, and group problem-solving and decision-making. Grant argues that rules and directives (i.e. written down directions) are suitable for communicating explicit knowledge among specialists and between specialists and non-specialists. Rules and directives are useful for tasks that are well-defined and to a great extent predictable. Group problem-solving and decision-making requires active interaction between participants and is needed for non-standardized tasks that are complex and unpredictable. Translating this to principles and rules, the more detailed knowledge expressed by rules is comparable to rules and directives and thus is useful for providing direction to relatively standard, predictable tasks. Principles, which are less precise, indicating desired outcome rather than the means to achieve that outcome, require more interaction and discussion in their application. They are the first choice when the organization is faced with disruptive technology.

Unpredictability is also apparent in the rapid decline in relevance of certain capabilities or the rapid emergence of unexpected parties exhibiting excellent capabilities. Examples are the decline of middlemen such as mortgage intermediaries and the rise of WhatsApp as an alternative to phone calls. Therefore, the enterprise architecture must be prepared for both decoupling and coupling of internal as well as external capabilities. This is done by carefully modeling the capabilities the enterprise needs, focusing on the correct scoping of capabilities and ensuring maximum independency between capabilities.

Unpredictability also necessitates a mindshift in the development of enterprise architecture. Refactoring should be a fundamental part of the architecture. This means, among other things, that architectural choices are evaluated for their retractability, that architectural choices are made at the latest possible moment instead of the first possible moment and that by rule architectural choices are provisional.

Summarizing, unpredictability requires fast reaction. However, not everything is equally unpredictable. Situationally applying a rule-based or principle-based approach provides the means to vary levels of freedom and hence flexibility. Careful scoping and designing of capabilities enables an enterprise to optimally exploit unpredictability in the relevance of internal capabilities and availability of external capabilities.

3.5.2 *Acting in a value network*

The boundaries of organizations are becoming less defined than they were and parties frequently switch roles. The same party may one moment act as client and the next as supplier—or competitor and client. For instance, an individual can both be a customer of bol. com buying books and a supplier offering their books through bol.com. Competitors and partners may emerge from unexpected directions. Only enterprises that are open to participation in fluid value networks will be successful. An example in case is the announcement of ING bank to become a platform organization and offer financial services from other financial institutions as well. This fluidity of roles has implications for the enterprise architecture.

A way of dealing with fluid value networks for enterprise architecture is to model the value network in terms of capabilities. From an enterprise perspective, the enterprise architect translates the ambitions and goals of the enterprise into the capabilities needed to realize these ambitions and goals. The next step is to model the way in which these capabilities collaborate. This collaboration can be modeled in terms of services delivered by one capability to another capability. Based on such a conceptual model, and dependent on the competences of the own organization as well as the interaction needs of using the services, decisions can be made on how to source each capability. If a party emerges that offers better services, i.e. excels in one of the capabilities, the organization may decide to switch.

A way to view collaboration between parties is the transaction-based approach on which DEMO (Design and Engineering Methodology for Organizations) is based [28]. DEMO breaks up a value chain or network into a tree of transactions between parties. A party in this case may be an individual, a business, a government organization or any other legal entity. A transaction consists of a request, promise, execution, delivery and acceptance. The transaction approach helps to clarify responsibilities. The promising party is the responsible party. Even if a party engages other parties to contribute to the execution of a transaction, it remains accountable to the asking party. Clear definition of transactions increases flexibility. In this sense, a transaction can be compared to a service. In both cases, a provider is responsible for the delivery of a well-defined unit of functionality to a consumer.

Summarizing, enterprise architecture can support participation in a value network by modeling it in terms of transactions between parties possessing valuable capabilities.

3.5.3 *Acting in a customer-centric world*

The rise of data-driven services offers consumers a lot of choice. Customers will no longer be loyal to enterprises that do not cater to their needs. In the past, as far as IT was concerned, enterprise architecture tended to focus on internal efficiency, whereas nowadays customer experience seems to be a main driver [30]. This asks for different architecture principles.

In the recent past, architecture principles about the use of IT were primarily focused on the values of robustness and efficiency [29,30]. This is illustrated by frequently used principles such as: (1) reuse before buy before build, (2) no redundancy, (3) shielding by firewalls and (4) standardization on technology. However, these principles are not aimed at providing an excellent customer experience. To do the latter, enterprises may need to experiment and take risks. They must learn to listen to their customers and start thinking outside-in.

Digital interaction processes offer lots of opportunities to get to know customers. However, enterprises must take care to use these data in a responsible manner and not to misuse the data they collect. This means being careful and transparent in how data are used and always keeping the interests and concerns of the customer in mind. In the architecture, this emerges among others in the form of principles concerning the use of data. This applies not only to data about customers collected by the enterprise in the execution of its service delivery, but also to the use of widely available data. For instance, the use of machine learning in decision-making carries the risk of treating customers in a biased manner. All this may lead to new principles, such as: (1) development by value-sensitive design, (2) use of customer data based on informed consent.

Summarizing, enterprise architecture stimulates customer centricity by formulating architectural principles from an outside-in perspective in which internal efficiency is not the primary driver, but acting in the interest of the customer, providing true value to the customer.

3.6 Enterprise architecture management function

Enterprise architecture provides the organization with the overview and insights necessary to make informed decisions on how to structure its products and services, processes, information flows and technology in a way that is aligned with its ambitions and strategy. The enterprise architecture models provide the required overview and insights. The enterprise architecture principles provide guidance on what to do or not to do when designing changes. The enterprise architecture management function is concerned with effectively applying these models and principles. Effectively applying enterprise architecture models and principles means applying them to provide direction to the change processes of the organization. For it is in these change processes that design decisions are being made, either explicitly or implicitly. Decisions that we want to be informed by enterprise architecture.

Decisions take place at various levels within the organization, ranging from strategic decisions at board level to operational decisions at for instance software development level. Enterprise architecture is relevant to all these levels of decision-making, but in different ways. At board level, the role of the enterprise architecture is to provide overview and to inform management about the impact and consequences of certain choices. Also, we see enterprise architects increasingly take the responsibility to proactively inform management about opportunities, often generated by the architectural choices. At operational level, the role of enterprise architecture is mainly to provide guidance in making specific design choices, either by providing relevant rules or by providing advice on specific solutions [3].

The way the enterprise architecture management function is organized differs between enterprises. Depending on the size of the enterprise, the number of architects may range from one employee fulfilling the role of architect for a part of his/her time to dozens of architects of various types spread over different departments. A common distinction is between enterprise architects who maintain a holistic view over the entire enterprise and solution architects who apply this enterprise architecture to guide the design of specific solutions, for instance a service to customers. Enterprise architects are usually centrally organized, either as a staff function below board level or as a central team within the IT department. Solution architects may be positioned within or near the development teams. The tasks of enterprise architects consist of keeping the enterprise architecture up to date and in line with the ambitions and strategy of the enterprise, developing roadmaps for realizing target architectures, advising the board about the applicability of technological innovations, implementing governance processes to ensure compliance with the enterprise architecture and educating the organization in enterprise architecture. Solution architects translate the models and principles of the enterprise architecture to specific guidelines for development teams, for instance in a so-called project-start architecture, model the architecture of specific solutions in collaboration with designers, monitor whether design decisions are in line with the architecture and act as advisor to development teams in cross-team issues.

The enterprise architecture management function faces various challenges in the fulfillment of its role. First, there is the question of mandate. Usually, it is not the architect who makes the final decision. In this respect, it is essential that the architects are backed by management. All too often, architects feel forced to sell architecture to the organization as if they themselves are the primary beneficiaries of the enterprise architecture. The main beneficiary of the enterprise architecture should be the board, however. That is why it is important that the enterprise architecture management function reports to the board directly, preferably to the CEO. It is the CEO who should take ownership of the enterprise architecture and who must understand and subscribe all choices made therein. In practice, however, the enterprise architects often report to the IT manager or CIO, limiting their scope to IT. This may restrain their effectiveness in aligning the enterprise architecture with the business strategy.

Effective application of enterprise architecture is also strongly related to its embedding in strategic dialogue as well as in solution development. The enterprise architecture management function must ensure that they can provide relevant insights at the moment of decision-making. Sometimes that may be a vision paper on the applicability of Cloud computing for the organization, other times that may be a specific solution pattern for communication with partners. Sometimes the insights needed can be simply derived from the existing architecture models and principles and sometimes a dedicated deliverable will have to be made. Architectural deliverables must be tuned to the stakeholders of these deliverables and architectural processes must be integrated with the organizations change processes.

The discipline of enterprise architecture is still relatively young. Different organizations show different levels of maturity of the enterprise architecture management function. As a discipline, it is far less established as for instance project management. The demands of digital business strategy and dealing with unpredictability, however, require a high architecture maturity level—especially, because the demands of fast response imply that architects cannot always fallback on premeditated models and visions, but need to "think on their feet" more.

Enterprise architecture maturity models are a means to support organizations in developing their enterprise architecture management function. Maturity models are conceptual models based on the idea that organizational competences develop through a number of anticipated, desired or logical stages from an initial state to a more mature state [31]. More mature means better equipped to fulfill its purpose. The basic components of a maturity model are (i) a number of overall maturity levels, (ii) a number of aspects or areas that can be developed along a predefined evolutionary path to achieve the defined maturity levels and (iii) descriptions of each step on the evolutionary path. In addition, a maturity model may contain suggestions on how to perform the various steps in terms of improvement actions.

Maturity models can be used with three different objectives in mind. First, they can be used to assess the current state of the architecture practices, i.e. how well is the enterprise architecture management function organized and how efficient or effective is it? What are its weak and strong points? Second, maturity models can be used for benchmarking, i.e. to make comparisons between enterprises. Of course, this objective can only be realized if all enterprises use the same maturity model and are willing to share their maturity scores. Third, maturity models can be used to improve the enterprise architecture management function. Dependent on an assessment of the current state, a maturity model may suggest adequate measures to grow to the next maturity level.

An example of a maturity model is the model developed by Ross et al. [32]. They discuss four stages that an organization passes through, making increasingly effective use of enterprise architecture: (1) business silo (IT applied to specific business needs, locally optimal business solutions), (2) standardized technology (central technology infrastructure), (3) rationalized processes (base of IT-enabled processes for core operations, shared and standardized business processes and/or data) and (4) business modularity (building on the core processes with plug-and-play processes built internally or externally). As an organization moves up through the stages, the strategic impact of IT increases. The organizational changes at each stage include new business processes, new management practices, new governance approaches and new attitudes about the role of IT. Ross et al. found in their research that large firms required on average five years per stage. They issue a warning that it is not possible to skip a stage. Each stage involves technology and organizational changes that prepare for the next stage. As the term suggests, to fully support a digital business strategy seems to require the stage of business modularity. Some organizations, however, are still struggling to get their operational backbone up and running, i.e. to reach the stage of rationalized processes. This is a serious threat to their business success. The maturity model of Ross et al. is primarily useful for assessing the current state of the architecture practices.

Another type of maturity model is the Dynamic Architecture Maturity Model, DyAMM, which is part of DYA [33]. DyAMM is designed and used for all three objectives mentioned above. It could be used to grow to level four of Ross et al. The DyAMM model distinguishes 17 aspects, called focus areas that together comprise an enterprise architecture practice. The focus areas are the development of architecture, use of architecture, alignment with business strategy, alignment with realization, relationship to the As-Is state, responsibilities and authorities, alignment with change portfolio, monitoring, quality assurance, management of the architectural process, management of the architectural products, commitment and motivation, implementation of the architectural role, architectural method, interaction and collaboration, architectural tools, budgeting and planning. The aim of DyAMM is to assist enterprises in increasing their enterprise architecture maturity step by step by developing each of the focus areas in a balanced manner. The idea behind DyAMM is that though each of the 17 focus areas must receive attention, this does not mean that each must be given equal consideration at the same time. For instance, not every focus area is equally relevant at the start: the use of architectural tools will certainly become a key concern at some point, but enterprises that are still in the phase of building up an architectural practice can focus more productively on aligning the architecture with the business strategy. Tools will have their turn. Furthermore, any given focus area need not be brought up to its full state of development right away. Each focus area has its own levels of maturity and the DyAMM model provides a matrix that shows how to alternately develop the different focus areas level by level. DyAMM distinguishes 12 overall maturity scales. For most enterprises, however, scale 6 will be more than adequate. Enterprises with a complex product portfolio and corresponding complex organization may aspire to scale 8 or even 10.

There is not one best way to organize the enterprise architecture management function. Its effectiveness very much depends on whether its implementation matches the size and organization of the enterprise. However, a maturity model such as the DyAMM model provides a useful tool to assess and subsequently develop the enterprise architecture management function to the required level.

3.7 Conclusion

The aim of enterprise architecture is to provide the structure to an enterprise that matches its strategic ambitions and enables the enterprise to turn strategy into execution. It does so from a holistic perspective, aiming for the seamless connection of products and services, processes, information flows and technology. The discipline of enterprise architecture consists of both the enterprise architecture artifacts, distinguishable into models and principles, and the enterprise architecture management function of developing and applying the enterprise architecture artifacts.

Digital sourcing in today's world puts certain requirements on enterprise architecture. Above all, it asks for the flexibility to quickly respond to changes in the environment and to flexibly start and end collaborations with other parties.

The enterprise architecture is an important enabler of digital sourcing by applying a service-oriented approach, modeling independent business capabilities at the right level of granularity, standardizing on interfacing instead of technology and formulating architectural principles from an outside-in, customer-centric perspective. The balance between robustness and flexibility can be supported by varying the level of normative statements using principles on one occasion and rules on another.

To be effective, the enterprise architecture management function must be aligned with the change processes in the organization, at all levels from strategic to operational, to be able to provide to-the-point advice at the moment of decision-making. This implies that the enterprise architecture management function tunes itself to the change processes in which the design decisions are made. In this effort, maturity models may function as useful checklists.

References

1. The Open Group: TOGAF version 9, p. 5 (2009).
2. McDonald, M.P.: The Enterprise Capability Organization: A Future for IT. *MIS Quarterly Executive*, 6(3), 179–192 (2007).
3. Berg, M. van den, Steenbergen, M. van: *Building an Enterprise Architecture Practice*. Springer, Dordrecht (2006).
4. Ward, J., Peppard, J.: *Strategic Planning for Information Systems*. 3rd edition, Wiley & Sons, Chichester (2002).
5. Versteeg, G., Bouwman, H.: Business Architecture: A New Paradigm to Relate Business Strategy to ICT. *Information Systems Frontier*, 8, 91–102 (2006).
6. Schekkerman, J.: *How to Survive in the Jungle of Enterprise Architecture Frameworks.*, 3rd edition, Trafford Publishing, Victoria, BC (2006).
7. Zachman, J.A.: A Framework for Information Systems Architecture. *IBM Systems Journal*, 26(3), 276–292 (1987).
8. The Open Group, http://www.opengroup.org/TOGAF-9.2-Overview
9. Lankhorst, M., et al.: *Enterprise Architecture at Work*. Springer, Heidelberg (2005).
10. Wagter, R., Berg, M. van den, Luijpers, L., Steenbergen, M. van: *Dynamic Enterprise Architecture: How to Make It Work*. Wiley, Hoboken (2005).
11. Wagter, R.: *Enterprise Coherence Governance*. Doctoral Thesis. Scholars' Press, Cambridge (2015).
12. Poort, E., van Vliet, H.: Architecting as a Risk- and Cost Management Discipline. Ninth Working IEEE/IFIP Conference on Software Architecture, 2–11 (2011).
13. SAFe. https://www.scaledagileframework.com/agile-architecture/.
14. SAFe 4.5 Introduction – Overview of the Scaled Agile Framework for Lean Enterprises. A Scaled Agile, Inc. White Paper (2017).
15. Berg, M. van den, Bieberstein, N., Ommeren, E. van.: *SOA for Profit, A Manager's Guide to Success with Service Oriented Architecture*. IBM, Sogeti, Paris (2007).
16. Amundsen, M., McLarty, M., Mitra, R., Nadareishvili, I.: *Microservice Architecture – Aligning Principles, Practices, and Culture*. O'Reilly Media, Portland, OR (2016).

17. Keen, P., Williams, R.: Value Architectures for Digital Business: Beyond the Business Model. *MIS Quarterly*, 37(2), 642–647 (2013).
18. Anthony, S.D., Viguerie, S.P., Waldeck, A.: *Corporate Longevity: Turbulence Ahead for Large Organizations.* Innosight, Executive Briefing, Spring (2016).
19. Pagani, M.: Digital Business Strategy and Value Creation: Framing the Dynamic Cycle of Control Points. *MIS Quarterly*, 37(2), 617–632 (2013).
20. Bharadwaj, A., El Sawy, O. A., Pavlou, P. A., Venkatraman, N.: Digital Business Strategy: Toward a Next Generation of Insights. *MIS Quarterly* 37(2), 471–482 (2013).
21. Ross, J. W., Sebastian, I. M., Beath, C., Mocker, M., Fondstad, N. O., Moloney, K. G.: Designing and Executing Digital Strategies. Proceedings of the International Conference on Information Systems (ICIS), 1–16 (2016).
22. Mesaglio, M., Hotle, M.: Pace-Layered Application Strategy and IT Organizational Design: How to Structure the Application Team for Success. Gartner, Stamford, CT, October 5 (2012).
23. Eusterbrock, T., van Steenbergen, M.: Principle-Based Approach in Enterprise Architecture practice; Finding the Sweet Spot, (2016). http://www.dya.info/sites/dya.info/files/attachments/1602028%20DYA%20Principle-based%20approach%20Enterprise%20Architecture_07.03.2016_0.pdf.
24. Black, J., Hopper, M., Band, C.: Making a Success of Principle-Based Regulation. *Law and Financial Markets Review* 1, 191–206 (2007).
25. Black, J.: Forms and Paradoxes of principles-Based Regulation. *Capital Markets Law Journal* 3(4), 425–457 (2008).
26. Burgemeestre, B., Hulstijn, J., Tan, Y. Rule-Based Versus Principle-Based Regulatory Compliance. Proceedings of the 2009 Conference on Legal Knowledge and Information Systems, JURIX 2009: The Twenty-Second Annual Conference, 37–46 (2009).
27. Grant, R.M. Toward a Knowledge-Based Theory of the Firm. *Strategic Management Journal*, 17, 109–122 (1996).
28. DEMO, http://www.ee-institute.org/en/demo
29. Boucharas, V., Steenbergen, M. van, Jansen, S. Brinkkemper, S.: The Contribution of Enterprise Architecture to the Achievement of Organizational Goals: A Review of the Evidence. In: Proper, E., Lankhorst, M.M., Schönherr, M., Barjis, J. and Overbeek, S. (Eds.), *Proceedings of the 5th International Workshop on Trends in Enterprise Architecture Research.* Springer, Berlin Heidelberg, 1–15 (2010).
30. Plessius, H., Steenbergen, M. van, Slot, R.: *Perceived Benefits from Enterprise Architecture.* Eighth Mediterranean Conference on Information Systems, Verona (2014).
31. Gottschalk, P. and Solli-Saether, H.: Maturity Model for IT Outsourcing Relationships. *Industrial Management & Data Systems*, 106(2), 200–212 (2006).
32. Ross, J.W., Weill, P., and Robertson, D.C.: *Enterprise Architecture as Strategy.* Harvard Business School Press, Boston, MA (2006).
33. Steenbergen, M. van, Bos, R., Brinkkemper, S., Weerd, I. van de, Bekkers, W.: Improving IS Functions Step by Step: The Use of Focus Area Maturity Models. *Scandinavian Journal of Information Systems*, 25(2), 35–56 (2013).

4

AGILE AND DEVOPS IN THE CONTEXT OF ENTERPRISE ARCHITECTURE AND IT ARCHITECTURE

Bill Schiano

4.1 Introduction

Bharadwaj [1] describes the role of digital business strategy as a fusion of formerly functional-level IT strategy and business strategy. Gartner [2] disputes this assumed elevation of IT, arguing that for over 30 years similar elevations had been expected following innovations in technologies with business potential, but did not materialize in most organizations. Whether or not IT is elevated, it must still continue to drive and support the new strategy along the four dimensions Bharadwaj outlines: scope, scale, speed, and sources of value creation and capture.

As Bharadwaj [3] notes, the IT infrastructure is now entangled with digital products and services. Enterprise architecture, here defined to encompass sometimes distinct roles of business architecture, technology/systems architecture, solutions architecture, and application architecture, is tasked with maintaining a longer-term view of the role and management of the entirety of IT infrastructure, even when much of it is provided outside the organization. Historically, this would mean extensive planning and modeling, but these traditional approaches are no longer viable in most organizations as agile development and DevOps move organizations away from occasional releases toward continuous delivery and even, in an increasing number of organizations, deployment.

As the scope of digital business requires expansion beyond individual projects, business units, and often organizations, the role of enterprise architecture becomes more important and the attendant complexity puts more pressure to increase agility just to keep up. Providing the elasticity needed to accommodate rapid changes in scale calls for agility and sourcing beyond the organization. Speed requires agility throughout the entire software supply chain. Finally, novel means of value creation need an architecture capable of supporting innovation in whatever forms are needed.

These IT trends facilitate, drive, and complicate sourcing IT from outside the organization. Particularly difficult are extant outsourcing contracts and relationships that had not anticipated what can be argued are radical changes in architecture and development.

In addition to the market and existing technology drivers pressuring innovation and agility, emerging technologies in Internet of Things (IoT) and artificial intelligence amplify the demand. IoT adds orders of magnitude more devices, but worse comes without accepted standards, massive security gaps, and the products and interfaces are evolving rapidly. Artificial intelligence-driven systems are enabling automation and previously prohibitively expensive systems and architectures by eliminating the need for human involvement.

4.2 The evolution of agility in the enterprise

Agile began as an approach to software development, popularized by the Agile Manifesto [4]. For organizations struggling to meet the demands of web-enabled systems with waterfall methodologies, agile had great appeal. Its impact on the effectiveness, efficiency, and morale of development groups was widely noted beyond the web development world and adoption began to spread. While many of the best practices emerge from organizations with massive "web-scale" operations, companies of all stripes have been rapidly adopting agile practices. As Figure 4.1 shows, by 2017, a majority of development teams were describing their methodology as agile.

The desire of organizations to be more nimble in the marketplace and able to adapt more smoothly internally has been a focus of management theory from the outset. More recently, the concepts of agility have been spreading across organizations far beyond the application to software development [6,7]. As internal organizations become more agile, they are increasingly constrained by their relationships with outside organizations. To realize their visions of enterprise agile, they expect and require their vendors to be agile and support their efforts. Velocity is the most common metric associated with agile, typically measured by the magnitude of stories delivered per sprint. Agile teams are also concerned with quality, effectiveness, and, increasingly, value [8].

In many organizations, budgeting has not caught up to the movement to agile, and is routinely still done in annual cycles. Agile development, by design, makes long-term estimation more difficult because it adapts over time, making resource needs difficult to project.

4.2.1 Lean enterprise

Many of the tenets of agile and DevOps overlap with the concepts of lean, which grew out of manufacturing, most notably the Toyota Production System. The principles of lean (eliminate waste, building quality, create knowledge, defer commitment, deliver quality, respect people, and optimize the whole) were ported to lean software development [9] and have been applied to companies as a whole [10, 11]. Toyota is of course well known for its management of outside vendors, and the move to lean organizations is similarly focused on the entire value chain.

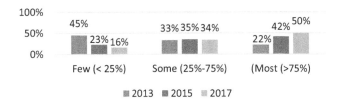

Figure 4.1 Agile adoption trends [5]

4.3 DevOps

Supporting digital business requires agility from all facets of IT work, not just development. As agile development progressed, the desire to implement ran into major impediments when the code was passed to operations. Weeks- and even months-long processes for integration were commonplace in many organizations, particularly larger ones, but made the shift to continuous deployment infeasible. DevOps tries to address some of the greatest constraints on achieving agility. The term "DevOps" emerged in 2009 following a talk at the O'Reilly Velocity 2009 conference [12]. In the intervening years, no standard definition of DevOps has emerged. Most definitions emphasize coordinating efforts of development and operations, focused on the application of agile principles and practices to facilitate more frequent delivery of higher quality systems which deliver greater value to the business. The concept has shown such strong appeal that in less than a decade, according to one survey [13], 78% of organizations have adopted DevOps, and of those, 30% company-wide, with another 28% adopting at the business unit or division level.

Teams delivering code frequently if not continuously, learning from it, and moving forward, is at the core of agile methods. In the early days of agile on websites, once code was ready, it was released immediately to customers. This is still the practice for many websites, but it may not be realistic for many enterprise systems. For instance, retail organizations may lock their systems in the fourth quarter to avoid system issues during their busiest season. Distinguishing delivery of working code from deployment and release of it is essential for enterprises. So finding ways to accommodate frequent/continuous delivery while protecting the integrity of enterprise systems became necessary. Some code may be deployed but not released to customers (similar to the DevOps concept of a feature flag, where code in the production system may be enabled or disabled by setting a simple parameter), while other code may be aggregated for deployment and eventual release [14,15]. This allows the agile developers to maintain momentum and get much needed feedback from clients without disrupting the business.

Much has been written about difficulties in alignment between business and IT, but intense, often overlooked, conflict also exists within IT itself. The development and operations organizations have a long history of tension, with each routinely blaming the other for the too common failure of systems. The conflict between dev and ops is rooted in their varying responsibilities, cultures, and world views. Table 4.1 outlines the stereotypes often attributed by each side to the other.

A major part of DevOps is improving the working relationship between dev and ops. It can be easy to dismiss the value of ops and simply see it as an easily outsourced commodity. The popular term "NoOps" reflects the drive for a state where ops does not require attention at all, and a predictably defensive reaction from ops [17]. But maximizing agility and treating the infrastructure as code will require careful thinking about ops, just as any code does, whether there is any in-house ops staff or not.

4.3.1 IT architecture

The fundamental tenets of service-oriented architecture, that architecture should be modular, well encapsulated, loosely coupled, discoverable, shareable, and distributable, have been widely accepted in theory for decades, going back to the advent of object orientation, but only in recent years, as the pressing need for agility combined with the availability of Cloud and nearly everything as a service (sometimes referred to as XaaS) has widespread

Table 4.1 Stereotypical differences between Dev and ops [16]

Dev's stereotypes of ops	Ops' stereotypes of Dev
Ponderously slow to act, whereas Dev feels agile and able to move quickly	Careless and lacks discipline; ops needs to perform heroics to keep the mess running
Wants to maintain the same old obsolete systems that cannot adapt to Dev standards	Likes to play with the latest "toys"
The department of "no" – there's always a reason something can't be done	Thinks anything is possible and there are no costs or other implications to its demands
Runs unreliable infrastructure that negatively affects Dev's credibility	Delivers lousy code that negatively affects ops' credibility
Not creative enough to understand the complex artistry of apps	Doesn't understand the real world, and creates unrealistic test environments
Just a bunch of process zealots and bureaucrats	Prima donnas who practice "art for art's sake"
Cobbles together infrastructure – it's not engineering	A bunch of hackers, not real professionals
Dev can do much better by replacing ops with the Cloud and supporting itself	Ops can do so much better by replacing Dev with packages software and SaaS

implementation of these principles been deemed feasible in many organizations. These attributes are not panaceas. Calibrating the degree of complexity, the size of the modules, and how they connect require sustained effort. This often falls to the enterprise architects, as any single agile initiative may not address these larger issues.

DevOps relies heavily on automation across all areas. Much of this involves self-service, where developers can "create environments, test and deploy code, monitor and display production telemetry" [18]. This self-service may extend to launching code through immutable infrastructure, where the only way code is deployed is through changes in version control, which then re-create the environments such as virtual machines, to prevent variance between production and the assumed code base [19]. Such variance is common – one telecom company found that only 50% of dev and test environments matched production [20] – and the cause of many bugs in production systems. This leads to system images being replaced frequently. At Netflix for instance, the average age of an Amazon Web Services instance is 24 days, and 60% are less than a week old [21]; 50% of Google's code is changed each month [22].

4.3.2 Magnitude of potential impact

Organizations implementing DevOps have reported staggering improvements. DevOps offers greater visibility into processes for the business [23]. The Walt Disney Company credits its DevOps initiative with enabling auto-scaling of its streaming sites, with hundreds of servers created on demand in less than 30 minutes, deployment time on many of its sites dropping from hours to minutes, and an 85% reduction in human errors [24]. The New York Stock Exchange went from 300 to 700 servers per admin and cut provisioning time from one to two days to 21 minutes [25]. While the 700:1 ratio is impressive, it is far less than Facebook's reported 25,000:1 [26]. HP cut development costs by more than 40%, saving over $40 million, and increased its "capacity for innovation" from 5% to 40% [27]. After facing highly publicized struggles with its systems, LinkedIn retooled with DevOps to deploy successfully multiple times daily [28]. Table 4.2 shows the difference in agile metrics between high-, medium-, and low-performing organizations.

Table 4.2 IT performance metrics [29]

Survey questions	High IT performers	Medium IT performers	Low IT performers
Deployment frequency For the primary application or service you work on, how often does your organization deploy code?	On demand (multiple deploys per day)	Between once per week and once per month	Between once per week and once per month[a]
Lead time for changes For the primary application or service you work on, what is your lead time for changes (i.e. how long does it take to go from code commit to code successfully running in production)?	Less than one hour	Between one week and one month	Between one week and one month[a]
Mean time to recover (MTTR) For the primary application of service you work on, how long does it generally take to restore service when a service incident occurs (e.g. unplanned outage, service impairment)?	Less than one hour	Less than one day	Between one day and one week
Change failure rate For the primary application or service you work on, what percentage of changes either results in degraded service or subsequently requires remediation (e.g. leads to service impairment, service outage, requires a hotfix, rollback, fix forward, patch)?	0–15%	0–15%	31–45%

a Low performers were lower on average (at a statistically significant level), but had the same median as the medium performers.

4.3.3 *Monitoring and analytics*

Historically, monitoring was used to keep track of the technical infrastructure and predict, detect, diagnose, and remediate issues. This was complex enough when dealing with just the hardware and operating systems within a single data center. As systems grew more distributed, monitoring evolved to manage remote locations, often in other organizations. The lower levels of the stack identify network bottlenecks and failure points as well as issues at the hardware and platform levels. While such narrow technical data can be helpful, it does not present a complete picture, and monitoring evolved to move up the stack into middleware, databases, and applications.

The focus on the full stack, from the lowest levels of infrastructure and hardware to the user interface, is an integral part of DevOps, to the point where full stack engineer is now a job title. To be agile, particularly if that involves continuous deployment, all levels of the stack need to be prepared for the changes needed to provide the desired functionality, and to ensure quality of service, the entire stack needs to be monitored.

Because many of the systems were opened up to customers and trading partners, the value of the monitoring data to those outside the information technology organization became apparent. To monitor effectively and provide value to such a range of constituents, organizations have moved from traditional blackbox monitoring, where nothing was known about what happens inside a server, service, or application, to whitebox monitoring, which provides much greater transparency and granularity [30]. Much of this information still comes from traditional log data, but Turnbull [31] notes that event tracking and metrics often prove more actionable. To facilitate the transparency, instrumentation of applications has become more common, with developers considering monitoring needs when designing and building apps, providing data feeds with a wealth of information. Building monitored applications requires thought in the design of the system to facilitate the subsequent monitoring [32]. As more applications are comprised of components and microservices, it will be even easier to get more data as each component or service will provide its own stream of data for monitoring along with the service.

The data gathered is crucial for the analytics process. The information available goes well beyond traditional network analytics and includes detailed information about applications and services that is useful to developers, ops, and business people across the organization interested in customer and/or user behavior. This commonly includes analysis of user counts, conversion rates, preferences, and behavior.

The skill set for this level of sophistication of analytics is a major change in many organizations, requiring massive data management of petabytes of raw data drawn from a complex array of heterogeneous distributed virtual servers (Etsy tracks over 800,000 metrics [33]), sophisticated understanding of architecture, and advanced knowledge of statistics to generate actionable insights.

4.3.4 Testing and Netflix's simian army

Organizations moving to DevOps need to accept that problems will happen, even if the failure rate may be lower. This comes as a shock in many organizations where failure has historically been chastised if not punished. It also requires changing the nature of service level agreements, or at least our reliance on them. The emphasis is on testing and monitoring and recovering quickly when the inevitable issues arise.

At the more extreme, and for many anxiety-provoking, level is the testing of code on production systems with active users. There are myriad terms for techniques for doing this: A/B testing, where alternative versions of code are deployed simultaneously to separate instances and customers are routed to one or the other based on any business rules that might be helpful, to see which version is more effective; canary rollouts, where code is deployed to subsets of users to see if there are problems; blue/green deployments, where two versions of the production system are maintained, and which one is available to users is alternated as new code is deployed; and dark launches, where code is placed onto production systems but not announced, allowing testing and enhancements until full release to users [34]. Netflix uses these techniques to conduct experiments to optimize the experience of their users [35].

There are three kinds of code: application, infrastructure, and test [36]. Much of software engineering theory evolved while focused on application code, and in many organizations, that is where developer resources are focused. But to achieve agility, a great deal of automation is needed in ops and QA, requiring code be implemented and, often, written.

Netflix has become famous for using such code and testing to limits previously unseen in large organizations. Its Chaos Monkey is designed to turn disable production systems to test claimed resiliency to failure. They later moved beyond the Chaos Monkey to an entire simian army, including Doctor and Janitor monkeys to remove unhealthy and unused instances, a Security Monkey to shut down any instances with violations, a 10–18 monkey for localization and internationalization issues [37]. They even implemented a Chaos Kong which would disable entire Amazon Web Services regions [38]. Many of the monkeys were made available to the public on GitHub, where Netflix to offer newer versions of services encompassing much of the same functionality (https://github.com/Netflix/SimianArmy).

In addition to being the most robust way to test claimed resiliency, such direct testing of the production environment sends a powerful signal about their willingness to stand behind their claims of reliability and, as long as most tests are passed, it enhances the organization's credibility.

4.4 Agility and DevOps beyond the boundaries of the organization

Distributing agile and DevOps work dramatically increases the complexity of managing it successfully in large part because agile processes are so communication intensive [39]. Many of the agile techniques to enhance communication were developed for co-located groups but many have been adapted to create virtual versions, including Kanban boards, burndown charts, standups, etc. Introducing cross-organizational issues on top of that complexity amplifies the problem.

A myriad of vendors, customers, and other organizations increasingly need to interact to function and support agility. Standards to support this are still evolving, so much of the work must be done more manually. In some cases, outsourced vendors have facilitated this. In other cases, outsourced vendors end up with enormous complexity to manage, essentially playing the familiar role of systems integrator, but in a far more dynamic environment.

4.5 Challenges for enterprises

4.5.1 Technical debt

The pressure to act and implement quickly often generates consequences in the long term. Cunningham [40] referred to the accumulation of such consequences as technical debt. Table 4.3 outlines Kruchten's [41] landscape of technical debt, with the implications for agile and outsourcing.

Table 4.3 Landscape of technical debt [42]

Source of technical debt	Implications
Architectural debt	Not considering how choices in elements impact others can reduce quality, impede scaling, and make maintenance slower and more expensive.
Structural debt	Poor design can impede efficiency and maintenance.
Test debt	Insufficient testing can lead to more defects in production and require more maintenance.
Documentation debt	This makes maintenance slower and more expensive.
Low internal quality	This can manifest in external issues, especially performance, and require more maintenance.
Code complexity	This can create inefficiency and increase maintenance expense.
Coding style violations	These make maintenance slower and more expensive and reuse less likely.
Code smells	These surface indications of potential problems with the code often reflect inefficiency, quality issues, and increased maintenance expense.

While taking on such technical debt might be sensible in the same way any debt can provide leverage, finding the time and resources to pay it off is difficult in most organizations as there is competition for the resources. In many cases, the debtor is unaware they have borrowed, particularly if components are outsourced.

The standard advice, obvious and easily given but far more difficult to follow, is to set aside resources to pay down this technical debt. Kim [43] recommends reserving 20% of the budget for non-functional requirements and reducing technical debt. This requires more discipline than many organizations have, particularly given the pressures to be responsive to the business. It also requires knowing what that has been incurred. Rather than responsible financiers regularly making interest and principal payments, many organizations behave more like failed gamblers scrambling to pay the vigorish only when not doing so constitutes an existential threat.

4.5.2 Technological change

Supporting an agile organization delivering continuously is a major technological undertaking, particularly if demands on the systems are also growing. Often all elements of the enterprise architecture need to change regularly. Both Etsy and Google have undergone five "entire rewrite(s) of their architecture from top to bottom" [44].

4.5.3 Organization change

Enhancing agility requires major changes in organizations, often altering power dynamics [45,46]. DevOps also requires rethinking how organizations meet audit and compliance standards. The greatest changes are in separation of duties, formerly handled by having developers hand off code to operations personnel who deploy and release it in production. DevOps achieves compliance through several mechanisms [47]:

- Automation. Deployment and release are handled by a system, rather than a person, which still constitutes separation from the person in development.
- Separate accounts. A temporary account is created for a developer to deploy and release code. This complies with the Payment Card Industry standard which requires separate accounts, but not necessarily separate people doing development and deployment.
- Independent checkpoints. Code is reviewed and signed digitally.

4.5.4 Scaling agile

Agile methodologies were developed for small project that could be completed by a single team. There are limits to the benefits of agile if it is only implemented at the project level in the development organization. The last decade has seen a rapid evolution of adaptations for scaling agile methods to the enterprise level. Finding ways to scale agile to enterprise level has become a cottage industry. Figure 4.2 shows some of the most common approaches in organizations in 2017. Many organizations are also creating hybrids of waterfall and other traditional methodologies and agile. All of the frameworks attempt to use agile principles to coordinate and aggregate work of small agile teams to accomplish larger enterprise goals. While not all of the frameworks describe a formal enterprise architecture role, each acknowledges to a varying extent, the need for a larger, longer-term view.

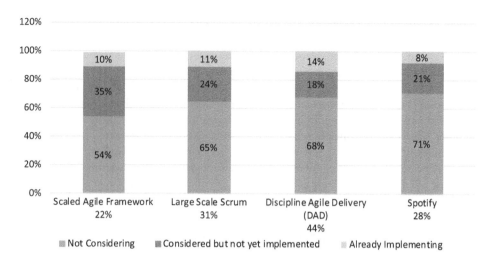

Figure 4.2   Enterprise agile framework adoption [48]

4.5.5   *Changing role of EA*

Enterprise architects have earned a reputation for being overly plodding; they are often accused of trying to boil the ocean while building models and frameworks. There is now, ironically, tremendous pressure to bring agile/lean principles to the work of enterprise architects. This requires a departure from starting with a massive, all-encompassing design/model, and the changes will be needed at every level of EA. In agile development, the concept of delivering a minimum viable product is a valuable framing to avoid gold plating/waste and delays. Enterprise architecture is working toward developing minimum viable architectures [49], but this quest is far more complex than minimum viable products, in no small part because EA isn't developed as a field, so establishing what constitutes an acceptable minimum is difficult.

The relationship between EA and the organization in many companies must also change. Architects can no longer expect to dictate how systems will be designed, developed, and implemented. Instead, the most effective EA groups are becoming more consultative, providing value just in time to dev and ops.

While agile was initially developed for small systems, at the enterprise level, it is proving helpful to have a conditional approach, where not all systems are treated the same. Two of the main criteria for this are the risk inherent in the systems and the level of innovation required. Gartner distinguishes mode 1 (linear and stable) and mode 2 (nonlinear and uncertain) [50]. Gartner also advocates pace-layering, distinguishing systems of record, innovation, and differentiation [51]. Forrester Research refers to systems of innovation, record, insight, and engagement [52]. The tolerance for risk on these dimensions varies depending on the nature of the system and the perceived need for speed/agility. The greater the granularity of the architecture, the more the gradations these distinctions can have.

4.6   Markets and contracts for agility

A mature or maturing agile organization dramatically complicates the classic "build or buy" dilemma. Forrester Research describes the choices as "build, compose, outsource, or buy" [53]. If the system is well architected, there is a great deal more granularity in the options. Beyond just the widely known and accepted infrastructure as a service, platforms as a service, and applications/software as a service, the application functionality has been further decomposed into components or services and now into microservices [54] and serverless/Functions as a Service [55].

Systems may employ scores, hundreds, and increasingly thousands of distinct components, many sourced from outside. In addition to traditional vendors, the open-source market is booming. The market for such small elements of code has exploded in recent years.

- There are now more than two million Java unique components in the Central Repository, almost three million unique JavaScript packages in npmjs.org, over 870,000 unique Python components housed in PyPI repository, and over 900,000 .NET components in the NuGet Gallery. There are also more than 900,000 containerized applications housed in Docker Hub [56].

And downloads have similarly grown, as reflected in Figure 4.3.

One survey of widely used repositories found that 5.9% of Java components, 6.2% of JavaScript components, and 3.6% of Python components contained at least one known vulnerability, and the average enterprise downloaded over 125,000 components annually [58]. Perhaps more troubling, only 16% of suppliers actively fix vulnerabilities and for them, the mean time to remediation is 233 days [59].

For many elements, it's a matter of entering a corporate purchasing card number and you are off and running. To further complicate matters, millions of components/services are open source and free for the taking. The governance process for open-source software has proved particularly challenging for organizations, with great risks of the software from both the security and legal perspective. Enforcing this is hard enough in a small development organization, but becomes impossible to do manually when myriad users and external

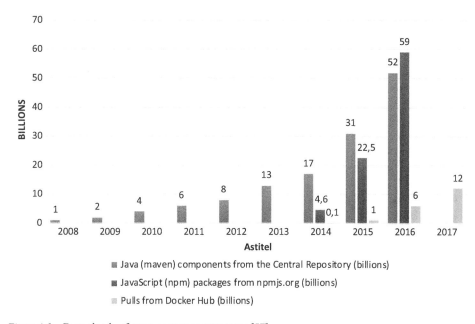

Figure 4.3 Downloads of open-source components [57]

Table 4.4 Percentage of work done manually, by performance [60]

	High performers (%)	Medium performers (%)	Low performers (%)
Configuration management	28	47	46
Testing	35	51	49
Deployments	26	47	43
Change approval processes	48	67	59

vendors may also be employing open source solutions, whether for complete applications or small components of them. The automated tools, including firewalls to prevent access to the components in the first place, are becoming more sophisticated and are an integral part of any effective governance program. Table 4.4 shows how much more is automated in high performing organizations.

DevOps now moves toward supply chain theory to broaden its scope in an emerging market. But because software is intangible, the degree of distribution and the number of vendors can be orders of magnitude greater than in manufacturing where the theory was formed and has already moved past manufacturing theory in terms of the speed and extent of automation throughout the chain.

Proper tools to support DevOps are critical. The toolset includes local development environments, version control, artifact repositories, testing, infrastructure automation, virtualization, and monitoring tools [61]. These tools are maturing rapidly and are routinely incorporating best practices. Cloud vendors are also evolving, offering much of the same functionality.

The use of automated code generation, sometimes referred to as low code, increases the speed of development and can be used by the user base producing their own code. When these tools first emerged decades earlier, they were often seen as not worth the trouble, as the resulting code was often buggy and inefficient. These objections are fading quickly in large part, not only because the tools themselves have improved dramatically, but also because processing power can offset some of the efficiency issues and time to market is often more important than efficiency or the highest quality levels.

Existing outsourcing relationships often struggle to adapt to the required level of agility. To support agility, many aspects of the traditional sourcing processes must change. The arms-length relationship with the client so common among outsourcers goes against the tenets of agile. But even organizations with close client relationships must still address challenges of distributed agile work, as well as educating clients about their role in agile processes. The contracts are often not amenable to agility and require contortions or renegotiation. Many outsourced firms are not staffed or organized for agile, although as agile matures, there are more new university graduates and experienced professionals with robust backgrounds in agile and even DevOps.

If the outsourced vendor has the entire lifecycle within its operation, they may better positioned for agile and DevOps than their clients. They have greater economies of scale in the monitoring and much of the work to be done can be held to standards set and audited within the organization [62]. Few organizations have the scale and skills to do all of their DevOps work in-house economically [63]. Thus, it is likely the vendor is still managing a complex software supply chain that extends beyond its boundaries, but they may still be in a better position to negotiate better deals with vendors and identify issues at one client that can be immediately addressed at others. But they may also be forced to collaborate with competitors, creating complex issues around coopetition and potentially encumbered by contract terms.

4.6.1 Sourcing strategy

Kleim [64], cited by Santy [65], offers seven steps involved in sourcing strategy:

* Determine the business case for or against outsourcing.
* Search for vendors.
* Select a vendor.
* Conduct negotiations.
* Consummate an agreement.
* Manage the agreement.
* Determine the business case to decide whether to renew, renegotiate, or terminate a contract.

All of the phases with the possible exceptions of managing the agreement and determining whether to renew face tremendous pressure to move more quickly. Complicating matters, many purchasing departments are not set up for agility and in fact are well designed as impediments to it. Creating formal business cases to justify purchasing outside code or services takes time both to create and to review. The expectation of pre-approving vendors with a rigorous process that can take weeks or months to complete creates delays in adding innovative vendors. Cloud, emerging technologies, microservices, and serverless are driving companies toward smaller vendors. The approval process may be too expensive to be worth doing for such small vendors, who may not be approved anyway because of stringent viability criteria emphasizing scale and track record of vendors. The search process itself has become more burdensome as the variety of vendors increases exponentially. Once viable vendors are found, many organizations require the detailed process for selecting vendors that may include several stages, including formal requests for proposal and perhaps trials of the products and services. Reaching an agreement may require multiple layers of authorizations, building further delay into the process.

4.6.2 Cloud

In addition to readily available infrastructure as a service to replace in-house data centers (or those housed at outsourcers), much of the code that once needed to be written in-house or outsourced is now readily available as Cloud services. And once a vendor is chosen, the contracts for Cloud are in many ways better. They are certainly easy, requiring only a brief form and a corporate purchasing number. The clickwrap agreements are standard, which reduces consolidation complexity if they need to be aggregated. But there are dramatic limits to customization and negotiation and most buyers don't even glance at the terms, which typically heavily favor the vendor.

Many Cloud vendors will not offer, perhaps because they cannot, full transparency into their systems. This is often a consequence of how they configure multi-tenancy to reduce their own costs. This introduces limits to what can be monitored, and to what extent.

4.7 Consulting

Organizations routinely look for help in making the move to agile. Every major consultancy purports to offer such services, from strategic advice and consulting to instrumental help and extra hands. Myriad boutique firms also compete in the space. But contracting for agile is more complex, particularly if clients want to move beyond time and materials billing. Some client organizations manage some of the risks and complexity of pricing by employing business outcome-driven contracts where the vendor is paid, at least in part, based on the results the organization achieves with the system. Such value-based pricing is becoming a more common component in contracts, but few vendors are interested in having it represent a major portion of their revenue stream.

Traditional full outsourcing is certainly still an option, but it is increasingly rare that a chosen external vendor would have all of the work and systems in-house. Given the rapidity of developments, particularly related to the IoTs, multisourcing has become a requirement for most enterprises. But the drive for integration and analytics as well as end-to-end service management has led to a need for the vendors to coordinate. The ecosystem has also grown to include customers. The increase in agility has been highly correlated with an increased focus on and involvement of customers.

4.8 Conclusion

Agility, driving both EA and DevOps, does not change the longstanding need to be open to outsourcing and to choose how and when to do so carefully. While it certainly requires detailed thought and heavy engagement of the client, lack of client engagement was often a complaint of outsourcing organizations, and there is long history of information systems research about improving the relationship between the two. Agility drives greater value to clients, which could help dramatically in bringing vendors and clients together.

References

1. Bharadwaj, A., El Sawy, O. A., Pavlou, P. A., & Venkatraman, N. V.: Digital Business Strategy: Toward a Next Generation of Insights. *MIS Quarterly*, 37(2), 471–482 (2013).
2. Nielsen, T.: *Maverick Research: CIOs Should Forget Digital Business and Concentrate on Core IT.* Gartner, Stamford, CT, October 7 (2016).
3. Bharadwaj, A., El Sawy, O. A., Pavlou, P. A., & Venkatraman, N. V.: Digital Business Strategy: Toward a Next Generation of Insights. *MIS Quarterly*, 37(2), 471–482, p. 472 (2013).
4. Beck, K., Beedle, M., Van Bennekum, A., Cockburn, A., Cunningham, W., Fowler, M., & Jeffries, R.: Agile Manifesto. (2001). http://www.agilemanifesto.org
5. Lo Giudice, D.: *The State of Agile 2017.* Forrester Research, Inc., Cambridge, MA, December 14 (2017).
6. Rigby, D. K., Sutherland, J., & Takeuchi, H.: Embracing Agile. *Harvard Business Review*, 94(5), 40–50 (2016).
7. Humble, J., Molesky, J., & 'O'Reilly, B.: *Lean Enterprise: How High Performance Organizations Innovate at Scale.* O'Reilly Media, Inc., Sebastopol, CA (2014).
8. Swanton, B., & Norton, D.: *Use the Right Metrics in the Right Way for Enterprise Agile Delivery.* Gartner, Stamford, CT, November 2 (2017).
9. Poppendieck, M., & Poppendieck, T.: *Lean Software Development: An Agile Toolkit: An Agile Toolkit.* Addison-Wesley, Boston, MA (2003).
10. Humble, J., Molesky, J., & O'Reilly, B.: *Lean Enterprise: How High Performance Organizations Innovate at Scale.* O'Reilly Media, Inc., Sebastopol, CA (2014).
11. Ries, E.: *The Lean Startup: How Today's Entrepreneurs Use Continuous Innovation to Create Radically Successful Businesses.* Crown Books, New York, NY (2011).
12. Sharma, S. (2017). *The DevOps Adoption Playbook* (Kindle ed.). Wiley IBM Press, Indianapolis, IN, Kindle location 743 (2017).
13. RightScale: RightScale 2017 State of the Cloud Report. p. 20 (2017). http://assets.rightscale.com/uploads/pdfs/RightScale-2017-State-of-the-Cloud-Report.pdf
14. Sharma, S. (2017). *The DevOps Adoption Playbook* (Kindle ed.). Wiley IBM Press, Indianapolis, IN, Kindle location 1069 (2017).

15. Humble, J., Molesky, J., & O'Reilly, B.: *Lean Enterprise: How High Performance Organizations Innovate at Scale.* O'Reilly Media, Inc., Sebastopol, CA, Kindle location 3430 (2014).
16. DeMartine, A., & Bittner, K.: The Seven Habits of Highly Effective DevOps. Forrester Research, Inc., Cambridge, MA, October 2, p. 3 (2014).
17. Humble, J., Molesky, J., & O'Reilly, B.: Lean Enterprise: How High Performance Organizations Innovate at Scale. O'Reilly Media, Inc., Sebastopol, CA, Kindle location 5523 (2014).
18. Kim, G., Debois, P., Willis, J., & Humble, J.: *The DevOps Handbook: How to Create World-Class Agility, Reliability, and Security in Technology Organizations.* IT Revolution, Portland, OR, Kindle location 461 (2016).
19. Kim, G., Debois, P., Willis, J., & Humble, J.: *The DevOps Handbook: How to Create World-Class Agility, Reliability, and Security in Technology Organizations.* IT Revolution, Portland, OR, Kindle location 2517 (2016).
20. Kim, G., Debois, P., Willis, J., & Humble, J.: *The DevOps Handbook: How to Create World-Class Agility, Reliability, and Security in Technology Organizations* (First ed.). IT Revolution, Portland, OR (2016).
21. Kim, G., Debois, P., Willis, J., & Humble, J.: *The DevOps Handbook: How to Create World-Class Agility, Reliability, and Security in Technology Organizations.* IT Revolution, Portland, OR, Kindle location 2588 (2016).
22. Kim, G., Debois, P., Willis, J., & Humble, J.: *The DevOps Handbook: How to Create World-Class Agility, Reliability, and Security in Technology Organizations.* IT Revolution, Portland, OR, Kindle location 2648 (2016).
23. Sharma, S. (2017). *The DevOps Adoption Playbook* (Kindle ed.). Wiley IBM Press, Indianapolis, IN, Kindle location 902 (2017).
24. Earnshaw, A.: Disney's DevOps Journey: A DevOps Enterprise Summit Reprise. https://puppet.com/blog/disney-s-devops-journey-a-devops-enterprise-summit-reprise, February 24 (2015).
25. Puppet: NYSE and ICE: Compliance, DevOps and Efficient Growth with Puppet Enterprise. Retrieved from https://www.puppet.com (2015).
26. Frazier, M.: Facebook Won't Hire You For Its Data Center. *Bloomberg Businessweek*, September 25 (2017).
27. Gruver, G., & Mouser, T.: *Leading the Transformation: Applying Agile and DevOps Principles at Scale.* IT Revolution, Portland, OR, Kindle location 106 (2015).
28. Kim, G., Debois, P., Willis, J., & Humble, J.: *The DevOps Handbook: How to Create World-Class Agility, Reliability, and Security in Technology Organizations.* IT Revolution, Portland, OR, Kindle location 1805 (2016).
29. Forsgren, N., Humble, J., Kim, G., Brown, A., & Kersten, N.: State of DevOps Report. https://www.puppet.com, p. 23. The 2017 DevOps Survey is the property of Puppet, Inc. and DevOps Research and Assessment, LLC. All rights reserved (2017).
30. Turnbull, J.: *The Art of Monitoring* (Kindle ed.): James Turnbull & Turnbull Press, New York, Kindle location 465 (2014).
31. Turnbull, J.: *The Art of Monitoring* (Kindle ed.): James Turnbull & Turnbull Press, New York, Kindle location 483 (2014).
32. Turnbull, J.: *The Art of Monitoring* (Kindle ed.): James Turnbull & Turnbull Press, New York, Kindle location 5399 (2014).
33. Kim, G., Debois, P., Willis, J., & Humble, J.: *The DevOps Handbook: How to Create World-Class Agility, Reliability, and Security in Technology Organizations.* IT Revolution, Portland, OR, Kindle location 3758 (2016).
34. Kim, G., Debois, P., Willis, J., & Humble, J.: *The DevOps Handbook: How to Create World-Class Agility, Reliability, and Security in Technology Organizations.* IT Revolution, Portland, OR, Kindle location 656 (2016).
35. Govind, N.: A/B Testing and Beyond: Improving the Netflix Streaming Experience with Experimentation and Data Science. *Netflix Technology Blog.* 13 July (2017). https://medium.com/netflix-techblog/a-b-testing-and-beyond-improving-the-netflix-streaming-experience-with-experimentation-and-data-5b0ae9295bdf
36. IT Revolution: *An Unlikely Union: DevOps and Audit: Information Security and Compliance Practices.* IT Revolution, Portland, OR (2015).
37. Izrailevsky, Y., & Tseitlin, A.: The Netflix Simian Army. *Netflix Tech Blog.* July 18 (2011). https://medium.com/netflix-techblog/the-netflix-simian-army-16e57fbab116

38. Basiri, A., Hochstein, L., Thosar, A., & Rosenthal, C.: Chaos Engineering Upgraded. *Netflix Technology Blog*. September 24 (2015). https://medium.com/netflix-techblog/chaos-engineering-upgraded-878d341f15fa

39. Diel, E., Marczak, S., & Cruzes, D. S.: Communication Challenges and Strategies in Distributed DevOps. Paper presented at the 2016 IEEE 11th International Conference on Global Software Engineering (ICGSE) (2016).

40. Cunningham, W.: The WyCash Portfolio Management System. *ACM SIGPLAN OOPS Messenger*, 4(2), 29–30 (1993).

41. Kruchten, P., Nord, R. L., & Ozkaya, I.: Technical Debt: From Metaphor to Theory and Practice. *IEEE Software*, 29(6), 18–21 (2012).

42. Kruchten, P., Nord, R. L., & Ozkaya, I.: Technical Debt: From Metaphor to Theory and Practice. *IEEE Software*, 29(6), 18–21 (2012).

43. Kim, G., Debois, P., Willis, J., & Humble, J.: *The DevOps Handbook: How to Create World-Class Agility, Reliability, and Security in Technology Organizations*. IT Revolution, Portland, OR, Kindle location 1178 (2016).

44. Kim, G., Debois, P., Willis, J., & Humble, J.: *The DevOps Handbook: How to Create World-Class Agility, Reliability, and Security in Technology Organizations*. IT Revolution, Portland, OR, Kindle location 3534 (2016).

45. Gruver, G., & Mouser, T.: *Leading the Transformation: Applying Agile and DevOps Principles at Scale*. IT Revolution, Portland, OR (2015).

46. Stoneham, J., Thrasher, P., Potts, T., Mickman, H., DeArdo, C., & Limoncelli, T. A.: *DevOps Case Studies: The Journey to Positive Business Outcomes*. IT Revolution, Portland OR (2016).

47. IT Revolution: *An Unlikely Union: DevOps and Audit: Information Security and Compliance Practices*. IT Revolution, Portland OR (2015).

48. West, M., & Norton, D.: *Market Guide for Enterprise Agile Frameworks*. Gartner, Stamford, CT, July 17, p. 4 (2017).

49. Erder, M., & Pureur, P.: *Continuous Architecture: Sustainable Architecture in an Agile and Cloud-Centric World* (Kindle ed.). Morgan Kaufmann, Waltham, MA (2016).

50. Norton, D.: *Bimodal in an Agile-Everywhere World*. Gartner, Stamford, CT, September 30 (2016).

51. West, M., & Norton, D.: *Market Guide for Enterprise Agile Frameworks*. Gartner, Stamford, CT, July 17 (2017).

52. Bartoletti, D.: *Take the Wheel: Build Your Cloud Computing Strategic Plan Now*. Forrester Research, Inc., Cambridge, MA, July 12 (2017).

53. Lo Giudice, D., & Condo, C.: *Master DevOps for Faster Delivery of Software Innovation*. Forrester Research, Inc., Cambridge, MA, November 21, 2017.

54. Balalaie, A., Heydarnoori, A., & Jamshidi, P.: Microservices Architecture Enables DevOps: Migration to a Cloud-Native Architecture. *IEEE Software*, 33(3), 42–52 (2016).

55. Hausenblas, M.: *Serverless Ops*. O'Reilly Media, Sebastopol, CA (2017).

56. Sonatype: 2017 State of the Software Supply Chain, p. 13. Retrieved from www.sonatype.com (2017).

57. Sonatype.: 2017 State of the Software Supply Chain, pp. 15–16. (2017). www.sonatype.com

58. Sonatype.: 2017 State of the Software Supply Chain, p. 17. (2017). www.sonatype.com

59. Sonatype.: 2017 State of the Software Supply Chain, p. 14. (2017). www.sonatype.com

60. Forsgren, N., Humble, J., Kim, G., Brown, A., & Kersten, N.: State of DevOps Report. https://www.puppet.com, p. 27. The 2017 DevOps Survey is the property of Puppet, Inc. and DevOps Research and Assessment, LLC. All rights reserved (2017).

61. Davis, J., & Daniels, K.: *Effective DevOps: Building a Culture of Collaboration, Affinity, and Tooling at Scale*. O'Reilly Media, Inc., Sebastopol, CA, Kindle location 3935 (2016).

62. Sharma, S. (2017). *The DevOps Adoption Playbook* (Kindle ed.). Wiley IBM Press, Indianapolis, IN, Kindle location 6853 (2017).

63. Sharma, S. (2017). *The DevOps Adoption Playbook* (Kindle ed.). Wiley IBM Press, Indianapolis, IN, Kindle location 6909 (2017).

64. Kliem, R.: Managing the Risks of Outsourcing Agreements. *Information System Management*, 16(3), 91–93 (1999).

65. Santy, S., & Sikkel, K.: Sourcing Lifecycle for Software as a Service (SAAS). Paper presented at the EPJ Web of Conferences (2014).

5

SUPPLY CHAIN COORDINATION AND INTEGRATION

Jos van Hillegersberg and Dissa R. Chandra

5.1 Introduction

Supply chains and business networks are dynamic, and subject to forces of disintegration and re-integration. Their structure is often large and complex. Still, agility is required to provide value to the end-customer. Agility and responsiveness require effective and efficient collaboration between organizations in the network. This can only be realized with properly designed and well-governed IT and information systems.

In this chapter, we review the business drivers for supply chain collaboration and the role of IT in disabling and enabling collaboration. We then discuss inter-organizational governance, as the interplay between technology and governance is an important part of sustainable collaboration. This can be viewed as a new type of alignment – the alignment between inter-organizational services, processes and governance, and the IT and systems that support it. We review types of Inter-Organizational System (IOS) and IOS governance (Section 5.4) and the role of IT and information systems (Section 5.5). As an example, we describe some aspects of Portbase, a logistics IOS illustrating network collaboration and IOS governance (Section 5.6). We conclude by discussing the state of the field and briefly point at the potential impacts of recent technologies.

5.2 Drivers for supply chains and networked business

As a result of drivers such as specialization, globalization and the increasing complexity of products/services, value chains usually consist of many tiers. Businesses in each tier fulfill a specific task to add value to the product/service. This specialization has many potential advantages. In [1], three types of advantages are given. (1) Disintegration advantages, related to the benefits of not having activities in-house that can be better sourced from external companies. One can think of focusing on core competencies that provide superior product/ service quality, cost, flexibility speed and innovation. As noted in [2], this also includes the benefit of modularization of products/services. (2) Location-specific advantages, such as placing specific product/service capabilities in geographical regions that offer certain policy, infrastructure or labor market benefits and (3) externalization advantages that encompass the benefits of co-specialization, organizational learning and relationship capital.

91

In [3], "vendor managed inventory (VMI), efficient customer response (ECR), and collaborative, planning, forecasting, and replenishment (CPFR)" are given as examples of vertical coordination. Clearly, to bring these benefits to the end-consumer, seamless integration is needed across the value chain. The coordination and collaboration that crosses supply chain tiers is referred to as *vertical integration*.

Each specific business function is a candidate for being outsourced and subsequently procured externally. The drivers and risks may vary based on the type of function that is externally sourced in the value chain. For example, drivers in logistics, procurement and IT partly overlap, but also differ (see Table 5.1). Compiling extant literature [4] gives a variety of factors that drive the externalization of the logistics function. For the outsourcing of the procurement function, a survey conducted with procurement managers finds that the presence of specific competences and product commoditization plays an important role [5]. Similarly, different factors are at play in the sourcing of IT services [6].

Within a tier of a value chain network, businesses perform similar tasks. For reasons such as location, regulation, market, specialization, etc., the number of players in a tier may vary. These players may simply co-exist, be in competition or cooperate. The reasons for cooperation can be many, such as risk sharing, gaining flexibility, cost reduction, knowledge exchange, innovation, complementing networks or services. Several scenarios can be thought of that require coordination and collaboration within a tier – *horizontal integration*. In [3], examples of reasons for horizontal collaboration are given: sharing private information, facilities or resources to reduce costs or improve service, manufacturers' consolidation centers (MCCs), joint route planning and purchasing groups.

Given the many drivers for externalization and outsourcing of business functions, one would expect to see very fine-grained business networks, with each business only providing highly specialized and focused functions and relying on the value network for everything else. Proponents of the dynamic value network envisage the dominance of smartly orchestrated networks in which capabilities are dynamically sourced and coordinated [7,8]. However, the same factors that drive the outsourcing of functions may also re-shift the

Table 5.1 Varying drivers for business function externalization

Externalization of logistics [10]	*Externalization of procurement [5]*	*Externalization of IT services [6]*
Logistics cost reduction	Contract manufacturer competence	Exploration of knowledge
Diverting capital investment	Lack of competencies at OEM	Innovation
Enhancement of business process	Product commoditization	Intellectual property
Expertise of 3PL service providers	Offshoring opportunity	Value network of client and/ or supplier
Focus on core competencies		Interaction and integration of resources
Reduction of warehouses and vehicles		Complementary competencies
Increasing of inventory turnover		Continuous improvement
Enhancement of flexibility in operations		Interaction and integration of resources
Access to emerging technology		Joint problem-solving
Productivity improvement		

balance toward insourcing or reshoring. Hartman et al. [9] find, based on 12 case studies of companies that insourced a previously outsourced manufacturing function, that external events often change, and conditions cause companies to reconsider their sourcing strategies. Re-integration decisions have recently been made by e-commerce giants such as Amazon. com that is moving away from contracting logistics services: "It has created its own logistics division and acts as its own freight forwarder" [10].

In summary, many drivers and counterforces determine the structure, composition and granularity of the value network. Outsourcing can have mixed effects on firm performance depending on the type of outsourcing and the context. Based on a survey of the literature, Lahiri [11] finds that "outsourcing involves tradeoffs between lowering cost and enhancing innovation capabilities". Moreover, the review shows that "a firm's careful balancing of vertical integration and strategic outsourcing for innovation helps achieve superior performance". It is also important to realize that outsourcing decisions that impact value network configurations are not fully rational. Changing environment, uncertainty and the bounded rationality of the decisions clearly play a role. Historical reasons, tradition, personal friendships and family ties, politics and trust can all be instrumental in value chain linkages and performance [12].

In the next section, we focus on the role of IT and information systems to enable effective collaboration and coordination in the supply chain. Drivers, such as shown in Table 5.1, only materialize if supported by effective IT. We introduce the literature in this area and then discuss various types of supply chain collaboration and coordination technology.

5.3 Responsive supply chain and the role of IT

The complex and dynamic structure of today's supply chains calls for mature levels of business network integration and agility. An agile business network is able to respond to largely unpredictable changes with ease [13]. Various related terms are used in the literature referring to similar abilities. In [14], the term responsive supply chain is used. The authors identify three major enablers: (1) value chain or a collaborative network of partners, (2) Information Technology (IT) and systems and (3) knowledge management. We have already discussed what drives the value chain structure. Now we focus on the systems and technology and their role as enabler or barrier.

How can technology and systems support the inter-organizational linkages between organizational nodes in the network? In addition to strategic and organizational barriers, IT systems continue to cause barriers to business integration: "both academia and industry observers have long been concerned about the continued slow, painful process and many cases of failure to realize the performance value of IOS" [15]. Technical complexity that can occur in inter-organizational integration goes beyond that of systems engineering within the organization. Inter-organizational processes will need to connect at least two systems embedded in different architectures and systems landscapes. Each organization involved will bring its own systems, procedures and practices to the table. Often, these have evolved over time and include proprietary technologies and customizations. The lack of a single dominant standard in most industries further increases the challenge [16].

In most organizations, Enterprise Resource Planning (ERP) systems account for an important part of the systems landscape or even form the backbone of the architecture [17]. Such systems have usually not been designed with seamless integration in mind. As a result, connecting legacy and ERP systems of various partners is technically highly complex. Enterprise Systems Integration projects may take years and huge investments to complete. The resulting "hard-wired" links often do not enable agile business networks that allow business partners to quickly connect their business processes [18]. Based on a Delphi panel study, Daniel and White [19] concluded that "ERP systems may be reaching a structural limit concerning their capabilities and adjunct technologies will be required to integrate multiple inter-organizational operations".

While agile business networks have been described in several conceptual studies, the lack of suitable ICT support has been a key hindrance to their success in practice. Traditional ICT support for connecting the nodes in business networks has been limited to the (often cumbersome) static horizontal and vertical integration of enterprise systems. The IT links established are usually limited to coordination and control at the operational level in the context of fixed collaboration patterns.

Theories and classifications can help in understanding the rich set of IT technologies and systems that are available to enable business network agility. In Table 5.2, we combine the well-known operational, tactical and strategic management decision levels with the typical phases of an inter-organizational transaction: search (finding a business partner), contract (setting up the agreement for value exchange), execute (running the inter-organizational process and exchanging value) and settle (providing a usually financial award for the services delivered). These four phases are similar to business action theory [20].

From Table 5.2, it is apparent that a single inter-organizational business transaction, such as the procurement of a series of valves from a sub-contractor for the manufacturing of an engine, can be supported by a variety of system functions and technologies. Typically, in each of the 12 areas of Table 5.2, some level of system support is present. This may range from very basic interaction and coordination using standard tools such as email and exchanges of text files and spreadsheets, to advanced supports using artificial intelligence, semantic integration technologies, robotic process automation and alike.

Experiences show that there often is a mis-alignment between IT and business [21]. This may even be more so in the IOSs sphere. In some areas, businesses may have adopted

Table 5.2 Classification and examples of systems supporting value networks

	Search	Contract	Execute	Settle
Strategic	Credit and reliability rating, risk management systems	Negotiation support systems, group support systems	Supply chain collaboration platforms	Supply chain finance systems
Tactical	Social media, information retrieval and search engines, text mining and analytics, communities of practice, e-markets	Contract management systems, business analytics, exception management	Inter-organizational process, performance monitoring	e-factoring, e-dispute and conflict handling, bonus and claims processing
Operational	Service and API catalogues and directories, search engines, service and data platforms	Business process execution systems, business process Rule engines, e-markets, smart contracts	Inter-organizational process integration platforms, e-markets	e-invoicing and e-payment, reconciliation

state-of-the art technologies where other inter-organizational processes may be largely manual or supported by basic email-based integrations that easily lead to errors and lack of oversight. Also, what links in the business network are supported by IOS and to what extent often seems arbitrary. In [15], based on a study among Chinese firms, the breadth and depth of IOS support is linked to organizational performance. The study concludes that "the balanced alignment between IOS depth and IOS breadth contributes to the firm's competitive performance, which implies that the firm gains long-term competitive advantage by maintaining balanced development in IOS depth and IOS breadth".

While business opportunities and technologies for business networking receive ample attention, many firms have only recently started to recognize the importance of a strategic view on IOS for supply chains. The structured and long-term assessment of IOS current and future developments for business networks are not often part of the strategic agenda. Some of the larger and innovative companies are taking initiatives in this area. Also, third parties, adopting e-commerce sharing and coordination models, are aiming at taking up coordination roles in the supply chain. Many projects run in this space are pushed by innovation projects, industry sector organization initiatives or R&D subsidized programs. Hopefully, more knowledge and experiences from these projects will lead to a higher priority for IOS, and more mature design and implementation practices.

In the following sections, we review strategies toward IOS implementation for business networks and give examples to illustrate opportunities and complexities.

5.4 Inter-organizational governance and configurations

IOSs can emerge on an ad hoc basis. While incidental successes can be achieved, a wide range of risks will threat the continuing collaboration. In [22], four types of risks are listed that may occur in IOS use. (1) Overgrazing: business partners may overuse the IOS, thereby degrading the service levels of other connected businesses. Fair use policies or pricing schemes can be introduced to manage this risk. (2) Fouling or contamination of the IOS: dumping incorrect data, missing data, incomplete transactions, etc. may all pollute the IOS, decreasing its value and trust that partners have in the IOS. Data integrity, data quality monitoring and transaction monitoring can be put in place to manage this risk. (3) Poaching: partners may poach common resources for their private gain against the original goals of the IOS. This risk can be managed by putting in place identity management, authorizations and security, and keeping logs of data access and updates. Repetitive audits or even continuously auditing IOS use can prevent this from happening. (4) Stealing: this related risk concerns outright abuse. Advanced security and access control including four-eye procedures can reduce this risk.

To ensure sustainable collaboration in value networks, some type of governance needs to be in place. The paradigm of the governance of collaboration is shifted from a static perspective toward a dynamic context-dependent perspective. For appropriate governance, the parties involved and their role need to be recognized and a governance process needs to be set up. Chandra and van Hillegersberg, based on the analysis of several Supply Chain Collaborations (SCCs), propose five general roles. These can be used to analyze the collaboration context to communicate the collaboration design, business model and governance to the potential business partners. The five roles are [23]:

- Member – Entity that is a member of a collaboration involved in the operational, tactical or strategical activities of the collaboration. They adopt shared services to support their supply chain activities. In order to maintain their access to these services, the members can invest into the IOS or pay per transaction.

- IOS provider – Providers deliver the IOS, either software and/or platform as a service, for supporting the coordinated supply chain activities enabling the collaborations. They are responsible to manage and maintain the IOS according to Service Level Agreements (SLAs) with its members.

- Partners – Outside the collaborations there may be companies that perform supply chain activities to support the collaboration. These companies are not direct members of the collaborations, but may get access to the shared system to fulfill their supporting role. However, their benefits are not a priority for the collaboration.

- Supporting partners – Other partners are typically sub-contracted. These are companies that support the IOS besides the partners and IOS provider(s). Examples of companies with this role are internet providers, IS developers to whom IOS providers outsource part or all of their software and/or platform development, universities, research institutes, associations and employee organizations.

- Orchestrator – Organizations that coordinate the supply chain activities inside the collaborations. These can be a separate third party, a joint venture, a virtual organization staffed by the partners involved, etc.

These roles can be assigned to separate organizations, or multiple roles could be performed by a single organizational unit. As the complexity of the collaboration quickly grows as the collaboration activities expand in breadth and depth, applying some form of inter-organizational governance is advisable. This can be achieved through applying a combination of formal and informal governance mechanisms.

Formalized governance mechanisms can take the form of contracts, regulations, policies and procedural approaches. Informal mechanisms are characterized by relationships rather than by bureaucratic structures. Examples are emerging relationships and norms, commitments and trust.

5.4.1 Configurations for inter-organizational collaboration

While the terminology in use is not always consistent, there are four basic configurations for inter-organizational collaboration. These are shown in Figure 5.1. These configurations each require governance. The type of governance that will be effective is related to the model used.

The description of the four types below is based on [24].

- Market, formed by contractual relationships between suppliers and buyers [25]. A market has certain features such as multiple suppliers of the same product or service and short-term partnerships which mainly occur during the transaction [26]. In this governance model, IOS providers can be seen as suppliers of a coordinating service and members can be seen as customers.

Market   Shared governance   Lead organization   NAO

Figure 5.1 Types of configurations for inter-organizational collaboration

- Shared governance, in which members participate in network governance without a separate and unique governance entity [27]. Collaborations applying this governance model are governed by regular meetings among members. In these collaborations, the members are collectively responsible for making decisions.
- Lead organization, in which a particular member coordinates major network-level activities and decision-making in a network [27]. This particular member takes sole responsibility of its inter-organizational collaboration. In a collaboration applying a lead organization governance model, the leading member should have adequate power – which could be acquired through market domination, law enactment or buyer-supplier relationship dependencies – over the remaining members. Centralized data in the IOS could be used by the leading member to gain a competitive advantage.
- Network Administrative Organization (NAO), which is a separate entity that is established to govern the network [27]. The NAO model provides inter-organizational collaborations with the benefits of having a neutral governance entity.

We follow [28,29] in viewing inter-organizational governance as a dynamic process and adopt a lifecycle view. In a way this is similar to the four-phased view of process transactions, though one has to keep in mind that IOS governance takes place at the network level, and thus is directing and steering the inter-organizational processes discussed before.

The governance lifecycle of inter-organizational collaboration follows these four phases [24,29].

5.4.2 *Pre-partnership collaboration*

Partnerships can be initiated in a variety of ways. Generally, the drivers for supply chain integration are at play. A business case can trigger the exploration of collaborative business initiatives, or external events, such as new regulation that requires value chain coordination, may trigger the pre-partnership phase. Markus and Bui [30] observe three ways to attract member participation in this phase. Drawing owners from all major segments of the community, providing for participants to have a say in decision-making, ensuring that owners do not profit financially at the members' expense. Ideally, in this phase already the appropriate mix of formal and informal governance mechanisms is initiated.

5.4.3 *Partnership creation and consolidation*

In this phase, the partnership between the organizations intensifies to prepare for the program delivery. During this phase, the alternative services, breadth and depth of collaborative services and processes are assessed. At the end of this phase, the selected service and related inter-organizational processes should be implemented and made ready to be used. The success of collaborations in this phase depends on the members' willingness to contribute financial, manpower and knowledge resources to the set-up as well as the willingness to exchange their information with other partners. This phase is crucial to the success of the next phases.

5.4.4 *Partnership program delivery*

In this phase, the services and inter-organizational processes are executed. Formal and informal governance mechanisms that have been defined are effectuated, evaluated and fine-tuned where needed. Payment schemes including transaction costs, incentive schemes, penalties and so on are settled. Decisions to adapt the partnership, such as the entry/exit of partners, are carried out. During the partnership delivery, service innovation projects can be started to extend and improve the collaboration and implement new services and processes.

5.4.5 *Partnership termination or succession*

There are several reasons for a partnership to end. The collaboration may have been set for a fixed time frame. Alternatively, the exit of partners or disrupted key resources may make the partnership no longer valuable. Despite formal or informal agreements, conflicts may occur and in the worst case these lead to termination of the partnership. Regulators can also make a partnership redundant. A changing law may take away the need for collaboration, or collaborations that are becoming too tight may turn out to be undesirable from an anti-trust law perspective. It is also possible that better alternatives become available and the current partnership becomes obsolete.

5.5 Role of IT in IOS and inter-organizational governance

As shown earlier (see Table 5.2), a variety of IT and systems can play a role in making inter-organizational integration happen. It is our view that the better the alignment between inter-organizational processes and IT, the more effective the partnership can be governed and the higher the chance for sustainable success. IOS governance is thus dependent on and influenced by the technologies that make IOS linkages happen. Since the rise of networking and Electronic Data Interchange (EDI) in the last decades of the previous century, methods and ITs that add to the possibilities for IOS have been introduced to make integrations easier, faster, smarter and agile. Without trying to give an exhaustive overview of the vast developments in this space, we illustrate some in this section.

The web service paradigm offers a set of technologies that directly enable agile business networks. Core to web service is the idea that organizations offer their services on the web in machine-readable format and accessible format on the Internet. The web service paradigm fundamentally offers a vision where anybody should be able to trade with everybody. While a range of specific technologies was introduced, the generic principles and elements are surveyed in [31]. The authors state that web service technology should offer semantic web technology to enable finding and comparing services and offers of vendors worldwide and negotiate and contract delivery conditions. Furthermore, ontologies should be incorporated to deal with the semantics of the business language and varying standards. While it is very likely that multiple semantic standards will be used, the web service technology should include ways to (semi-)automatically map between these standards. Finally, the varying business logics and rules should be supported. To make this all work, a web services framework should offer a way to describe the web service goal, semantics, ontology, pre- and post-conditions, input and output data, composition and flow details such as what other services area called or need to be called before and after the service. In addition, execution details such as error messages and performance and scalability need to be specified. Integrity needs to be assured such that invoked services notify that they have understood the message call and are able to execute the service request. In the case of a failed service, some sort of compensation (or roll-back) needs to be available to make complex message orchestrations possible.

Clearly, these goals are very ambitious. Still, over the last decades the services paradigm has evolved and promising methods, tools and applications have become available.

Large tech-companies and innovative organizations have published web service APIs that are often heavily used and have become an important part of their business services portfolio. Think of the Google maps and Google translate API, Amazon books API and Twitter data API. Also, in business, basic web services APIs have become commonplace. In areas such as finance and banking and mobile services, web services have become standard for services such as stock trading or getting currency exchange information, interest rates, etc. [32].

SMEs offering specialized services have also started to explore the opportunities of the web service paradigm. In [33], a scenario is developed where warehouse space is found and contracted through web services across multiple vendors automatically. In a recent study, an architecture and prototype is developed to show how ecommerce companies can integrate to logistics companies using web services to integrate the return process of shipments [34]. 12Returns.com is a company that commercializes such a scenario by handling returns of goods for ecommerce companies through a set of Cloud-based services. The web services offered by 12Returns connect to the ecommerce client and logistics companies that support in handling the returns [35].

Web services can also bring advanced capabilities and knowledge to the value network of companies that would not be able to afford this in-house. In [36], the authors show that the latest advances in sales forecasting algorithms can be seamlessly integrated in ecommerce planning processes using services-based integration. A service provider can offer a customized forecast based on product and historical sales data, and return the forecast to the service requester. Such a service is clearly positioned higher in the value chain than standardized fully automated services.

The integration of services is greatly simplified if a business ontology is available that defines core business terms, their meaning and relationships. Using such ontologies, semantic standards for business interoperability can be defined and services can use these to specify the joint business process and service specifications. XML is often used as a language as a basis for these standards. In many industries, such standards are developed. Depending on the industry and parties involved, the quality varies. Standards can be in a rudimentary phase, offering only support for the most basic processes, or standards may have matured offering a wide range of process and data definitions. The complexity of semantic standards or too many alternatives to choose from may hamper integrations. Still, it is advisable to scan the market for available semantic standards. A lot of efforts and knowledge has usually gone into their development and they can give a project a kick start [37].

Cloud computing and various orchestration solutions offered in the Cloud can aid in facilitating inter-organizational collaboration [34]. In particular, the emergence of iPaas, Integration Platform as a Service, offers Cloud-based integration services that bring many benefits of previously complex and expensive enterprise integration platforms to the Cloud. Using flexible pricing models and scalable architectures, iPaas can evolve with business integration offering also a low entry point for Small and Medium Enterprises. In [38], iPaas is defined as: "a suite of cloud services that enable users to create manage, and govern integration flows connecting a wide range of applications without installing or managing any hardware or middleware". While iPaas are still emerging, required core functionalities include the ability to interface to a variety of web service and API technologies, providing support for security, compliance and synchronization when setting up and executing web service orchestrations [39]. Moreover, iPaas can support in joint governance, data sharing policies and business model execution of the collaborative business.

5.6 Portbase: an example of an integration hub

To illustrate the theories and technologies discussed, we give the examples of Portbase, its governance and how it provides business integrations.

Portbase provides logistics services around the port of Rotterdam. Our description here is a summary of [24] that gives a more detailed case study based on an interview with the managing director and secondary sources. The collaboration has a fairly long history and has evolved over time into delivering a rich set of services supporting collaboration among hundreds of companies around the large sea-port.

Over the years, Portbase has connected an increasing number of agents, barge operators, shipbrokers, customs, empty depots, exporters, importers, forwarders, Food & Consumer Product Safety Authority, inspection stations, port authorities, selection points, companies, rail infrastructure managers, rail infrastructure operators, traction suppliers, road haulers and terminals. By the end of 2016, Portbase had 3,900 companies as members and 14,000 users who were involved in 82 million transactions within the system. Today, Portbase's PCS has been implemented in The Rijkswaterstaat Maritime Navy and several Dutch ports: Rotterdam, Amsterdam, Harlingen, Zeeland Seaports (Vlissingen and Terneuzen), Dordrecht, Scheveningen, Den Helder, Gronigen Seaports (Delfzijl and Eemshaven) and Moerdijk.

Portbase has four functions: dangerous goods declaration, customs, logistics and navigation. The services are used in all Dutch ports to guarantee synchronized data between its *members*. Nowadays, Portbase offers 43 services to support its community. Through these services, Portbase provides standardization of information that is being exchanged in the port community. The services provided through each function are available by using several application modules contained in a modular architecture approach. Services are built using a platform, which is developed by Oracle frameworks and tools. Portbase *members* also have access to build their own services on top of Portbase's platform – e.g. ProRail's Wagonload Information System.

In order to develop these services, Portbase collaborates with IT companies and service providers that support its *members*. The *members* pay Portbase access fees based on their transaction for exploitation and development of the services on Portbase's platform. *Members* can choose for relatively high transaction fees, or subscription fees plus lower transaction fees. Portbase's balance sheet is break-even and proves its standing as a non-for-profit company. Portbase issues monthly invoices for the *members*.

Portbase is in the *partnership program delivery phase*. Ownership is shared between the Port of Rotterdam Authority (75%) and the Port of Amsterdam Authority (25%). Both port authorities are represented on the *Supervisory Board*, together with other Portbase's main business partners (Figure 5.2).

Portbase can be viewed as an orchestrator connecting processes between partners such as the shippers and forwarders, logistics companies and government agencies. Portbase has an Advisory Board and the Supervisory Board that enables stakeholders to be involved in decision-making. Both the port authorities of Rotterdam and Amsterdam invest in Portbase. Portbase offers two financial plans for funding the *operational cost* that gives the *members* flexibility in deciding on the plan that fits their needs.

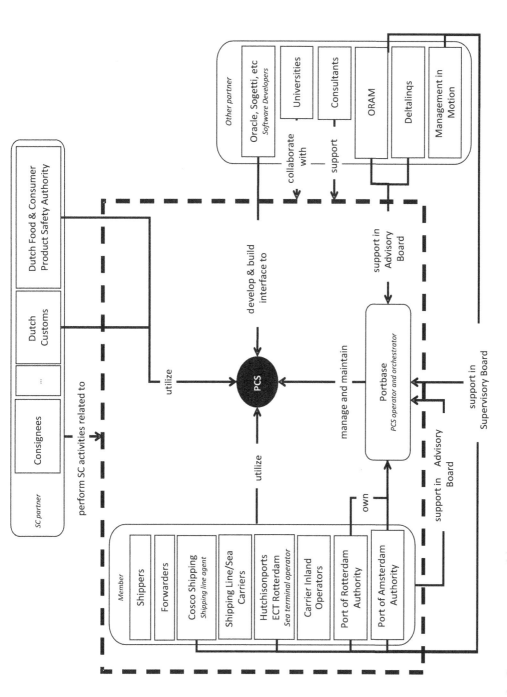

Figure 5.2   Governance structure of the port community system

5.7 Discussion and conclusion

A range of drivers causes business networks and supply chains to form often complex and dynamic network structures. Horizontal and vertical linkages are needed to coordinate, share risk, innovate and generate optimal value. While IT and systems can both be an enabler and a disabler of smooth collaboration, it has often been the latter. Complex architectures and legacy enterprise systems have made cross-organizational integration a cumbersome job. Moreover, organizational challenges are complicating matters further. Still, value that can be generated if borders can be crossed trigger many projects to build IOSs.

Design and implementation projects can benefit from a clear positioning of the processes and systems to be built. The transaction phase (search, contract, execute and settle) and level (operational, tactical and strategic) can help to identify the goal and development path of the joint services, processes and systems.

Any IOS requires governance. Governance is needed to ensure sustainable operation, monitor performance and facilitate high-level decisions regarding the collaboration. A mix of formal and informal mechanisms can be designed. Through the phases of collaboration, governance can evolve and mechanisms can be evaluated and adjusted.

Modern IT and systems offer more possibilities to build IOS that can be efficiently operated and effectively governed. The web service paradigm is evolving and especially integration platforms as a service fit well to the increasing need for agile collaboration. Especially as semantic standards are becoming available, efforts to build semantic integrations are less difficult to engineer.

The Portbase example illustrates how both technology and governance can evolve over decades to keep on adapting to the changing needs of the stakeholders and actors involved. It shows that careful design of the governance structure and mechanisms ensures that many companies can benefit.

The field of IOS can benefit from several recent developments. Robotic Process Automation (RPA) offers an alternative way to APIs as RPAs can mimic labor-intensive integration tasks that human users used to perform. The RPA Bot can operate on top of existing user interface screens of legacy systems. While perhaps not the most elegant solution, the RPA does not need extensive work on defining and building services and APIs [40].

Blockchain technologies can provide a secure and neutral way to record distributed transactions between organizations. Future research and field tests need to demonstrate in what scenarios this will generate value and how these technologies fit in the toolbox of the IOS systems engineer. Semantic web technologies enabling linking open data sets offer an alternative way to created pooled resources that can solve part of the integration puzzle. Decades after their inception, IOS continue to be the champions' league of systems design and governance, requiring high skills, high stakes and high rewards.

References

1. Kedia, B.L., Mukherjee, D.: Understanding Offshoring: A Research Framework Based On Disintegration, Location and Externalization Advantages. *J. World Bus.* 44(3), 250–261 (2009).
2. Kotlarsky, J., Oshri, I., Hillegersberg, J. van, Kumar, K.: Globally Distributed Component-Based Software Development: An Exploratory Study of Knowledge Management and Work Division. *J. Inf. Technol.* 22(2), 161–173 (2007).
3. Cruijssen, F., Cools, M., Dullaert, W.: Horizontal Cooperation in Logistics: Opportunities and Impediments. *Transp. Res. Part. E. Logist. Transp. Rev.* 43(2), 129–142 (2007).

4. Khan, H., Hussainy, S.K., Khan, A., Khan, K., Farooq, U., Mir, M.M.: Drivers of Outsourcing and Selection Criteria of 3rd Party Logistics Service Providers. *Oper. Supply Chain Manag. Int. J.* 10, 240–249 (2017).

5. Brewer, B.L., Ashenbaum, B., Carter, J.R.: Understanding the Supply Chain Outsourcing Cascade: When Does Procurement Follow Manufacturing Out the Door? *J. Supply Chain Manag.* 49(3), 90–110 (2013).

6. Murthy, C., Padhi, S.S., Gupta, N., Kapil, K.: An Empirical Investigation of the Antecedents of Value Co-Creation in B2B IT Services Outsourcing. *Bus. Process Manag. J.* 22(3), 484–506 (2016).

7. Mowshowitz, A.: Virtual Organization: A Vision of Management in the Information Age. *Inf. Soc.* 10(4), 267–288 (1994).

8. Heck, E., Vervest, P.: Smart Business Networks: How The Network Wins. *Commun. ACM* 50(6), 28–37 (2007).

9. Hartman, P.L., Ogden, J.A., Hazen, B.T.: Bring It Back? An Examination of the Insourcing Decision. *Int. J. Phys. Distrib. Logist. Manag.* 47(2–3), 198–221 (2017).

10. The Global Logistics Business Is Going to Be Transformed by Digitisation. https://www.economist.com/briefing/2018/04/26/the-global-logistics-business-is-going-to-be-transformed-by-digitisation

11. Lahiri, S.: Does Outsourcing Really Improve Firm Performance? Empirical Evidence and Research Agenda. *Int. J. Manag. Rev.* 18(4), 464–497 (2016).

12. Kumar, K., van Dissel, H.G., Bielli, P.: The Merchant of Prato-Revisited: Toward a Third Rationality of Information Systems. *MIS Q.* 22(2), 199–226 (1998).

13. Van Oosterhout, M., Waarts, E., Van Hillegersberg, J.: Change Factors Requiring Agility and Implications for IT. *Eur. J. Inf. Syst.* 15(2), 132–145 (2006).

14. Gunasekaran, A., Lai, K., Edwin Cheng, T.C.: Responsive Supply Chain: A Competitive Strategy in a Networked Economy. *Omega* 36(4), 549–564 (2008).

15. Zhang, C., Xue, L., Dhaliwal, J.: Alignments between the Depth and Breadth of Inter-Organizational Systems Deployment and Their Impact on Firm Performance. *Inf. Manage.* 53(1), 79–90 (2016).

16. Ahn, H.J., Childerhouse, P., Vossen, G., Lee, H.: Rethinking XML-Enabled Agile Supply Chains. *Int. J. Inf. Manag.* 32(1), 17–23 (2012).

17. Kumar, K., van Hillegersberg, J.: Enterprise Resource Planning: Introduction. *Commun. ACM* 43(4), 22–26 (2000).

18. Hillegersberg, J. van, Moonen, H., Dalmolen, S.: Coordination as a Service to Enable Agile Business Networks. In: Kotlarsky, J., Oshri, I., Willcocks, L.P. (eds.) *The Dynamics of Global Sourcing Perspectives and Practices*, pp. 164–174. Springer, Heidelberg (2012).

19. Daniel, E.M., White, A.: The Future of Inter-Organisational System Linkages: Findings of an International Delphi Study. *Eur. J. Inf. Syst.* 14(2), 188–203 (2005).

20. Lind, M., Goldkuhl, G.: Coordination and Transformation in Business Processes: Towards an Integrated View. *Bus. Process Manag. J.* 14(6), 761–777 (2008).

21. Suh, H., Hillegersberg, J., Choi, J., Chung, S.: Effects of Strategic Alignment on IS Success: The Mediation Role of IS Investment in Korea. *Inf. Technol. Manag.* 14(1), 7–27 (2012).

22. Kumar, K., Van Dissel, H.G.: Sustainable Collaboration: Managing Conflict and Cooperation in Interorganizational Systems. *MIS Q. Manag. Inf. Syst.* 20(3), 279–299 (1996).

23. Chandra, D.R., Hillegersberg, J. van.: The Governance of Cloud Based Supply Chain Collaborations. In: *2015 IEEE International Conference on Industrial Engineering and Engineering Management (IEEM)*, pp. 1608–1612. IEEE Press, New York (2015).

24. Chandra, D.R., Hillegersberg, J. van.: Governance of Inter-Organizational Systems: A Longitudinal Case Study of Rotterdam's Port Community System. *Int. J. Inf. Syst. Proj. Manag.* 6(2), 47–68 (2018).

25. Lowndes, V., Skelcher, C.: The Dynamics of Multi-Organizational Partnerships: An Analysis of Changing Modes of Governance. *Public Adm.* 76(2), 313–333 (1998).

26. Grant, G., Tan, F.B.: Governing IT in Inter-Organizational Relationships: Issues and Future Research. *Eur. J. Inf. Syst.* 22(5), 493–497 (2013).

27. Provan, K.G., Kenis, P.: Modes of Network Governance: Structure, Management, and Effectiveness. *J. Public Adm. Res. Theory.* 18(2), 229–252 (2008).

28. Chandra, D.R., van Hillegersberg, J.: Governance Lifecycles of Inter-Organizational Collaboration: A Case Study of the Port of Rotterdam. *Proc. Comput. Sci.* 121, 656–663 (2017).

29. Wilding, R., Pilbeam, C., Alvarez, G.: Nestlé Nespresso AAA Sustainable Quality Program: An Investigation into the Governance Dynamics in a Multi-Stakeholder Supply Chain Network. *Supply Chain Manag. Int. J.* 15(2), 165–182 (2010).

30. Markus, M.L., Bui, Q.: Going Concerns: The Governance of Interorganizational Coordination Hubs. *J. Manag. Inf. Syst.* 28(4), 163–198 (2012).

31. Fensel, D., Bussler, C.: The Web Service Modeling Framework WSMF. *Electron. Commer. Res. Appl.* 1(2), 113–137 (2002).

32. Data, Financial, Analytics API Categories See Big Growth. https://www.programmableweb.com/news/data-financial-analytics-api-categories-see-big-growth/research/2018/05/21

33. Hillegersberg, J., Boeke, R., Heuvel, W.-J.: The Potential of Webservices to Enable Smart Business Networks. In: Vervest, P., Heck, E., Pau, L.-F., Preiss, K. (eds.) *Smart Business Networks,* pp. 349–362. Springer, Heidelberg (2011).

34. Aulkemeier, F., Paramartha, M.A., Iacob, M.-E., van Hillegersberg, J.: A Pluggable Service Platform Architecture for E-Commerce. *Inf. Syst. E-Bus. Manag.* 14(3), 469–489 (2016).

35. 12Return Developer Portal. http://developer.12return.com/

36. Aulkemeier, F., Daukuls, R., Iacob, M.-E., Boter, J., van Hillegersberg, J., de Leeuw, S.: Sales Forecasting as a Service. In: Proceedings of the *18th International Conference on Enterprise Information Systems,* pp. 345–352. SCITEPRESS, Portugal (2016).

37. Folmer, E., Oude Luttighuis, P., van Hillegersberg, J.: Do Semantic Standards Lack Quality? A Survey among 34 Semantic Standards. *Electron. Mark.* 21, 1–13 (2011).

38. Serrano, N., Hernantes, J., Gallardo, G.: Service-Oriented Architecture and Legacy Systems. *IEEE Softw.* 31(5), 15–19 (2014).

39. Theilig, M.-M., Pröhl, T., Zarnekow, R.: Requirements Analysis for an Open iPaaS: Exploring the CSP, ISP, and SME View. *AMCIS 2018 Proc.* (2018).

40. Suri, V.K., Elia, M., van Hillegersberg, J.: Software Bots – The Next Frontier for Shared Services and Functional Excellence. In: Oshri, I., Kotlarsky, J., Willcocks, L.P. (eds.) *Global Sourcing of Digital Services: Micro and Macro Perspectives,* pp. 81–94. Springer, Heidelberg (2017).

6

OFFSHORE OUTSOURCING

Hans Solli-Sæther and Petter Gottschalk

6.1 Introduction

IT outsourcing can be defined as:

> the process whereby an organization decides to contract-out or sell the firm's IT assets, people and/or activities to a third party supplier, who in exchange provides and manages these assets and services for an agreed fee over an agreed time period.
>
> *[1, p. 3]*

Strategic drivers for outsourcing may be that the company wants to achieve economies of scale in production, increase efficiency through the use of a specialized supplier, gain access to highly qualified labor, settle or restructure unprofitable work processes. The offshore outsourcing of white-collar work has grown rapidly since the early 21st century [2,3]. The digital workforce of countries such as India and China are only paid a fraction of the minimum wage enjoyed by that of Western firms.

Offshore outsourcing or just offshoring is "the practice among US and European companies of migrating business process overseas to India, the Philippines, Ireland, China and elsewhere to lower costs without significantly sacrificing quality" [4, p. 14]. Following the fall of Communism in 1989, most Eastern European countries started the long road to democracy and a market economy [5], and from the mid-1990s commercialization and mass distribution of the Internet gained prominence. Internationalization and technology development enabled the global sourcing of cross-border products and services, and Western companies have increasingly gained access to cheap labor from Eastern Europe and Asia over the last three decades. Today, there are two main types of jobs in the global labor market. The first is production-related jobs in the export industries, for example in sectors such as maritime and furniture, while the second is knowledge-intensive jobs in service industries in sectors such as IT, banking and finance. According to Jensen and Pedersen [6], the offshoring of IT and other types of administrative services flows to destinations with available talent pools (e.g., Asia, Central and Eastern Europe). IT offshore outsourcing means using an offshore provider to handle some of an enterprise's IT work [7]. More specifically, it implies contracting with a third party (supplier) based at an offshore location (which usually means in a

105

developing country and separated from the client by an ocean) to accomplish some work for a specified length of time, cost and level of service [8].

Outsourcing and offshoring has become a common business practice in many Western companies, but far from all businesses succeed. Some companies that do not succeed choose to take back the product or service. Backsourcing is defined as "retrieving previously outsourced activities as contracts expire or terminate" [9, p. 165]. Ejodame and Oshri [10] also describe backsourcing as the process where a client firm brings previously outsourced services from a supplier back in-house. According to Veltri, Saunders and Kavan [11], there are two main reasons for backsourcing decisions: first, outsourcing has failed and backsourcing is viewed as a solution to correct outsourcing problems, and second, external and internal changes may motivate firms to backsource activities to respond to new opportunities created by these changes. Typical problems encountered by companies are higher than expected production costs, unexpected transaction costs, lower quality than expected, a knowledge gap between customer and supplier, and lack of control over resources and features. A US survey shows that as many as 70% of US companies have negative experiences with offshoring of IT and that 25% of these companies have brought their services back in-house [10].

A decision to outsource, offshore or backsource implies that the company has to consider costs, resources and its relationship with a partner. In the case of backsourcing, it must also understand knowledge re-integration [10]. Recently, Law [12] introduced the path-dependent pattern or path creation on outsourcing, explaining why firms continue to use outsourcing as a preferred governance mode despite experiencing low performance. Organizational crises and the perception of backsourcing as a success are two elements that enable significant mindful deviations from outsourcing practices and the development of a backsourcing path.

The purpose of this chapter is to provide a basis for understanding organizational maturity for outsourcing, offshoring and backsourcing, as well as showing the characteristics and dominant issues that follow the various levels of maturity.

6.2 Theoretical background

6.2.1 Maturity models

Maturity models have been used in organizational and management research since the 1970s. According to King and Teo [13], such models can describe a variety of phenomena, such as the life cycle or growth of organizations and products. These models assume predictable patterns, preferably called stages or levels in an organization's growth, product sales or application of technology. These levels can be characterized by the fact that they: (1) are sequential by nature, (2) occur in a hierarchical progression that is not easily reversible and (3) contain a number of organizational activities and structures.

6.2.2 Maturity model for outsourcing, offshoring and backsourcing

The development of the maturity model for outsourcing, offshoring and backsourcing has taken place over time, and is based on a targeted research process that first involved the development of a conceptual and theoretical model, then empirical testing of the model and later a revised model [13,14,15]. The revised maturity model shown in Figure 6.1 identifies five stages — internal function, internal service function, outsourcing, offshoring and backsourcing — as explained below [15].

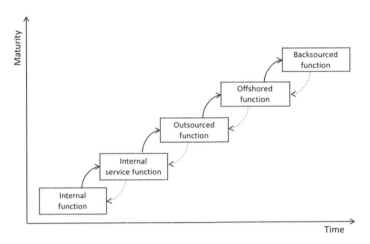

Figure 6.1 Maturity model for outsourcing, offshoring and backsourcing, adapted from Solli-Sæther and Gottschalk (2015)

- Stage one – Internal function. This is the traditional organization where the company manages and maintains an internal IT function. At this stage, efficiency in internal work processes, access to skilled resources and maintaining a good relationship between the IT function and the line of business are important.
- Stage two – Internal service function. An in-house service function delivers services back to the line of business based on documented agreements for services; for example, IT consulting, systems integration, application development and maintenance, and IT infrastructure operation. At this stage, IT costs and resources are still issues, but the significant difference is that the relationship between the IT service function and the line of business is more formal.
- Stage three – Outsourced function. An outsourced function involves a budget, assets such as hardware, software and personnel, and the management of the entire function. At this stage, a contractual relationship is established between the client and the supplier organization, which leads to dramatic changes in the relationship – transactions are formal, control mechanisms change from behavioral control to output control and the personal relationship changes from manager and employee to client and supplier.
- Stage four – Offshored function (or offshore outsourcing). An offshored function delivers IT services from overseas, typically for lower costs. Important issues are reduced production costs, access to qualified resources and partnership quality. The client and the supplier are geographically disparate; they may have different languages, cultures and time zones, and are often asymmetrical in knowledge and economic power.
- Stage five – Backsourced function. A backsourced function is a reverse from outsourcing or offshoring. Due to the termination of a contract, an organization brings IT back either in part or totally. The challenges include cost minimization and operational efficiency, availability of resources and knowledge re-integration, and re-establishment of governance structure.

All stages are conceptualized, so that they are significantly different from each other. There is no overlap in content between the stages, and no stage is perceived as a subcategory of another stage. Each stage is transferable to an empirical setting as the phenomena described are taken from real-life business practices.

6.3 Framework for analysis

Applying dominant problems to stages-of-growth models indicates an existing pattern of primary concerns that firms face for each theorized stage [16]. Kazanjian and Drazin [17] claim that maturity models, implicitly or explicitly, share a common underlying logic. Organizations undergo transformations in their design characteristics, which enable them to face the new tasks or problems that growth elicits. The problems, tasks or environments may differ from model to model, but most models suggest that stages emerge in a well-defined sequence, so that the solution of one set of problems or tasks leads to the emergence of a new set of problems or tasks that the organization must address. Benchmark variables are often used to indicate the characteristics in each stage of growth and to demonstrate that transitions occur throughout the stages. Table 6.1 serves as a framework for analyzing the stages of growth for the sourcing decisions and indicates a set of benchmark areas such as costs, resources and partnership.

6.3.1 Dominant problems and benchmark areas

The first area for benchmarking is *costs*. Cost considerations are an important issue in all sourcing decisions. The first step is to measure the baseline IT service and its associated costs. In making the initial outsourcing decision, companies are concerned about their internal production costs, and they will choose outsourcing where the market is cheaper or better than their own IT services. An argument for the offshore outsourcing decision is the lower labor costs overseas. When companies decide to backsource, managers use arguments such as "external production costs are higher than expected" and "unanticipated transaction costs"

Table 6.1 Framework for analysis, adapted from Solli-Sæther and Gottschalk (2015)

Areas for benchmarking \ Stage	Stage one: Internal function	Stage two: Internal service function	Stage three: Outsourced function	Stage four: Offshored function	Stage five: Backsourced function
Costs	Efficiency in business process	Establish baseline for service levels and costs	Lower production costs due to scale economies	Cost reduction due to cheap labor Unanticipated transaction costs	Re-establish operational efficiency in-house
Resources	Access to qualified labor	Professionalization of the service function	Access to top-class resources	Resource flexibility, better access to skilled developers Knowledge gap between client and supplier	Regain control of resources
Partnership	Maintaining internal relationships	More formal relationship between line of business and service function	Formal contractual relationship between client and supplier	Client-supplier differences in terms of geography, time zones, language and cultures	Re-establish internal governance structure

[11,18,19]. As such, cost concerns follow maturation. Regardless of the source, the goal is to minimize costs and achieve operational efficiency.

The second area of benchmarking is *resources*. Companies have to integrate and exploit IT services, internally or from a supplier, to produce competitive services. In running an in-house IT function, there may be a challenge accessing skilled resources. Companies can try to professionalize the IT function by organizing IT as an internal service function. An outsourcing agreement may potentially give the organization access to world-class resources, but the challenge is still to integrate and exploit strategic IT resources from the supplier together with the client company's own resources. If the organization loses control over resources and service function, it is difficult to accelerate the pace of innovation [11]. In offshoring, the knowledge, which earlier could be transferred between people in the same organization or country, now has to be transferred between business professionals in the client company and IT professionals in the supplier company in the low-cost country. In bringing IT back in-house, resource availability is once again a critical factor for success.

The third area of benchmarking is *partnership*. Relationship issues between the internal staff function and line of business may arise because of differences in the professional culture, i.e., between the IT professionals and the business professionals. An internal service function will typically have some kind of documented agreement with the line of business, regulating governance structure, service level and fees for service. An outsourcing contract has the purpose of facilitating exchange and preventing opportunistic behavior between the two parties; however, contractual issues may arise. In an offshoring relationship, the parties have to handle geographic distances, cultural differences, language barriers and time zones. Backsourcing implies the re-establishment not only of systems but of personnel and governance procedures [9,11].

6.3.2 *Path of evolution*

As indicated above, there may be a general path or trend from an in-house staff function (stage one), via an in-house service function (stage two) to an outsourced function (stage three), followed by an offshored function (stage four), and then potentially a backsourced function (stage five). The most obvious path is from the initial stage one, via intermediary stages two, three and four, to the final stage five. However, other paths are possible. For example, some stages may be bypassed, and also, a temporary return to an earlier stage may be possible.

6.4 Two business examples

In this section, two business examples are used to illustrate the stages-of-growth model and the analytical framework. This approach was selected to understand the inherent complexities and the underlying constructs, in addition to debating the economies of offshore outsourcing. According to Yin [20], the case study method is preferred when examining contemporary events, especially when the focus is on a contemporary phenomenon within some real-life context. The case study's unique strength is its ability to deal with the full variety of evidence, including documents, artifacts, interviews and observations. Two cases of offshore outsourcing information systems development (ISD) relationships were selected with the following similarities: Nordic client companies with suppliers from South-East Asia (India and Bangladesh), and client companies whose aim is to save money and access a skilled work force. The cases provided a broad base of offshore outsourcing practices, suggesting that the case in each cooperating constellation would be of interest.

6.4.1 Data collection and analysis

Data were collected in two steps: first during 2011–2013 through 12 interviews, and second with two additional follow-up interviews in 2017. In-depth interviews following a semi-structured approach were employed as the data collection method. For each case, six interviewees were selected among the participating organizations, both the client and supplier side were covered. The duration for each interview was between one and two hours. Interviews took the form of personal meetings – in person or via Skype. The same researchers conducted all interviews to assure consistency. The questions were addressing ISD, dominant problems, benchmark variables, description of the evolution and the economies of outsourcing. Each interview was documented as soon after the interview as possible to preserve accuracy. The initial interviews were of exploratory character, whereas follow-up interviews were targeted to discuss relevance of the model.

For the purpose of this study, a content analysis approach was applied, as data needed to be analyzed and interpreted [21]. In the analysis, pertinent patterns and similarities in the responses were looked for and identified. The individual cases served as the evidentiary base for the study. The purpose was not to portray any single one of the relationships, but rather to synthesize the lessons learned, which were dispersed throughout the separate, cross-case issues. Below, the results from the case studies are presented and discussed with respect to stages-of-growth, dominant problems and benchmark areas, and evolutionary path. To illustrate the application of the analytical framework presented in the previous section, the two client organizations are analyzed based on the relevant parameters of the analytical framework (costs, resources and partnership).

6.4.2 Case one

Stages-of-growth. The client company is a leading Northern European supplier of electronic payment and information solutions (named: Payco). Payco operates in five countries: Denmark, Norway, Sweden, Finland and Estonia. Payco offshored part of its application development and application maintenance to a global service supplier based in India back in 2003. Every year, a number of calls were made for individual project contracts. Over the years, Payco had developed a standardized set of sourcing models by outlining the tasks/roles that were sourced to the offshore service supplier, the tasks/roles retained by Payco, organizational structures, methodology used to operate the model (e.g., scrum or Waterfall) and key sourcing governance mechanisms. These sourcing models included sourcing of application maintenance, application development and managed service production support and test center. All aimed at increasing the offshore rate, and hence resource flexibility and cost reduction. According to Payco's sourcing manager, "The motivations for offshore outsourcing was increased flexibility, lower labor costs, greater innovation and access to skilled developers."

The ISD project studied was the "Web Portal." The one-year project used scrum methodology to develop and maintain the application. The teams had daily scrum meetings, backlog meetings, weekly meetings and live demo meetings with business unit(s). All project team members were trained in scum methodology and some members were certified. According to Payco's project manager, the two companies had built trust and communicated well using English as a common business language during their long relationship. The supplier provided employees with an internal cultural training program to help them understand Nordic values and culture, as stated by the supplier's on-site coordinator. Software development by the offshore team finished in time and on budget, having met the technical and quality requirements. Payco's project was successful since the project goals were achieved.

Dominant problems and benchmark areas. Cost considerations were an important issue in all Payco's sourcing decisions. An argument for the decision to offshore was the lower labor costs overseas. According to Payco's sourcing manager: "Home country consultants do not have the same low level of costs as our outsourcer." All software was tested and quality checked. Payco's project manager stated, "The control activity was merely aimed to ensure the deliverables were in accordance with quality specifications." The performance pricing model fixed milestone-based pricing for defined deliverables, i.e., four new releases of the Web Portal. Although transaction costs were significant, such as follow-up, travel and control costs, these did not offset production cost advantages for the global service supplier. As stated by the supplier's scrum master, "Achievement of goals were important to our team members, because success would influence bonuses and future careers."

During the long-term relationship, Payco had learnt to integrate and exploit IT services, from the supplier, to deliver competitive services. The offshore outsourcing agreement gave Payco access to world-class resources, and the two parties had built standardized procedures for integrating and exploiting strategic IT resources from the supplier together with Payco's own resources. For example, the parties had developed a project handbook, which specified the general approach for projects, including the scope, resources, knowledge management, project management processes, quality, agreements, project methodology and contacts.

As Payco's IT manager characterized employees at the supplier, "They have high procedural skills, but they sometimes have trouble seeing the solution in a business context." The supplier's onsite coordinator, co-located with the client company in a Nordic country, maintained the dialogue on business requirements including release planning, and prioritization of tasks.

During their long-term relationship, the two companies had built trust, achieved common values, and they communicated well using English as a common business language. Payco's project manager emphasized that earlier successful experiences made them confident that they could achieve success again: "Our trust in the offshore team was high from the start and it remained high for the rest of the project." This was confirmed by the supplier's on-site coordinator: "We have worked together in more than ten years and we have a very good relationship." Key governance mechanisms, such as contract with deliverables, quality requirements, and commercial terms, suppliers review of deliverables and participating in scrum meetings, escalation points for any sourcing issues, milestone-based payments, were established and recognized by both parties. The supplier investigated expectations and perceptions of partnership quality. According to the supplier's project manager: "A customer satisfaction questionnaire was sent every six months."

Evolutionary path. Payco had matured into offshore outsourcing (stage four) over time. Focus on costs had driven the company toward an ever cheaper, more efficient and flexible production of services. However, Payco has realized that tight cost control, access to and control of resources and expertise, and the long-term commitment from both parties were essential for success, as summarized in Table 6.2.

6.4.1 *Case two*

Stages-of-growth. The client company is a leading provider of open-source web application acceleration software (named: Webco). The software development began in 2005 as an idea by Norway's largest online newspaper. Today, leading websites all over the world rely on this software, including Facebook, Twitter, eBay and The New York Times. The supplier, a software development provider, is a Norwegian IT consultant and offshoring company, with administrative offices in Norway and a main services and development department in Bangladesh. The supplier, a small- to medium-sized enterprise, offers IT development and maintenance services to European organizations. It was founded in 2010, reflecting the managers' previous experiences with offshoring to Bangladesh and India. The client had no experience with offshoring software development activities to low-cost countries. According to Webco's CEO, "The main motivations for the arrangement were lower development costs, better access to skilled developers, and contributions to local community development."

The offshore project studied was the "Administrative Console." The project was defined as a scrum-based software development project with a duration period of 15 months. The purpose of the project was to develop software to configure the web accelerator. Webco signed a contract with the supplier in Norway, which gave it access to a systems development team of IT workers in Bangladesh. Webco's project owner was responsible for the program development, which included a description of user stories and architecture.

The supplier office in Norway assisted and coached the process, including helping with the scrum methodology, communications and culture building; the plan was that Webco would communicate directly with the offshore team after a start-up period. Webco's project was not successful because of delays and poor quality of source code.

Dominant problems and benchmark areas. Webco decided to purchase system development services from a supplier in a low-cost country. The expectations of low production costs and high quality of the development work were not met. The poor quality of the software developed by the offshore team, the demand for extra quality assurance and the need for extensive reprogramming of the software by Webco's onshore team meant that the project was not finished on budget and schedule. Webco took over the software programming and spent approximately a year rewriting and improving the code. In this case, higher than expected transaction costs ruined the cost advantages of the supplier, and Webco subsumed the system development.

During the project, two development teams, one onshore in Norway and one offshore in Bangladesh, worked closely together. These teams were established across organizational borders with the intention of improving understanding of the business process, providing insight into both business and technical challenges, as well as using each other's professional expertise. Initial trust was soon diminished, and high knowledge-based trust was never achieved due to the offshore team's poor product performance. According to Webco's CEO, the offshore team did not have the necessary competence: "They didn't have the same professional level as our onshore team, and thus knowledge transfer became difficult." This was confirmed by the supplier's scrum master: "There were a lack of quality in code for some sprints, and the client was not very happy." In addition, the supplier's lack of business understanding made the software development work difficult and the supplier's commitment to quality declined. The problem of supplier competence strongly influenced the backsourcing decision.

To facilitate relationship, building a special "on-boarding program" was initiated by the supplier's office in Norway. According to a project member of the supplier, there were physical meetings between members of the onshore and offshore teams over a one-week period. The aim was to increase motivation, shorten start-up time and bridge the gap between the client's onshore team and the supplier's offshore team. According to Webco's project owner, "The need for this program became clear when we sensed a cultural and organizational mismatch between the onshore and offshore team during the initial face-to-face meeting."

To reduce this gap, training of the offshore team took place to teach them about the aim and objectives, project organization, roles, responsibilities, processes, methods, expectations and culture. In addition, the supplier's project coach trained the offshore team in the scrum methodology. The intentions were good; requirements and needs were specified in contract, but it proved time-consuming to build a trusting relationship. The great challenge Webco faced was the achievement and the enforcement of agreed terms.

An effective communication and operations structure had to be established in each organization and between both parties, but this was too time-consuming. The discovery of flaws in the contract motivated backsourcing.

Evolutionary path. Webco took a huge step from an in-house function (stage one) to an offshored function (stage four), as they had no previous experience with offshore outsourcing. This proved to be problematic as the software development project was not finished on budget, was delayed for several months, and the quality of the source code was poor. In addition, the established management structure worked poorly. Webco took the system development back under internal control, and the project was subject to additional costs for rewriting the source code. The result of backsourcing (stage five) was risk reduction, higher quality of source code and lower maintenance costs. See Table 6.2 for a summary of the case.

6.4.4 Lessons learned

First, these two business examples demonstrate that both companies tried to justify their sourcing strategy based on evaluating the possibilities for production cost savings. In addition, transaction costs such as meetings, training, travel and control costs were significant and influenced the sourcing decisions. Second, client companies experienced different levels

Table 6.2 Two business examples

Client organization	Situation/stage	Dominant problems	Evolutionary path
Payco – Northern European supplier of electronic payment and information solutions	Application development and maintenance offshored to a global service supplier based in India	Transaction costs did not offset production cost advantages of the global service supplier Had built standardized procedures for how to integrate and exploit resources Well-established governance structure among partners for different sourcing models, training program to understanding values and cultures	Payco had matured into offshore outsourcing Cost control, resource control and long-term commitment essential for offshoring success
Webco – Provider of open-source web application acceleration software	Application development offshored to a consultant company in Bangladesh	Budget overruns, schedule not met and low quality of source code Knowledge gap between parties, low knowledge-based trust between teams Cultural and organizational mismatch	Webco's step from in-house to offshored function proved to be problematic Backsourcing decision aimed to reduce risk and cost, and to improve source code quality

of success in integrating and exploring suppliers' resources with their own resources. Although the intention behind offshoring was to gain access to world-class resources from the supplier, this was not achieved in one of the cases. The knowledge of client business practices was particularly difficult to transfer to a supplier in another culture. Third, outsourcing contracts provided a legally bound, institutional framework in which each party's rights, duties and responsibilities were codified and the goals, policies and strategies underlying the arrangement were specified. In addition, partnership was a complement to overcome constraints in the adaptation and execution of contracts. In case one, Payco and its supplier had a long-term commitment and had established a governance structure that nourished continuity and flexibility when change and conflicts did arise. In case two, there were no such governance structures that could help.

6.5 Return to the beginning or a step forward?

The suggested multidimensional analytical framework incorporating areas such as costs, resources and partnership concerns, as suggested by Solli-Sæther and Gottschalk [15], indicates that companies undergo transformations in their design characteristics, which enable them to face the new tasks or problems that growth elicits. These areas may explain why service functions are steadily on the move.

Economic theories address performance, such as high economic benefits, low transaction costs, effective contracts, good principal-agent cooperation and efficient division of labor. Neo-classical economic theories regard every business function as a production function [22], where their motivation is driven by profit maximization. According to Henisz and Williamson [23], transaction cost economics is a comparative contractual approach to economic organization in which the action resides in the details of the transactions on the one hand and governance on the other. In transaction cost economics, firms are hypothesized to take sourcing decisions to minimize the sum of production and transaction costs [24]. Following production and transaction cost theories, the sourcing of the IT service function will continuously be on the move, looking for the best opportunity to lower costs. At one point in time an outsourcing or offshoring decision is reasonable; later, because of changing conditions, backsourcing may lower the costs.

The central tenet in resource-based theory is that the unique organization of resources is the real source of competitive advantage [25]. A company's resources include not only physical assets such as infrastructure and information systems but also its competencies. The ability to leverage distinctive internal and external competencies relative to a specific environmental situation affects the performance of the company. Thus, the value potential of an outsourcing or offshoring arrangement is to gain access to the supplier's resources. A firm's own resource endowments, particularly its intangible resources, are difficult to change except over the long term, and even more difficult if the client and supplier are not located in near proximity. Although human resources may be mobile to some extent, capabilities may not be valuable as some of them are based on firm-specific knowledge, and others are valuable when integrated with additional individual capabilities and specific firm resources [26]. Client companies may lose control over outsourced services, and there may be large knowledge gaps between the client and the supplier [11].

Every outsourcing contract has the purpose of facilitating exchange and preventing opportunism, but outsourcing contracts can also be characterized by long durations of inter-partner dependency and unanticipated contingencies in uncertain environments. A contract alone is insufficient to guide outsourcing arrangements, cooperation is also needed [27]. Cooperation is an improvement process through mutual forbearance in the allocation of resources, such that one party is made better off and no one is worse off than it would otherwise be. Poppo and Zenger [28] argue that contracts and relational governance are not substitutes but complements.

Digitalization occurs in each step of the maturity model. At the stage of backsourcing, the digital perspective has transformed the in-house function in terms of automization and intelligence. After the stage of backsourcing, a new iteration of maturity steps can emerge, where digital outsourcing is not just a matter of systems, but also a matter of business functions. We can see a never-ending spiral where exploration and exploitation of digital opportunities take place in an interaction between internal and external digital service functions over time.

6.6 Conclusion and implications

The path of outsourcing is important, as it may be argued that backsourcing is a return to the beginning, where this organizational change is seen as a waste of time. The suggested stages-of-growth model indicates a path of evolution from the in-house function(s), via the outsourced and offshored function, and finally to a backsourced function. It is not a return to the beginning, but something that has been altered. As time passes, a company's product and services change, and so do the internal production processes. As a consequence, its focus on IT costs, resources and relationships changes and matures. Moves may be caused by production and transaction cost economics, contract shortcomings and opportunistic behavior.

For practitioners, a stages-of-growth model represents a picture of evolution, where the current stage can be understood in terms of both the history and the future. According to Burns and Stalker [29], companies can use maturity models to identify which stage they are in, particularly when using the characteristics of each stage. Having positioned their firm, the particular model has the potential to help managers in identifying upcoming issues and, thus, provides a framework for planning and orchestrating the evolutionary journey. Using the benchmark variables suggested for a specific model may provide practitioners with a set of considerations that may deserve special attention. Therefore, the concept of stages-of-growth models should enable practitioners to better understand, manage and plan for the evolution in their firms [13]. According to Burns and Stalker [29], an important feature of a stages-of-growth model is that it can identify for management where major transition points occur and also the change factors that need to be managed if staged growth is to be accomplished effectively.

For researchers, the stages-of-growth models have the potential for creating new knowledge and insights into organizational phenomena. Such models represent theory-building tools that conceptualize evolution over time. The stages-of-growth model for outsourcing, offshoring and backsourcing represents a theory to be explored and empirically validated. Further research should carry out empirical testing of the framework. Another promising direction for further study could be a more thorough analysis of how digitalization will change outsourcing strategies and decisions.

It remains an interesting question to explore how automation and robotics influence digital supply chains, and how government initiatives will succeed in bringing back formally offshored jobs. Digitalization alone is not a reason to favor or dismiss backsourcing. However, the traditional offshoring practices are increasingly counterbalanced by rising labor costs in offshoring countries and new technologies.

References

1. Kern, T., & Willcocks, L. P.: Exploring Relationship in Information Technology Outsourcing: The Interaction Approach. *European Journal of Information Systems*, 11, 3–19 (2002).
2. Rai, A., Maruping, L., & Venkatesh, V.: Offshore Information Systems Project Success: The Role of Social Indebtedness and Cultural Characteristics. *MIS Quarterly*, 33, 617–641 (2009).
3. Shao, B. B. M., & David, J. S.: The Impact of Offshore Outsourcing on IT Workers in Developed Countries. *Communications of the ACM*, 50, 89–94 (2007).
4. Venkatraman, N. V.: Offshoring without Guilt. *MIT Sloan Management Review*, 45, 14–16 (2004).
5. Knutsen, T.: The Democratisation of Eastern Europe 1989–2004. A Closer Look at How Latvia, Poland, Slovakia, Hungary and Bulgaria Have Handled the Challenges of Economic Development, Good Governance, Nationalism and Xenophobia. PhD thesis, University of Bergen, Bergen (2009).
6. Jensen, P. D. Ø., & Pedersen, T.: The Economic Geography of Offshoring: The Fit between Activities and Local Context. *Journal of Management Studies*, 48, 352–372 (2011).
7. Oshri, I., Kotlarsky, J., & Willcocks, L.: Managing Dispersed Expertise in IT Offshore Outsourcing: Lessons from Tata Consultancy Services. *MIS Quarterly Executive*, 6, 53–65 (2007).
8. Oshri, I., Kotlarsky, J., & Willcocks, L. P.: *The Handbook of Global Outsourcing and Offshoring* (2nd ed.). Palgrave Macmillan, London (2011).
9. Bhagwatwar, A., Hackney, R., & Desouza, K. C.: Considerations for Information Systems "Backsourcing": A Framework for Knowledge Re-Integration. *Information Systems Management*, 28, 165–173 (2011).
10. Ejodame, K., & Oshri, I.: Understanding Knowledge Re-Integration in Backsourcing. *Journal of Information Technology*, 33, 136–150 (2018).
11. Veltri, N. F., Saunders, C. S., & Kavan, C. B.: Information Systems Backsourcing: Correcting Problems and Responding to Opportunities. *California Management Review*, 51, 50–76 (2008).
12. Law, F.: Breaking the Outsourcing Path: Backsourcing Process and Outsourcing Lock-In. *European Management Journal*, 36, 341–352 (2018).
13. King, W. R., & Teo, T. S. H.: Integration between Business Planning and Information Systems Planning: Validating a Stage Hypothesis. *Decision Science*, 28, 279–308 (1997).
14. Gottschalk, P., & Solli-Sæther, H.: Maturity Model for IT Outsourcing Relationships. *Industrial Management & Data Systems*, 106, 200–212 (2006).
15. Solli-Sæther, H., & Gottschalk, P.: Stages-of-Growth in Outsourcing, Offshoring and Backsourcing: Back to the Future? *Journal of Computer Information Systems*, 55(2), 88–94 (2015).
16. Kazanjian, R. K.: Relation of Dominant Problems to Stages of Growth in Technology-Based New Ventures. *Academy of Management Journal*, 31, 257–279 (1988).
17. Kazanjian, R. K., & Drazin, R.: An Empirical Test of a Stage of Growth Progression Model. *Management Science*, 35, 1489–1503 (1989).
18. Barthélemy, J.: The Hidden Costs of IT Outsourcing. *Sloan Management Review*, 42, 60–69 (2001).
19. Larsen, M. M., Manning, S., & Pedersen, T.: Uncovering the Hidden Costs of Offshoring: The Interplay of Complexity, Organizational Design, and Experience. *Strategic Management Journal*, 11, 3–19 (2013).
20. Yin, R. K.: *Case Study Research: Design and Methods.* Sage Publications, Thousand Oaks, CA (2009).
21. Patton, M. Q.: *Qualitative Research and Evaluation Methods.* Sage Publications, Thousand Oaks, CA (2002).
22. Williamson, O. E.: The Modern Corporation: Origins, Evolution, Attributes. *Journal of Economic Literature*, 19, 1537–1568 (1981).
22. Henisz, W. J., & Williamson, O. E.: Comparative Economic Organization – Within and between Countries. *Business and Politics*, 1, 261–277 (1999).
24. Anderson, S. W., Glenn, D., & Sedatole, K. L.: Sourcing Parts of Complex Products: Evidence on Transactions Costs, High-Powered Incentives and Ex-Post Opportunism. *Accounting, Organizations and Society*, 25, 723–749 (2000).
25. Barney, J. B.: Is the Resourced-Based "View" a Useful Perspective for Strategic Management Research? *Academy of Management Review*, 26, 41–56 (2001).
26. Hitt, M. A., Bierman, L., Shumizu, K., & Kochhar, R.: Direct and Moderating Effects of Human Capital on Strategy and Performance in Professional Service Firms: A Resourced-Based Perspective. *Academy of Management Journal*, 44, 13–28 (2001).

27. Lou, Y.: Contract, Cooperation, and Performance in International Joint Ventures. *Strategic Management Journal*, 23, 903–991 (2002).
28. Poppo, L., & Zenger, T.: Do Formal Contracts and Relational Governance Function as Substitutes or Compliments? *Strategic Management Journal*, 23, 707–725 (2002).
29. Burns, T., & Stalker, G. M.: *The Management of Innovation*. Tavistock, London (1961).

7

IMPACT SOURCING (SOCIALLY RESPONSIBLE OUTSOURCING)

Ron Babin and Brian Nicholson

7.1 Introduction

The world of global outsourcing is driven by organizations' need for lower cost, greater reliability and the need to constantly innovate. As the last three decades have shown, work that can be done electronically, using digital technology, can be done anywhere. Hence, the practice of Global IT Outsourcing (GITO) relies on moving work to low-cost locations, where skilled labour is plentiful and cheap. From the perspective of North America and Europe, this is often called off-shoring, which has contributed to a robust outsourcing industry in regions such as India, Africa, China and south-east Asia. These regions also contain some of the highest populations of poverty, sometimes referred to as the bottom of the pyramid.

We discuss research on this topic from the last decade in three sections. Section 7.2 describes our initial 2008–2009 research of the background for Corporate Social Responsibility (CSR) in outsourcing, with an identification of the need for industry standards. Section 7.3 describes the Rockefeller Foundation's uptake of CSR in outsourcing starting in 2011 and provides an assessment of Socially Responsible Outsourcing (SRO) today. Section 7.4 describes 2018 plans for the global industry standards for SRO, now referred to as Impact Sourcing. These standards are being defined by an industry consortium called the Global Impact Sourcing Coalition (GISC).

First a short definition from the GISC [1]:

> Impact Sourcing is business practice where companies prioritize suppliers that intentionally hire and provide career development opportunities to people who otherwise have limited prospects for formal employment. Impact sourcing has been shown to provide many business benefits, including access to new sources of talent, higher levels of employee engagement, and lower attrition rates, while offering employees their first step into a career ladder that leads to economic self-sufficiency through income growth, skills development and professional advancement.

7.2 2008–2011 corporate social responsibility in global outsourcing

We began our research on social responsibility in outsourcing in 2008. At that time, we described the concept as Corporate Social Responsibility (CSR) in Global IT Outsourcing

(GITO). Initial descriptions of the concept and implications for the industry are outlined in a 2009 paper "Corporate Social and Environmental Responsibility in Global IT Outsourcing" [2]. A more detailed description is provided in our 2012 book *Sustainable Global Outsourcing* [3].

Global IT outsourcing (GITO) generally refers to third-party management of IT assets and services, including people and knowledge content, which are delivered on a coordinated fashion across multiple national locations [4]. GITO is an accepted practice in many business organizations and even regarded by some as a fundamental business capability.

In contrast to GITO, corporate social responsibility is less clearly defined. Crane, Matten and Spence [5] point out that "definitions of CSR abound, and there are as many definitions of CSR as there are disagreements over the appropriate role of the corporation in society." Matten and Moon [6] provide a more current and comprehensive definition of CSR, including environmental issues: "CSR is a cluster concept which overlaps with such concepts as business ethics, corporate philosophy, corporate citizenship, sustainability and environmental responsibility." CSR is recognized by some as a business strategy to define and defend an organization's position in the marketplace. For example, Michael Porter and Mark Kramer propose the concept of Shared Value [7] as a framework to blend CSR with corporate strategy. As many organizations and their stakeholders increase their expectations regarding social and environmental issues, we posit that CSR expectations will be applied to outsourcing vendor. Similarly, buyers will expect their IT outsource vendors to deliver the same level of CSR performance which they provide to their own customers.

A CSR lens on global outsourcing reveals how outsourcing affects a broader set of stakeholders than just shareholders. The costs of outsourcing to both local and global society, and to the environment are weighed against the benefits to the corporations and their shareholders.

The research question guiding this inquiry is this: how do social responsibilities affect current and future business knowledge and capabilities in global sourcing of IT and business services that rely on IT? We begin to answer this question first by examining the challenges identified in the literature and through empirical investigation.

Since January 2008 we have focused on understanding the nature and impact of CSR on the outsourcing market, examining the perspectives of outsourcing buyers, vendors and advisors. In the following sections, we describe two challenges we identified of implementing CSR for both buyers and vendors as indicated in the relevant literature. Following this we present the results of our empirical work followed by the implications for business knowledge and capabilities of outsourcing buyer, provider and advisor organizations

7.2.1 Social responsibility issues

The topic of corporate social responsibility and global IT outsourcing has attracted considerable academic interest. The range of research and opinion is wide; pessimists posit that outsourcing is an example of unfettered, irresponsible corporate profit maximization. Conversely, optimists argue that outsourcing is an attractive economic mechanism for sharing wealth globally. Table 7.1 summarizes the range of views on CSR in GITO.

Table 7.1 Views on CSR issues in Global IT Outsourcing

	CSR outsourcing issue	Authors
Pessimists	• Global outsourcing represents profit maximization for the rich and offers limited benefits for other groups, extending growing gap between rich and poor in developing countries. The rich simply get richer as a result of global IT outsourcing, "deepening income inequalities in the developing world and deepening income inequalities in the developed world after the onset of the so-called information economy."	Payaril [8]
	• Transnational corporations (TNCs) are "designed, constructed and maintained to make money for the interests of those that own them."	Blinder [9] Jones [10]
	• Global IT outsourcing in the context of stateless, placeless and heartless TNCs is dangerous for society, and requires an expanded vision to "generate socially positive outcomes."	
	• Software houses with "precarious employment contracts, Taylorized work processes in software factories without support of union organization and poor attention to health and safety do not offset the improved income and economic status of global software work (GSW) performed primarily in India."	Sahay, Nicholson and Krishna [11]
Optimists	1 Outsourcing can be seen as a mechanism for sharing wealth on a global basis. CSR and ethical trading, especially for global consumer branded products and services, as well as collective action toward an International Labour Organization fair-work agenda, can improve labour conditions in developing country global value chain participants.	Knorringa and Pegler [12] De George [13]
	2 "Outsourcing promotes efficiency; helps developing countries by providing jobs where unemployment is very high, involves transfer of information technology and knowledge and encourages the educational process in less developed countries so that people are trained for new types of work provided by information technology and helps cut the costs of goods and services."	

7.2.2 Social responsibility standards

Crane et al. [5] refer to the recent "rise in prominence of CSR" as well as "a burgeoning number of CSR standards, watchdogs, auditors and certifiers aiming at institutionalizing and harmonizing CSR practices globally." Several industries such as apparel manufacturers, mining and forestry have created CSR standards and codes of conduct for their industries. Often these standards were developed in response to pressures from unions, non-governmental organizations (NGOs) and multi-stakeholder organizations. Back in 2009 the GITO industry had not defined any CSR standards. However, at least four potentially relevant CSR standards were appropriate to the global IT outsourcing industry. The first is the Global Reporting Initiative (GRI) which provides a consistent standard for reporting CSR activities [14]. The second is the SA8000 standard from Social Accountability International (SAI) which defines global standards for working conditions. Third ISO 26000 defines a set of standard practices across all industries for CSR activities. The fourth standard is the United Nations

Table 7.2 International CSR standards

Global Reporting Initiative (GRI)	GRI provides a "trusted and credible framework for sustainability reporting that can be used by organizations of any size, sector or location." GRI was developed over the last 20 years and is now broadly recognized by many organizations as a standard for corporate responsibility and sustainability reporting. GRI provides a public record of organizations which have voluntarily provided their sustainability reports. By 2018, over 12,000 organizations had registered with GRI and approximately 30,000 GRI reports were available online.
SAI's SA8000	This standard has been adopted by almost 3,800 facilities in 61 countries around the world. Much of the rationale for SAI came from the 1990s realization that "sweat-shop labour" and child labour were frequently used to produce global branded products that were both fashionable and expensive. SAI certification provides assurance to end consumers that products and services are delivered from facilities with fair working conditions for employees.
ISO 26000	This standard provides a guide for organizations to voluntarily adopt CSR practices. With participation from about 80 countries and many stakeholder groups, ISO 26000 is recognized as a universal standard, across most industries. The ISO 26000 standard addresses core CSR subjects including governance, human rights, labour practices, the environment, fair operating practices, consumer issues, community involvement and development.
UN Global Compact	The fourth standard, the UN Global Compact, is a set of ten universally accepted principles in the areas of human rights, labour, environment and anti-corruption. The Compact is focused on businesses, requiring CEO endorsement and annual reporting. The Compact's overarching mission is to help build a more sustainable and inclusive global economy. To date, over 9,600 companies in 161 countries and over 4,000 non-businesses have signed the Global Compact.

(UN) Global Compact, which defines ten universal CSR principles. Table 7.2 summarizes the standards.

In summary, looking back to our analysis in 2009, the topic of CSR in global IT outsourcing had gained attention from researchers presenting challenges to outsourcing vendors and buyers who we argued must have the business knowledge and capabilities to understand and address social issues related to outsourcing. Second, government and non-government organizations began to define and monitor standards for corporate social activities, which are applicable in varying degrees to global IT outsource vendors. We argued that vendors and clients must have knowledge and capability to understand and comply with appropriate CSR standards.

To understand more about the CSR knowledge and capability challenges, back in 2009 we interviewed senior executives who are actively involved as outsourcing buyers, vendors or advisors. Interviews included representatives from two major North American banks, two consumer product companies, two global outsource vendors and three legal and accounting advisory firms.

We conducted a focus group with a panel of four subject experts and an audience of 50 participants from industry and academia.

In the interviews, the survey and the focus group we discussed the following topics. The phrasing of each question was altered slightly for buyers, suppliers and advisors.

- When making outsourcing decisions do you consider CSR capabilities in your evaluation criteria?
- What components of CSR are most important (such as employee support, environmental stewardship, working environment, community involvement)?
- How do buyers give preference to CSR factors in outsourcing decisions?
- Do you expect CSR considerations will become more important in future outsourcing contracts?

From these data we identified three key directions related to the CSR business knowledge and capability.

Direction #1: CSR in outsourcing is relevant.

Several interviewees suggested that the CSR factor in outsourcing decisions was new, they had not seen any of these issues previously and they expected CSR to be an important issue in the near future. One advisor commented on a recent client request for explicit CSR capabilities in a request for proposal (RFP) for outsourcing services. A recurring theme across all interviews was that environmental concerns, such as carbon emissions, will be an important social issue "in the very near future." One advisor mentioned that "carbon credits [as an environmental issue] have received more attention than CSR." For some outsource vendors, attention to environmental sustainability presents both an economic advantage and potentially a reputation advantage, as mentioned by executives from two large global outsourcing firms.

So our findings in 2009 were that knowledge and capability requirements are becoming clear: CSR capabilities within the outsourcing industry will become mandatory for ongoing success. As we describe later in this chapter, this CSR capability in outsourcing was further defined as Impact Sourcing.

Direction #2: CSR will be driven by consumer and employee stakeholder concerns.

A recurrent theme from interviewees and at the focus group was a responsiveness to consumer pressures regarding CSR issues. Consumer product organizations have established CSR frameworks to manage products that may be tainted by CSR issues such as child labour or worker safety. Many interviewees expressed the importance of the perception of their employees. It was felt that young employees have higher expectations of their employer's CSR, especially as young workers replace the retiring baby boom generation. The implication is that employers, especially in global IT outsourcing firms which rely heavily on "bright young talent," need a strong positive CSR profile to attract and retain employees (Bhattacharya et al.) [15]. A corollary of this is that organizations will need to develop a capability to communicate with key stakeholder groups such as employees and customers. The communication must include the ability to understand stakeholder CSR expectations and the ability to effectively describe how well the outsourcing buyers and vendors are living up to those expectations.

Direction #3: Due diligence is a required component in CSR; beware of CSR cynicism.

Several advisors suggested that a thorough walk-through of CSR capability, in the due diligence phase of contracting, is the best way to ensure that the provider "can live up to the CSR requirements of the buyer." However, most buyers rarely or never validate an outsource vendors' CSR claims. Although several global CSR standards are defined, no one in the interviews or focus group was able to quickly identify CSR outsourcing standards or norms other than the buyer's own expectations for CSR. Several interviewees cautioned that CSR may become a marketing message, lacking substance, for some organizations. Organizations may quickly respond to consumer concerns with slick marketing messages rather than substantive CSR programmes. One interviewee expressed caution against "green-washing" on environmental issues. At the focus group, panel members cautioned against CSR hypocrisy "being good at home, but bad abroad." However, as one panel member commented, with corporate transparency enabled through global access to information on the Internet, "organizations can no longer say one thing and do another." However, panel members did argue that large global organizations with strong brands will be less likely to substitute image in place of facts.

Outsource buyers will need to develop knowledge and capabilities that are able to verify outsource provider CSR claims, through audit or other mechanisms. The role of third-party advisors may fill this skill gap, where the advisor has specialist knowledge in CSR regulations and standards. As Section 7.3 suggests, certification is a likely outcome from the development of the Impact Sourcing Standard. Although initially proposed in 2009, certification could only begin in 2018 or later.

7.2.3 CSR knowledge and capability

From our 2009 research and the literature review, we argued for the need for CSR knowledge and capabilities in buyer and provider global IT outsourcing organizations. We proposed five knowledge and capability areas – each area has different implications for domestic outsourcing clients and for global vendors. The five knowledge and capability areas are as follows:

1   Understand relevant CSR regulatory requirements. Global IT outsourcing requires both buyers and vendors to be aware of government and NGO standards and regulations. Knowledge will be required of relevant regulations and now they should be applied to the outsourcing environment.
2   Anticipate stakeholder CSR expectations. Direction #2 above describes how employees and customers will influence CSR requirements, implying that organizations must anticipate their expectations. A capability will be needed that allows an organization to monitor and manage stakeholder expectations.
3   Operationalize CSR capabilities. Our research shows that CSR is not a short-term or transitory issue. The challenges of social issues, environmental issues and developing standards will require organizations to embed CSR capabilities into ongoing operations. This will require knowledge and capabilities of overall CSR functions and how they are deployed within the organization.
4   Respond to CSR inquiries. Honest and forthright communications will be needed to confront potential stakeholder cynicism described in Direction #3. The key capability needed will be effective communication skills related to CSR.
5   Develop a CSR culture through hiring and education. CSR will be a long-term issue to which organizations must adapt. Organizations will need an ongoing programme of hiring and education that builds a culture of social and environmental responsibility. A positive CSR profile will be helpful in attracting and retaining promising young talent. The knowledge and capability required here will be focused on assessing and reinforcing CSR concepts in the organization and its participants.

From the 2009 perspective, there was much work and further research ahead on this import-ant global topic, which is now described in sections 7.2 and 7.3.

7.3 2011–2016: an assessment of Socially Responsible Outsourcing (aka Impact Sourcing)

In 2011 the Rockefeller Foundation identified the need to work with impoverished popula-tions, using the concept of global outsourcing to provide skills and income at the bottom of the pyramid. Notably, this initiative developed from the Rockefeller's focus on digital jobs in Africa. Building on the success of the Impact Finance model, the new term of Impact Sourc-ing was coined. Working with the Monitor Group consultancy, the Rockefeller Foundation supported the development and testing of Impact Sourcing business models, with research on key interventions needed to advance the concept of Impact Sourcing. The 2011 working paper produced by the Monitor Group (now part of Deloitte) provided the first detailed global analysis of the Impact Sourcing opportunity [16].

The Rockefeller Foundation engaged the Everest Group in 2014 to conduct an in-depth assessment on how the growth of Impact Sourcing could be accelerated by creating a da-ta-driven Impact Sourcing model. The 2014 study "The Case for Impact Sourcing" exam-ines the benefits of the Impact Sourcing model for business process service delivery [17]. However, for a variety of reasons the take-up of Impact Sourcing did not accelerate as many had hoped, which was cause for some introspection. In part, the 2008–2009 global recession and the slow economic recovery of the following years may have impeded the uptake of CSR issues in many organizations, particularly in the outsourcing industry.

A 2016 discussion panel at the International Conference on Information Systems (ICIS) examined the positive and negative impacts of Impact Sourcing, examining the core IT management issues with broader societal issues. The panel provided a balanced discussion, concluding that although the Impact Sourcing market is growing it is not a guaranteed success. Many challenges still need to be addressed, such as the rise of the gig-economy with online outsourcing – firms such as Upwork [18] provide a global sourcing network for individual tasks, which may create a form of Impact Sourcing for marginalized groups such as youth and women. This phenomenon is explored by Malik, Nicholson and Heeks [19] who conclude that although many individuals failed to launch and struggled to earn minor amounts, a "significant number were able to earn a reasonable living from online outsourc-ing," again a mixed but encouraging message for Impact Sourcing.

7.4 2017 onwards – the future of Impact Sourcing: the GISC

In 2017, Business for Social Responsibility (BSR) with sponsorship from the Rockefeller Foundation created the GISC, which is a collaborative initiative of influential global buyers and vendors of business services who are committed to Impact Sourcing. The initial focus of GISC is to create an Impact Sourcing Standard. From the GISC website [1]:

> Global Impact Sourcing Coalition is a forum of the world's leading companies com-mitted to incorporate and scale impact sourcing as a business strategy. Members of the coalition are united behind a shared commitment to advocate for this inclusive employment practice and demonstrate how impact sourcing leads to business growth and employee diversity and engagement. Member companies share a commitment to provide skills training and career advancement opportunities for individuals around

the world who previously had limited employment prospects. The Global Impact Sourcing Coalition will create a globally accepted standard and approach for impact sourcing. This will help global buyers scale up their commitment and employ a consistent approach across markets, while empowering service vendors to communicate their impact sourcing capabilities and impact through a common methodology that meets their clients' needs.

Current (2018) members consist of 25 Regular Members including Bloomberg, Facebook, Google, Microsoft, Nielsen and Tech-Mahindra, and 18 Associate Members including Avasant Foundation, Everest Group, the Global Sourcing Council, IAOP and the University of Manchester. The current list of all members can be found at GISC.BSR.org/members.

GISC is actively working with members and interested organizations to define the Impact Sourcing Standard. The Standard will allow "companies to be flexible and to adapt their Impact Sourcing initiatives to the unique demographics and priorities of the regions that they are operating in." Notably, the Impact Sourcing Standard relies on SA8000 and ISO 26000 standards described in Table 7.2 as well as International Labour Organization (ILO) standards.

Development of a global, consistent standard will be beneficial to many organizations. Without a standard, anyone can claim that their services are Impact Sourcing compliant. The GISC standard will allow organizations to become certified themselves or to require that their suppliers are certified as meeting Impact Sourcing Standard requirements. Further, benchmarks and best practices can be developed that will allow new entrants to quickly become Impact Sourcing compliant by learning from others.

The Standard consists of five sections, each with a set of specific requirements. Table 7.3 summarizes the requirements. The full set and current description of the Impact Souring Standard can be found at the GISC website, at GISC.BSR.org.

In 2017–2018 the International Association of Outsourcing Professionals (IAOP) conducted an assessment of global Impact Sourcing by inviting organizations to submit a profile of their Impact Sourcing activities, for the first annual Impact Sourcing Award. Twenty-four organizations responded in late 2017 and Awards were presented at the IAOP Outsourcing World Summit in February 2018. Judges relied on the GISC standards in Table 7.3 to evaluate the submissions. Subsequent to the award ceremony a research team at Ryerson University began a thematic analysis of the 24 profiles and conducted a content analysis of the organizations' websites, to understand the current trends and realities for Impact Sourcing. The research team grouped findings into five categories, which are (1) Benefits, (2) Partnerships, (3) Strategy, (4) Challenges and (5) Promotion. A summary of the each category is provided below [20].

1   Benefits of Impact Sourcing. Applicants cited many commercial benefits such as cost efficiency and workforce benefits such as ability to attract low-cost labour and reduced attrition. Impact sourcing was often seen as a mechanism for entry to new markets and was perceived to improve the brand value of the company. In addition to commercial benefits, of course social benefits were highly cited, such as helping marginalized individuals and their families and overall help to the community. Most companies clearly targeted a specific group, such as persons with disabilities, refugees, military veterans and women and girls. Most organizations had established specific goals and metrics such as number of new jobs created, number of persons helped, improvement in literacy and education levels.

Table 7.3 GISC Impact Sourcing Standards

Standard section	Requirements
1 Commitment to Impact Sourcing	1.1 Organizational commitment to employ, advance in employment and offer equal opportunities in all employment practices to people who were previously long-term unemployed, first-time employed or informally employed
	1.2 Publish a statement of commitment to Impact Sourcing
	1.3 Appoint a top executive to be responsible for Impact Sourcing compliance
2 Recruitment and Hiring	2.1 Periodic review of recruiting and hiring processes and policies to ensure that they comply with intent of Impact Sourcing
	2.2 Train hiring managers and recruiters to identify and offer job opportunities to Impact workers
	2.3 Ensure that no employment fees or costs are borne by Impact Workers
	2.4 Adopt non-discrimination and equal opportunity policies
	2.5 Offer reasonable adjustments for all applicants and employees with disabilities
	2.6 For purposes of quantification, count only Impact Workers who have been employed at full wages for six months or more
3 Remuneration and Benefits	3.1 Pay Impact Workers at least the minimum wage, including allowances and benefits, required by local law
	3.2 Compensate Impact Workers equally and with the same benefits as non-Impact Workers doing the same job
4 Training and Career Development	4.1 Provide onboarding, training and development opportunities for Impact Workers, at the same level as offered to all other employees
	4.2 Establish clear performance and promotion criteria for Impact Workers
5 Management Systems	5.1 Create systems that measure and evaluate the success of Impact Workers within the organization
	5.2 Maintain documented information to demonstrate conformity with the Impact Sourcing Standard
	5.3 Regularly review and continually improve Impact Sourcing policies and procedures

2   Impact Sourcing Partnerships. All applicants identified the criticality of partnerships in creating a successful Impact Sourcing operation; no Impact Sourcing venture can succeed without a network of supportive partnerships. First, government support can be helpful, in terms of funding and resources, and legitimization (certification, license, etc.). Second, NGOs and charities such as the Rockefeller Foundation can be helpful. Third, an important link with educational institutions, from schools, technical training centres, to colleges and universities, provides education and future career potential for workers. Finally, business partnerships are important, as clients and supporters of the Impact Sourcing venture.

3   Impact Sourcing Strategy. A variety of strategies were defined, but each strategic model had a very clear structure, purpose and expected value. Of interest are some strategies that have begun to embrace machine learning and artificial intelligence to augment impact source workers.

4   Challenges for Impact Sourcing. Like any start-up venture, Impact Sourcing firms must surmount initial sales, marketing and operational challenges. Just because an

organization or business unit is designed for Impact Sourcing does not guarantee success or that customers will automatically buy those services. Again, the importance of partnerships was cited as a key factor on overcoming start-up challenges. A second challenge for Impact Sourcing firms is the nature of their location, serving needy communities often in regions with poor and unreliable infrastructure services such as electricity, transportation and Internet access.

5   Promotion of Impact Sourcing. Because Impact Sourcing is a relatively new concept, it must be promoted by members of the industry, including associations such as IAOP and GISC. This can be complex given the dual goals of business and social improvement. In addition to industry promotion, internal efforts are required to explain the benefits of Impact Sourcing to individual business units.

7.5 Conclusion

With increasing interest in global sourcing and Impact Sourcing, the Impact Sourcing Standard would be welcomed by global outsourcing industry participants (as suggested in Section 7.2) so that specific goals can be defined and measured, by committed Impact Sourcing participants. Carmel et al. suggest that "impact sourcing [should] focus on the dimensions that make up the impact… and therefore it is critical that our research focus on its measurement" [21]. For example, GISC defines three social impact goals which are aligned with the UN 2030 Agenda for Sustainable Development; the goals are: (1) income growth for people from disadvantaged or vulnerable backgrounds, (2) career opportunities for employees to learn transferable skills for future job opportunities, long-term career advancement and increased remuneration, and (3) poverty reduction through formal employment with the ability to support families, invest in improved housing, education and healthcare [22]. The expectation for the future of Impact Sourcing is that defined standards, measurements and outcomes will be established and potentially vendors and buyers of global business services will be able to certify compliance with the Impact Sourcing Standard. As we see from the GISC website and from the applicants to the IAOP Impact Sourcing awards, both large and small, local and global organizations are adopting Impact Sourcing, in the developed nations of North America and Europe as well as in the developing nations of Asia, Latin America and Africa. Impact Sourcing is relevant to all.

Global outsourcing is a well-accepted practice in most large organizations. The concept of CSR in outsourcing, socially responsible sourcing or Impact Sourcing is still relatively new. Although many have great expectations for Impact Sourcing, a set of global standards that can be measured and monitored is needed, and is being developed by GISC, to provide evidence of the societal impact. Many case examples suggest that Impact Sourcing can fundamentally create positive change for impoverished populations. Academic researchers increasingly examine, theorize and explain Impact Sourcing, with recent contributions by Sandeep and Ravishankar [23] exploring detailed Impact Sourcing examples in India and Khan et al. [24] describing the need to balance commercial and social logics to understand the challenges of Impact Sourcing.

7.5.1 *Expectations for Impact Sourcing*

It is safe to say that the take-up of Impact Sourcing, since its introduction in 2011 and the definition of GISC standards in 2017, has been lackluster. Indeed, the Ryerson research team found that Google keyword search for Impact Sourcing returned only 166 results in 2017, suggesting Impact Sourcing has a very low profile "for a practice with such a promise." Additionally, the research team found very few industry reports, the last being published in 2012, and "business magazines such as HBR and the Economist did not show a single article with Impact Sourcing in the title." As well, Impact Sourcing failures are now being examined in the literature, one case being Indigena Solutions, a Canadian Aboriginal Impact Sourcing firm that ceased business operations in 2017 [25] after a six-year struggle for profitability.

So, what are the expectations for Impact Sourcing? First, a long-term sponsor such as Business for Social Responsibility and the GISC organization are needed to continually promote the concept. Perhaps this is a role for the UN or another similar global organization. Second, ongoing education of outsourcing buyers and providers is required, at industry events such as the IAOP Outsourcing World Summit or the GSA Global Sourcing Summit.

Business education programmes globally should include Impact Sourcing in the curriculum so that Impact Sourcing is as well understood as Impact Investing, Socially Responsible Investments and other CSR business practices. When graduating students understand Impact Sourcing, they will be equipped to apply these concepts throughout their careers. Third, the public's attention is required, so that Impact Sourcing becomes a mainstream concept. This could be accomplished through global awareness campaigns by the larger members of GISC. From the analysis of the 2018 IAOP Impact Awards, it appears that there is no lack of Impact Sourcing providers, but what is lacking is demand from large traditional outsource buyers. Focusing public attention on large financial institutions, consumer packaged goods, manufacturers, etc. will create more opportunity for existing and new Impact Sourcing providers. The growth of Impact Sourcing in developing nations of Asia, Latin America and Africa will be driven by the buyers of Europe and North America. Fourth, successful Impact Sourcing firms will need to expand, to scale up. A few large Impact Sourcing providers have been able to replicate their success in different geographies but many Impact Sourcing firms are still very small, helping hundreds but not yet thousands. To grow, the Impact Sourcing model must be adaptable; lessons learned from one model location can be re-used to start many more locations. As an example, Teleperformance, one of the 2018 IAOP Global Impact Sourcing Award winners, has hired 25,000 Impact Sourcing workers since 2014 and has developed a global model for continuing this growth.

Lastly, a comment on a potential growing threat to Impact Sourcing. The concept of labour arbitrage, where low-cost workers perform tasks in off-shore locations, has been a fundamental enabler in global outsourcing. Impact Sourcing is a further adaptation of labour arbitrage, with lower skilled and low-cost workers. The rise of artificial intelligence (AI), machine learning and other advanced technologies threatens to displace low-cost labour, and may threaten Impact Sourcing. If an AI robot such as Apple's Siri, Amazon's Alexa, IBM's Watson or IPSoft's Amelia can replace call centre operators or back-office workers, and provide many additional benefits of never getting tired or sick, never taking time off, never asking for a raise, etc., then perhaps demand for human-based outsourcing will decline, including Impact Sourcing. These are early days for AI, but developments in this field and practical commercial deployments are proceeding rapidly.

Despite these threats, significant change and growth for Impact Sourcing should come through the GISC and an accepted global Impact Sourcing Standard that will encourage large multinational corporations to participate in Impact Sourcing. As suggested in our early research, there is still much more development to come on this topic. A decade after our research began, the IAOP Global Impact Souring Awards (GISA) demonstrate strong interest, participation and progress from industry. We look forward to the next decade of Impact Sourcing.

References

1. See http://gisc.bsr.org
2. Babin, R., Nicholson, B.: Corporate social and environmental responsibility in global IT outsourcing. *MIS Quarterly Executive*. 8(4), 123–132 (2009).
3. Babin, R., Nicholson, B.: *Sustainable global outsourcing: Achieving social and environmental responsibility in global IT and business process outsourcing* (Vol. 16). Palgrave Macmillan, London (2012).
4. Lacity, M., Willcocks, L.: *Global information technology outsourcing: In search of business advantage*, Wiley, Chichester, 2001, and Sahay S., Nicholson, B., Krishna, S., *Global IT outsourcing: Software development across borders*. Cambridge University Press, Cambridge (2003).
5. Crane, A., Matten, D., Spence, L.: *Corporate social responsibility, readings and cases in global context*. Routledge, London, p. 5 (2008).
6. Matten, D., Moon, J.: "Implicit" and "explicit" CSR: A conceptual framework for a comparative understanding of corporate social responsibility. *Academy of Management Review*. 33(2), 404–424 (2008).
7. Kramer, M. R., Porter, M.: Creating shared value. *Harvard Business Review*. 89(1/2), 62–77 (2011).
8. Parayil, G.: The digital divide and increasing returns: Contradictions of informational capitalism. *The Information Society*. 21, pp. 41–51 (2005).
9. Blinder, A.: "Offshoring: The next industrial revolution?." *Foreign Affairs*. 85(2), 113–123 (2006).
10. Jones, M.: The transnational corporation, corporate social responsibility and the 'outsourcing' debate. *The Journal of American Academy of Business*. 6(2), 91–97 (2005).
11. Sahay, S., Nicholson, B., Krishna, S.: *Global IT outsourcing: Software development across borders*. Cambridge University Press, Cambridge, pp. 254–255 (2003).
12. Knorringa P., Pegler, L.: Globalisation, firm upgrading and impacts on labour. *Royal Dutch Geographical Society*. 97(5), 470–479 (2006).
13. De George, R.: Information technology, globalization and ethics. *Ethics and Information Technology*. 8, 29–40 (2006).
14. Global reporting initiative: Sustainable reporting guidelines. (2006). http://www.globalreporting.org/ReportingFramework/ReportingFrameworkDownloads/
15. Bhattacharya, C.B., Sen, S., Korschun, D.: Using corporate social responsibility to win the war for talent. *MIT Sloan Management Review*. 49 (2), 37–44 (2008).
16. Job Creation through Building the Field of Impact Sourcing. March 14, 2011. https://www.rockefellerfoundation.org/report/job-creation-through-building-the-field-of-impact-sourcing/
17. The case for impact sourcing. Everest Group. September 2014. http://www.everestgrp.com/wp-content/uploads/2014/09/RF-The-Case-for-Impact-Sourcing-Final-approved_vf.pdf
18. See https://www.upwork.com
19. Malik, F., Nicholson, B., Heeks, R.: Understanding the development implications of online outsourcing. In International Conference on *Social Implications of Computers in Developing Countries*. Springer, Cham, May, pp. 425–436 (2017).
20. Castillo, N., Grewal, P.: Impact sourcing: A qualitative study of practices, benefits and challenges. forthcoming (2020).
21. Nicholson, B., Babin, R., Lacity, M. C. (Eds.): *Socially responsible outsourcing: Global sourcing with social impact*. Palgrave MacMillan. London. Chapter 2 "The Impact of Impact Sourcing" by Carmel, E., Lacity, M., Doty, A., pp. 16–47 (2016).
22. From GISC "Building More Inclusive Global Supply Chains," February (2017).
23. Sandeep, M., Ravishankar, M.: Social innovations in outsourcing: An empirical investigation of impact sourcing companies in India. *The Journal of Strategic Information Systems*. 24(4), 270–288 (2015). Sandeep, M., Ravishankar, M.: Impact sourcing ventures and local communities: A frame alignment perspective. *Information Systems Journal*. 26(2), 127–155 (2016). Sandeep, M., Ravishankar, M.: Sociocultural transitions and developmental impacts in the digital economy of impact sourcing. *Information Systems Journal*. 28(3), 563–586 (2018).
24. Khan, S., Lacity, M., Carmel, E.: Entrepreneurial impact sourcing: A conceptual framework of social and commercial institutional logics. *Information Systems Journal*. 28(3), 538–562 (2018).
25. Babin, R., Nicholson, B., & Young, M. (2020). Indigena Solutions, Tensions in an Aboriginal IT Impact Sourcing Firm. Journal of Global Information Management (JGIM), 28(2), 202–224. doi: 10.4018/JGIM.2020040109

8

SAMURAIS AND NINJAS

Ambidexterity @ AXA Konzern AG

Antje Susanne Koch, Pieter M. Ribbers and
Anne-Françoise Rutkowski

8.1 Introduction

What do Japanese warriors and traditional organizations with more than 100 years of company history have in common [1]?

In the 16th and 17th centuries, Ninja warriors, as open-minded to new experiences warriors, were associated with the term "agility"; whereas Samurai combatants, stable and reliable armed forces, were correlated with the term "stability". The ambidextrous management of both Ninjas and Samurais were the recipe for success for Japanese armed forces to win crucial battles or fend off enemies [1]. Samurais and Ninjas were equally vital for the Japanese combat units in order to win their decisive battles.

About 500 years later, organizations find themselves in similar situations as Japanese warriors: nowadays, it is crucial for traditional organizations to jointly maintain a stable environment (e.g. reliable and efficient IT), as well as being able to implement new innovations (e.g. state-of-the-art technology). They need to be ambidextrous (e.g. from the Latin ambi- "on both sides" and -dexter "right-handed")[1] in order to simultaneously master both Samurais and Ninjas with contrasting strategies, processes, values and attitudes. Ambidexterity puts the company in the position to overcome disruptive innovations, to ensure survival, to sustain agility or – in other words – to gain additional power [2]. However, ambidexterity does not solely emerge on enterprise-wide level. Ambidexterity also occurs on different levels within an organization, e.g. on business unit, department or functional level, namely within IT (as IT ambidexterity) or within IT functions (as bimodal IT). Henceforth, IT ambidexterity and bimodal IT are also important organizational building blocks that contribute to the overall business success.

The fourth – IT/digital driven – industrial revolution forced organizations to step up the pace of change [3]. Thus, it is not surprising that industry in particular the information-intensive industry – as first movers and pioneers when it comes to introducing new IT and digital applications – is affected by this development. As of today, companies in many industries could not keep up with the digital development, e.g. photography and newspaper [4,5]. Besides photography and newspaper, digitalization has left its mark on other industries. Therefore, it is only a question of how and in which way the other industries, notably the insurance industry, are and will continue to be affected by this development.

Ambidexterity research has already investigated the paradoxes and the nature of ambidexterity in IT transformation programs [6], how IT ambidexterity impacts organizational agility [7] and also how the role of IT agility and IT ambidexterity supports digital business transformation [8]. They identified the six ambidexterity areas: (1) IT portfolio decisions, (2) IT platform design, (3) IT architecture change, (4) IT program planning, (5) IT program governance and (6) IT program delivery. Furthermore, they demonstrated that IT ambidexterity enhances organizational agility by facilitating operational ambidexterity which, in turn, depends on the level of environmental dynamism. Lastly, they confirmed that IT agility positively influences the IT function's digitization support, whereas IT ambidexterity has a moderating effect on this relationship.

Interestingly, the way that organizations deal with Samurais and Ninjas (respectively Samurai IT and Ninja IT) in present times has not been addressed yet. Therefore, this explorative case study conducted at AXA Konzern AG in Germany aims to shed more light on the current situation. Furthermore, the objective of this research is to explore how traditional organizations with more than 100 years of company history, such as AXA Konzern AG, deal with ambidexterity, IT ambidexterity and bimodal IT in order to overcome disruptive innovation and sustain the organizational success.

The German AXA Konzern AG is the local unit of AXA S.A. – "the AXA Group". Headquartered in Paris, France, the AXA Group is among the largest insurance companies worldwide with about 107 million clients and approximately 165,000 employees. Based on its 150 years of history, AXA Konzern AG has already faced many technological challenges and has, so far, successfully mastered all of them. However, now being confronted with digitalization, disruptive innovations, insurtechs and its own digital and agile transformation, AXA Konzern AG has started its own journey in how to handle these opportunities and potential threats. This chapter describes ambidexterity, IT ambidexterity and bimodal IT in AXA Konzern AG's business strategy, IT strategy and the corresponding exploitative and explorative initiative examples to overcome all the current hurdles.

The remainder of the chapter is organized as follows: Section 8.2 presents the theoretical background. The nature of the case of AXA Konzern AG is introduced in Sections 8.3 and 8.4. Conclusion, discussion and directions for future research close this contribution and can be found in Section 8.5.

8.2 Theoretical background

8.2.1 Disruptive innovation

According to Christensen's theory [9], disruptive innovation is defined as a process in which small companies/start-ups with few resources challenge established incumbent organizations (often with more than 100 years of company history) by focusing on their neglected less-profitable business segments. In doing so, the intruders are succeeding in this segment by offering appropriate products, services or functionalities at mostly lower prices. In contrast, sustained innovation describes the introduction of new innovations/technologies which upgrade or improve existing products or services for mainstream markets of specific organizations [10,11].

Christensen's theory also describes the response and corresponding recommendations for incumbents caused by the emergence of disruptive innovations. At first glance, new technology investments appear not very interesting for traditional organizations because these investments are just attractive for a limited number of customers and not alluring for the mainstream market. Therefore, incumbents rarely invest in these brand new technology trends. Yet, it goes even beyond this; these organizations have such deeply entrenched management processes that disruptive innovation investments will be automatically rejected [9,12]. This puts traditional organizations at risk of "simply oversleep" new trends, products, services and technologies.

Christensen and Overdorf [10] recommend three strategies for established incumbent organizations to overcome this detriment and to foster breakthrough innovation and technologies: first, creating new organizational structures within corporate boundaries in which new processes can be developed; second, spinning out an independent organization from the existing organization and, third, developing new processes by acquiring new disruptive intruders and start-ups.

8.2.2 Ambidexterity

The roots of ambidexterity can be found in organizational theory. Generally, (organizational) ambidexterity describes the ability to combine two opposing components, respectively the competence to simultaneously track the two disparate objectives: the exploration of new possibilities and the exploitation of old certainties [13,14,15]. Exploration describes the ability to combine (existing) skills and resources in a new way to generate new competencies and opportunities. Attributes such as risk taking, experimentation, play, loosely coupled systems, path breaking, flexibility, discovery, innovation, emerging markets and technologies are associated with this term. Conversely, mechanical structures, tightly coupled systems, path dependence, routinization, control, bureaucracy, stable markets and technologies function as idioms for exploitation. Thus, exploitation indicates the efficient usage of existing resources and capabilities through known processes [2,8,15]. Summarized in the popularized words by March [15,5]: "The essence of exploitation is the refinement and extension of existing competencies, technologies and paradigms. ... The essence of exploration is experimentation with new alternatives".

8.2.3 IT ambidexterity, bimodal IT and digital ambidexterity

Ambidexterity does not only exist on organizational-wide level, but also occurs within IT departments. Consequently, IT ambidexterity describes "the ability of firms to simultaneously explore new IT resources and practices (IT exploration) as well as exploit their current IT resources and practices (IT exploitation)" [7, p. 398]. IT exploration focuses on the ability to put emerging IT trends, methodologies and skills into practice with the aim of entering new product-market domains. In contrast, IT exploitation comprises the ability to implement such up-coming trends into the existing IT assets with the aim to improve their organizational effectiveness and efficiency. Evidently, the focus on IT ambidexterity – the joint consideration of Ninja IT and Samurai IT – within an organization is more promising in terms of enterprise performance, compared to just focusing on one of the two elements within an organization [2].

Today, IT ambidexterity, especially as IT function, is discussed in organizations and media as "bimodal IT". This term and concept of IT division was designed and popularly introduced by Gartner at the end of 2012 [16] (Table 8.1). In line with the definitions of ambidexterity and IT ambidexterity, Gartner [17, online] describes bimodal IT as "the practice of managing two separate but coherent styles of work: one focused on pre-dictability, the other on exploration. Mode 1 is optimized for areas that are more pre-dictable and well-understood. It focuses on exploiting what is known, while renovating the legacy environment into a state that is fit for a digital world. Mode 2 is exploratory, experimenting to solve new problems and optimized for areas of uncertainty."

Table 8.1 Characteristics of traditional and digital IT [adapted from 18]

	Exploitation (Traditional IT, Mode 1, Industrial IT, Core IT)	*Exploration (Digital IT, Mode 2, Agile IT, Fast IT)*
Goal	Stability	Agility and speed
Culture	IT-centric	Business-centric
Customer proximity	Remote from customer	Close to customer
Trigger	Performance and security improvement	Short-term marked trends
Value	Performance of services	Business moments, customer branding
Focus of services	Security and reliability	Innovation
Approach	Waterfall development	Iterative, agile development
Applications	Systems of record	Systems of engagement
Speed of service delivery	Slow	Fast

As anticipated, two opposing bimodal IT components – traditional IT and agile IT – can also be found in IT departments. Thereby, traditional IT and agile IT can be classified into four different archetypes of bimodal IT (always depending on e.g. the organizational set-up, the IT department structure and agile transformation status within the organization) – (1) project-by-project bimodal IT: approach which describes bimodal IT on project-based level; (2) sub-divisional bimodal IT: concept that structurally subdivides the IT function into the two distinct groups of agile IT and traditional IT; (3) divisionally separated bimodal IT: approach that establishes the agile IT function completely outside of the traditional IT function and (4) reintegrated bimodal IT: concept which describes an already established bimodal IT and currently yields the benefits of the agile IT and traditional IT split [19].

However, in times of digitalization and digital transformations, ambidexterity becomes digital ambidexterity. Henceforth, digital ambidexterity encompasses the equilibrate application of digital exploration and digital exploitation, in terms of agility vs. stability, short-term vs. long-term IT investments and digital innovation vs. manufacturing philosophy [20].

8.3 The case of AXA Konzern AG

8.3.1 Data collection

The purpose of this explorative case study was to investigate the Samurais and Ninjas (respectively Samurai IT and Ninja IT) within its real-life context. Furthermore, we wanted to gain a better understanding of this emerging "ambidexterity phenomenon", to gather new theoretical insights and to generate new ideas and hypotheses [21]. Common sources of evidence in doing exploratory case studies comprise direct observations, interviews, archival records, documents,

Table 8.2 Primary and secondary research resources

Primary sources	Secondary sources
Websites: e.g. www.axa.com; www.axa.de	Gesamtverband der Deutschen Versicherungswirtschaft (GDV – General Association of the German Insurance Industry)
Twitter Accounts: e.g. @AXA; @AXADeutschland; @AXALab	Newspaper: e.g. Koelnische Rundschau (Germany); Landbote (Switzerland); Sueddeutsche Zeitung (Germany); Koelner Stadtanzeiger (Germany)
Books: e.g. Desaegher, C. 1995. The History of AXA, Levallois: HM Editions, France; Couwez, M.-C. and Ganong, P. 2002. AXA – Diary of a Journey, Group AXA, Paris, France Presentations: e.g. Ambition 2012 – Investor Conference; Ambition 2020; Ambition 2020 – Media Conference; Unternehmenspräsentation Annual Reports: e.g. Annual Report 2016 Youtube Videos: e.g. Interview with AXA's CIO	Specific finance- and insurance-related information: e.g. Experten Report für Versicherungs- und Finanznachrichten (expert report for insurance and financial news); IT Finanzmagazin – Das Fachmagazin für IT und Organisation bei Banken, Sparkassen und Versicherungen (IT Finanzmagazin – The Specialist Magazine for IT and Organization at Banks, Savings Banks and Insurance Companies); Versicherungsmagazin (Insurance Magazine); Versicherungswirtschaft heute (Insurance Industry Today)

participant observation and physical artifacts [22]. Therefore, the research that was conducted at AXA is mostly based on direct observations, as well as publicly and AXA-internally available information in the form of the following primary and secondary sources (Table 8.2).

8.3.2 AXA S.A. and AXA Konzern AG

AXA S.A. – "the AXA Group" – is a French multinational insurance and financial services company. Since 2008, AXA has been among the first insurance brands worldwide with operating primarily in regions in Western Europe, North America, Asia Pacific and Middle East. AXA's operational and core competences are life and savings insurances, property-casualty (non-life) insurances, as well as asset management. In 2016, the AXA Group was present in 64 countries, had 166,000 employees worldwide, served 107 million clients and generated total revenues of €100,2 billion.

Headquartered in Cologne, AXA Konzern AG is a major insurance and financial services company in Germany. Originally founded in 1893 as Kölnische Feuer-Versicherungs-Gesellschaft (commonly known as Colonia), AXA Konzern AG's history has been formed by several important mergers and acquisitions, especially in the last 30 years. First, the former Colonia was merged with Nordstern (1990) and Albingia (2000). It is worth noting that even before these mergers, Nordstern and Albingia already had more than 100 years of their own history. Second, as a response to the German reunification in 1991 and the increasing convergence within Europe, Colonia formed a new holding structure with the Colonia Konzern AG as the German holding in 1991. In 1993, the majority shareholder was the French Stat Union des Assurances de Paris (UAP). In 1997, with the acquisition of UAP by AXA S.A. ("the AXA Group"), Colonia joined one of the largest insurance and financial services companies in the world – now known as AXA Colonia Konzern AG. Since September 2001, the company has been known as AXA Konzern AG. With the acquisition of DBV-Winterthur in 2009, AXA Konzern AG has significantly strengthened its position in the German insurance market.

Today, AXA Konzern AG is among the fifth largest insurance and financial services organization in its home market of Germany. By the end of 2016, AXA Konzern AG achieved a consolidated net profit of €545 million and underlying earnings of €569 million. In the same year, AXA employed about 9,400 employees in Germany.

8.3.3 *Characteristics and challenges of the insurance industry*

Selling insurance contracts and financial services are clearly not include physical products; thus, almost everything at AXA Konzern AG revolves around intangible products. Thereupon, the insurance sector embodies very well-developed information processing capabilities and is considered as an information-intensive industry [23,24]. The higher the information intensive industry, the more important is for information processing to business success and the more dependent these organizations are on IT [25,26]. Consequently, industries with high information-intensive processes are particularly affected by IT developments, and, thus, by digitalization and digital transformation – as already pointed out in the introduction. According to the Gesamtverband der Deutschen Versicherungswirtschaft (GDV – General Association of the German Insurance Industry), the insurance sector is currently determined by the following three main characteristics and challenges:

- Insurtechs: New technological developments such as big data, cloud computing and internet of things (IoT) provide ample possibilities to offer (new) insurance services, products and technologies. Newly founded small companies and start-ups – so-called insurtechs – are taking advantage of using these recent opportunities. In doing so, insurtechs, with having just a small administration, are succeeding by offering appropriate insurance functionalities, products and services quicker and at mostly lower prices [27]. While originating in low-end or new-market footholds and do not targeting on mainstream customers until quality reaches their standards, insurtechs fulfill the criteria of being described as a disruptive innovation for the insurance sector [11].
- Changed customer behavior: Changed technological developments lead to changed customer behavior. The communication between customer and insurance company via electronic interaction channels (e.g. smartphones, tablets, Facebook and Twitter) has greatly increased in recent years. In order to remain accessible to their customers, insurance companies must be able to keep pace with these rapidly evolving technological developments [28].
- Volatile markets and low interest rates: Insurers, which have to manage and profitable invest high amount of customer deposits, are affected by these capital market developments. Profitable sources of revenues in the form of share earnings, dividends and interest rates have been eliminated. Henceforth, insurers need to find new (secure) investment opportunities for customer funds in future.

Moreover, the Gesamtverband der Deutschen Versicherungswirtschaft also reported that the German insurance industry is also particularly affected by the following two current trends:

- Demographic change in Germany: Medical progress, healthier lifestyle, rising prosperity and better human working conditions are increasing the average life expectancy of the German population. Henceforth, this affects also the insurance customer structure in terms of e.g. higher customer average age and the associated higher costs. This is increasing the importance of the market segment "seniors".

- Extensive legislation and regulatory frameworks: Germany is regarded as a much regulated country. Thus, strict legislation and several regulations from the Bundesaufsicht für Finanzdienstleistungen (BaFin – German Federal Financial Supervisory Authority) as well as detailed regulatory framework such as VVG-Reform, BGH and BVerfG rulings, IFRS, Solvency II and EU Mediator Directive determine their day-to-day insurance operations.

8.3.4 IT @ AXA Konzern AG

The AXA Groups and AXA Konzern AG's digital and IT transformation is very much supported and driven by the global and local CEO and CIO. The importance of IT, and therefore the role of the CIO within AXA, is a role which reports directly to the CEO, as with other members of the c-suite. Responsible for approximately 700 IT and digital employees, the CIO manages an IT landscape and IT systems for about 9,000 users within Germany.

As in many IT departments of large and traditional organizations, also the IT at AXA Konzern AG also faces the conflict of "efficiency vs. innovation": IT needs to ensure stable and robust operations, continuous efficiency improvements and digital change implementations. Previously, topics such as hardware, licenses for standard software (e.g. Microsoft Office, SAP) and purchases of individual software through service contracts dominated the IT departments. Today, application platforms provided by cloud providers, software licenses being replaced by software-as-a-service (SaaS) and custom software developments being developed by local product teams, are the day-to-day CIO concerns. To ensure IT efficiency and IT effectiveness, innovation and stability, AXA Konzern AG is currently driving its own agile transformation. In the agile transformation, various IT teams – predominantly software development teams – are being transformed from the traditional to the agile way of working. The focus of agile teams changed from end-to-end processes and strict release cycles to on-going implementations to allow IT to "respond to business needs with incremental and frequent changes in a speed as fast as every two to three hours." Initially, it was planned that about 50% of the IT teams will work in agile mode by 2020. With the appointment of the new CIO, this transition accelerated. The target is to establish a product- and customer-oriented organization by Q1 2019, adopting the agile way of working – where reasonably possible – of more than 50%. Thereby, the exact percentage of teams working in agile mode by Q1 2019 is not predefined yet; it will be the result of a bottom-up process involving all IT staff, the consideration of strategic and extrinsic factors, as well as core beliefs, intrinsic factors and the constraints of the individual teams.

Being currently in the middle of its own agile transformation, AXA Konzern AG's IT can currently be classified in the archetype "Subdivisional Bimodal IT". Henceforth, its IT function is presently structurally subdivided into two distinct groups: one operates in traditional mode, the other one in agile mode [19]. Consequently, finding the right balance in terms of departmental organization, managerial attention, strategic focus, monetary investments and skilled employees between Samurai IT and Ninja IT is a major challenge in these times. As well as other information-intensive financial services organizations (e.g. ING in the Netherlands), AXA Konzern AG expects to set aside rigid structures in order to develop into a more flexible organization through the introduction of agile teams. To get the maximum out of the agile transformation, not only IT teams but also the company-wide business teams – if applicable – will gradually switch to the agile way of working. Henceforth, the demand management entities, comprising business owners and business consultants of the IT-interfacing entities, will be part of the new product- and customer-oriented organization. Whether AXA

Konzern AG operates in future in one of the bimodal IT archetype quadrants or rather in a unimodal or a multimodal IT function model will indicate further IT function developments.

8.4 Ambidexterity @ AXA Konzern AG

As already indicated in the introduction, ambidexterity, IT ambidexterity and bimodal IT and their corresponding explorative and exploitative initiatives currently of particular interest of present times. Therefore, many companies have anchored these matters into their strategic plans in order to appropriately target and manage them. Although it is argued that organizations need a standalone digital transformation strategy [29], the reality appears rather different. Business strategy and IT strategy, especially in traditional organizations with more than 100 years of company history, are still two distinct – albeit intertwined – strategies. However, the four key decisions for digital transformation strategies (use of technologies, changes in values creation, structural changes and financial aspects) are usually covered by today's business and IT strategies. This is also the case at the AXA Group's, respectively AXA Konzern AG's, business strategy plan (named "Ambition 2020") and IT strategy plan. Even when both strategic plans have different objectives, both plans clearly indicate the digital transformation key decisions, as well as ambidexterity and their explorative and exploitative components.

8.4.1 Ambition – AXA's business strategy

Studying AXA's major strategic plans "Ambition 2012", "Ambition 2015" and "Ambition 2020" shows that – besides some smaller local strategic initiatives – these three strategic plans have dominated AXA's development over the last 15 years. Ambition 2012, Ambition 2015 and Ambition 2020 are global strategic initiatives and, thus, have been initiated by the AXA Group. Needless to say, these strategic plans and the corresponding strategic targets have been filtered down to all subsidiaries.

Therefore, all strategic plans also impact the local units, including the German AXA Konzern AG.

First, Ambition 2012, as AXA Group's first communicated strategic plan, was introduced in 2004. Ambition 2012 pursued two fold with financial and non-financial targets on the one hand, financial goals such as doubling revenues and trebling underlying earnings over the period 2004–2012; and, on the other hand, non-financial targets such as becoming the industry's preferred company for shareholders and employer of choice for its employees, as well as increasing customer centricity for its clients. Several initiatives were undertaken to accomplish these goals, namely the acquisition of the Swiss Winterthur Group in 2007.

Second, Ambition 2015, published in 2012, listed all targets that AXA should reach by 2015. Due to customers' fundamentally changing behavior, Ambition 2015's official main focal point was to "becoming a leading digital insurance company with a physical network to build a differentiated customer experience". The following five pillars of Ambition 2015 have been defined to achieve this aspiration: (1) selectivity – spotlighted on portfolio restructuring and growth positioning in mature markets; (2) acceleration – consisted of selective investments in high growth markets, e.g. Asia; (3) efficiency – focused on overall financial targets; (4) trust and achievement – targeted the stakeholder through e.g. brand management and finally (5) achievement and customer centricity – focal pointed customers, especially in mature markets, as well as fundamental structural changes, e.g. restructuring IT, creating synergies between all networks and modernizing distribution networks.

Third, whereas the main focus of Ambition 2015 was on selectivity, acceleration and efficiency, Ambition 2020 clearly spotlights the customer needs in a challenging economic environment. AXA seeks to create more and new ways for customer interaction via fast and simple multichannel processes and new innovation ecosystems, while the customer experience with insurance should be revolutionized. In order to achieve these ambitious targets, AXA has formulated the strategic targets based on the two pillars "Focus" and "Transform". First, the exploitative pillar Focus strives for sustainable growth and robustness, in continuity with Ambition 2015. Therefore, AXA is going to invest in selective growth areas such as health, protection and P&C commercial lines which also require more frequent customer contacts and allows the insurer to get closer to the customer. Active capital management is to balance the internal growth needs of the company to further increase the cash flows and the shareholder return in the form of dividends and to maintain a robust financial structure. Second, the explorative pillar Transform encompasses AXA's development from a pure insurance provider, or simply a "bill payer", toward a partner to its customer. This future-oriented pillar regarding AXA's digital transformation includes the key messages: new customer experience (B2B2C, new services, digital), from payer to partner (innovation, prevention, care) and adapt capabilities (e.g. engagement, employee training and employee recruitment) as well as shift the portofolio mix in order to reduce the financial risks and diversify towards technical risks. Henceforth, as already indicated by the pillar's name, Focus clearly focuses on securing AXA's stability, whereas Transform spotlights on AXA's agility and transformation.

As already indicated in the introduction, ambidexterity – the simultaneous management of Ninjas and Samurais – is becoming increasingly important in companies. As can be seen in AXA's three strategic plans, AXA ascribes much attention to this topic. While in Ambition 2012, the targets were formulated rather hazily; the future aims in Ambition 2020 have been clearly specified: AXA must take targeted actions to ensure its stability and agility in the rapidly changing world. In fact, successfully managing AXA's ambidexterity is AXA's current business strategy, named Ambition 2020.

8.4.2 *Explorative and exploitative business initiatives*

Various explorative (referable to the pillar Transform) and exploitative (referable to the pillar Focus) initiatives have emerged as an outcome of Ambition 2020. Through these initiatives, AXA has put its strategy into action in order to strengthen the organization and to promote its digital transformation. "NWOW," which represents the exploitative initiative, as well as "AXA Innovation Campus", which symbolizes the explorative initiative, is presented below in more detail.

First, "New Way of Working" (NWOW), an already proven and successfully implemented scheme at many young and innovative firms, was implemented as an exploitative initiative of AXA Konzern AG in 2017. NWOW encompasses, among other things, an open-space concept for all offices and buildings as well as desk-sharing. Therefore, all German offices are in the process of being rebuilt according to the open-space concept and will be divided into five different zones: "all in one" (standard work zones), "communication" (communication and meeting areas), "regeneration" (creative space and relaxation zones), "organization" (work equipment in one place) and "concentration" (quiet work areas). The classic office will disappear. There will no longer be single work places – even for members of the board. Employees are not tied to a specific work place anymore and will be encouraged to exchange interdisciplinary. Furthermore, employees are allowed to make use of zone number six: "work@home". They can spend up to two days a week in their home office and will be equipped accordingly so they can work at home.

AXA Konzern AG expects a more agile corporate culture, increased project work, more innovative ideas, faster decision-making, more employee self-responsibility and increased interdisciplinary cooperation from NWOW – the latter especially between business and IT.

Second, insurtechs – as agile, flexible, cost-efficient and customer-oriented providers of insurance services – are the opposite of traditional and long-established insurance organizations. Consequently, insurtechs are substantial challengers and disruptive innovators within this industry. This has also been recognized by AXA Konzern AG. Following Christensen's [10,11] recommendation strategies (creating new organizational structures within corporate boundaries in which new processes can be developed, spinning out an independent organization from the existing organization, and developing new processes by acquiring new disruptive intruders and start-ups) to overcome such detriments, one of their approaches to face this challenge was the foundation of "AXA Innovation Campus" in 2015. In the name of AXA Innovation Campus, AXA Konzern AG promotes and cooperates with start-ups that develop and offer insurance-related products and services, namely in the field of e-health, lead generation, big data, mobile and retirement planning. AXA Konzern AG promotes start-ups by investing capital and providing insurance benefits, as well as offering its infrastructure, such as customer and sales network and employee expertise. Two of the latest examples supported by AXA Innovation Campus are the recently founded start-ups Nello and Optionspace. Nello upgrades existing intercom systems with WLAN features and, thus, front door activities can be handled via smartphone app. Optionspace offers via online platform free office spaces which can be rented on a flexible basis with a minimum rental period of just one month. AXA Konzern AG supports both start-ups with corresponding insurances.

AXA Innovation Campus' aim is to identify, develop and manage innovative ideas within the insurance industry, to invest in compelling ideas and to participate in their development and scaling, thereby transferring the knowledge and culture from start-ups to AXA and their employees and to organize and emphasize its innovation strengths. Among other innovation initiatives, AXA Konzern AG has founded AXA Innovation Campus to spot innovative ideas that could generate added value for customers. Developing innovative ideas during daily business is highly restricted due to AXA Konzern AG's employees' time constraints. Thus, start-ups, which AXA Konzern AG has recently targetted/pigeon-holed as (einsortieren) potential eligible candidates, have developed e.g. an application which tracks lost motor vehicles, boats and busses in the internet by using artificial intelligence; a software package which translates linguistic content into mathematics; a software package which can answer any kind of questions and a claims management tool which can automatically calculate damage totals based on photos.

However, even when NWOW and AXA Innovation Campus are so-called business initiatives supporting AXA Konzern AG's current business strategy, their IT dependency is obvious: NWOW is currently being implemented, among other things, to overcome the local separation – and with it the associated "silo thinking" – between business and IT and should actively promote this cooperation. Moreover, AXA Innovation Campus does not only promote start-ups with the business focus; but, as can be derived from the examples mentioned above, mostly start-ups which develop software or similar technical applications and those then arouse interest to be implemented at AXA Konzern AG IT department in the long run.

8.4.3 Big Bets – accelerating AXA's IT strategy

In 2013, the AXA Group released a new IT strategy to support AXA's digital transformation. This new IT strategy consists of six pillars: (1) partnership – comprises the boundary dissolvability between business and IT and within IT, (2) fast IT – encompasses topics such as innovation and co-location, (3) core IT – includes the modernization of AXA's core systems, (4) cost efficiency – discusses all cost-saving activities, (5) data – consists of all data-related activities and finally (6) security – contains all IT security topics to be handled by business and IT. Relatively parallel in time, AXA launched the "Big Bets," an implementation strategy and implementation concept to accelerate the new IT strategy. Big Bets should put the IT strategy into action. The six Big Bets, each referring to one or more IT strategy pillars, are characterized as follows:

- Big Bet 1 – Fast IT: The first Big Bet comprises all activities regarding fast IT, such as the introduction of sharing knowledge, innovations and assets between all developers working worldwide for AXA, the implementation of new concepts such as agile development, co-location and pair programming and the usage of public clouds whenever possible.
- Big Bet 2 – Data management: The second Big Bet examines all management activities including data; namely the data management of analytical data (e.g. customer data, needed to identity cross-selling activities to customers) and operational data (e.g. financial data, needed for year-end closing).
- Big Bet 3 – Cost efficiency: The third Big Bet drives cost optimization realized through the two sub-initiatives: Big Bet 3a – de-duplicating systems which are not close to the business (e.g. reducing the number of document storage software and systems) and Big Bet 3b – moving all possible infrastructure to the cloud.
- Big Bet 4 – Core IT systems: The fourth Big Bet comprises all future activities including AXA core IT systems, namely investing in the best available systems and software on the market for all insurance core procedures.
- Big Bet 5 – Operating model: The fifth Big Bet targets the re-organization of AXA's IT operating model. The current IT operating model has been in place for about 12 years. Due to the digital development, it is time to re-structure the IT operating model to be prepared for all future challenges and themes.

Comparable to AXA's business strategy, ambidexterity also becomes apparent in AXA's IT strategy and in the Big Bets – represented in core IT (pillar 3 and Big Bet 4) and fast IT (pillar 2 and Big Bet 1). On the one hand, these concepts should secure AXA's daily operations, and, on the other hand, these should guard AXA's future adaption at the same time.

8.4.4 Explorative and exploitative IT initiatives

The Big Bets should accelerate AXA's IT strategy. Thereby, it is a program which has been introduced on group level, but which should help the local entities to transform their IT and all related processes and structures in order to successfully master the digital transformation. Every local entity – often in collaboration with the AXA Group – has enforced its own initiatives to implement the Big Bets. The "COR.FJA Life Factory," representing the exploitative initiative as a part of Big Bet 4 (core IT systems), and the "Data Innovation Lab," which illustrates the explorative initiative as part of Big Bet 2 (data management), are presented in more detail.

First, as already mentioned earlier, AXA Konzern AG has emerged from a wide range of mergers. The mergers of the former insurance firms Concordia, Nordstern, Albingia, Colonia, UAP and Winterthur have formed the AXA Konzern AG of today. All insurance companies have been involved in AXA Konzern AG's development; in particular, AXA Konzern AG's current IT. Comparable to other big and traditional organizations that emerged from several mergers, AXA Konzern AG has also a very heterogeneous IT [e.g. 30].

The reasons behind this heterogeneous IT can be found within the AXA Konzern AG's IT integrations. Despite the recommendation, a complete IT integration was not performed with every merger due to cost and time saving [e.g. 31,32]. Henceforth, AXA Konzern AG's wide range of mergers with partial and marginal IT integrations has led to a diverse IT. To overcome this heterogeneous IT for the life insurance sector, AXA Konzern AG has started to implement the new central management platform "COR.FJA Life Factory". This five-year project encompasses COR.FJA Life Factory implementation, as well as the transfer of all existing insurance contracts and policies from the old life sector IT systems to the new platform. Thereby, the new IT platform will replace the "smorgasbord" of all current life sector IT systems. Henceforth, this exploitative initiative – the unified IT platform – is the foundation for a more efficient and digital business model of AXA Konzern AG's life sector.

Second, "insurance is at its core a construct of data and models…". Thus, the topic "data" itself and all data-related topics, namely analytics, are of great importance in insurance companies – so, naturally, also for the entire AXA Group and the German AXA Konzern AG. Thereupon, AXA Konzern AG founded the "Data Innovation Lab" in Cologne in 2017 to transfer all data-related topics, such as analytics, big data, artificial intelligence and machine learning, into the insurance world. Thereby, AXA Konzern AG chose to build a dedicated lab for all data innovations because these units are set up with a mandate to coordinate the development of ideas and support the scaling-up of the most promising ones [33]. Within its Data Innovation Lab, AXA Konzern AG focuses on innovation in data storage and data analysis. As usual in such labs, AXA Konzern AG dispenses large project teams and fixed structure and prefers to rely on agile methods. Employees from a wide range of business sectors work together in interdisciplinary teams in vitreous conference rooms and open-space offices. Altogether, this is the third Data Innovation Lab of the entire AXA Group – following Paris and Singapore. Later on, it is planned on global level that the Data Innovation Lab will be part of REV.

However, even when the COR.FJA Life Factory and the Data Innovation Lab are IT-driven initiatives, the entire business neverthless benefits from these investments. The COR.FJA Life Factory has not only been implemented to update the current IT landscape; with the COR.FJA Life Factory the business departments are able to offer new insurance contracts and new insurance solutions for the life sector. Offering digital insurance contracts would not have been possible with the old IT systems. Moreover, the Data Innovation Lab enables the business department to evaluate the existing data (e.g. client data) in order to develop new business ideas and create new business segments.

8.4.5 Outsourcing – current activities of AXA Konzern AG and the AXA group

Traditionally, insurers are organizations with an average in-house production depth of approximately 80–90%. Thereupon, the proportion of general outsourced production activities for insurance products is approximately 10–20%. In contrast, the in-house production depth within the automotive industry is on average less than approximately 25%, i.e. 25% or less of all products are assembled in-house, whereas 75% or more are produced externally through e.g. joint ventures. Consequently, the overall outsourcing ratio in the insurance sector is relatively low compared to other sectors, namely the automotive branch. On average, the duration of contractual outsourcing lasts three years or less. Outsourcing contracts within insurance organizations mainly refer to association work (e.g. with Gesamtverband der Deutschen Versicherungswirtschaft), networking and information exchange.

By virtue of their information-intensive character, IT outsourcing in particular plays an important role within insurance companies. IT outsourcing in the insurance sector, namely of IT infrastructure, IT applications and IT services, is well established and has reached a high level of maturity. As of today, IT infrastructure outsourcing is one of the top IT outsourcing priorities within financial services organizations. Remaining relatively constant in most IT areas, only application development indicates an explicit trend toward more outsourcing in the future. Reasons for IT outsourcing have changed in the past years; while cost savings were the main target already a few years ago – and still are – today's emphasis is focused on qualitative objectives such as focusing on the insurance core business. Furthermore, dynamic markets and innovative technology force the change of IT sourcing models. The (contractual) relationship between insurance company and IT service provider needs to be more flexible in design, changeable at short notice and easily replaceable. These changes are creating the prerequisites for e.g. the integration of cloud-based solutions in existing insurance IT application landscapes.

AXA anchored IT outsourcing as an important strategic pillar within its IT strategy and its Big Bets, particularly in Big Bet 3b and Big Bet 1. As previously described, Big Bet 3b encompasses cost efficiency by moving all possible infrastructure to the cloud ("IT infrastructure outsourcing") and Big Bet 1 comprises all fast IT activities, namely IT innovation ("IT innovation sourcing"). IT innovation sourcing describes i.e. the increasing speed and impact of the adoption of technology-driven innovation in the organization by collaboration with innovative specialists. Consequently, ambidexterity in AXA's IT strategy and the Big Bets also becomes evident while examining the Samurais and Ninjas of AXA's IT (out)sourcing.

8.4.6 *Explorative and exploitative outsourcing initiatives*

Various initiatives have been introduced by AXA Konzern AG and the AXA Group to facilitate and speed up long-existing IT outsourcing activities, namely IT infrastructure outsourcing. Furthermore, several new IT sourcing initiatives, notably IT innovation sourcing, have been developed in order to strengthen AXA's position within the market. Henceforth, IT infrastructure outsourcing (representing the exploitative initiative), as well as IT innovation sourcing (illustrate the explorative initiative) is presented in more detail.

First, as in other industries, many financial services companies also founded their own IT subsidiaries which have been running the entire or partial IT operations for their holdings and financial insurance groups. German insurance companies particularly outsource IT infrastructure components to their IT subsidiaries. Mostly, these holding internal IT service providers bundle all infrastructure components and activities of the entire insurance group within a few data processing service centers (worldwide). This enables stable and reliable multi-platform infrastructure operations, as well as – even more important – cost-effective IT processes.

In line with other European traditional insurance groups (e.g. Allianz, Generali), AXA Services, as IT subsidiary within the AXA Group, hosts AXA's infrastructure and offers additional business application services, namely SAP services. In 2017, AXA Services employed about 4,000 FTE professionals in 15 countries worldwide, ranging from Europe, the United States to India. Thereby, depending on the particular IT application, AXA Services offers local and global services, whereas global services encompass 24/7 development and maintenance across all countries. However, AXA Services does not alone but in turn has outsourced several infrastructure operations to e.g. IBM. For instance, in this "infrastructure on demand" outsourcing service, IBM will provide on-demand mainframe, server and storage services and consulting to AXA Services, helping them to transform its data center and processes, reduce operating costs and also improve the service quality to its customers.

While the importance of infrastructure services is steadily declining in times of digital transformation, the significance of cloud computing services is dramatically gaining in importance. Whether choosing a cloud-based provider for data storage or outsourcing to virtual infrastructure using SaaS, cloud computing is often easier and cheaper to maintain compared to traditional legacy systems. Furthermore, it often encompasses software and hardware including corresponding updates which in the long run save time and budget. Thereupon, in terms of infrastructure services, cloud computing provides a solid fundament for all agile modes of operation within the entire AXA Group and AXA Konzern AG.

Depending on the country's privacy policy, more and more of AXA's IT applications are being moved to the cloud. Consequently, the overall organizational outsourcing behavior is changing. Infrastructure applications are no longer outsourced to AXA Services, but instead infrastructure applications are outsourced to AXA's private or third-party cloud providers. Henceforth, this exploitative initiative of moving IT services, especially infrastructure applications, to the IT subsidiary AXA Services as well as the cloud focuses on cost optimization, as well as reliable, secure and future-oriented infrastructure provision for the entire AXA Group.

Second, since AXA's employees' capacity is used to run the daily insurance business, developing innovative ideas during working hours is highly restricted due to the staff members' time constraints. Furthermore – broadly speaking – traditional large financial services organizations, such as AXA, often have "a kind of dusty image" and, thus, cannot be classified as an innovation accelerator/pioneer. Their usual corporate innovation processes are often too costly, slow and inflexible. Thereupon, as suggested by Christensen and Overdorf [10], innovation and generating new ideas has to happen in a different environment or by acquiring new disruptive intruders and start-ups.

Yet, insurtechs and fintechs are considered as digital disrupters of the financial services industry. Due to their innovative nature, insurtechs are able to develop and implement new insurance ideas and solutions quickly and inventively. In IT innovation sourcing, AXA Konzern AG, as well as the AXA Group, wants to harness the power of innovations from insurtechs. Consequently, AXA is developing various explorative initiatives to support the collaboration with insurtechs and, thus, are planning to drive their own IT innovation.

In addition to the previously described AXA Innovation Campus, since 2015, the Group has been very active in the innovation space with the creation of various business units and the launch of new services to the benefit of the customers. AXA's innovation ecosystem, made of 7 dedicated units, is orchestered by AXA Next.

- The start-up studio Kamet aims to create innovative entrepreneurs and companies in the insurance and asset management sector. Kamet supports those companies and entrepreneurs by supplying resources (advice, methods, structures and financing) in order to launch, incubate or build new partnerships.
- The fintech and insurtech specialized investment fund – AXA Strategic Ventures, endowed with 450 million Euro – invests in start-ups in the area of enterprise software, fintech, consumer tech and digital health around the world.
- AXA Partners helps corporate clients to enrich their customers' experience by implementing innovative global solutions in assistance services, specialized insurance and credit protection.
  - Global Enterprises management builds multi-facetted partnerships with out One AXA Enterprise Partners to drive Business-to-Business growth across all AXA assets in the AXA entities and lines of business.
  - Maestro Health is a technology-enabled employee health and benefits administration company on a mission to deliver better outcomes at lower cost.
  - AXA Emerging Customers makes insurance accessible, affordable adn relevant to 4 billion low income to mass market customers who remain vulnerable to unforseen events.

- AXA Climate helps communities and business tackle climate risks, with solutions combining parametric insurance (automated, data-driven), real-time alerting services and adaption services to climate change.

IT innovation sourcing – as explorative initiative – should help the AXA Group to accelerate IT innovation within the insurance business, provide new (IT) services and interaction possibilities with clients, as well as leverage acquisition for new products and offerings.

However, both illustrated sourcing initiatives – IT infrastructure and IT innovation outsourcing – concern both business and IT. IT infrastructure outsourcing to AXA Services and the cloud can be seen more as a pure IT initiative, but the business is stuck without secure, stable running and cost-effective IT systems. Selling insurance products without IT is impossible. Additionally, IT innovation sourcing can be considered as a mere IT initiative, but it also affects business since the insurtech cooperation should accelerate business and IT. However, both AXA's sourcing initiatives clearly demonstrate that business and IT cannot be seen as separate components anymore; they are intertwined and dependent on one another. Henceforth, also IT sourcing clearly forces AXA's business and IT units into one.

8.5 Conclusion, discussion and directions for further research

As well as other big European insurers, AXA Konzern AG has been forced by disruptive innovations and the digital transformation to rethink and restructure itself. Therefore, it is necessary to reorganize the unprecedented gap between exploitation and exploration and to manage the resulting ambidexterity accordingly. As extensively outlined in this conference paper, AXA Konzern AG tackles this challenge by concretely addressing ambidexterity, as well as the management of ambidexterity, in its business and IT strategy. Furthermore, several exploitative (e.g. NWOW, COR.FJA Life Factory, AXA Services) and explorative initiatives (e.g. AXA Innovation Campus, Data Innovation Lab) have been introduced to speed up AXA Konzern AG's digital transformation.

However, even when AXA Konzern AG is in the midst of the renewal process and its digital transformation journey is still on-going, the following academic research results are supported by this case: Gregory et al. [6, p. 76] stated that "the choice between IT efficiency and IT innovation is not an either-or decision but more a both-and decision." True, both Samurais and Ninjas are needed to the master the digital innovation at AXA Konzern AG's. Furthermore, this case also examined and confirmed some of the sixth ambidexterity areas listed by Gregory et al. [6], such as IT portfolio decisions (e.g. IT efficiency vs. IT innovation), IT architecture change (e.g. IT integration vs. IT replacement) and IT program planning (e.g. IT program agility vs. IT project stability).

Yet, being currently classified in the archetype "Subdivisional Bimodal IT," AXA Konzern AG's IT function is structurally subdivided into two distinct groups: one operates in traditional mode, the other one in agile mode [19]. Whereas in the traditional mode, business and IT usually operate in two different business units, in agile mode, business and IT generally work in integrated teams. Thereby, a business employee (the so-called product owner) is part of approximately ten members IT team. Within this team, the product owner is the person who knows the business requirements, who "translates" the business requirements into IT assignments, who manages the IT implementation orders and, thus, guides the entire IT team. As a consequence, the agile IT transformation does not only require an IT team reorganization from the traditional to the agile operation mode; the business teams also need to adapt their way of working accordingly, e.g. they need to appoint a product owner acting as "connector" between business and IT.

As this product owner example demonstrates, an IT function transformation using bimodal IT and operating in traditional and agile mode is not possible without the simultaneous business transformation. Presently, the aspect of "transforming the business function using bimodal businesses" [adapted from 19] has not been addressed yet.

As already mentioned in academic literature [e.g. 6] and also demonstrated in this case, digital transformations, the management of ambidexterity and bimodal IT, as well as the shift of an entire group to agile working methods, all exert considerable new demands on structures, processes and relational mechanisms of enterprise governance of IT [34]. As in most big organizations, IT is not equal to IT: there are different types of IT, namely global IT, local IT, agile IT, traditional IT and product-driven IT. Every IT function has its own IT systems, its own organization, its own employees and, thus, needs its own regulation to govern all activities. Nowadays, it is not sufficient enough simply to redefine the existing structures, processes and relational mechanisms of enterprise governance of IT. New forms of enterprise governance of IT have to be formulated, notably agile IT governance and traditional vs. agile operating IT governance. First, agile IT teams demand governance for collaboration within agile teams, but also in the context with the business department. Second, bimodal IT requires new forms of structured collaboration between agile and traditional IT teams, as well as interaction with the corresponding business department. Thereupon, this new partnership forces new definitions, structures, processes and relational mechanisms of enterprise governance of IT.

Furthermore, enterprise governance of IT is not only of particular importance within IT management and its related territories; enterprise governance of IT also plays a crucial role for the future design of business and IT alignment. Ambidexterity, IT ambidexterity, bimodal IT and the digital and agile transformation will significantly reduce, maybe even dissolve the split of business and IT. This development is also supported by the ever-increasing dispersion of IT (e.g. through mobile applications) into business segments. Thereupon, it will remain interesting as the future development of business IT alignment at AXA Konzern AG is created. Presently, this statement can be applied: "IT as a service provider was yesterday – joint business and IT teams are the future" [35].

Note

1 Oxford English Dictionary: Definition of "ambidextrous"; Retrieved 25.02.2018 at https://en.oxforddictionaries.com

References

1. Quack, K.: Ein bisschen bi schaded nie – ganz im Gegenteil, sagt Gartner (2015). Retrieved 01.09.2017 at https://www.computerwoche.de/a/ein-bisschen-bi-schadet-nie-ganz-im-gegenteil-sagt-gartner,3219396
2. He, Z.-L., Wong, P.-K.: Exploration vs. Exploitation: Am Empirical Test of the Ambidexterity Hypothesis. *Organization Science*. 15, 481–494 (2004).
3. Schwab, K.: *The Fourth Industrial Revolution*. Penguin Random House, London (2016).
4. Lucas, H.C., Goh, J.M.: Disruptive Technology: How Kodak Missed the Digital Photography Revolution. *The Journal of Strategic Information Systems*. 18, 46–55 (2009).
5. Utesheva, A., Cecez-Kecmanov, D., Schlagwein, D.: *Understanding the Digital Newspaper Genre: Medium vs Message*. European Conference on Information Systems (ECIS) (2012).
6. Gregory, R.W., Keil, M., Muntermann, J., Maehring, M.: Paradoxes and the Nature of Ambidexterity in IT Transformation Programs. *Information Systems Research*. 26, 57–80 (2015).
7. Lee, O.-K., Sambamurthy, V., Lim, K. H., Wei, K.K.: How Does IT Ambidexterity Impact Organizational Agility. *Information Systems Research*. 26, 398–417 (2015).

8. Leonhardt, D., Haffke, I., Kranz, J., Benlian, A.: *Reinventing the IT Function: The Role of IT Agility and IT Ambidexterity in Supporting Digital Business Transformation.* 25th European Conference on Information Systems (ECIS), Guimaraes, Portugal (2017).

9. Christensen, C.M.: *The Innovator's Dilemma: When New Technology Cause Great Firm to Fail.* Harvard Business School Press, Boston, MA (1997).

10. Christensen, C.M., Overdorf, M.: Meeting the Challenge of Disruptive Change. *Harvard Business Review.* 78, 66–76 (2000).

11. Christensen, C.M., Raynor, M., McDonald, R.: What Is Disruptive Innovation?. In: *The HBR's Must Reads 2017,* Harvard Business School Publishing Corporation, Boston, MA (2017).

12. Christensen, C.M., Raynor, M.: *The Innovator's Solution: Creating and Sustaining Successful Growth.* Business School Press, Boston, MA (2003).

13. Cao, Q., Gedajlovic, E., Zhang, H.: Unpacking Organizational Ambidexterity: Dimensions, Contingencies, and Synergistic Effects. *Organization Science.* 20, 781–796 (2009).

14. Gibson, C.B., Birkinshaw, J.: The Antecedents, Consequences, and Mediating Role of Organizational Ambidexterity. *Academy of Management Journal.* 47, 209–226 (2004).

15. March, J.: Exploration and Exploitation in Organizational Learning. *Organization Science.* 2, 71–87 (1991).

16. Aron, D., McDonald, M.: Taming the Digital Dragon: The 2014 CIO Agenda. (2013). Retrieved 31.08.2017 at http://www.gartner.com/imagesrv/cio/pdf/cio_agenda_insights2014.pdf

17. Gartner: From the Gartner IT Glossary: What Is Bimodal?. (2017). Retrieved 31.08.2017 at https://research.gartner.com/definition-whatis-bimodal?resId=3216217&srcId=1-8163325102

18. Horlach, B., Drews, P., Schirmer, I.: Bimodal IT: Business IT Alignment in the Age of Digital Transformation. *Multikonferenz Wirtschaftsinformatik (MKWI).* 3, 1417–1428 (2016).

19. Haffke, I., Kalgovas, B., Benlian, A.: Options for Transforming the IT Function Using Bimodal IT. *MIS Quarterly Executive.* 16, 101–120 (2017).

20. Piccinini, E., Hanelt, A., Gregory, R.W., Kolbe, L.M.: Transforming Industrial Business: The Impact of Digital Transformation on Automotive Organizations. In: 36th Conference on Information Systems, Forth Worth, USA (2015)

21. Yin, R.: *Case Study Research: Design and Methods,* 5th Edition, Sage, Los Angeles, CA (2014).

22. Yin, R.: Applications of Case Study Research, SAGE, London (2012).

23. Earl, M.J.: *Management Strategies for Information Technology.* Prentice Hall, Upper Saddle River, NJ (1989).

24. McFarlan, W.: Information Technology Changes the Way You Compete. *Harvard Business Review.* 62, 98–103 (1984).

25. Porter, M.E., Millar, V.E.: How Information Gives You Competitive Advantage. *Harvard Business Review.* 63, 149–160 (1985).

26. Teubner, R.A., Mocker, M.: Strategic Information Planning: Insights from an Action Research Project in the Financial Services. Industry Working Paper, ERCIS – European Research Center for Information Systems (3). (2005). Retrieved 28.09.2017 at https://www.econstor.eu/bitstream/10419/58420/1/517263610.pdf

27. Baum, A., Schreiber, F.: The Current InsurTech Landscape: Business Models and Disruptive Potential. (2017). Retrieved 02.02.2018 at https://www.ivw.unisg.ch/~/media/internet/content/dateien/instituteundcenters/ivw/studien/ab-insurtech_2017.pdf

28. Puschmann, T.: Fintech Business. *Information Systems Engineering.* 59, 69–76 (2017).

29. Hess, T., Benlian, A., Matt, C., Wiesboeck, F.: Options for Formulating a Digital Transformation Strategy. *MIS Quarterly Executive.* 15, 123–139 (2016).

30. Batelaan, M., Veltman, J.: Vijf Mythes Over Postfusie ICT-Integratie. *Management & Informatie.* 5, 50–58 (2002).

31. Giacomazzi, F., Panella, C., Pernici, B., Sansoni, M.: Information Systems Integration in Mergers and Acquistions: A Normative Model. *Information & Management.* 32, 289–302 (1997).

32. Wijnhoven, F., Spil, T., Stegwee, R., Tjang A Fa, R.: Post-Merger IT Integration Strategies: An IT Alignment Perspective. *Journal of Strategic Information Systems.* 15, 5–28 (2006).

33. McKinsey: Digital Disruption in Insurance: Cutting through the Noise. (2017). Retrieved 30.11.2017 at https://www.mckinsey.com/industries/financial-services/our-insights/digital-insurance

34. Van Grembergen, W., De Haes, S.: *Enterprise Governance of Information Technology – Achieving Strategic Alignment and Value.* Springer Science + Business Media, LLC, New York (2009).

35. AXA Switzerland: Business IT Alignment History – Example from AXA Winterthur (Switzerland). Presentation of AXA Winterthur (Switzerland) from CIO Andreas Maier at Konferenz für Wirtschaftsinformatik at 15.02.2017, St. Gallen (Switzerland). Retrieved 04.04.2017 at http://www.wi2017.ch/de/videos

9

CAN OUTSOURCING IMPROVE COMPETITIVE ADVANTAGE IN DIRECT RETAIL BANKING?

Julia Kotlarsky and Jan Teckemeyer[1]

9.1 Introduction

Banks are exposed to pressure from several directions. While banks are still suffering from the aftermath of the financial crisis, customers are becoming more demanding and discerning, regulators are adding more burdens to front- and back-office processes and the policy of low interest rates is further lowering margins. Comparing the risk-weighted returns of European banks, the average of 0.5% implies that most European banks currently do not earn their cost of capital, which emphasises the need for the banks to improve their margins. The direct or online banks – type of banking that has been growing since the 1990s and can be distinguished from traditional retail banks since they do not possess physical branches and communicate with their customers only via telephone, email and their web portal – are specifically affected by this pressure since banks of this type tend to be focused on keeping their costs on a low level and their structure lean. For such banks outsourcing presents an attractive proposition as it opens a possibility for reducing costs without making visible changes in the way the bank is "facing" its customers (via web-based interface). However, before embarking on an outsourcing journey, it is important to understand whether a high degree of outsourcing means that a bank loses its core competences in banking and therefore only acts as a manager of different external service providers. To address this challenge, we conducted research study aiming to assess suitability of value-creating activities of a direct bank to outsourcing, and the implication of outsourcing to bank's competitive advantage.

The core idea behind a direct bank's strategy is to build up and sustain a price leadership positioning compared to other banks. The prerequisite to reach that aim is to gain a high market share. Consequently, direct banks can benefit from economies of scale – through lowering the fixed cost per transaction – and economies of scope – through the usage of efficient IT-based processes. Direct banks typically compete with the traditional retail banks by using mass marketing, using automated transaction processes and only selling a small number of products, thus being able to offer better conditions than traditional retail banks due to cost advantages. However, what do we know about how direct banks compete and what helps

---

1 Empirical work reported in this study is based on research that Jan Teckemeyer has done during his Master study at Aston University

them to survive in this world populated by highly experienced providers of financial services (all top outsourcing vendors e.g. IBM, TCS, Accenture, Infosys that offer variety of financial products) and online giants that offer credit cards (e.g. Amazon) or online payment facility (e.g. Google Wallet)?

As a point of departure, we undertook an in-depth analysis of a direct bank's value chain.

9.2 Understanding the value chain of a direct bank

The banking value chain consists of product development, acquisition and sales, transaction processing and support activities (see Figure 9.1). Instead of manufacturing and delivering tangible goods, banking products such as loans, securities, current accounts and IPOs are developed, sold, processed and serviced. Related secondary activities within the banking value chain include human resources, technology development, risk management and governance.

9.2.1 Product development

Besides the development of new banking products, product management includes the provision, controlling and elimination of products. It might also comprise the design of product bundles or the combination of bank products with other consumer goods with the aim to facilitate cross-selling and to increase customer loyalty. Product development can contribute to value creation when development times can be kept shorter and when innovative products can be offered at competitive prices.

9.2.2 Acquisition and sales

Many retail banks define the acquisition and sales as their key activity since it is the only process directly visible to the customer. This entails two main activities: the management of the chosen sales channels and the actual sales processes. Direct banks use impersonal and semi-personal sales channels only: telephone, mail and internet.

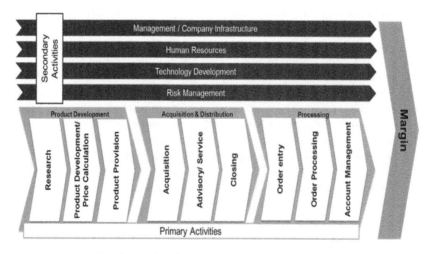

Figure 9.1 Generic retail banking value chain

The primary goal of a retail bank's sales activities is to gain new customers and to intensify existing customer relationships. Many customers only use one product category – their checking account – at their primary bank while products from other categories such as loans or pension insurances are held at other banks. Customers often perceive direct banks only as a low-cost provider of checking accounts and credit cards. For more complex products, e.g. building loans, many direct banking customers prefer traditional retail banks offering face-to-face advisory in their branches.

9.2.3 Transaction processing

Transaction processing typically includes deposit business, lending business, securities settlement and payments. Each of these high-level processes contains more granular processes such as order entry, order processing and account management. All transaction processing activities are closely linked and interdependent to the respective sales activities. Since these activities are high-volume routine tasks, the key challenge for banking institutes lies in balancing optimal quality, speed and cost.

Payments in Europe work according to international standards such as Single Euro Payments Area (SEPA), which was one of the reasons why the processing of payments was one of the first banking business processes to be outsourced in a majority of banks.

In the area of payments banks increasingly face competition from online payment providers such as PayPal or Google Wallet which attract users with an easy handling and lower fees. Even Facebook set up a payment system allowing users to buy goods with virtual credits.

Due to the higher automation of the securities processes, sales and processing can operate independently. Most direct banks outsource their securities processing since they do not see it as a core competence but seek to benefit from the securities service.

9.3 To outsource or not to outsource? Comparison of three direct banks

To understand implications of outsourcing to competitive advantage in direct retail banking, we conducted in-depth study of three direct banks, all based in Germany. These banks varied in their size, focus on target customers, product portfolio and main channels used to reach customers (see Table 9.1).

9.3.1 Bank 1: Online Bank

The *Online Bank* is a true "born digital" – established in the late 90s it was one of the first movers in direct banking to offer the internet as the only sales channel. It offers a call centre only as a back-up channel for service enquiries (company presentation). The main target group of the bank are well-educated people with a high income who do not need any financial advisory and who are not dependent on a certain location. The bank positions itself as a "price and quality leader" with a free current account and over-average conditions for savings accounts and consumer loans. The bank's strategic principle is to make most of its costs variable through outsourcing of almost all of its operational activities. This allows the bank to operate by a relatively small number of staff and to cope easily with fluctuations in demand: if only a few products are being sold, there will be few service requests as well. The bank claims that the outsourcing brings a savings potential of up to 40% for some processes.

Table 9.1 Comparison of the three bank's characteristics focusing on their business models

Characteristics	Online Bank	Top 3 Direct Bank	Advisory Bank
Date of foundation	Late 1990s	Before 1970	Before 1950
No. of employees	10–50	>1,000	50–250
Balance sheet total	<€1 bn	>€50 bn	N/A
No. of customers	>100,000	>1,000,000	>3,000
Target customers	Freelancers and employees with above average income being not bound to a specific location	Mainstream, including people who normally do not prefer direct banking	High net worth customers, typical private banking customers
Product portfolio	Standard products, from current accounts and consumer loans to pension plans. Also offers some non-financial products such as magazines	Standard products, almost all developed in-house.	Most standard products focus on investment products
Main channels	Website (outsourced call centre as back-up)	Website, call centre	Personal advisor, call centre, website
Advisory offered	No	Yes, but limited	Yes
Transaction processing	Outsourced (except loan processing)	In-house	In-house

9.3.2 Bank 2: Top 3 Direct Bank

The Top 3 *Direct Bank* has a similar strategic approach as the Online Bank to address customers: above-average conditions and a few standardised products are offered to the customers while the service is limited to the website and a call centre which also offers advisory services. The target group is the mainstream population having no need in a physical branch and extensive personal consultations. In the recent years, the bank was able to reduce the interest rates paid on deposits and still keep their customers loyal. The reason was the high service standard (the bank received various awards for customer satisfaction) which encouraged customers to stay even though the bank does not have the best prices in the market anymore.

The processes of the Top 3 Direct Bank are focused on automation and efficiency. The concept of simple and standardised products for the mainstream fits together with the aim not to use tailor-made procedures which usually lead to manual interruptions of the automated processes.

9.3.3 Bank 3: Advisory Bank

The *Advisory Bank* serves their customers online and on the phone (through a call centre) and additionally, for more complex questions, advises the customers at their homes. Over time this Bank transformed from a traditional private bank with a physical presence to a mixed business model that combines direct banking with a "mobile sales force" that rely on freelance advisors who visit the customers at home. Thus, in comparison to other direct banks, the Advisory Bank puts a greater focus on the personal relationship with their customers.

Since 80% of the Advisory Bank's IT development expenses have gone into regulatory topics, the bank found outsourcing to help with reducing IT development costs to comply with

Table 9.2 Illustration of the three banks' sourcing strategy – in-house activities marked in white, outsourced functions in grey

Function		Online Bank	Top 3 Direct Bank	Advisory Bank
Product development	Research			
	Product development	(grey)	(grey)	(grey)
	Product provision	(grey)	(grey)	(grey)
Acquisition and sales	Acquisition	(grey)		
	Advisory and services	(grey)	(grey)	
	Closing	(grey)		
Processing	Order entry	(grey)		
	Order processing	(grey)		
	Account management	(grey)		
Secondary activities	Management/company infrastructure			
	Human resources	(grey)		
	Information technology	(grey)	(dark grey)	(grey)
	Risk management/ governance/quality management	(grey)		
	Maturity transformation	(grey)		

new regulatory requirements. Reliance on a third party to support IT and regulatory processes helps the bank to keep costs for adjustments in the processes or IT that are necessary due to new requirements such as SEPA and the Foreign Account Tax Compliance Act (FATCA).

Building upon the value chain model introduced above, Table 9.2 summarises the sourcing strategy of the three banks. As it demonstrates, management, governance and product development are the only activities that are mainly kept in-house by all three firms.

The case of the Online Bank highlights that almost all activities that do not directly contribute to the competitive advantage can be outsourced if the bank possesses the skills and experience to effectively govern and steer the outsourcing relationships with their service providers. Another factor that is important when considering the potential scope of outsourcing is the profile of target customers of the respective bank and their expectations regarding customer services. For instance, the complexity of outsourcing customer service is higher in a bank that offers extensive advisory to their customers than in a bank that relies on automated transactions through the website. However, how does outsourcing affect bank's ability to compete? We address this question in the next section.

9.4 Value chain and outsourcing: the impact on competitive advantage of direct banks

9.4.1 *Product development in direct banking*

Banking products are usually perceived as being standardised commodities which banks cannot use to differentiate themselves from competitors. Nevertheless, in direct banking it is regarded as a core competence. Different from traditional banks that rely on local presence and personal relationship between bank advisors and their customers as main reasons to choose a certain branch-based retail bank, direct banks are mainly chosen for price and possibly flexibility reasons. That means the product development plays a central role since it determines the price policy and the composition and design of the product. By contrast, since the personal relationship to the customer is not the primary concern, the front-office activities – acquisition and sales – do not necessarily belong to the key activities of direct banks.

The current account, which is often the central product of a direct bank to gain new customers, becomes therefore a key focus of product development efforts. This entails market and competitor research, the design of the product according to market demand and the integration of the product in all service and processing activities. This activity cannot be outsourced in direct banks since otherwise the bank would lose control over its key differentiation factor.

Regarding the number of products, the Online Bank and the Top 3 Direct Bank offer all standard bank products but they keep the number of products low in order to keep the procedures within sales and processing simple. In contrast, the Advisory Bank offers a higher number of products, especially investment products, since their freelance sales force is capable of covering the higher requirements for advisory.

9.4.2 Acquisition and sales in direct banking

The sourcing of sales and customer service activities (e.g. call centre services) depends on the approach taken by a direct bank to their target customer population. The Online Bank only targets a group of customers which is completely autonomous in financial decisions and does not need any advice. In contrast, the Top 3 Direct Bank focuses on a broad mainstream target group for which good conditions form their main priority but which also expects a high standard customer service and advisory. The relevance of the customer service call centre is significantly lower for the Online Bank compared to the Top 3 Direct Bank. The Online Bank operates the call centre to ensure a provision of basic services in case problems with the website occur or customers have additional questions. In contrast, the Top 3 Direct Bank as well as the Advisory Bank regards the call centre as one of the main channels to communicate with the customer and keep this function in-house. While the Top 3 Direct Bank also targets the "internet generation" with a high affinity towards technology, it also wants to reach customers who expect personal advisory on the phone. In the case of the Advisory Bank, the focus on the personal relationship to the customer is even stronger. These factors explain the preference either to outsource the call centre or to keep it in-house.

However, as we have learnt from the Online Bank, outsourcing of the customer service call centre only works through extensive control measures and through careful selection of a partner that is able to understand the DNA of the bank and make it transparent while handling customer requests. Since customer service processes are defined in great detail by the responsible service manager within the bank, the key know-how remains in the bank. It helps to reduce the risk that the service provider becomes more knowledgeable in executing the processes than the bank, thus making the bank dependent on the provider.

When considering the nature of the sales activity in direct banks, it is apparent that the Online Bank's sales is more suitable for outsourcing compared to the other two banks due to the fact that the Online Bank was able to codify the activity more and to reduce its complexity.

9.4.3 *Transaction processing in direct banking*

Different from many other contexts where transaction processing is regarded as one of the most suitable processes for outsourcing as it typically entails high-volume and repetitive activities, does not require customer contact and can be separated from other processes, we have observed the opposite in direct retail banking. The Top 3 Direct Bank and the Advisory Bank do not outsource any processing activities while the Online Bank outsourced all processing services except loan processing which is more complex and more difficult to codify compared to other processing activities, and often requires interaction with the customer and credit decision to be taken by the bank.

Yet, transaction processing is typically not regarded as a core competence and could be outsourced to specialised service providers that can provide such commodity services cheaper, faster and possibly better than a bank could internally. However if internal capabilities in this area are highly developed as in the case of the Top 3 Direct Bank that already reached a high optimisation degree for their processes internally, outperforming specialised service providers, outsourcing is not expected to improve operational performance. Additionally, both the Top 3 Direct Bank and the Advisory Bank highlighted that keeping the processing in-house allows a more efficient and flexible product development process since product development, front office and back office can work closely together to develop a product.

However when outsourcing transaction processing, the Online Bank most strongly emphasises the need to pay special attention to cost management of their providers and to constantly benchmarking other providers on the market.

9.4.4 *Governance and support activities in direct banking*

In direct banking, the need for outsourcing governance, which includes quality management, provider management and service level management, is strongly associated with degree of outsourcing. While all parties in our study were in agreement that certain governance measures are a minimum requirement to operate in the market, it is only in the case of the Online Bank which is outsourcing majority of its processes, governance is seen as one of the key activities within the firm which attracts considerable attention by the board members and involves additional costs associated with extensive management of outsourcing relationships. Treating outsourcing governance as core competency, the Online Bank relies on internal staff to monitor service providers and to prevent losing know-how.

For example, internal audit, anti-money laundering and compliance are done by service providers but responsibility and liability remain in-house.

For direct banks that have high degree of outsourcing, it is important to recognise that, as in the case of Online Bank, investment in outsourcing governance allows the firm to gain access to suppliers' capabilities and to effectively steer service providers, which is necessary to be able to benefit from flexibility in reacting to market demands while offering competitive prices to customers. In such circumstances, even though governance does not directly create value for the customer, this activity should be regarded as a core competence that provides a sustainable competitive advantage.

Information Technology was the only support activity partially outsourced by all of the three banks as it is seen as less critical for outsourcing. For instance, the Top 3 Direct Bank outsourced the computer centre and other commodity services, the Online Bank outsourced all IT functions except a small team which steers the external providers.

9.5 Lessons learnt: what contributes to competitive advantage in direct banking?

Internal skills and capabilities that a bank developed over time as well as the size and target market play a significant role in deciding about the right sourcing strategy. For example, being "digital born," Online Bank has based its business model on online channels and use of outsourcing service providers from the beginning, and therefore developed sound skills and capabilities required to manage outsourcing relationships since its foundation. The Top 3 Direct Bank, however, benefited from its long history of investing extensive resources in internal process optimisation and automation and which is superior to what local service providers could offer.

Table 9.3 lists the three banks' core competences and explains their role in providing the firms with a sustainable competitive advantage.

Being put under pressure by regulators and customers, banks are embarking on outsourcing as one of the ways to increase their profitability and to improve their competitive positioning. Considering that there is a trend towards further standardisation of banking processes and availability of mature service providers, it is likely that more banks will outsource various processes and services. Nevertheless, as the case of the Top 3 Direct Bank shows, an operating model based on internal process automation and optimisation might also provide a competitive advantage.

Our research suggests that there are no activities that would always be suitable for outsourcing in the direct banking context; however, there should always be alignment between sourcing strategy and activities that can support the bank's business model (especially its target customers and products) most effectively. For example, it would not be advisable for a

Table 9.3 Summary of the three banks' competitive advantages

Bank	Core competence	Comment
Online Bank	Outsourcing governance and provider management	Extensive experience in outsourcing governance lets the bank effectively outsource a majority of the operational activities
	Product development	Product managers also engage in governance activities and thereby ensure that all transactions concerning a product can effectively be steered
Top 3 Direct Bank	Process automation and optimisation (overall)	Leads to superiority of internal processes in terms of costs, time and quality
	Product development	Connected to process optimisation: products are designed in accordance with automated and simplified processes
	Customer service	High standard customer service allowed the bank to retain customer base while decreasing interest rates
Advisory Bank	Product development	Product development takes place in teams of staff from different operational functions. Ensures an alignment of all activities when launching a new product.
	Sales (freelance, sales force, call centre, website)	The sales force provides individual advisory while the call centre and website guarantee availability when needed

bank that relies on personal customer relationships and offers complex advisory to outsource its customer service activities as the Online Bank did. A bank's outsource practices should be supported by constant attention of top management and profound governance and steering capabilities.

Interestingly, neither of the three banks is engaged in any offshore sourcing activities. One of the main reasons lies in reputational concerns which offshoring might entail. Another factor is the size of the companies since offshore activities are likely to require a higher minimum volume to compensate for higher governance cost compared to domestic sourcing. Higher transaction costs associated with legal, cultural, geographical and language barriers is an additional argument against offshoring. Global players like Deutsche Bank that operate their own captive centres are examples of bigger companies for which offshoring is a more attractive option.

Bibliography

1. Accenture. The Future of Payments: Convergence, Competition and Collaboration. (2012). [Online]. Available at: http://www.accenture.com/SiteCollectionDocuments/gb-en/Accenture-The-Future-of-Payments-Convergence-Competition-and-Collaboration.pdf
2. Amit, R., and Zott, C.: Value Creation in E-Business. *Strategic Management Journal*. 22(6/7), pp. 493–520 (2001).
3. Aron, R., and Singh, J.: Getting Offshoring Right. *Harvard Business Review*. 83(12), pp. 135–143 (2005).
4. ATKearney.: Banking in a Digital World. (2013). [Online]. Available at: https://www.at-kearney.com/documents/10192/3054333/Banking+in+a+Digital+World.pdf/91231b20-788e-41a1-a429-3f926834c2b0
5. Beimborn, D.: *Cooperative Sourcing – Simulation Studies and Empirical Data on Out-Sourcing Coalitions in the Banking Industry*. Gabler: Wiesbaden (2008).
6. Bharadwaj, A., Sawy, O., Pavlou, P., and Venkatraman, N.: Digital Business Strategy: Toward a Next Generation of Insights. *Management Information Systems: MIS Quarterly*. 37 (2), pp. 471–482 (2013).
7. Broedner, P., Kinkel, S. and Lay, G.: Productivity Effects of Outsourcing: New Evidence on the Strategic Importance of Vertical Integration Decisions. *International Journal of Operations and Production Management*. 29 (2), pp. 127–150 (2009).
8. Casu, B., Girardone, C. and Molyneux, P.: *Introduction to Banking*. Financial Times Prentice Hall, Harlow (2006).
9. Dedrick, J., Carmel, E. and Kraemer, K.: A Dynamic Model of Offshore Software Development. *Journal of Information Technology*. 26(1), pp. 1–15 (2011).
10. Deloitte Consulting LLP. Kicking It Up a Notch – Taking Retail Bank Cross-Selling to the Next Level. (2012). [Online]. Available at: http://www.deloitte.com/assets/Dcom-UnitedStates/Local%20Assets/Documents/FSI/us_fsi_KickingItUpaNotch_7913.pdf
11. Financial Times. Big Banks on Thin Ground with Margins. (2013). [Online]. Available at: http://www.ft.com/cms/s/0/fec67a80-5d76-11e2-ba99-00144feab49a.html#axzz2tDoSNgA4
12. Gonzalez, R., Llopis, J. and Gasco, J.: Information Technology Outsourcing in Financial Services. *The Service Industries Journal*. 33(9–10), pp. 909–924 (2013).
13. Goo, J., Huang, C., and Hart, P.: A Path to Successful IT Outsourcing: Interaction between Service-Level Agreements and Commitment. *Decision Sciences*. 39(3), pp. 469–506 (2008).
14. Güttler, A. and Hackethal, A.: *How ING-DiBa Conquered the German Retail Banking Market*. Technical Report, European Business School, Geneva (2006).
15. Hamel, G. and Prahalad, C.: The Core Competences of the Corporation. *Harvard Business Review*. pp. 79–91, May–June (1990).
16. Hamoir, O., McCamish, C., Niederkorn, M. and Thiersch, C.: Europe's Banks: Verging on Merging. *The McKinsey Quarterly*. Issue 3, pp. 116–125 (2002).
17. Lacity, M., Solomon, S., Yan, A. and Willcocks, L.: Business Process Outsourcing Studies: A Critical Review and Research Directions. *Journal of Information Technology*. 26(4), pp. 221–258 (2011).

18. Lamarque, E.: Identifying Key Activities in Banking Firms: A Competence-Based Analysis. In: Sanchez, R. and Heene, A. (editors) *Competence Perspective on Managing Internal Process, Advances in Applied Business Strategy*, Volume 7, Emerald Group Publishing Limited, London, pp. 29–47 (2005).

19. Morschheuser, B., Zerndt, T., Alt, R., Bons, R. and Puschmann, T.: *Banking 2020 – zwischen Individualisierung und Standardisierung*. CC Sourcing, St. Gallen (2014).

20. Oshri, I., Kotlarsky, J. and Willcocks, L.: *The Handbook of Global Outsourcing and Offshoring*. 3rd edition, Palgrave Macmillan, London (2015).

21. Pond, K.: *Retail Banking*. Global Professional Publishing, Kent, ON (2014).

22. Porter, M.: *Competitive Advantage: Creating and Sustaining Superior Performance*. Free Press/Collier Macmillan, New York/London (1985).

23. PwC. Retail Banking 2020 - Evolution or Revolution. (2014). [Online]. Available at: http://www.pwc.com/en_GX/gx/banking-capital-markets/banking-2020/assets/pwc-retail-banking-2020-evolution-or-revolution.pdf.

24. The Boston Consulting Group: Operational Excellence in Retail Banking. (2013). [Online]. Available at: https://www.bcg.com/documents/file72591.pdf

25. Tiwari, R. and Buse, S.: *The German Banking Sector: Competition, Consolidation and Contentment*. Background Paper. Hamburg University of Technology, Hamburg (2006).

PART 2

Inter-organizational relations and transfer

In Chapter 10 Plugge and Janssen reflect on the question of governing and orchestrating relationships with multiple vendors. When managing multisourcing relationships, firms have to pay additional attention to guard the scope of services provided by each vendor and to orchestrate their activities to create synergies. Tensions between the vendors may arise as their objectives might be conflicting and their relationship may have a competitive nature. This research aims at developing a better understanding of governance under these conditions. The analysis comes to the conclusion that an inter-organizational governance is needed that includes governance mechanisms to decrease potential uncertainties and deal with the competitive nature. In particular, a responsible entity (individual or team) at each party is required that develops a coherent strategic plan, monitors relationships, and enforces governance mechanisms.

IT outsourcing, especially in the case of digital outsourcing, may entail significant knowledge transfer when moving services to another sourcing partner. In Chapter 11 Krancher discusses the literature on this topic and analyzes its implications for digital business strategy and agility, based on the findings of 35 studies. Knowledge transfer during the phase in which the service is handed over to a new supplier is one of the most critical and least understood aspects of outsourcing and offshoring projects. A key finding from the review is that months or even years of scaffolded practice through learning tasks are often required before suppliers have acquired sufficient domain-specific knowledge to take over the service. These findings suggest that, to harness the potentials associated with digital business strategy and agility while doing outsourcing or offshoring, clients may need to rely on long-term, embedded relationships vendors, on learning tasks and feedback, and on technologies that reduce complexity.

In Chapter 12 Wende and Mertel focus on the communication challenges between key people on both ends of a transition project. Effective communication during the transition phase is critical for achieving an effective and efficient outsourcing situation. In this chapter the authors illustrate a method, KAIWA, for managing challenges that emerge around the human interaction, which includes the transfer of implicit knowledge.

Outsourcing relations are formalized by a contract. In Chapter 13 Stuurman discusses a number of trends that need attention when designing and implementing contracting structures in the context of digital outsourcing transactions. First, partnerships introduce a significant focus on the actual process of communication and cooperation, including dealing with disputes, rather than 'only' KPI-driven service delivery. Second, digital outsourcing as an enabler for transforming organizations usually requires input from a range of capabilities. As a result, a growing range of subcontractors is being involved in the delivery of services. However, in the contractual architecture, this is often not reflected. Finally, third, the impact of growing compliance pressure on the chain of parties involved in the delivery of services. Privacy and, for specific organizations, cyber security are leading themes in this respect. Compliance becomes a multi-party issue. Very significant penalties and increased reputation risk are strong incentives for drafting adequately protective contractual arrangements (including auditing down the chain).

10

GOVERNING AND ORCHESTRATING RELATIONSHIPS IN OUTSOURCING WITH MULTIPLE VENDORS

Albert Plugge and Marijn Janssen

10.1 Introduction

Today, firms are not able to neglect the impact of the digitalization on their business [1]. As a result, business processes transform into digital end-to-end–oriented processes that even go beyond their own organization. When firms have outsourced their information systems, vendors have to cater for digitalization too as information systems are intertwined with business processes. Literature revealed that single outsourcing vendor relationships have declined and are replaced by smaller selective contracts provided by multiple vendors [see for example 2, 3]. Multisourcing outsourcing can be defined as 'a one-to-many relationships, in which one client uses multiple vendors while the division of labor is jointly negotiated and understood by all parties to the agreement' [4, p. 8]. The authors of [5] argue that as an effect of a firm's digital business strategy vendors share digital infrastructure. This implies that sourcing vendors need to work together, for instance by means of sharing technical insights, while they also operate in a competitive environment at the same time. Managing the tension of collaboration and competitions requires strong governance mechanisms.

Managing multiple vendors is much more complex in comparison to managing a single vendor [6] due to the many dependencies. Additional management attention is required to guard the boundaries related to the scope of services provided by each vendor and governance is needed to ensure coordination of their activities for both service delivery and digital innovation. Governance and communications are needed to ensure that vendors do not compete and work together to fulfill the clients need. In general, communication results in more effective governance [7]. In contrast to dyadic relationships, multisourcing relationships create an inherent coordination problem in which activities and resources from client and various vendors need to be coordinated. As each party in a multisourcing relationship can be considered as a fragmented or monolithic system, sourcing governance is needed to manage interdependencies between systems and vendors. Establishing sourcing governance structures encourages a firm's behavior to achieve their business performance goals [7]. Although each vendor aims to create business value for the client, the conditions of each stakeholder might be different and at the same time they might compete for market share. This may result in tensions between parties as vendors' objectives might be conflicting as they are also intertwined competitors [8,9]. Therefore, governance of the relationship is necessary to ensure the proper functioning of a multisourcing outsourcing relationship.

The authors of [10] called for more research on multisourcing in the post-contract stage, specifically on how governance mechanisms affect interdependent relationships. The aim of this research is to develop a better understanding of governance in multisourcing relationships. This has been given scant attention in outsourcing literature. Multisourcing can only be understood by using multiple theories. The governance of resources is investigated by focusing on how resources are coordinated and which resources the organizations are dependent on. As governance is related to coordinating the activities of multiple organizations, we opted for the *Coordination Theory* (CT) to study the interdependencies between the parties involved. As both client and vendors are dependent on each other, the *Resource Dependency Theory* (RDT) was used to investigate how vendors' resources effect the client.

The remainder of this chapter is organized in the following way. Section 10.2 provides the background of both CT and RDT. Section 10.3 presents a research approach that is based on a case study methodology. Section 10.4 relates to the findings of the empirical case study, highlighting a client and three IT vendors. In Section 10.5 we discuss the findings by using the two theories and finally we present our conclusions in Section 10.6.

10.2 Literature background

In this study both concepts from governance, CT, and RDT will be used to understand multisourcing relationships.

10.2.1 Governance in multisourcing relationships

In the 2010s both scholars and practitioners agreed on a common understanding of multisourcing, to use two or more external vendors as part of an outsourcing arrangement [11]. We built on [12, p. 211] who define multisourcing 'as the situation where a client firm delegates projects and services to multiple external vendors who must, at least partly, work cooperatively to achieve the client's business objectives'. Multisourcing relationships results in new challenges with regard to the way that the dependencies among vendors and the client can be coordinated, roles and responsibilities between client and vendors, and decision-making among parties is determined. This is the domain of sourcing governance, which represents the framework for decision rights and accountabilities to encourage desirable behavior in the use of resources [7]. Enterprises generally design three kinds of governance mechanisms: (1) decision-making structures, (2) alignment processes, and (3) formal communications [7]. Often a distinction between contractual and relational governance is made. Some scholars address the importance of contractual governance agreements to manage the relationship [13]. Specifying long-term contracts is complex and inherently incomplete because firms have to deal with uncertainty and unanticipated obligations. Hence, firms should govern an outsourcing relationship beyond traditional contractual agreements and also consider relationships [14,15]. The relational governance concept largely grows out of the work of [16]. Importantly, relational governance attempts to address some of the deficiencies in contract governance: the failure to account for social structures within which the inter-firm exchanges are embedded, and the overestimation of hazardous elements in the exchange [17]. The authors of [18] found that relational governance was realized most frequently by means of effective knowledge sharing, communication, trust, and viewing the vendor as a partner. Literature suggests that contractual governance and relational governance influence each other and can be perceived as complements in that both need to be strong to produce positive outsourcing outcomes [19]. In this study both forms of governance will be taken into account.

10.2.2 Coordination and orchestration

CT has been applied to design the relationships between systems (Malone and Crowston 1990) as well as the design of processes [20]. The authors of [21, p. 87] define coordination as 'the process of managing interdependencies between activities'. As scholars disagree about the definition of interdependence, it is difficult to formulate an exact description [22]. Based on our literature review, interdependence is the extent to which tasks in a network require various elements, e.g. departments and people, to work with one another [adapted from 23]. Based on our literature review, interdependence is the extent to which the tasks and decisions in a network require various resources (e.g. departments, people) to work with one another [23]. The authors of [24] described three types of dependencies, namely flow, sharing, and fit dependencies. Flow dependencies relate to an activity that produces a resource that is used by another activity. Next, sharing dependencies occur when multiple activities share the same resources. Finally, fit dependencies arise when multiple activities collectively produce a single resource. These types of dependencies can be managed by means of coordination mechanisms. As different dependencies may occur, different types of coordination mechanisms can be identified, e.g. standardization, coordination by plan, and coordination by mutual adjustment [25]. Standardization can be characterized as establishing routines to coordinate activities. Orchestration is a particular kind of coordination form and is studied in various domains such as value chains [26], business services [27], eGovernment [28], and relationships [29]. We define orchestration as the ability of a firm to manage interdependency challenges by means of coordinating process steps [adapted from 26]. While coordination uses a process view to identify interdependencies and allocate relevant mechanisms, orchestration, however, focuses on the ability of organizations to apply mechanisms to manage interdependencies.

The goal of an orchestrator, which can be perceived as an organizational entity, is to ensure that different organizational dispersed units cooperate in a concerted fashion [26]. With regard to an orchestrator two modes of operation can be distinguished, namely: customer servicing mode and service delivery mode, consecutively characterized as front office and back office [30].

10.2.3 Resource-dependency theory

RDT addresses the organizational necessity of firms to adapt to environmental uncertainty while coping with complex interdependencies [31,32]. Essentially, the central proposition of the RDT is that organizations must be able to procure critical resources from the external environment in order to survive. Access to external resources is a widely adopted strategy and a primary stimulus for organizations to engage in interactions with others [33]. RDT focuses on a wide range of choice behaviors that can be applied by organizations to manage external dependencies. Examples include coping with interdependencies, adaptation, reduction of uncertainty, and power and influence [25,31]. As multisourcing relationships include various parties, the dependency between multiple actors becomes important as they influence each other. Over time, this may result in changes of power and dependency in the relationship between organizations. However, multisourcing relationships are based on the premise that the nature of exchanges (e.g. information, services) between clients and vendors is determined by the client perception of their inter-organizational dependence (power) and the degree of uncertainty within the multisourcing environment. Therefore, it can be argued that in cases of a high interdependence between client and vendors parties have to invest in building relationships to decrease the level of uncertainty. Related to a multisourcing relationship, the client holds a contractual position in the network and influences the number of vendors to be governed (span of control). The determinant of power is dominant in shaping outsourcing relationships. Therefore, we will use this view in our research.

10.3 Research approach

Since empirical research related to governing multisourcing relationships is limited, the aim of this research is to develop a better understanding in this field. Due to the complex nature of multisourcing relationships, we opted for an exploratory, case-study–based research. This would gain us a deep understanding of the phenomenon under study [34]. Case study research is one of the most common qualitative methods used in the field of information systems [35]. A case study approach does not allow statistical generalization since the number of entities as described in case studies is too small. However, our main objective is to expand and generalize theories (analytical generalization) and not to enumerate frequencies (statistical generalization) [34]. Applying a semi-structured interview method as a research instrument is useful to select data and information for exploratory-descriptive studies that may be extended later [36]. We use two main criteria to select a multisourcing case study. First, we identify the aspect of type of Information Technology (IT) services as IT multisourcing arrangements are perceived to be complex due to interdependencies between parties [12]. Depending on the vendors' type of IT services (e.g. IT infrastructure, application maintenance, application development), governance in delivering services may vary. Second, the role of each vendor in a multisourcing relationship can differ. Some vendors are only responsible for the delivery of their own services while others are assigned with the responsibility to integrate IT services delivered by various vendors, which, however, affects the degree of coordination. We selected a case study in which a client outsourced their entire IT function to the market and multiple vendors are involved in the provisioning of IT services.

As such a large variety of IT services were outsourced (selection criterion one). Three global IT vendors have been contracted in which one operated as IT infrastructure vendor and the other two as IT service integrators (selection criterion two). All vendors are acting in the field of IT outsourcing specifically.

10.3.1 Data collection and analysis

We collected data by conducting in-depth interviews with both the client's and the vendors' staff members, including IT executives, transition managers, service delivery managers, contract manages, and experts positioned across the firm. In this way, we avoid 'elite bias'. The interviews were semi-structured and based on a protocol that included open questions on how to improve governance. In total, we conducted 19 interviews and all interviewed participants had been engaged in the multisourcing relationship. This was to ensure internal consistency within the multisourcing landscape. As the interviews were confidential, we anonymized the company names as listed in Table 10.1. The varying hierarchical levels of the

Table 10.1 Case study characteristics

Party	Focus	Geographical position	Type of services	Start of the contract	Length of the contract	Generation	Number of FTE transferred
Client		Europe	Complete IT function is outsourced			Second generation	800
Vendor 1	Focus on infrastructure	Top 3 global vendor	IT infrastructure service desk, workplace automation	2009	Seven years	Extended contract period (first time)	350
Vendor 2	Service integrator (old world)	Top 3 European vendor	Application development, Application maintenance	2010	Five years	Extended contract period (first time)	450
Vendor 3	Service integrator (new world)	Top 5 Indian vendor	Application development, Application maintenance	2008	Five years	First contract	N.A.

interviewed staff members prevent potential limitations of the evolving phenomenon from arising. The interviewees were asked to describe their role in the multisourcing relationship and specifically how they dealt with governance. Interviews varied from 60 minutes to 90 minutes in duration. Additional information was gathered from three contracts, governance schedules, and satisfaction reports. All the interviews were then transcribed, and the transcripts were sent to the participants to be confirmed.

When executing our qualitative research concept, maps are used to guide us through the process of data analysis. Since knowledge is fairly nonlinear, concepts can be seen as organized networks. By selecting and organizing relevant information, we are able to identify links between concepts, so that we can fathom the data [35]. Interview data of the staff members were translated into concept maps. As a result of the coding process, we were able to create more insight in relevant concepts and relationships.

10.4 Findings

10.4.1 Context of the multisourcing case study

The case study is positioned in the retail market, and concerns a company (the client) that provides services in Europe. Importantly, the client's business processes are highly dependent on IT to fulfill customers' need in time (e.g. ordering systems, logistic function, replenishment, retail payments). Today, the client is expanding their portfolio as online business is growing while new store formats are developed to extend the range of products. In order to retain their competitive position in the market the client had to decrease their IT cost level. To accomplish this, they decided to outsource various IT functions to the market. In the sourcing ecosystem, the client holds a dominant position toward three key vendors. Vendor V1 is responsible for IT infrastructure services that are geographically dispersed among various data centers. Vendor V2, who acts as a service integrator, provides services related to various legacy applications, also called the 'old world'.

Next, Vendor V3 also acts as service integrator, however, related to Cloud services enabling applications which support the new business strategy (e.g. online shopping). In addition, the client extended the ecosystem by contracting 60 smaller IT vendors all acting as subcontractors providing services to the three key vendors (see Figure 10.1, label S). The empirical setting for this case study focuses on collaboration between the client and the three core IT vendors.

10.4.2 Governance between the client and its vendors

10.4.2.1 Inter-organizational governance

While studying the multisourcing relationship, we found that the focus of the client was on utilizing resources at the lowest costs and, in doing so, paid insufficient attention to the coordination of the multi-vendor relationship. This immaturity is reflected in a lack of a coherent inter-organizational structure, strategy, and plan related to the coordination of various roles, activities, and responsibilities of each party. Addressing the determinant strategy, we find that the way in which the client governs the multisourcing landscape is ambiguous. For example, the execution of IT infrastructure-related IT tasks can be allocated to Vendor 1 or Vendor 2, depending on the client employees' knowledge and experience. This resulted in fierce discussions between vendors and the client regarding the boundaries of IT services. Addressing the inter-organizational structure of the multisourcing landscape, we find that at

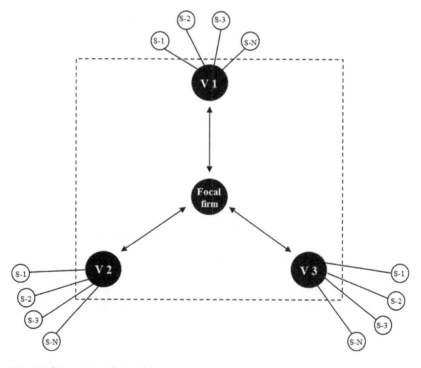

Figure 10.1 Multisourcing relationships

the start of the relationship the client did not describe the position of each vendor and third parties and their mutual relationship. In particular, our analysis of documentation revealed that the responsibilities and boundaries of vendors' service agreements, including their position and mandates in the landscape, were vague with regard to the exact type of IT service that is to be provided.

> Previously, our organizational structure and strategic plan was weak as we exchanged vendors quite often. We created more stability in the landscape as each vendor is authorized to deliver IT services within an IT domain for two years. In turn, vendors are more willing to set up OLA's with their competitors to ensure end-to-end delivery of IT services.
>
> *(Source: CIO client)*

> The client have setup a strategic plan that describes the boundaries of each IT domain but this plan is not sufficient. In fact, the existing plan can be seen as high level with limited details, actually it's a workflow diagram that lacks concrete activities such as organizational roles and responsibilities.
>
> *(Source: Account executive Vendor 2)*

The absence of a coherent strategic plan describing the position, role, and mandate of each party resulted in fierce discussions about service provisioning between the client and its vendors over time. For example, we found that the deployment of software technology partners (e.g. Oracle, Microsoft) by the client is based on an ad hoc approach. Vendor 2 and Vendor 3, which provide application services, are responsible for the deployment of software and the relationship with technology partners. However, when initiating new IT projects, the client decided to choose for technology partners directly without any involvement of Vendor 2 and Vendor 3. Consequently, the client's ad hoc decision-making in this area resulted in multiple misunderstandings and debates between client and vendors and between vendors and technology partners with regard to technical and financial issues. Importantly, both Vendor 1 and Vendor 2 were selected originally to develop and implement software technology projects, which is conflicting with the client's selection of software technology partners to fulfill these activities.

Addressing the determinant of roles, our study revealed a lack of governance agreements. The roles and corresponding responsibilities of the employees of the client and the vendors are not described and implemented. At the start of each client-vendor relationship, all parties had the intention to set up clear roles and responsibilities to govern the relationship. However, interviews revealed that due to a lack of management attention the client and vendors did not address this aspect in a proper way. In addition, we found that no regular meeting structures had been developed and implemented consciously. Meetings between the client and each vendor were organized ad hoc, while inter-organizational meetings were bypassed. The result was insufficient alignment between parties as developments on the side of both client and vendor were not shared and assessed on their impact by each party.

Figure 10.2 depicts the formal and informal inter-organizational dependencies within the multisourcing landscape. The straight lines (A) represent the formal contractual and relational agreements between the focal firm and its vendors. The dotted lines (B) represent the informal service agreements between Vendor V1 toward Vendor 2 and Vendor 3.

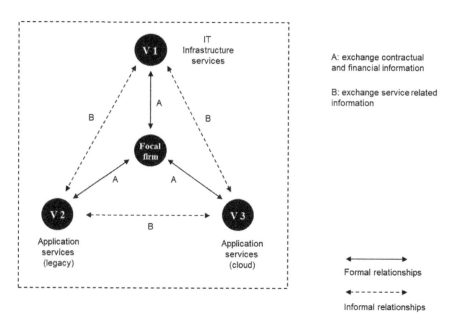

Figure 10.2 Inter-organizational governance

10.4.2.2 *Contractual governance*

Our interviews show that the way in which the client coordinates the multisourcing relationship is predominantly based on the financial contract and targets related to each vendor. This approach leads to a lack of inter-organizational governance while relational and substantive aspects were neglected. We found that vendors were reluctant in allocating resources to staff future projects in advance. When projects were initiated, vendors addressed severe staffing problems as resources were not available. This way of working resulted in a delay of projects and it affected the service delivery performance negatively. Moreover, fierce financial disputes arose between the client and vendors that were related to the scope and the content of the contracts (e.g. changes are in scope or out of scope of the contract).

> The contracts are fiercely negotiated meaning that we got the best price. However, the vendors established their 'B teams' as their resources are cheaper. Too much focus on getting the lowest price resulted in strict rules from the vendors. For instance, each change is discussed from a financial perspective (in or out of scope of the contract).
>
> *(Source: Program manager client)*

As the client focuses on achieving financial benefits based on the agreed contracts, we perceived an opportunistic behavior. This behavior is reflected, for instance, in setting up short-term contracts with technology partners instead of doing business with their selected key vendors. The client's motivation to use this approach was to create a competitive market exploiting external resources offering services at lowest cost. When studying the contracts between the client and the selected vendors, we noticed that the contracts and the related schedules were only described on a high level. Many details were postponed to the transition phase. Examples include the service scope, roles, responsibilities, meeting structures, and steering mechanisms. Based on the interviews, it became clear that the fierce time pressure during the outsourcing selection and the contract negotiation phase resulted in incomplete contacts.

Importantly, these inconsistencies were not repaired during the transition phase or the service delivery phase. Interestingly, we found that the contracts with the three key vendors include a clause that allows the client to terminate the contract within 60 days.

> Related to the degree of contractual flexibility, we set up contracts with a strong focus on flexibility. There are no long term commitments agreed with our vendors. The contracts include a clause in which we agreed a 60 day termination period with no financial commitments. Vendor 3 wanted to agree a multiyear BIG contract, however, we do not give anything more than 60 days.
>
> *(Source: IT manager client)*

> Contracts run out on short notice (60 days) with no single commitment from the client. The client is micro managing the contracts, resources and utilization. Their culture and behaviour in the retail business is insufficient to manage and coordinate IT, instead it's a hostile environment!
>
> *(Source: global head of software Vendor 3)*

The client's rationale is that if a vendor is not able to provide a sound service performance over time they have the right to select and switch to a new vendor. Although the vendors agreed to this clause, their perception is that the client is repressing the relationship strictly focusing on achieving financial benefits. As a result, the vendor has a short-term view and is not prepared to commit resources and invest in long-term commitments.

10.4.2.3 Relational governance

Interviews show that less attention is paid to investing in the relationship between the client and its vendors over time. We did not find evidence that the personal bonds between the client and the vendor counterparts were strengthened. In contrast to building relationships, both the client and the vendors focused on controlling the contracts in a rigid way. Particularly, the relationship between the client and its vendors creates a tension as the client plays a dominant role by playing off the vendors against each other. For example, the client's approach to select technology partners instead of the key vendors under study decreased the degree of trust on the vendors' side. The absence of regular meetings and the strict contractual clauses underpin the lack of relational governance. Consequently, the lack of trust on strategic level of both the client and the vendors affects the operational performance of the vendors significantly as the vendors are not willing to allocate employees in view of uncertain projects with regard to services or projects.

> There is a lack of trust in the relationship towards our vendors. The basic attitude of all parties, however, is based on mistrust instead of trust. The type of deal is financially driven which is an influencing factor that lead to this lack of trust.
>
> *(Source CIO client)*

> There is an unbalance regarding power and dependency as we apply a strong power behavior. We have the opinion that we know how IT services should be provided by the vendors instead of managing the delivery and relationships.
>
> *(Source: Sourcing manager client)*

Since the start of the relationship limited attention was given to improving the relationship with the client. Recently, we introduced the third relation manager. From an operational view, too much time is spend that refer to issues of the past. It's all about facts versus expectations.

(Source: Account executive Vendor 1)

Although the contract includes governance mechanisms for conflict resolution (e.g. escalation mechanisms), the client did not intervene in service boundary conflicts between vendors. The client has the opinion that vendors have to solve any conflicts themselves. Hence, the relationship between the client and vendors was negatively influenced as the degree of trust between parties further decreased.

10.4.3 Governance between vendors

10.4.3.1 Inter-organizational governance

The absence of a coherent strategic inter-organizational structure that describes the position, role, and mandate of each party in the multisourcing landscape had a severe impact on the governance between vendors. As the number of key vendors increased over time (see Table 10.1), the lack of the client's inter-organizational coordination between the vendors leads to ad hoc governance between vendors. Clear strategic roles and division of responsibilities were missing.

Today, there are no back-to-back agreements (OLAs) that are related to the cooperation between parties. This lead to disproportional alignment between client and vendors, which increases the costs.

(Source: Account executive Vendor 1)

We do cooperate with other vendors on an operational level. At a strategic level, however, we do not have in-depth relationships and discuss strategic developments.

(Source: Account executive Vendor 2)

The multisourcing culture is 100% better compared to the start because vendors implemented operational IT processes. This lead to more successful delivery of IT services.

(Source Delivery program manager Vendor 3)

Importantly, we find multiple interdependencies between the vendors as service provisioning is interrelated. Vendor 1 is responsible for IT infrastructure services while Vendor 2 and Vendor 3 are responsible for managing applications running on top of the infrastructure. As clear boundaries of IT services were not described, multiple misunderstandings occurred with regard to maintenance activities, which resulted in a decrease of service performance toward the client. We found that in the case of the client's request to configure applications Vendor 1 as well as Vendor 2 did not respond as each had the impression that the other party would take the action. Interestingly, while clear client directions were missing the vendors initiated inter-vendor meetings to align and coordinate their service provisioning. As a result of multiple disputes between all parties, the client developed a strategy to improve the coordination of the multisourcing landscape. A strategic multisourcing framework was created that determines the scope of IT services and the way of working related to major IT projects of each vendor for a period of two years. As a result, the vendors experienced more stability as the roles, responsibilities, and mandates of each party on a strategic level were described unambiguously. Moreover, the interviews revealed that the degree of trust between the client and the vendors increased significantly.

We found a strong interdependency between Vendor 2 and Vendor 3 equal toward Vendor 1 and other third parties due to their role as service integrator. As Vendor 2 and Vendor 3 are not in control of the contracts with these parties, both vendors experienced various conflicts in delivering an end-to-end service performance to the client.

> Agreements regarding end-to-end services do not fit. The client holds us responsible for meeting end-to-end KPIs. However, SLAs provided by various parties (e.g. other vendors, third parties) are not aligned. As the client is responsible for managing the contract to all parties, they are responsible for SLA alignment.
>
> *(Source: Manager service integration Vendor 2)*

Due to their role as contract owner the client is responsible to verify if the service conditions (e.g. SLAs, KPIs) as part of the end-to-end services are reflected in the contracts of Vendor 1 and third parties. We find that the client neglected this activity, which resulted in a breach of service level agreements (SLAs) of Vendor 2 and Vendor 3 regularly. In fact, Vendor 2 and Vendor 3 are dependent on their persuasiveness to other parties to ensure a sound service performance. Our research shows that informal relationships with other parties become more important when compared to contractual relationships.

10.4.3.2 Contractual governance

Studying the contracts we find that the structure of all contracts is strictly based on dyadic relationships. Since Vendor 2 and Vendor 3 are dependent on Vendor 1 in supporting the client's digital end-to-end processes, their mutual interdependencies are described in the contract. Interviews revealed that the service delivery of multiple vendors and third parties is stressed regularly as various SLAs are breached resulting in a decrease of the service performance to the client. We noticed that during the outsourcing relationship Vendor 2 and Vendor 3 set up Operational Level Agreements (OLAs) with Vendor 1 and third parties as a way of working to improve the end-to-end service performance. After implementing these OLAs, the satisfaction reports showed an increase of service performance. This was executed independent of the client's involvement.

> The contracts are dyadic by nature, there are no mutual agreements to exchange services between vendors. We experience a lot of informal relationships between vendors to deliver services in a successful manner. We also experience compensation behavior as vendors fulfill tasks that should be done by the client.
>
> *(Source: Account manager Vendor 1)*

> We experienced that vendors are also competitors. They all fight against each other in achieving to win a piece of the landscape at the cost of their competitors.
>
> *(Source: CIO client)*

> Various contracts such as with Vendor 1 and Vendor 3 are contradictory as they have an overlap. This resulted in fierce disputes towards Vendor 3 about projects, responsibilities

and off course fees. We even defined a non-aggression pact. Later, we improved our mutual relationship with Vendor 3 to settle our disagreements and focused on improving the delivery of services to the client.

(Source: Account executive Vendor 1)

To minimize management attention, the client decided to consolidate the multisourcing landscape by decreasing the number of subcontractors (60 parties). Their services will be divided among the three vendors under study. Interestingly, we found that during the selection phase of Vendor 1 the client primarily transferred staff to Vendor 1 that focuses on application maintenance tasks, whereas Vendor 2 also performed these types of task. However, as the boundaries between the vendors' service scope are not well defined and described conflicts arose with regard to the question which vendor was officially responsible for service provisioning. After two years of discussions, both the client and Vendor 1 and Vendor 2 decided to retransfer staff of Vendor 1 to Vendor 2 to streamline the operational application maintenance tasks. This retransferred activity contributed to clear service boundaries, and, subsequently, an increased service performance.

10.4.3.3 Relational governance

As a result of unclear strategic roles and responsibilities and lack of structure (e.g. meetings, forecasts), vendors experienced a strong degree of distrust between each other. In particular, the vendors' inability or unwillingness to cooperate in delivering IT services to the client affected their relationship negatively. With regard to the mutual relationship between the vendors, our study demonstrates that Vendor 2 focuses on solving problems first while Vendor 1 requires the client's approval first before solving the problem. This example shows that the employees' behavior with regard to organizational procedures influences the relationship toward the client and between the vendors. With regard to conflict resolution, we find that during the first two years of the relationship Vendor 1 applied an aggressive sales strategy at the cost of their competitors. Their behavior resulted in multiple conflicts between the vendors.

The key vendors are too focused on fulfilling their own tasks which result in much finger pointing between parties. Actually, more interaction between vendors is needed as they are mutually dependent on each other. That's why multisourcing requires tactical coordination. Moreover, we have the opinion that the client should manage the interaction between vendors which is not set up right now.

(Source: Account manager Vendor 1)

As the client was not willing to interfere in these type of conflicts, Vendor 2 and Vendor 3 limited their cooperation with Vendor 1, which resulted in a decrease of service performance of Vendor 1. This shows that multisourcing relationships between vendors are intertwined as IT services involve multiple vendors. Ultimately, the client did intervene by means of a strategy change creating clarity for each party. As a result, conflicts between vendors decreased while the level of trust increased. In turn, the vendors' willingness to cooperate improved positively.

10.5 Discussion

Applying governance, CT, and RDT as a lens, we investigate the types of dependencies and subsequently the coordination mechanisms that are used to manage interdependencies.

Related to the governance area between the client and the vendors, our research shows a lack of coordination between all parties. The various roles, activities, and responsibilities of each party were not clear. Studying the interview analyses and contracts, we found that the client is coordinating the delivery of IT services by the vendors based on dyadic relationships. Related to IT service delivery, a flow type of dependency is used for managing the dependencies between clients and vendors. For instance, technical application resources provided by the vendors are used by the client's resources to use applications from a functional perspective. As a result of the indistinctness with regard to multiple interdependencies between parties, the client and the vendors experience coordination problems. The sharing and fit type of dependency of [25] categorization was not found. Consequently, strategic and tactical information was not shared between the client and the vendors, resulting in a deterioration of service performance. Coordination mechanisms such as coordination structure, strategy, and plan were not defined. Importantly, the authors of [37] argue that coordination is essential to leverage digital resources in building a digital strategy and create value. The coordination mechanism that is used by the client for an individual vendor is based on standardization of work processes to support service delivery. Only routines and work instructions are established. The coordination of IT activities that reflects the relationship between the client and the vendors, however, reveals that no particular coordination mechanism is used. Based on our analyses of the type of dependency used, we conclude that the coordination mechanisms in place are not suitable for coordinating the dependencies. Coordination by standardization of work processes is not able to deal with ad hoc situations [38]. We argue that to apply coordination in a more structured way the mechanism coordination by plan will deal with unclear responsibilities, functions, and roles. Moreover, the coordination mechanism mutual adjustment would fit in the relationship between the client and the vendors to deal with unanticipated events. Applying these mechanisms may decrease the vagueness of the vendors' strategic role and position and, therefore, improve service performance to the client.

Addressing the governance area that includes mutual activities between the vendors, we identified two types of dependencies, namely (1) sharing type of dependency and (2) fit type of dependency. There is a sharing type of dependency between Vendor 1 and both other vendors with regard to the exchange of information. We found that at an operational level information was exchanged by employees of Vendor 2 and Vendor 3 to prevent underperformance of their IT services. According to the literature [39], this type of dependence seems consistent since multiple activities (e.g. application maintenance, IT infrastructure) share the same resource (e.g. information). Next, a fit type of dependency is found that is related to the integration of end-to-end services by Vendor 2 and Vendor 3. As Vendor 2 and Vendor 3 were held responsible by the focal firm for service integration tasks, their employees shared technical information among all parties that was related to application work-a-rounds, reporting information, and IT tooling. This is also consistent with literature [24] as a fit type of dependency is related to multiple activities (e.g. information and services from separate vendors) that collectively produce a single resource (e.g. digital end-to-end process and service). Our analysis shows that originally no specific coordination mechanisms were used to exchange information between the vendors. The vendors experienced severe coordination problems in managing mutual interdependencies resulting in a breach of service levels regularly. During the outsourcing relationship, vendors established various types of coordination mechanisms independently of the client. Two types of coordination mechanisms were introduced. Coordination by plan was implemented to exchange information related to knowledge management while the type of mutual adjustment was used to support the integration of end-to-end services. Remarkably, the client did not play a role in encouraging the vendors to establish coordination mechanisms. There was no cooperative relationship between the client and the vendor as the client's financial measurements were leading. This finding is consistent with literature as a high level of interdependence indicates a strong cooperative relationship [40,41]. Based on our analysis of the vendor interviewees, an explanation can be found in the client's rationale to focus on achieving financial benefits and apply a procurement strategy to their IT vendors. This is consistent with literature related to outsourcing non-core activities, such as retail suppliers and facility service vendors (e.g. cleaning, security), that focus less on strengthening the relationship and creating loyalty [42] as a means to improve service delivery. The overall case study findings are summarized in Table 10.2.

Interviews show a lack of both client and vendors orchestration capability to govern the relationships. We did not find evidence that each party established a dedicated organizational entity (e.g. orchestrator) to manage tasks, cross-functional processes, allocating resources and manage conflicting goals. Essentially, all parties governed these tasks as regular tasks similar to internal governance tasks. This lack of orchestrating entity may explain the governance challenges as identified between client and vendors and between vendors. The results of our study identify that the implementation of an orchestrator, related coordination mechanisms, and regular adaptation are perceived to be critical factors. Client interviewees explained that at the start of the multisourcing arrangement their opinion was to manage the dyadic relationships toward the vendors as high-level service boundaries were determined. However, practice revealed that interdependencies between client and vendors and between vendors had to be governed intensively (e.g. services, architecture, finance). We argue that each party should apply a holistic view with regard to multisourcing relationships, and implement an organizational entity to orchestrate governance-related tasks. Hence, an organizational entity forms a prerequisite to limit governance issues and create an opportunity to cater for digitalization effectively.

Using the concept of the RDT, first we focus on the construct power-dependency and subsequently on the construct uncertainty. Addressing the construct power-dependency we

Table 10.2 Case study findings related to coordination

Governance area	Coordination focus area	Example	Type of relationship	Type of dependency	Coordination mechanism
Area 1: between client and vendor	Client and single vendor	Providing a single services (e.g. AD, AM, service desk, IT infrastructure)	Dyadic	Flow	Standardization
	Client and multiple vendors	Generic information sharing (e.g. strategy, policies, risks)	Triadic	Flow	N.A.
Area 2: between vendors	Multiple vendors working together	Application and IT infrastructure alignment (e.g. knowledge management)	Triadic	Sharing	Coordination by plan
	Multiple vendors working together	Vendors B and C act as service integrators providing end-to-end services	Triadic	Fit	Mutual adjustment

found that as the client is responsible for managing the interdependencies between the vendors, their position can be described as powerful. This means that their hierarchical level is strongly influencing their organizational position in the multisourcing landscape [43,44]. On the one hand, the vendors' solutions are relatively unique due to the degree of customization and the provisioning of end-to-end services. On the other hand, the vendors perceive the client's account as attractive due to their annual revenue and position in the market.

However, when terminating the contracts switching costs for both the client and the vendors are high as their transaction costs will increase due to the search for alternatives and initiating a transition. Remarkably, the example of short-term contract termination shows that the contractual exit barrier between the client and the vendors is low in some areas, whereas other exit barriers are high. A long-term outsourcing relationship having low exit barriers is inconsistent with literature [41,42]. An explanation of our findings might be that due to their contracts and encouraging competition among vendors the client perceives their position as power dominant while they characterize the vendors' position as dependent. Interviews with the vendors' representatives reveal that their IT services are essential for the client's digital business strategy. Examples include online ordering, distribution, and replenishment. When the vendors' IT services underperform, the client's businesses might be at risk resulting in a decrease of their customer satisfaction. From this view, the vendors' position can be considered as power dominant too, equal to the client's power position.

10.6 Conclusion

Although companies are more and more using multisourcing relationships, empirical research on relationships remains scarce. Our study aims to contribute by partially filling this gap. Multisourcing is a multi-faceted domain, which needs to be tackled using a variety of theories and methods in which outsourcing vendors and clients are dependent on each other that can be understood by the RDT. The use of resources needs to be managed, which requires coordination mechanisms. Coordination mechanisms should be designed for the management and governance of clients and vendors in multisourcing relationships. The exchange of services and information of both the client and the vendors are intertwined, and, as such, are highly interdependent on each other that require governance mechanisms. Governance should achieve the objectives of both parties to avoid conflicts.

We contribute to the outsourcing literature by creating insight in how client and vendors deal with multisourcing relationships and the exposition of the way in which multisourcing arrangements are governed and orchestrated. Our findings illustrate that both contractual and relational governance are needed to manage the complex arrangement among the parties. Contractual governance should reflect interdependencies, not only between client and vendors, but also between vendors. Clear responsibilities need to be defined to avoid that problems are not tackled or that it is to clear who is in charge. Relationship procedures and processes need to be in place to coordinate the dependencies. Also, conflict resolution mechanisms are needed as part of the governance mechanisms. A lack of coherent governance mechanisms results in multiple misunderstandings between client and vendors and between vendors, which lowers performance. The high interdependence seems to be best managed by creating strong ties between vendors and client in which all the parties need to invest. Effective governance mechanisms will facilitate smooth communication and can decrease potential uncertainties, while the degree of mutual trust between parties can be strengthened. To make multisourcing a success an orchestration entity at each party is needed, which requires more research on governing relationships.

Our research also aims to contribute to the vendor's best practices. Most fundamentally, our research demonstrates that clients have to develop a coherent strategic plan describing the position, role, and mandate of each party. This requires an inter-organizational governance structure that needs to be monitored over time to prevent fierce discussions about service provisioning between the client and its vendors. Moreover, the client plays an important role in creating a power and dependency balance between all parties. In doing so, the degree of trust between parties will increase that contribute to the performance of the arrangement as a whole. From a vendor perspective, mutual operational agreements (OLAs) have to be set up and governed to improve end-to-end service performance. In addition, we argue that vendors invest in employees' behavior to solve problems first and settle formal approvals later. This way of working influences the relationship toward clients and other vendors positively. The ability and willingness to adapt to changing client circumstances is a prerequisite for retaining business and staying competitive.

We conclude that governing multisourcing relationships requires a view in which the dependencies between multiple vendors are also coordinated. This study contributes to clients and vendors involved in IT multisourcing relationships in that it increases their awareness of the multiple factors that affect the way in which these relationships are governed. Clients and vendors may benefit from the insights of this research by setting up inter-organizational structures and corresponding contracts. From a managerial perspective, our results suggest that assessing the governance of a multisourcing relationship is a prerequisite for both clients and vendors to meet the objectives as stated at the start. Our research demonstrates that clear governance structures and mechanisms and an orchestrating entity are seen as critical in multisourcing relationships to support a client in applying a digital business strategy.

References

1. Mithas, S., Smith, R.H., Tafti, A., Michell, W.: How a Firm's Competitive Environment and Digital Strategic Posture Influence Digital Business Strategy. *MIS Quarterly*. 37, 2, 511–536 (2013).
2. Oshri, I., Kotlarski, J., Willcocks, L.P.: *The Handbook of Global Outsourcing and Offshoring*. Palgrave Macmillan, London (2009).
3. Beulen, E., Ribbers, P., Roos, J.: *Managing IT Outsourcing. Governance in Global Partnerships*. 2nd ed., Routledge, London (2011).
4. Dibbern, J., Goles, T., Hirschheim, R., Jayatilaka, B.: Information Systems Outsourcing: A Survey and Analysis of the Literature. *Data Base Adv. Inf. Syst*. 34, 4, 6–102 (2004).
5. Bharadwaj, A., El Sawy, O.A., Pavlou, P.A., Venkatraman, N.: Digital Business Strategy: Toward a Next Generation of Insights. *MIS Quarterly*. 37, 2, 471–482 (2013).
6. Bapna, R., Barua, A., Mani, D., and Mehra, A.: Cooperation, Coordination, and Governance in Multisourcing: An Agenda for Analytical and Empirical Research. *Inf. Res. Syst*. 21, 4, 785–795 (2010).
7. Weill, P., Ross, J.: *IT Governance: How Top Performers Manage IT Decision Rights for Superior Results*. Harvard Business School Press, Boston, MA (2004).
8. El Sawy, O. A., Pereira, F.: *Business Modelling in the Dynamic Digital Space: An Ecosystem Approach*. Springer, Heidelberg (2013).
9. Plugge, A.G., Janssen, W.F.W.A.H.: Governance of Multivendor Outsourcing Arrangements: A Coordination and Resource Dependency View. In Oshri, I., Kotlarsky, J., Willcocks, L.P. (eds.), *Governing Sourcing Relationships*, LNBIP 195, pp. 78–97, Springer-Verlag Berlin, Heidelberg (2014).
10. Herz, T. Ph., Hamel, F., Uebernickel, F., Brenner, W.: Deriving a Research Agenda for the Management of Multisourcing Relationships Based on a Literature Review. In AMCIS 2010 Proceedings, paper 357 (2010).
11. Su, N., Levina, N.: Global Multisourcing Strategy: Integrating Learning from Manufacturing into IT Service Outsourcing. *IEEE Trans. Eng. Mgt*. 58, 4, 717–729 (2011).

12. Wiener, M., Saunders, C.: Force Coopetition in IT Multisourcing. *J. Strat. Inf. Syst.* 23, 210–225 (2014).

13. Lioliou, E., Zimmermann, A., Willcocks, L.P., Gao, L.: Formal and Relational Governance in IT Outsourcing: Substitution, Complementarity and the Role of the Psychological Contract. *Inf. Syst. J.* 24, 503–535 (2014).

14. Lee, Y., Cavusgil, S. T.: Enhancing Alliance Performance: The Effects of Contractual-Based Versus Relational-Based Governance. *J. Bus. Res.* 59, 8, 896–905 (2006).

15. Rai, A., Keil, M., Hornyak, R., Wüllenweber, K.: Hybrid Relational-Contractual Governance for Business Process Outsourcing. *J. Mgt. Inf. Syst.* 29, 2, 213–256 (2012).

16. Macneil, I. R.: *The New Social Contract: An Inquiry into Modern Contractual Relations.* Yale University Press, New Haven, CT, and London (1980).

17. Xiao, J., Xie, K., Hu, Q.: Inter-Firm IT Governance in Power-Imbalanced Buyer–Supplier Dyads: Exploring How It Works and Why It Lasts. *Eur. J. Inf. Syst.* 22, 5, 512–528 (2012).

18. Lacity, M.C., Khan, S.A., Willcocks, L.P.: A Review of the IT Outsourcing Literature: Insights for Practice. *J. Strat. Inf. Syst.* 18, 3, 130–146 (2009).

19. Kim, Y.J., Lee, J.M., Koo, C., Nam, K.: The Role of Governance Effectiveness in Explaining IT Outsourcing Performance. *Int. J. Inf. Mgt.* 33, 850–860 (2013).

20. Crowston, K., Osborn, C.: A Coordination Theory Approach to Process Description and Redesign. In Malone, T.W., Crowston, K., Herman, G.A. (eds.), *Organizing Business Knowledge.* MIT Press, Cambridge, MA (2003).

21. Malone, T.W., Crowston, K.: The Interdisciplinary Study of Coordination. *ACM Computing Surveys (CSUR).* 26, 1, 87–119 (1994).

22. Rockart, J.F., Short, J.E.: IT in the 1990s: Managing Organizational Interdependence. *Sl. Mgt. Rev.* 30, 2, 7–17 (1989).

23. Cheng, J.L.C.: Interdependence and Coordination in Organizations: A Role-System Analysis. *Acad. Mgt. J.* 26, 1, 156–162 (1983).

24. Malone, T.W., Crowston, K., Lee, J., Pentland, B., Dellarocas, C., Wyner, G., et al.: Tools for Inventing Organizations: Toward a Handbook of Organizational Processes. *Mgt. Sci.* 45, 3, 425–443 (1999).

25. Thompson, J.D.: *Organizations in Action.* McGraw-Hill, New York (1967).

26. Hinterhuber, A.: Value Chain Orchestration in Action and the Case of the Global Agrochemical Industry. *L. R. Plan.* 35, 6, 15–635 (2002).

27. Sadiq, W., Racca, F.: *Business Services Orchestration: The Hypertier of Information Technology.* Cambridge University Press, Cambridge (2004).

28. Janssen, M.F.W.H.A., Gortmaker, J., Wagenaar, R.W.: Web Service Orchestration in Public Administration: Challenges, Roles and Growth Stages. *Inf. Syst. Mgt.* 23, 2, 44–55 (2006).

29. Hurmelinna-Laukkanen, P., Olander, H., Blomqvist, K., Panfilii, V.: Orchestrating R&D Networks: Absorptive Capacity, Network Stability, and Innovation Appropriability. *Euro. Mgt. J.* 30, 6, 552–563 (2012).

30. Bovaird, T.: E-Government and E-Governance: Organizational Implications. In Khosrow-Pour, D. B. A. (eds.), *Practicing E-Government: A Global Perspective.* Idea Group Publishing, Hershey, PA, 43–61 (2005).

31. Pfeffer, J., Salancik, G.R.: *The External Control of Organizations.* Harper and Row, New York (1978).

32. Pfeffer, J., Salancik, G.R.: *The External Control of Organizations: A Resource Dependence Perspective.* 2nd ed. Stanford University Press, Stanford, CA (2003).

33. Nord, W.R.: The Study of Organizations through a Resource-Exchange Paradigm. In Gergen, K.J., Greenberg, M.S., Willis, R.H. (eds.), *Social Exchange. Advances in Theory and Practice*, pp. 119–139. Plenum Press, New York (1980).

34. Yin, R.K.: *Case Study Research: Design and Methods.* Sage Publications, London (2009).

35. Orlikowski, W.J., Iacono, C.S.: Research Commentary: Desperately Seeking the "IT" in IT Research – A Call to Theorizing the IT Artifact. *Inf. Syst. Res.* 12, 2, 121–134 (2001).

36. Denzin, N. K.: *The Research Act: A Theoretical Introduction to Sociological Methods.* McGraw-Hill, New York (1978).

37. Peppard, J., Ward, J.: *The Strategic Management of Information Systems: Building a Digital Strategy.* 4th Edition. Wiley, Chichester (2016).

38. Mintzberg, H.: *Structure in Fives: Designing Effective Organizations*. Prentice Hall Business Publishing, Englewood Cliffs, NJ (1983).
39. Malone, T.W., Crowston, K.: What Is Coordination Theory and How Can It Help Design Cooperative Work Systems? In Proceedings of the 1990 ACM Conference on Computer-Supported Cooperative Work, Los Angeles, CA, pp. 357–370 (1990).
40. Fink, R.C., Edelman, L.F., Hatten, K.J., James, W.L.: Transaction Cost Economics, Resource Dependency Theory, and Customer-Supplier Relationships. *Ind. Corp. Ch.* 15, 3, 497–529 (2006).
41. Gulati, R., Sytch, M.: Dependence Asymmetry and Joint Dependence in Interorganizational Relationships: Effects of Embeddedness on a Manufacturer's Performance in Procurement Relationships. *Adm. Sci. Q.* 52, 32–69 (2007).
42. Casciaro, T., Piskorski, M.J.: Power Imbalance, Mutual Dependence and Constraint Absorption: A Closer Look at Resource Dependency Theory. *Adm. Sci. Q.* 50, 167–199 (2005).
43. Brass, D. J.: Power in Organizations: A Social Network Perspective. In Moore, G., Witt, J.A. (eds.), *Research in Politics and Society. The Political Consequences of Social Networks*. JAI Press, Greenwich, CT, pp. 295–323 (1992).
44. Cendron, B.V., Jarvenpaa, S.L.: The Development and Exercise of Power by Leaders of Support Units in Implementing Information Technology-based Services. *J. Strat. Inf. Syst.* 10, 121–158 (2001).

11

KNOWLEDGE TRANSFER IN THE TRANSITION PHASE

Review of the literature and implications for digital business strategy and agility

Oliver Krancher

11.1 Introduction

Any outsourcing or offshoring project initially goes through a so-called transition phase, i.e., the phase during which the service is handed over to a new service delivery unit (SDU), which can be a vendor or a captive centre [1,2]. The key challenge in transitions is to enable the new SDU to take over the service as quickly as possible. This requires the transfer of critical resources, including hardware [3], software [4], and knowledge [5]. In many cases, the most difficult of these transfers is the transfer of knowledge, or knowledge transfer (KT). While KT was rather unproblematic in earlier domestic outsourcing arrangements in which clients transferred their IT staff, along with their knowledge, to vendors [6], staff transfer is not an option anymore in the age of offshoring. Engineers will not accept being relocated to another country while earning a fraction of their former salaries. Thus, in many contemporary sourcing arrangements, transitions involve a KT process during which the new SDU acquires knowledge from the incumbent SDU, i.e., the unit that provided the service thus far.

KT in the transition phase is one of the most critical [7] and least understood [8] aspects of sourcing arrangements. Managers often highly underestimate the efforts and challenges associated with KT in transitions, assuming that KT resembles other asset transfer processes [8,9]. It is not uncommon that managers plan transition phases of a few weeks [1,9] although managers experienced with transitions concede that it may take, in some instances, five years until the new SDU has acquired enough knowledge to display the performance levels of the incumbent SDU [9,10]. It is thus of little surprise that unanticipated costs for KT during transition are a principal reason for offshoring failures [11]. The critical nature of KT during transition is further elevated by the fact that transitions are no one-off in the life of a client. Many clients are engaging in their second- and third-generation outsourcing projects [2,12]. These organizations need to manage transitions each time they switch a vendor. The difficulty of switching vendors, rooted in the problematic nature of KT, is widely acknowledged in practice and theory. Willcocks and Lacity conclude that "the single most threatening aspect of outsourcing is the substantial switching costs" [13,4]. The most popular theoretical perspectives in outsourcing research, transaction cost economics [14], and the knowledge-based view [15] also emphasize the problematic nature of transferring knowledge (or human assets) to the new SDU. Hence, a thorough understanding of KT during transitions is essential both for practice and theory of outsourcing and offshoring.

The critical nature of KT during transitions has recently given rise to a vibrant stream of research on the topic. In light of this quickly increasing body of work, the goal of this chapter is twofold. First, it summarizes the current state of research about KT in the transition phase. Second, it theorizes how the two recent developments that are in the focus of this book, digital business strategies [16,17] and the increasingly important role of agility [18], are related to KT during transitions.

The chapter proceeds follows. It first summarizes two foundational literature streams on which research on KT during transitions draws heavily: the literatures on KT and expertise. It then provides a review of 35 published studies on KT in the transitions phase. The review focuses on four themes: (1) types of knowledge, (2) the mechanisms through which knowledge is transferred, (3) contextual factors that affect KT, and (4) the management of KT. The key findings from the review are (1) that knowledge about the software application is often the most critical knowledge, (2) that learning tasks are often the most effective KT mechanism, (3) that the knowledge recipient's expertise and distances of various types are important context factors, and (4) that these contextual factors affect the need for management efforts by the client. Building on the findings from the review, I discuss implications for KT during transition in the age of digital business strategies and the quest for agility. I present three specific recommendations: (1) cultivate embedded, concurrent-sourcing relationships, (2) organize KT around learning tasks and feedback, and (3) reduce the need for learning by hiding complexity. The discussion suggests that the effective execution and management of transitions will be vital for organizations that strive to leverage digital business strategies and agility while doing outsourcing or offshoring.

11.2 The foundations: the literatures on KT and expertise

Although research on KT in the transition phase draws on a variety of perspectives, two have been particularly influential: the broader literature on KT and the literature on expertise. This section provides brief summaries of these two literature streams.

11.2.1 The KT literature

With the increasing interest in knowledge-based perspectives on organizations since the 1990s [19,20], a substantial body of literature on KT has emerged [21,23]. Although this literature is not concerned with the specifics of the transition phase in outsourcing or offshoring projects, it has served as a foundation for much of the research on the transition phase.

Among the most influential studies are those by Garbriel Szulanski and Wenpin Tsai. Szulanski examined the transfer of best practices between different organizational units within a firm. He found that although the literature at the time emphasized motivational factors (i.e., the source's willingness to share knowledge and the recipient's willingness to accept knowledge), these factors hardly correlated with KT outcomes. Of much greater importance were knowledge-related factors, in particular the recipient's *absorptive capacity* (i.e., their ability to assimilate and apply new knowledge to commercial ends), *causal ambiguity* (i.e., uncertainty about the factors of production and their interaction), and *arduous relationships* (i.e., the extent to which the source-recipient relationship is laborious and distant) [21]. Szulanski also demonstrated that KT is a long process, rather than a one-off event, and that different factors come into play at different stages of the process [24]. The recipient's absorptive capacity was by far the most important factor during those stages (implementing, ramp-up, and integrating) in which the recipient is supposed to acquire knowledge. A key concept in Szulanski's arguments, as well as in the broader KT literature, is *tacit knowledge*, i.e., knowledge that is rooted in action and that cannot be transferred by communication [25]. Tacit knowledge contributes to causal ambiguity and it makes individual exchanges in embedded relationships important. Tsai [22] further delved into the role of relational factors. He demonstrated the importance of the *network position* that an organizational unit occupies within the organization. The more central the network position, the more does the unit benefit from KT, in particular if the absorptive capacity of the unit is high.

Subsequent studies on KT corroborated the importance of relational and knowledge-based characteristics. In a meta-analysis of research on KT, Van Wijk and Jansen [26] found that the factors with the highest correlations with KT outcomes were relational factors (trust, tie strength, a centralized network position, shared vision, cultural distance, and the number of relationships) and the knowledge-related factors of causal ambiguity and the recipient's absorptive capacity.

Although these findings provided important foundations for research on the transition phase in outsourcing and offshoring, two boundary conditions of the KT literature should be kept in mind when transferring its insights to outsourcing or offshoring settings. First, with few exceptions, the KT literature focuses on the collective knowledge that one organizational unit (or organization) possesses and that another organizational unit (or organization) attempts to acquire. Examples of *collective knowledge* include organizational routines and shared language [20,27]. Yet, without empirical examinations of transitions, it is not clear whether the most critical process in transitions is the transfer of collective knowledge or of individual knowledge, such as individual cognitive schemas of application domains and applications.

Second, the recipient in the KT literature is typically an organizational unit that, while attempting to acquire knowledge from another unit, is already competent in the execution of its task. It seeks additional knowledge in order to improve its performance, rather than in order to be able to perform its task in the first place. For instance, Szulanski examined how well a recipient unit was able to incorporate a specific best practice (a specific organizational routine) from another unit into its existing operations, not how a newly created recipient unit learned to perform its basic mission. In contrast to the KT literature, the literature on expertise shows greater interest in the individual level of analysis and in the initial acquisition of competence.

11.2.2 The expertise literature

Long before the recent interest in KT in organizational studies, the expertise literature has set out to explore the nature and the acquisition of expertise. At the heart of this research are the questions of *why* particular individuals excel in their performances of particular tasks (i.e., the nature of expertise) and *how* their superior ability has come about (i.e., the process of expertise acquisition).

Substantial insights into the organization of expertise came from the seminal work by William Chase and Hebert Simon on perception in chess [28]. They found that expert chess players did not outperform novice chess players in the task of memorizing and reproducing randomly created chess positions, while they strongly outperformed novices if the chess positions exhibited a typical pattern (i.e., a pattern that can occur in real chess plays). From this observation, Chase and Simon concluded that expertise does not result from superior general memory abilities but from *domain-specific cognitive schemas* that allow chunking information to familiar higher-order units. In the context of chess, these cognitive schemas include typical patterns of chess positions that chess masters learned over thousands of matches. Elaborating on these ideas, subsequent research has established that expertise resides in cognitive schemas that are (1) *highly organized* (i.e., many linkages between concepts), (2) *highly automated* (i.e., experts rely on the schemas in an effortless, immediate, intuitive way), and (3) *domain specific* (i.e., they enable superior performance only in a relatively narrow domain). For instance, illustrating organization, Adelson [29] found that novice programmers comprehend source code based on the syntax expressed in individual lines of codes, whereas expert programmers relate lines of codes into a hierarchy of concepts. In a similar vein, Doane et al. [30] found that UNIX experts had much greater knowledge of the relationships between UNIX structures than novices. This knowledge allowed UNIX experts to perform complex commands (composite commands), which novices failed to perform although they had been instructed on them. These examples show that experts differ from novices in the organization of their cognitive schemas: The experts' schemas include more relationships and more powerful higher-order concepts, which allows experts to aggregate information to higher-order chunks. Expert knowledge is not only well organized, but also highly automated. Chess grandmasters can devise excellent moves within few seconds, and, in simultaneous chess, they can defeat dozens of less experienced players at the same time. Illustrating the domain specificity of expertise, Voss et al. [31] found that expert chemists are essentially novices in solving political science problems, much like Chase and Simon's chess players are novices in the task of recalling randomized chess positions.

How do experts acquire their well-organized, automated cognitive schemas that enable them to quickly assimilate new information and solve complex problems within a domain? Expertise research concurs that it takes *long periods of deliberate practice* to become an expert [32,33]. Practice implies that learners need to perform the task in which they want to become experts in order to become more proficient. Deliberation means that learners need to reflect about their practice and to be coached about ways to improve it [32,33]. Long periods of practice imply that it typically takes 10 years, or 10,000 hours, of deliberate practice in a particular domain in order to become expert in it [32]. While practice, deliberation, and coaching are essential for acquiring expertise according to the expertise literature, codified information is not. As Ericsson and colleagues put it: "Knowledge management systems rarely, if ever, deal with what psychologists call knowledge" [34,3]. While most of the expertise literature has put greater emphasis on advanced skill acquisition (transition from proficient to expert level) than on early skill acquisition, research on cognitive load theory extends expertise research to the process of early skill acquisition. This research recommends scaffolded practice, i.e., learning based on simplified task tasks that match the learner's expertise level [35,36]. Scaffolded practice allows learners to engage in practice tasks while it reduces the risk of cognitive overload.

Table 11.1 compares key aspects of the KT and the expertise literatures. The literatures focus on different knowledge-acquiring (or learning) entities. While, with few exceptions [23], the KT literature focuses on organizational units that are already proficient in their task, the expertise literature focuses on individuals at various expertise levels. The literatures also differ in their conceptualizations of knowledge. While the KT literature views knowledge as pieces of explicit and tacit knowledge that entities may or may not possess, the expertise literature views knowledge as personal domain-specific cognitive schemas that vary in organization and automation. Both literature streams have contributed important knowledge. While the KT literature emphasizes context factors (e.g., absorptive capacity), the expertise literature emphasizes the mechanisms through which knowledge is acquired.

Table 11.1 Summary of the literatures on KT and expertise

	KT literature	*Expertise literature*
Entity that acquires knowledge	Organizational unit already proficient in its task	Individual at various expertise levels
Nature of knowledge	Explicit and tacit knowledge	Domain-specific cognitive schemas that vary in organization and automation
Key findings	The extent to which a unit acquires knowledge from another unit strongly depends on knowledge-related factors (e.g., absorptive capacity) and relational factors (e.g., network centrality).	Individuals acquire expertise through years of domain-specific deliberate practice, initially supplemented by scaffolding.

11.3 What we know about KT in the transition phase: a review of the literature

This section provides a review of the literature on KT in the transition phase in information systems (IS) research. Since the essence of transitions is to enable a new service delivery unit (SDU) to provide its service, the review is limited to studies that examine unidirectional KT to a new SDU (which may be a vendor or a captive centre). This excludes papers that examine KT from an SDU to the client [37,38] and papers that examine bidirectional knowledge flows [6,39,40]. Studies are included in the review if they give insights into the KT to a new SDU, even if the terms transition or KT are not used. Since the focus in this book lies on IS work, we included only studies that refer to IS tasks, such as application development, application maintenance, technical support, or infrastructure operations. Thirty-five papers met these criteria and were included into the review. All topic areas that are in the focus of this review are well represented in this literature sample, with most work focusing on KT management (23 studies), followed by KT mechanisms (19 studies), context factors (17 studies), and knowledge categories (14 studies).

11.3.1 Knowledge categories

The literature provides substantial insights into the types of knowledge that are transferred during transitions. Table 11.2 shows important knowledge categories, their definitions, and key findings related to the categories. While the first four categories refer to different types of knowledge, the subsequent categories refer to different domains of knowledge.

Individual vs. Collective Knowledge. Not surprisingly, research on transitions draws heavily on the different types of knowledge that are distinguished in the broader KT or outsourcing literature. A number of studies mention the distinction between individual and collective knowledge (see Table 11.2 for definitions). There is some agreement that both individual and collective knowledge matter in transitions [2,41,42]. For instance, at an individual level, engineers in the new SDU have to learn the structure of the existing software applications [1]. At a collective level, the new SDU builds up transactive memory systems (i.e., distributed knowledge about who knows what) [43]. Moreover, the client and the new SDU build up new collaboration processes [1]. While studies emphasize individual and collective knowledge, there is little research that systematically compares the criticality of individual with collective knowledge in transitions. Thus, it is unclear whether KT during transitions is often difficult because of challenges related to the acquisition of individual

Table 11.2 Findings related to types of knowledge

Knowledge categories	Definitions (examples in parentheses)	Key findings
Individual vs. collective	• Individual knowledge: Knowledge possessed by individuals (e.g., programming skills, an engineer's mental models about a particular software application) • Collective knowledge: Knowledge possessed by collective entities such as teams or organizations (e.g., work routines, transactive memory systems, shared knowledge) [27]	Transitions involve the acquisition of both individual knowledge (e.g., individuals learning to perform the outsourced task) and collective knowledge (e.g., units adjusting their routines to the new set-up) [2,41–43].
Explicit vs. tacit	• Explicit knowledge: Knowledge that can be communicated without losing its value (e.g., passwords) • Tacit knowledge: Knowledge that would lose its value when being communicated (e.g., programming skills, mental models about a particular software application) [25]	Transitions involve the transfer of both explicit and tacit knowledge [5,11,41–45].
Embedded vs. non-embedded knowledge	• Embedded knowledge: Knowledge that is anchored in local (e.g., societal, organizational) meanings (e.g., the British tax system) • Non-embedded knowledge: Knowledge that can be interpreted irrespective of local meanings (e.g., meaning of crash test simulation models) [46,47]	Although the transfer of embedded knowledge is often challenging [46,48,49], the transfer of non-embedded knowledge may be equally difficult [47].
Specific vs. generic knowledge	• Specific knowledge: Knowledge that loses much of its value when being redeployed to another client (e.g., knowledge about a custom-built software application) • Generic knowledge: Knowledge that can be redeployed to other clients without significant loss of value (e.g., programming skills) [14]	Although the transfer of client-specific knowledge demands substantial involvement from the client and often causes cost overruns [11,50], the transfer of generic knowledge can be equally challenging and involve significant efforts [47].
Business knowledge (or application domain knowledge)	Knowledge about the application domain for which an information system is built (e.g., knowledge about the client's business) [51]	Especially in application development projects, the transfer of business knowledge is difficult given that business knowledge is often highly embedded in the client's local context [8–10,48,52–57].

Knowledge categories	Definitions (examples in parentheses)	Key findings
Technical knowledge	Knowledge about hardware and software programming [51]	In some transitions, technical knowledge plays a relatively unimportant role because the engineers in the new SDU already possess the required technical knowledge [5,8,11,49,52,57]. In other transitions, the engineers in the new SDU lack technical knowledge [47,54].
Application knowledge	Knowledge about the software application, its structure, functionality, and behaviour [51]	Especially in software maintenance projects, application knowledge tends to be the most difficult knowledge to transfer [5,10,11,57,58].
Process knowledge	Knowledge about tools, techniques, methods, approaches, and principles used in software development [51]	Process knowledge can be critical [5], in particular if the new SDU lacks experience with business software development [49]. In other projects, process knowledge was found to be less critical [8,57]. However, the client and the new SDU may need to develop new processes for their collaboration [1].

knowledge (e.g., engineers struggle to acquire mental models of applications) or of collective knowledge (e.g., clients and vendors struggle to fine-tune their collaborative processes). In other words, it is unclear whether KT during transitions is primarily an individual learning problem or a collective learning problem.

Explicit vs. Tacit Knowledge. As Table 11.2 shows, many studies evoke the dichotomy of explicit and tacit knowledge that goes back to Polanyi [25]. Interestingly, this dichotomy is more salient in the theoretical arguments than in empirical investigations. Few studies have attempted to measure the amount of explicit versus tacit knowledge that is transferred or needs to be transferred during transitions.

Embedded vs. Non-Embedded Knowledge. Interpretive research on transitions emphasizes the challenges that arise due to the embedded nature of knowledge [46,48,49]. For instance, in one project with an English client, Indian engineers struggled to understand the business logic of a software package that was supposed to support the administration of social security benefits because the Indian engineers were not familiar with the concept of a State-supported welfare system [46]. Interestingly, however, Leonardi and Bailey [47] presented a case in which non-embedded knowledge was very difficult to transfer. They showed that requests sent from two different onshore sites (the United States and Mexico) were highly similar in the nature of knowledge they required, suggesting that the needed knowledge was not of an embedded nature. Yet offshore engineers required substantial help in order to be able to interpret the requests and work on them.

Specific vs. Generic Knowledge. Relatively few studies focus on the distinction between specific and generic knowledge. Dibbern, Winkler, and Heinzl found that transitions suffer from greater extra costs if the required knowledge was highly specific to the client [11]. In a similar vein, Deng and Mao found that the acquisition of client-specific knowledge ("learning about client" in their terms) affected project costs [50]. While specific knowledge may therefore be difficult to transfer, Leonardi and Bailey [47] showed that even the transfer of generic ("occupational" in their terms) knowledge can involve substantial costs. The relatively weak attention to specific versus generic knowledge in the literature is somewhat surprising given that specificity is a key construct of transaction cost economics [59] and of the knowledge-based view [15], theories that are popular in outsourcing and offshoring research.

Domains of Knowledge. A key question in many studies is what domains of knowledge are most salient in the KT process. While many studies build on the dichotomy of business and technical knowledge advocated in particular by Amrit Tiwana's early research [60,61], recent work has relied on more complex taxonomies that also distinguish application knowledge and process knowledge [5,51,57,58]. Research relying on the classic distinction between business and technical knowledge points to the key role of *business knowledge*, in particular in application development projects [48,52,53]. Business knowledge is often specific to the client. Engineers in the new SDU frequently lack business knowledge at the outset of transitions and, hence, struggle to understand requirements and their context [54]. In contrast, *technical knowledge* is typically generic. For example, skills in a programming language are typically applicable to many clients. Since engineers can leverage generic technical knowledge acquired in prior projects, problems related to technical knowledge are often much less salient during transitions [5,49,57], although the transfer of technical knowledge can be an issue in projects that involve many junior engineers in the new SDU [47,54].

Although the business-technical dichotomy has been influential in research on transitions, a number of studies reveal that especially in application maintenance projects, *application knowledge* is often the most difficult knowledge to transfer [5,57,58]. It is well known from software maintenance research that maintainers need to acquire highly elaborated cognitive schemas of the structure of the particular software application in order to be able to maintain the software. The process of acquiring these schemas may require years of application-specific practice [62,63]. Not surprisingly, the acquisition of application knowledge can be a key challenge during transitions, which are typically planned to take weeks or months. In line with these ideas, a multiple-case study by Krancher and Dibbern [57] showed that application knowledge was the knowledge domain that was most salient in interviews, that best predicted cognitive load on vendor engineers, and that engineers found most difficult to transfer. *Process knowledge* may also be important to transfer, in particular when the new SDU lacks experience in business application development. For example, Levina and Vaast [49] reported that teams in the Russian captive centre were initially unaware of structured deployment processes, although the teams were able to learn these processes after some time. In another study, Chua and Pan [5] interpreted that the lack of process knowledge was a reason for having to retain experienced onshore staff. Conversely, Krancher and Dibbern [57] reported that in the software maintenance outsourcing cases studied, the engineers in the new SDU found it straightforward to adjust to the clients' maintenance processes.

In sum, research on knowledge domains concurs that business knowledge and application knowledge are often difficult to transfer during transition, while technical and process knowledge are often rather unproblematic, unless in cases of inexperienced SDUs and engineers.

11.3.2 KT mechanisms

The literature gives insights into a large variety of KT mechanisms, i.e., of activities aimed at helping the new SDU to acquire knowledge from the incumbent SDU. Table 11.3 provides an overview of the mechanisms along with definitions and key findings related to each mechanism.

Table 11.3 Findings related to KT mechanisms

Context factors	Definitions	Key findings
Knowledge recipient's expertise/absorptive capacity	• Knowledge recipient's expertise: The power of domain-specific cognitive schemas in the knowledge recipients' long-term memory [67] • Knowledge recipient's absorptive capacity: The knowledge recipient's ability to utilize outside knowledge [11]	The knowledge recipient's expertise or absorptive capacity affects KT efforts [9,11,54], the choice and effectiveness of particular KT mechanisms [41,42,53,67], and the extent to which knowledge recipients can self-manage the KT process [70].
Experts' availability and motivation	• Experts' availability: The extent to which experts have free capacity to support the KT • Experts' motivation: The experts' willingness to contribute to KT	Expert's availability and their motivation to share knowledge are critical for KT [1,2,9,52,58,70,71].
Distance (cultural, geographic, semantic, temporal, status, cognitive)	• Cultural distance: Differences in shared values, norms, beliefs, and assumptions between groups (such as nations or organizations) [11] • Geographic distance: The spatial distance between experts and knowledge recipients [11] • Semantic distance: The extent of language barriers between experts and knowledge recipients [11] • Temporal distance: The time-zone difference between experts and knowledge recipients [49] • Status distance: The degree to which knowledge recipients and experts differ in deference and respect for each other according to shared beliefs • Cognitive distance: Differences in taken-for-granted beliefs, perspectives, and mental models at the individual level [8,46]	Although distance of various types often introduces boundaries and thereby hampers KT [48,49,56], distance is less problematic at high levels of knowledge recipient's expertise [11,41,42,70] and at low levels of task complexity [44].
Social capital	Resources embedded in the relationship between experts and knowledge recipients. Resources include network ties, trust, norms, identity, and knowledge [66,72].	Social capital affects the experts' ability and willingness to share knowledge and the knowledge recipients' willingness to ask questions [66].
Turnover	The frequency at which engineers leave the SDU unit	Since high turnover often requires redoing the KT [11] and reduces experts' motivation to share knowledge [66], client managers should take actions to reduce turnover, such as through contractual governance and through socialization efforts [58].
Task complexity	The extent to which a task involves many elements, to which the relationships between these elements are sophisticated, and to which changes in the world interfere with the task [67]	Higher task complexity requires higher amounts of direction in order to reduce cognitive load to a manageable level [67]. High task complexity also makes transitions riskier [9].

Formal Information Sharing. Formal information-sharing mechanisms are planned mechanisms that convey information about a knowledge domain to recipients. The most prominent formal information-sharing mechanisms are documents and presentations. There is a strong emphasis on formal information-sharing mechanisms in many transitions, in particular at early stages of transitions [1,5,44,52]. Some evidence suggests that documents and presentations can indeed help convey useful knowledge about the location of expertise [43,65] and about the client [64], in particular if they incorporate stories (events, facts, and experience in the context of specific situations) [45]. Formal information-sharing mechanisms are appealing mechanisms because they promise the efficient broadcasting of knowledge to many recipients (such as the attendants of a presentation or the readers of a document) [53]. Moreover, especially documents are appealing because they promise the ability to capture knowledge, making it available beyond the point when the personnel of the incumbent SDU leaves [68]. Despite such positive expectations, longitudinal case studies that examined at which point new SDUs were able to take over their task (the ultimate goal of transitions) shed a rather negative light on the potential offered by formal information sharing. A number of case studies show that documents and presentations rarely enable engineers to take over the tasks that clients expect them to take over [5,10,11,47,52,53,57,67]. For instance, Krancher and Dibbern made the following observation about software maintenance transitions:

> [The engineers in the new SDU] initially struggled to make sense of documents. They were able to understand many documents only after they had worked on related tasks. Put differently, documents did not enable them to solve tasks, but solving tasks enabled them to understand documents.
>
> *[57, p. 4412]*

Such a rather pessimistic perspective on the potential offered by documents and presentations is in line with the concept of tacit knowledge. A fundamental idea behind the concept of tacit knowledge is that knowledge that can be communicated (e.g., through documents and presentations) is only a relatively minor facet of the knowledge that enables competent human action [25,69].

Socialization. Many transition projects rely strongly on socialization mechanisms, including site visits, teleconferencing, and instant messaging [58,65,66]. Although the managers in some projects initially fail to anticipate the need for socialization, they often increase the use of these mechanisms after observing initial disappointing work outcomes [11,48]. Socialization mechanisms stimulate informal communication, which offers a number of potential benefits: helping develop transactive memory systems [65], allowing to rapidly clarify queries [48,66], helping the engineers in the new SDU to deepen their knowledge about the client [64], and helping the client to gain a better understanding of the needs of the new SDU [66]. In a survey study, Williams found support for the importance of socialization by showing that client embedment, a construct highly related to socialization, predicts KT outcomes [64]. Socialization efforts need some time to become effective given that engineers in the new SDU initially often hesitate to request help through informal communication channels [58,66,70].

Feedback. Some transitions rely on feedback mechanisms such as quizzes and playback [5,58]. These mechanisms are feedback mechanisms because they provide the people involved in KT with information about the outcomes of KT activities (e.g., learning). Feedback mechanisms help not only to judge the effectiveness of KT but also to discover and to align different understandings [5,58]. Moreover, feedback mechanisms stimulate communication by inviting engineers in the new SDU to ask questions [58]. Stimulating communication may be necessary in particular in offshoring projects that involve countries with high power distance, such as India, where engineers initially often hesitate to ask questions [58,67].

Learning Tasks. Among the most important mechanisms in transitions are learning tasks, i.e., authentic tasks from the domain in which knowledge shall be transferred [67]. Learning tasks include on-the-job training, where the engineers of the new SDU work on real tasks or observe engineers of the former SDU perform their task [5], and support simulation, where the engineers of the new SDU work on tasks that occurred in the past [5]. Learning tasks trigger active cognitive processing in the domain of the particular task, helping engineers to acquire powerful mental models of the task domain [67]. In many case studies, the engineers of the new SDU were able to take over work only after they had engaged in a number of learning tasks in the domain [5,10,11,47,52,53,57,67]. This is consistent with the expertise literature, which suggests that people acquire competence mostly through the active cognitive engagement that is stimulated by practice in the task domain [32].

Direction. Although learning tasks are essential during transitions, they risk cognitively overloading knowledge recipients [11,67]. An effective, and often necessary, strategy for avoiding cognitive overload is direction, i.e., providing knowledge recipients with hints on how to solve a particular learning task. Although studies have used different terms such as direction [67], specification [11], and defining requirements [47], the key commonality among these notions is the principle that experts scaffold the problem-solving process that knowledge recipients encounter during the work on learning tasks by providing hints on how the particular task can be solved. Direction is different from information-sharing mechanisms in that direction is specific to a particular tasks (e.g., the list of changes in a database that are required for a particular change request) whereas information sharing refers to information of a knowledge domain (e.g., information about the structure of the database and the meaning of fields in the database).

To summarize, although many transitions heavily rely on formal information-sharing mechanisms such as documents, case study evidence suggests that learning tasks and direction are critical to enable the SDU to take over work.

11.3.3 *Context factors*

The literature points to a variety of context factors that affect KT. Table 11.4 provides an overview of context factors along with definitions and key findings. Context factors make KT easier or more difficult, they affect which KT mechanisms are appropriate, or they engender greater need for client management efforts. Context factors are initially exogenous factors in the sense that they are given rather than subject to choice. Yet, over the course of transitions, context factors can change endogenously due to the emergent KT outcomes.

Knowledge Recipients' Expertise or Absorptive Capacity. A key context factor is the knowledge recipient's expertise or absorptive capacity. Some studies rely on the individual-level concept of expertise, i.e., the power of cognitive schemas in the knowledge recipients' long-term memory [28,35]. Other studies rely on the highly related concept of absorptive capacity [5,11], an organizational-level concept that was originally developed in an analogy to individual-level concept of expertise [73] but then often reapplied to the individual level of analysis. Expertise affects KT in at least three ways. First, expertise affects the choice and effectiveness of KT mechanisms. Chen and McQueen [41] observed that low expertise called for more structured KT mechanisms such as formal information-sharing mechanisms. Krancher and Dibbern [67] found that although knowledge recipients learned

Table 11.4 Findings related to context factors

Context factors	Definitions	Key findings
Knowledge recipient's expertise/ absorptive capacity	• Knowledge recipient's expertise: The power of domain-specific cognitive schemas in the knowledge recipients' long-term memory [67] • Knowledge recipient's absorptive capacity: The knowledge recipient's ability to utilize outside knowledge [11]	The knowledge recipient's expertise or absorptive capacity affects KT efforts [9,11,54], the choice and effectiveness of particular KT mechanisms [41,42,53,67], and the extent to which knowledge recipients can self-manage the KT process [70].
Experts' availability and motivation	• Experts' availability: The extent to which experts have free capacity to support the KT • Experts' motivation: The experts' willingness to contribute to KT	Experts' availability and their motivation to share knowledge are critical for KT [1,2,9,52,58,70,71].
Distance (cultural, geographic, semantic, temporal, status, cognitive)	• Cultural distance: Differences in shared values, norms, beliefs, and assumptions between groups (such as nations or organizations) [11] • Geographic distance: The spatial distance between experts and knowledge recipients [11] • Semantic distance: The extent of language barriers between experts and knowledge recipients [11] • Temporal distance: The time-zone difference between experts and knowledge recipients [49] • Status distance: The degree to which knowledge recipients and experts differ in deference and respect for each other according to shared beliefs • Cognitive distance: Differences in taken-for-granted beliefs, perspectives, and mental models at the individual level [8,46]	Although distance of various types often introduces boundaries and thereby hampers KT [48,49,56], distance is less problematic at high levels of knowledge recipient's expertise [11,41,42,70] and at low levels of task complexity [44].
Social capital	Resources embedded in the relationship between experts and knowledge recipients. Resources include network ties, trust, norms, identity, and knowledge [66,72].	Social capital affects the experts' ability and willingness to share knowledge and the knowledge recipients' willingness to ask questions [66].
Turnover	The frequency at which engineers leave the SDU unit	Since high turnover often requires redoing the KT [11] and reduces experts' motivation to share knowledge [66], client managers should take actions to reduce turnover, such as through contractual governance and through socialization efforts [58].
Task complexity	The extent to which a task involves many elements, to which the relationships between these elements are sophisticated, and to which changes in the world interfere with the task [67]	Higher task complexity requires higher amounts of direction in order to reduce cognitive load to a manageable level [67]. High task complexity also makes transitions riskier [9].

most effectively from learning tasks irrespective of their level of expertise, expertise affected how strongly the cognitive load imposed by learning tasks needed to be reduced through direction, simple-to-complex sequencing, and supportive information. Second, expertise affects the management efforts required from the client. Knowledge recipients with high expertise are in a better position to self-manage KT than are knowledge recipients at low levels of expertise [70]. Moreover, low levels of expertise bear a strong risk for vicious circles of negative outcomes, declining trust, and weak helping behaviours. Client management actions are required to break these circles [58,66,70,74]. Third, expertise affects the effort for KT. The lower the expertise, the higher the costs and time required for KT [9,11,47,54]. In light of the first two effects of expertise, higher costs and longer transition durations are a straightforward consequence from the higher need for cognitive load reduction mechanisms and for client management efforts, both of which typically demand effort from the client. Interestingly, expertise is not only a context factor but also the key outcome from KT [67]. This makes KT a dynamic processes where the outcomes from initial activities strongly affect subsequent activities [53,74].

Experts' Availability and Motivation. While expertise is a critical property of the knowledge recipients, key properties of the experts involved in KT are their availability and motivation. Especially when the knowledge recipients' expertise is low, the availability of experts and their motivation to share their knowledge with the knowledge recipients become critical [1,2,9,52,58,70,71]. Motivation may depend on a number of factors. First, experts are more willing to support KT if the client offers a perspective for attractive future work to them as individuals [58,66] and, in the case of between-vendor transitions, to the incumbent vendor [4,12]. Experts' motivation may also suffer from high turnover rates of SDU personnel. From the experts' perspectives, high turnover rates make KT a Sisyphean task, where they have to start KT from scratch many times [66]. Somewhat relatedly, motivation depends on a number of tightly related attitudes and beliefs held by experts, such as their general attitudes towards offshoring (in case of offshoring), outcome expectations, and trust in the new SDU [70,75,76]. These attitudes are often a result from turnover and from initial work outcomes [70,75].

Distance. The literature abounds with descriptions of how distances of various types hamper KT. Types of distances include cultural [41,42,48,56,58], geographic [11,58], semantic [11,48], temporal [49], status-related [49], and cognitive [46]. Interestingly, although these distances are of different kinds, they are similar in their effects on KT. They present barriers for social interaction, making thus KT more difficult and calling for greater amounts of client management involvement [11,49,58,70]. For instance, although offshore employees may initially have lower status than client employees and although this hampers social interaction and KT, client managers can raise the status of offshore employees by symbolic action that treats offshore employees as team members equal to client employees [49]. Although distances of various types all hamper KT, they do not hamper KT in all projects to the same extent. Some evidence suggests that distance is less problematic when the knowledge recipients' expertise is relatively high [11,41,42] and when tasks are rather simple, such as in the case of infrastructure outsourcing [44]. Consequently, in such cases less client management effort is required to overcome KT barriers [70].

Social Capital. Although most studies rely on the negative notions of distance (or differences) to explain barriers to interaction during KT, some work relies on the positive but highly related notion of social capital [49,66]. Social capital refers to resources embedded in the relationship between experts and knowledge recipients, including network ties, trust, shared norms and identities, and shared knowledge [66,72]. There is evidence that social capital facilitates KT [39]. This is not surprising given that some of the dimensions of social capital are positive equivalents of negative notions of distance. For instance, shared knowledge is largely equivalent to (lack of) cognitive distance. Other dimensions of social capital go beyond notions of distance. For instance, trust between experts and knowledge recipients can enable effective KT even under adverse distance configurations, such as when cultural and semantic differences are large [66,70,75].

Turnover. In particular in offshoring projects, turnover in the new SDU is often a problem [11,58,66]. Turnover often hits projects severely, requiring them to redo the KT [11] and reducing the experts' motivation to share knowledge [66]. The critical role of turnover also bears one interesting insight for the types of knowledge involved in transitions: It suggests that individual, rather than collective, knowledge is key. For, if only collective knowledge (e.g., practices, transactive memory systems) were critical, projects would be largely unaffected by the departure of individuals, with hardly any need for KT to be redone.

Task Complexity. Not surprisingly, KT in transitions related to complex tasks is more difficult than in transitions related to simple tasks [9,54,67]. Task complexity is to some extent exogenous because it depends, for instance, on the maturity and complexity of the software [9]. Task complexity is, however, also subject to choice given that managers may purposefully assign tasks to the new SDU based on task complexity [10,67].

In conclusion, the knowledge recipient's expertise is among the most critical context factors influencing KT efforts and the choice of KT mechanisms. Distance and low expert motivation complicate KT but can be mitigated by strong client management efforts.

11.3.4 KT management

The literature reveals five important KT management mechanisms: formal transition governance, boundary spanners, staff selection, team-based organization, and coexistence. Table 11.5 gives an overview including definitions and key findings.

Formal Governance. Case studies show that transitions often require substantial efforts for formal governance from the client [5,11,58]. Formal governance is often critical because it helps promote social interaction and break vicious circles of disappointing outcomes, weak social interaction, and weak learning [58,70,74,75]. Among the most important formal governance mechanisms are exit criteria, monitoring of KT outcomes, communication structures, task assignment, and transition plans. Clients may formally specify exit criteria, i.e., criteria that need to be fulfilled for the transition to be considered complete [2,44,70,10]. These criteria may dictate at which point the vendor takes over the majority of the work, which is a critical decision in any transition [10]. Clients may also monitor KT outcomes, such as by examining the types and numbers of questions asked by SDU personnel [47,53], and they compare these questions to the requirements according to exit criteria. Exit criteria and their monitoring are what the IS project control literature calls outcome control because they refer to the learning outcomes of the transition process [70,79]. Many clients and vendors find it important to define formal structures for regular communication such as through steering committees [2], other types of regular meetings [58], and mirroring. In mirroring, the vendor deliberately mirrors the organizational structure of the client in order to facilitate communication [1,65,43]. Although sometimes not acknowledged as part of KT management, task assignment is also a critical mechanism for managing KT [8,47,66,70]. Since learning tasks are among the most essential KT mechanisms, the assignment of particular tasks to particular engineers in the new SDU helps clients to make sure that engineers have sufficient learning opportunities [8,47,66,70] and that these learning opportunities fit

Table 11.5 Findings related to KT management

KT management mechanism	Definition	Key findings
Formal transition governance	The client management's attempts to influence behaviour in transitions through written and/or authority-based mechanisms	Formal transition governance mechanisms, such as exit criteria, monitoring, and task assignment, help promote social interaction and break vicious circles [58,74,75].
Boundary spanners	Individuals who have the formal role of facilitating KT (nominated boundary spanners) or who facilitate KT (boundary spanners-in-practice) by helping to establish connections between client and vendor [77]	Middle managers are in a strong position to act as boundary spanners-in-practice by treating offshore employees as team members equal to client employees [49,58].
Staff selection	The client's efforts to influence the selection of SDU engineers	Both in offshore outsourcing and in captive offshoring, clients often influence the selection of vendor staff to ensure minimum levels of initial expertise and communication skills [5,11,58,70].
Team-based organization	An organizing mode that views SDU engineers and client personnel as part of the same team (rather than SDU engineers as suppliers)	Team-based organization helps promote ongoing support by the client's engineers [5,49,66].
Coexistence	The simultaneous presence of experts from the client or the former SDU and of engineers from the new SDU.	Since coexistence is essential for the vendor's learning processes [78], too short coexistence phases can substantially delay the time after which the vendor is able to perform the service [74].

their level of expertise [67]. Last but not least, transition plans (or transition guides) can be an important mechanism for KT management, in particular in large-scale transitions [5]. Transition plans are blueprints for the activities to be conducted during KT [5]. The definition of communication structures, task assignment, and transition plans are what the IS project control literature calls behaviour control because they refer to the procedures through which knowledge is to be transferred [70,79].

Boundary Spanners. A second management mechanism is the institution of boundary spanners (or offshore coordinators or middlemen). Nominated boundary spanners are individuals whose formal role is to act as a bridge between the client and the SDU and to thereby facilitate KT. In contrast, boundary spanners in practice are individuals who act as a bridge without being formally assigned the role of boundary spanners [77]. Boundary spanners fulfil a number of functions such as coordinating both teams, cultivating and intensifying relationships, eliminating status differences, filling cultural gaps, and overcoming communication barriers [49,58,80]. The client's middle managers, with their strong knowledge of the project and their power to influence engineers, are in a strong position to act as boundary spanners [49,58].

Staff Selection. In many projects, clients make efforts to select the individuals working in the new SDU. Interestingly, clients select staff not only in captive offshoring, where the client concludes employment contracts with the individuals in the captive centre [5], but also in offshore outsourcing [11,58], where clients exert influence on staff selection by vendor managers. Since staff selection helps influence the engineers' initial expertise levels (by selecting individuals with substantial prior experience in the applications and technologies relevant in the project) and since their expertise is critical, staff selection can help strongly reduce transition durations [74]. But clients may select staff to influence not only their initial expertise but also their communication skills, helping thus to promote effective social interaction during KT [11,58].

Team-Based Organization. A fourth important KT management mechanism according to the literature is team-based organization, i.e., a mode in which SDU engineers and client personnel are seen as members of the same team rather than SDU engineers seen as suppliers to the client team. A supplier-based organizing mode often evokes the expectation that SDU engineers should be able to independently perform their work without the help of the client engineers [5,66]. Moreover, a supplier-based organizing mode reinforces status differences between client and SDU [49]. In contrast, a team-based organizing mode helps sensitize client engineers for the need to ongoingly support SDU engineers. Team-based organization is thus a strategy to ensure sufficient cognitive load reduction for SDU engineers even after formal KT has been completed.

Coexistence. Last but not least, decisions related to coexistence can have important impact on KT. Coexistence denotes the time during which experts and engineers from the new SDU are simultaneously present in the project. While some clients may decide that experts and SDU engineers are co-present over the course of an entire project (i.e., concurrent sourcing) [78], a more typical scenario is that after some time experts are released and are, hence, no longer available to help the engineers from the new SDU. Using simulation methods, Krancher and Dibbern [74] showed that short coexistence durations can have strong negative impact on transitions if the knowledge recipients' expertise is relatively low. In such conditions, too short coexistence durations result in SDU engineers being cognitively overloaded for relatively long time, giving rise to long periods of unsatisfactory performance and weak learning.

11.3.5 Summary

Taken together, the literature on transitions echoes a number of findings from the broader KT and expertise literatures but also goes beyond these literatures in a number of ways. The findings in two areas are largely consistent: KT *mechanisms* and context factors. While the expertise literature emphasizes that long periods of practice through scaffolded learning tasks are essential KT mechanisms, the literature on transitions is very much in line with this assertion. Studies abound with accounts of how projects initially attempted to transfer knowledge through formal information-sharing mechanisms but then managed to hand over the service to the new SDU only after the engineers from the new SDU had sufficient opportunities to work on learning tasks (authentic or real tasks). This points to an important potential for improving practice. Practitioners should be sensitized for the need for learning tasks, and for the limitations of popular information-sharing mechanisms such as documents. The findings on *context factors* are also highly consistent with the reference literature, in particular with the KT literature.

In line with that literature, the knowledge recipient's expertise, or absorptive capacity, turned out to be a key factor in many studies. Moreover, the important role of various types of distance and of social capital is highly consistent with the important role of relational factors in the KT literature.

While the literature on transitions thus invigorates findings from the reference literature around KT mechanisms and context factors, it goes beyond the reference literature in the other two topic areas covered by this review. With regard to *knowledge categories*, the important role of turnover and the accounts of cognitively overloaded individuals in the new SDU suggest that the transfer of individual, or personal [25], knowledge is often the most critical issue. Although more research is needed to compare the relative importance of individual with collective knowledge, the tentative conclusion that individual knowledge and individual learning are key in transitions would have important implications for practice. In practice, vendors often attempt to make their delivery robust to the departure of individuals, advertising their structured approaches for capturing knowledge [43]. A more successful approach for vendors might be to openly admit that their ability to provide the service strongly depends on the expertise of particular individuals and to deliberately manage this personal knowledge, rather than to attempt to obviate the need for it. The literature also gives important insights into knowledge domains. Going beyond the prevailing business-technical knowledge dichotomy, a number of studies have shown that, in application outsourcing, the most critical domain of knowledge is often application knowledge. Oftentimes, SDU engineers are able to take over tasks only after they have acquired sufficiently powerful cognitive schemas of the structure and functioning of existing software applications, typically through a relatively long period of practice.

The literature on transitions also goes beyond the KT and expertise literature in its findings on KT management, a topic that has enjoyed relatively little attention in the reference literature. The key finding is that the more adverse the circumstances in transitions (e.g., low knowledge recipient's expertise, high distance in many dimensions), the greater the management efforts required from the client. Moreover, the need for team-based structures and the findings related to coexistence suggest that, in some cases, permanent coexistence of the client's experts and SDU engineers may be the most effective way to avoid knowledge losses.

11.4 KT in transitions: implications in the era of digital business strategy and agility

While the preceding review provides a synthesis of themes that turned out important in the past, the remainder of this chapter draws on and extrapolates these findings to discuss implications from these findings for a future in which two themes are likely to gain importance: digital business strategy and agility.

As described in greater detail in other sections of this book, *digital business strategy* describes an organizational strategy in which IS are not seen as a separate function that exists independent of other business functions; instead, digital business strategy emphasizes how digital resources and business activities have become inseparable in attempts to create differential impact with digital technology [16]. Digital business strategy draws thus on a relational (or fusion) perspective of technology and social action in which technology and social action are not separate things but tightly entangled or inseparable [81,82]. For instance, it is difficult to separate a firm's digital products from technology since many digital products would not exist without the technology. Rather than to ask how an IS function can be aligned with the rest of an organization, the question becomes what the organization can do with digital resources in order to create and maintain competitive advantage. This draws attention to design moves, i.e., the ways in which organizations recombine, reconfigure, or design digital resources to change products or processes in response to market opportunities or competitors' action, and to design capital, i.e., the ways in which existing digital resources and knowledge enable or constrain these moves [83].

Agility is an organization's or a team's ability to rapidly create and react to change and to learn from it while focusing on customer value [18]. Agile organizations are able to quickly seize competitive market opportunities by quickly re-assembling digital resources and knowledge [84]. Although the concept of agility is highly related to digital business strategy, agility emphasizes the speed of change while digital business strategy emphasizes the relational nature of change.

The era of digital business strategy and agility is characterized not only by increasing desires for digital business reconfiguration and agility but also by new opportunities offered by technology. These opportunities are related to digital business strategy and agility in that they may enable organizations to more effectively implement digital business strategies and to increase agility. These technology-based opportunities include modular microservice-based architectures [85,86], digital ecosystems [87], and Cloud technologies [88].

We next discuss how desires and opportunities in the era of digital business strategy and agility are related to the findings from our literature review. From these considerations, we draw three normative implications for how to deal with KT in transitions in this new era: cultivate long-term, embedded, concurrent-sourcing relationships; accelerate learning by organizing KT around learning tasks and feedback; and reduce the need for learning by hiding complexity. Table 11.6 gives an overview of desires, opportunities, findings from our literature review, and the posited implications.

Table 11.6 Implications for the era of digital business strategy and agility

Desires and opportunities in the era of digital business strategy and agility	*Key findings of the literature on KT during transitions*	*Implications in the era of digital business strategy and agility*
Desire: Ability to reconfigure and recombine digital resources while not affecting their stability	• Application and business expertise are important. • The acquisition of sufficient expertise may take years. • In the absence of sufficient expertise held by the SDU, social ties are essential to reduce cognitive load.	Cultivate long-term, embedded, concurrent-sourcing relationships
Desire: Agility Opportunity: Technologies that enable rapid feedback	Learning tasks and feedback enable effective learning.	Accelerate learning by organizing KT around learning tasks and feedback
Opportunity: Technologies that reduce complexity	Cognitive load is often the bottleneck that limits the ability to change digital resources.	Reduce the need for learning by hiding complexity

11.4.1 Cultivate long-term, embedded, concurrent-sourcing relationships

At the heart of the concept of digital business strategy lies the desire to be able to reconfigure and recombine digital resources to enact new business opportunities [83]. At the same time, these reconfiguration or recombination moves shall not adversely affect existing operations. Three findings from our review of the literature on KT in transitions suggest that these desires pose *enormous cognitive and coordinative challenges*. A first finding is that strong business and, in particular, application knowledge are required to design and perform changes in digital resources that do not affect existing operations while allowing new business opportunities [5,70]. Engineers need powerful mental models of existing digital resources (i.e., application knowledge) before they are able to effectively change them. If these changes shall serve to enable novel business opportunities, strong knowledge of the organization's business is likely to be required as well. Engineers, who lack intimate familiarity with the client's existing digital resources and with the client's business, are likely to overlook ways to leverage existing digital resources or to overlook side effects that the changes have on existing operations and products. Moreover, strong cognitive schemas about existing infrastructures will help reduce the cognitive load on engineers, leaving them sufficient mental capacity to think about how to recombine and reconfigure the resources for innovation. Second, acquiring such strong application and business expertise often takes long time, in many cases years [9,10]. It is only through the repeated engagement in a variety of real or realistic tasks in the particular software applications that engineers will acquire such levels of expertise [57]. Third, if the SDU engineers lack such expertise, they will be cognitively overloaded unless social ties to experts allow them to obtain direction and information.

These findings suggest that a *new vendor*, who lacks familiarity with a client's existing digital resources and with the client's business, will typically be *unable*, for a relatively long time, to reconfigure and recombine the client's digital resources to create new business opportunities while not affecting the client's operations. The vendor's engineers would be unlikely to possess such application and business expertise given their lack of familiarity with the client's specific software applications. Even transitions with KT efforts of a few months are unlikely to elevate the vendor engineers' expertise to a level that would enable such transformative competent action. Instead, years of practice with a client's applications and business are likely to be required before the vendor engineers' expertise is high enough. However, transition durations of several years are neither economically viable nor desirable in terms of agility.

If years of practice are required but not economically viable, how can clients ensure that sufficient expertise is present while still relying on offshoring or outsourcing? A powerful solution is to cultivate long-term, embedded, concurrent-sourcing relationships with vendors. By long term, I mean that clients should seek to build relationships over many years. Although contracts need not necessarily be many years long, clients may need to offer a constant perspective for future business to the vendor, which may lead vendors to make long-term commitments for key personnel. Such long-term relationships will allow vendor engineers to acquire deep expertise in the client's applications and business in order to be able to guide the client at a transformative level. By embedded, I mean that vendor engineers collaborate with client personnel in team-based organizing forms. Such embedded forms provide the foundation for ongoing mutual support, which is essential to reduce the enormous cognitive load associated with transformative moves. By concurrent sourcing [78], I mean that the client keeps in-house experts involved in the projects. In-house experts will grant greater continuity of expertise. Their expertise will be needed to guide those SDU engineers who have not yet several years of working experience with the client. Positive side effects of retaining in-house experts include that these in-house experts also help the client to control projects more effectively [79] and that they reduce the dependency on the vendor, mitigating hold-up risks [10,14].

11.4.2 Accelerate learning by organizing KT around learning tasks and feedback

A key facet of the desire for greater agility lies in the speed at which organizations are able to realize and implement opportunities for innovation by modifying digital infrastructure. While typical lead times for changes in digital infrastructure were in the range of years some years ago, organizations now increasingly strive for lead times in the range of weeks [89,90]. Clearly, transition durations of months or years do not align well with such desired lead times. This is why clients should cultivate long-term embedded relationships with their SDU to make sure that expertise is retained rather than needs to be transferred for each new project. However, even in long-term embedded relationships not all required expertise may be on board from the beginning. Especially projects that strive for innovation will likely need not only to access existing expertise but also to engender quick learning in unfamiliar areas.

Research on transitions suggests that learning tasks and quick feedback are effective mechanisms to engender such quick learning. The concept of learning tasks implies that teams should do, rather than plan, the recombination and reconfiguration moves they are considering. If engineers need to acquire knowledge about new technologies or about applications or business areas with which they are not familiar, engineers may attempt to acquire this knowledge by working on a number of tasks in these areas (e.g., a number of simple tasks that occurred in the past), rather than by studying documents. The claim that learning tasks rather than formal information sharing are effective strategies for learning under high innovation pressures is also in line with research that found traditional organizational memory systems to be inappropriate in turbulent environments [17]. Quick feedback implies that teams should perform these moves and observe the outcomes as quickly and frequently as possible. This will help business users and engineers quickly build mental models of potential moves and their prerequisites, complications, and consequences. Moreover, by relying on learning tasks and feedback, engineers will rapidly learn the specifics of new technologies that are involved in the moves. The key role of learning tasks and feedback is also corroborated by organizational research on collaboration projects, which found that experimenting through active learning activities is key [91].

Although organizations may find it difficult to change their processes towards quicker feedback, recent research suggests that Cloud technologies can serve as an enabler in this mission [92]. Due to its on-demand self-service characteristic [93], Cloud technology allows engineers to instantly set up infrastructure and to instantly make changes to such infrastructure. Thus, Cloud technology can help accelerate feedback processes and learning [94].

11.4.3 Reduce the need for learning by hiding complexity

As argued above, the era of digital business strategy and agility will yield a strong increase in the cognitive and coordinative demands on SDUs. The speed at which digital infrastructures are created, reconfigured, and recombined and the complexity of existing infrastructures (e.g., the number of applications, the number of interfaces) might increase. SDU engineers require strong cognitive schemas of these increasingly large and entangled infrastructures.

Their cognitive schemas need to be so powerful that engineers are able to think about these existing infrastructures and still have sufficient cognitive capacity to think about innovative changes to digital infrastructures. These increasing cognitive demands may make any outsourcing or offshoring attempts, which necessitate transitions of years, economically prohibitive, unless deliberate attempts are made to reduce complexity.

Fortunately, technologies that help reduce complexity by hiding information are increasingly powerful and common. Three such important technologies are microservices, digital ecosystems, and Cloud computing. Microservices are a strategy to encapsulate elementary business functionality in a reusable service [85,86,95]. Microservices hide the complexity that lies behind the implementation of the service to those that want to consume the service. This helps reduce cognitive load in attempts to recombine existing digital infrastructures because engineers need not process any information related to the inner workings of the service. A highly related concept is modularity [96]; microservices enable a modular architecture of digital resources. Digital ecosystems, such as the Salesforce AppExchange or Heroku Elements, provide existing, often relatively small, applications or application components that organizations can reuse and recombine [87]. They hide the complexity that lies behind the implementation of the application or application component. Cloud services are on-demand self-services that include virtualized infrastructure (Infrastructure-as-a-Service), application environments (Platform-as-a-Service), or ready-to-use software (Software-as-a-Service). Cloud services hide the complexity by abstracting away the details behind setting up infrastructure, environments, and readily configure software components [94]. The use of these three technologies reduces cognitive load by eliminating information elements that engineers need to process. Thus, the use of these technologies may serve to counterbalance the increased cognitive demands through the increasing variety of existing applications and the increased need for speed. Organizations that manage to leverage these technologies to a great extent may even be able to shorten transition durations and, hence, need to rely to a lesser extent on long-term, embedded, dual-sourcing relationships. Whether and under what circumstances transitions will thus become simpler or more complex remains an intriguing question for future research.

11.5 Conclusion

KT during transitions is one of the key issues in outsourcing and offshoring relationships. The critical nature of KT has given rise to a vibrant stream of research that has examined what knowledge needs to be transferred, through what mechanisms knowledge can be transferred effectively, how context factors influence KT, and how KT can be effectively managed. This research has invigorated some findings from the broader KT literature and from expertise literature. These findings include that the knowledge recipients' expertise is among the most important context factors and that learning tasks (i.e., practice based on authentic tasks) are among the most effective KT mechanisms, although many projects initially rely on formal information-sharing mechanisms (e.g., documents). Research on transitions goes also beyond reference literatures by revealing what categories of knowledge are critical in IS transitions and how KT can and should be managed. Although evidence is not yet conclusive, findings suggest that in many transitions the transfer of individual, rather than of collective, knowledge is the key bottleneck, and that application knowledge is often the most important knowledge domain. A key finding on KT management is that the more adverse the circumstances (e.g., low knowledge recipient's expertise, high distances in a number of dimensions), the more client management involvement is needed.

While these findings stem from the past, they are also informative in a future in which digital business strategy and agility will become increasingly important. The findings sensitize for the high amounts of expertise that are required to understand existing digital resources and for the long time it takes to build such expertise. At a time when rapid innovation by reconfiguring and recombining digital resources is much sought, the need for such expertise is unlikely to decline. Clients may therefore need to cultivate long-term, embedded, concurrent-sourcing relationships with vendors to ensure that expertise is retained. KT approaches based on learning tasks and feedback, rather than based on documents, are likely to become even more needed to satisfy the need for quick learning and agility. Although cognitive demands may increase with the increasing variety of existing digital resources and with the increasing demand for agility, the era of digital business strategy and of agility also offers new technologies that may help reduce cognitive demands by hiding complexity. These technologies include microservices, digital ecosystems, and Cloud computing. Organizations that leverage these technologies may even be able to shorten transition durations. Future practice and research will yield insights into whether and how important these changes are, how they interact, and how they will inform KT during transitions.

References

1. Tiwari, V. Transition during Offshore Outsourcing: A Process Model. In The 30th *International Conference of Information Systems*, Phoenix, AZ, 2009.
2. Beulen, E. and V. Tiwari, Parallel Transitions in IT Outsourcing: Making It Happen. In *Global Sourcing of Information Technology and Business Processes*, I. Oshri and J. Kotlarsky, Editors. 2010, Heidelberg: Springer, pp. 55–68.
3. Ravindran, K., Asset Transfer in IT Outsourcing: Divesting Commodities or Inviting Investment?, In *The Dynamics of Global Sourcing. Perspectives and Practices*, J. Kotlarsky, I. Oshri, and L. Willcocks, Editors. 2012, Heidelberg: Springer, pp. 39–60.
4. Sia, S.K., W.K. Lim, and K.P. Periasamy, Switching IT Outsourcing Suppliers: Enhancing Transition Readiness. *MIS Quarterly Executive*, 2010. 9(1): pp. 203–213.
5. Chua, A.L. and S.L. Pan, Knowledge Transfer and Organizational Learning in IS Offshore Sourcing. *Omega*, 2008. 36(2): pp. 267–281.
6. Blumenberg, S., H.T. Wagner, and D. Beimborn, Knowledge Transfer Processes in IT Outsourcing Relationships and their Impact on Shared Knowledge and Outsourcing Performance. *International Journal of Information Management*, 2009. 29(5): pp. 342–352.
7. Carmel, E. and P. Tjia, *Offshoring Information Technology: Sourcing and Outsourcing to a Global Workforce*. Cambridge: Cambridge University Press, 2005.
8. Madsen, S., K. Bødker, and T. Tøth, Knowledge Transfer Planning and Execution in Offshore Outsourcing: An Applied Approach. *Information Systems Frontiers*, 2015. 17(1): pp. 67–77.
9. Smite, D. and C. Wohlin, Strategies Facilitating Software Product Transfers. *IEEE Software*, 2011. 28(5): pp. 60–66.
10. Williams, C. and S. Durst, Exploring the Transition Phase in Offshore Outsourcing: Decision Making Amidst Knowledge at Risk. *Journal of Business Research*, 2019. 103: pp. 460–471.
11. Dibbern, J., J. Winkler, and A. Heinzl, Explaining Variations in Client Extra Costs between Software Projects Offshored to India. *MIS Quarterly*, 2008. 32(2): pp. 333–366.
12. Chua, C.E.H., et al., Client Strategies in Vendor Transition: A Threat Balancing Perspective. *The Journal of Strategic Information Systems*, 2012. 21(1): pp. 72–83.
13. Willcocks, L. and M.C. Lacity, *Global Sourcing of Business and IT Services*. London: Palgrave Macmillan, 2006.
14. Williamson, O.E., Transaction-Cost Economics: The Governance of Contractual Relations. *The Journal of Law & Economics*, 1979. 22(2): pp. 233–261.
15. Conner, K. and C. Prahalad, A Resource-Based Theory of the Firm: Knowledge versus Opportunism. *Organization Science*, 1996. 7(5): pp. 477–501.
16. Bharadwaj, A., et al., Digital Business Strategy: Toward a Next Generation of Insights. *MIS Quarterly*, 2013. 37: pp. 471–482.

17. Pavlou, P.A. and O.A. El Sawy, The "Third Hand": IT-Enabled Competitive Advantage in Turbulence Through Improvisational Capabilities. *Information Systems Research*, 2010. 21(3): pp. 443–471.

18. Conboy, K., Agility from First Principles: Reconstructing the Concept of Agility in Information Systems Development. *Information Systems Research*, 2009. 20(3): pp. 329–354.

19. Grant, R.M., Toward a Knowledge-Based Theory of the Firm. *Strategic Management Journal*, 1996. 17(10): pp. 109–122.

20. Spender, J.C., Making Knowledge the Basis of a Dynamic Theory of the Firm. *Strategic Management Journal*, 1996. 17: pp. 45–62.

21. Szulanski, G., Exploring Internal Stickiness: Impediments to the Transfer of Best Practice within the Firm. *Strategic Management Journal*, 1996. 17(1): pp. 27–43.

22. Tsai, W., Knowledge Transfer in Intraorganizational Networks: Effects of Network Position and Absorptive Capacity on Business Unit Innovation and Performance. *Academy of Management Journal*, 2001. 44(5): pp. 996–1004.

23. Ko, D.G., L.J. Kirsch, and W.R. King, Antecedents of Knowledge Transfer from Consultants to Clients in Enterprise System Implementations. *MIS Quarterly*, 2005. 29(1): pp. 59–85.

24. Szulanski, G., The Process of Knowledge Transfer: A Diachronic Analysis of Stickiness. *Organizational Behavior and Human Decision Processes*, 2000. 82(1): pp. 9–27.

25. Polanyi, M., *Personal Knowledge. Towards a Post-Critical Philosophy*. Chicago, IL: The University of Chicago Press, 1962.

26. Van Wijk, R., J.J. Jansen, and M.A. Lyles, Inter-and Intra-Organizational Knowledge Transfer: A Meta-Analytic Review and Assessment of Its Antecedents and Consequences. *Journal of Management Studies*, 2008. 45(4): pp. 830–853.

27. Lam, A., Tacit Knowledge, Organizational Learning and Societal Institutions: An Integrated Framework. *Organization Studies*, 2000. 21(3): p. 487.

28. Chase, W.G. and H.A. Simon, Perception in Chess. *Cognitive Psychology*, 1973. 4(1): pp. 55–81.

29. Adelson, B., Problem Solving and the Development of Abstract Categories in Programming Languages. *Memory & Cognition*, 1981. 9(4): pp. 422–433.

30. Doane, S.M., J.W. Pellegrino, and R.L. Klatzky, Expertise in a Computer Operating System: Conceptualization and Performance. *Human-Computer Interaction*, 1990. 5(2): pp. 267–304.

31. Voss, J.F., et al., Problem-Solving Skill in the Social Sciences. In *The Psychology of Learning and Motivation*, G.H. Bower, Editor. 1983, Stanford, CA: Stanford University. pp. 165–213.

32. Ericsson, K.A., R.T. Krampe, and C. Tesch-Römer, The Role of Deliberate Practice in the Acquisition of Expert Performance. *Psychological Review*, 1993. 100(3): p. 363.

33. Dreyfus, H.L. and S.E. Dreyfus, Peripheral Vision: Expertise in Real World Contexts. *Organization Studies*, 2005. 26(5): pp. 779–792.

34. Ericsson, K.A., M.J. Prietula, and E.T. Cokely, The Making of an Expert. *Harvard Business Review*, 2007. 85(7/8): pp. 115–121.

35. Sweller, J., J.J.G. Van Merriënboer, and F.G.W.C. Paas, Cognitive Architecture and Instructional Design. *Educational Psychology Review*, 1998. 10(3): pp. 251–296.

36. Van Merriënboer, J.J.G., R.E. Clark, and M.B.M. De Croock, Blueprints for Complex Learning: The 4C/ID-Model. *Educational Technology Research and Development*, 2002. 50(2): pp. 39–64.

37. Cha, H., D. Pingry, and M. Thatcher, Managing the Knowledge Supply Chain: An Organizational Learning Model of Information Technology Offshore Outsourcing. *Management Information Systems Quarterly*, 2008. 32(2): p. 7.

38. Teo, T.S. and A. Bhattacherjee, Knowledge Transfer and Utilization in IT Outsourcing Partnerships: A Preliminary Model of Antecedents and Outcomes. *Information & Management*, 2014. 51(2): pp. 177–186.

39. Zimmermann, A., et al., Sourcing In or Out: Implications for Social Capital and Knowledge Sharing. *The Journal of Strategic Information Systems*, 2018. 27(1): pp. 82–100. doi:10.1016/j.jsis.2017.05.001

40. Lee, J.-N., The Impact of Knowledge Sharing, Organizational Capability and Partnership Quality on IS Outsourcing Success. *Information & Management*, 2001. 38(5): pp. 323–335.

41. Chen, J. and R.J. McQueen, Knowledge Transfer Processes for Different Experience Levels of Knowledge Recipients at an Offshore Technical Support Center. *Information Technology & People*, 2010. 23(1): pp. 54–79.

42. Chen, J., P.Y. Sun, and R.J. McQueen, The Impact of National Cultures on Structured Knowledge Transfer. *Journal of Knowledge Management*, 2010. 14(2): pp. 228–242.

43. Kotlarsky, J., H. Scarbrough, and I. Oshri, Coordinating Expertise across Knowledge Boundaries in Offshore-Outsourcing Projects: The Role of Codification. *MIS Quarterly*, 2014. 38(2): pp. 607–627.
44. Hawk, S., W. Zheng, and R.W. Zmud, Overcoming Knowledge-Transfer Barriers in Infrastructure Management Outsourcing: Lessons from a Case Study. *MIS Quarterly Executive*, 2009. 8(3): pp. 123–129.
45. Wende, E., G. King, and G. Schwabe, *Exploring Storytelling as a Knowledge Transfer Technique in Offshore Outsourcing*. Auckland, New Zealand: International Conference on Information Systems, 2014.
46. Nicholson, B. and S. Sahay, Embedded Knowledge and Offshore Software Development. *Information and Organization*, 2004. 14(4): pp. 329–365.
47. Leonardi, P.M. and D. Bailey, Transformational Technologies and the Creation of New Work Practices: Making Implicit Knowledge Explicit in Task-Based Offshoring. *MIS Quarterly*, 2008. 32(2): pp. 159–176.
48. Imsland, V. and S. Sahay, 'Negotiating Knowledge': The Case of a Russian–Norwegian Software Outsourcing Project. *Scandinavian Journal of Information Systems*, 2005. 17(1): p. 3.
49. Levina, N. and E. Vaast, Innovating or Doing as Told? Status Differences and Overlapping Boundaries in Offshore Collaboration. *MIS Quarterly*, 2008. 32(2): pp. 307–332.
50. Deng, C.-P. and J.-Y. Mao, Knowledge Transfer to Vendors in Offshore Information Systems Outsourcing: Antecedents and Effects on Performance. *Journal of Global Information Management (JGIM)*, 2012. 20(3): pp. 1–22.
51. Iivari, J., R. Hirschheim, and H. Klein, Towards a Distinctive Body of Knowledge for Information Systems Experts: Coding ISD Process Knowledge in Two IS Journals. *Information Systems Journal*, 2004. 14(4): pp. 313–342.
52. Feng, Y., H. Ye, and S.L. Pan, Delivering Knowledge across Boundaries: A Process Model of Knowledge Delivery in Offshoring Projects. *Pacific Asia Conference on Information Systems*. Taipei, Taiwan, 2010.
53. Schott, K. Vendor-Vendor Knowledge Transfer in Global ISD Outsourcing Projects: Insights from a German Case Study. *PACIS*, 2011.
54. Vlaar, P., P. van Fenema, and V. Tiwari, Cocreating Understanding and Value in Distributed Work: How Members of Onsite and Offshore Vendor Teams Give, Make, Demand, and Break Sense. *MIS Quarterly*, 2008. 32(2): p. 5.
55. Park, J.Y., K.S. Im, and J.S. Kim, The Role of IT Human Capability in the Knowledge Transfer Process in IT Outsourcing Context. *Information & Management*, 2011. 48(1): pp. 53–61.
56. Wende, E., et al. Why They Do Not Understand – A Model of Knowledge Discourse in the Transition Phase of Globally Distributed Projects. In System Sciences (HICSS), 2013 46th Hawaii International Conference On. IEEE, 2013.
57. Krancher, O. and J. Dibbern. Knowledge in Software-Maintenance Outsourcing Projects: Beyond Integration of Business and Technical Knowledge. In The *48th Hawaii International Conference on System Sciences*, Kauai, HI, 2015.
58. Gregory, R., R. Beck, and M. Prifling, Breaching the Knowledge Transfer Blockade in IT Offshore Outsourcing Projects – A Case from the Financial Services Industry. In The *43th Hawaii International Conference on Systems Sciences*. Big Island, HI, 2009.
59. Williamson, O.E., The Economics of Organization: The Transaction Cost Approach. *American Journal of Sociology*, 1981. 87(3): pp. 548–577.
60. Tiwana, A., Knowledge Partitioning in Outsourced Software Development: A Field Study. In *Twenty-Fourth International Conference on Information Systems*. 2003. pp. 259–270.
61. Tiwana, A., An Empirical Study of the Effect of Knowledge Integration on Software Development Performance. *Information and Software Technology*, 2004. 46(13): pp. 899–906.
62. Banker, R.D., et al., Software Errors and Software Maintenance Management. *Information Technology and Management*, 2002. 3(1–2): pp. 25–41.
63. Boh, W.F., S.A. Slaughter, and J.A. Espinosa, Learning from Experience in Software Development: A Multilevel Analysis. *Management Science*, 2007. 53(8): pp. 1315–1331.
64. Williams, C., Client–Vendor Knowledge Transfer in IS Offshore Outsourcing: Insights from a Survey of Indian Software Engineers. *Information Systems Journal*, 2011. 21(4): pp. 335–356.
65. Oshri, I., P. Van Fenema, and J. Kotlarsky, Knowledge Transfer in Globally Distributed Teams: The Role of Transactive Memory. *Information Systems Journal*, 2008. 18(6): pp. 593–616.

66. Zimmermann, A. and M. Ravishankar, Knowledge Transfer in IT Offshoring Relationships: The Roles of Social Capital, Efficac and Outcome Expectations. *Information Systems Journal*, 2014. 24(2): pp. 167–202.
67. Krancher, O. and J. Dibbern. Learning Software-Maintenance Tasks in Offshoring Projects: A Cognitive-Load Perspective. In *The 33rd International Conference on Information Systems*. Orlando, FL, 2012.
68. Cognizant. How to Conduct Knowledge Transfer Efficiently. 2002 June 6th, 2014; Available from: http://www.cognizant.com/InsightsWhitepapers/amseries-kt.pdf.
69. Tsoukas, H., Do We Really Understand Tacit Knowledge. The Blackwell Handbook of Organizational Learning and Knowledge Management, 2003: pp. 410–427.
70. Krancher, O. and S.A. Slaughter, Governing Individual Learning in the Transition Phase of Software Maintenance Offshoring: A Dynamic Perspective. In *The 46th Hawaii International Conference on System Sciences*, Maui, HI, pp. 4406–4415, 2013.
71. Beulen, E., V. Tiwari, and E. van Heck, Understanding Transition Performance during Offshore IT Outsourcing. *Strategic Outsourcing: An International Journal*, 2011. 4(3): pp. 204–227.
72. Nahapiet, J. and S. Ghoshal, Social Capital, Intellectual Capital, and the Organizational Advantage. *Academy of Management Review*, 1998. 23: pp. 242–266.
73. Cohen, W.M. and D.A. Levinthal, Absorptive Capacity: A New Perspective on Learning and Innovation. *Administrative Science Quarterly*, 1990. 35(1): pp. 128–152.
74. Krancher, O. and J. Dibbern, Managing Knowledge Transfer in Software-Maintenance Outsourcing: A System-Dynamics Perspective. In *Information Systems Outsourcing: Towards Sustainable Business Value*, R. Hirschheim, A. Heinzl, and J. Dibbern, editors. Springer: Heidelberg, pp. 223–243, 2014.
75. Zimmermann, A., K. Raab, and L. Zanotelli, Vicious and Virtuous Circles of Offshoring Attitudes and Relational Behaviours. A Configurational Study of German IT Developers. *Information Systems Journal*, 2013. 23(1): pp. 65–88.
76. Westner, M. and S. Strahringer, Determinants of Success in IS Offshoring Projects: Results from an Empirical Study of German Companies. *Information & Management*, 2010. 47(5): pp. 291–299.
77. Levina, N. and E. Vaast, The Emergence of Boundary Spanning Competence in Practice: Implications for Implementation and Use of Information Systems. *MIS Quarterly*, 2005. 29(2): pp. 335–363.
78. Tiwana, A. and S.K. Kim, Concurrent IT Sourcing: Mechanisms and Contingent Advantages. *Journal of Management Information Systems*, 2016. 33(1): pp. 101–138.
79. Kirsch, L.J., The Management of Complex Tasks in Organizations: Controlling the Systems Development Process. *Organization Science*, 1996. 7(1): pp. 1–21.
80. Strasser, A. and M. Westner. Knowledge Transfer in IS Offshoring: Processes, Roles, and Success Factors. In *PACIS*, 2015.
81. Orlikowski, W.J. and S.V. Scott, Sociomateriality: Challenging the Separation of Technology, Work and Organization. *The Academy of Management Annals*, 2008. 2(1): pp. 433–474.
82. Riemer, K. and R.B. Johnston, Clarifying Ontological Inseparability with Heidegger's Analysis of Equipment. *MIS Quarterly*, 2017. 41(4): pp. 1059–1081.
83. Woodard, C.J., et al., Design Capital and Design Moves: The Logic of Digital Business Strategy. *MIS Quarterly*, 2013. 37(2): pp. 537–564.
84. Sambamurthy, V., A. Bharadwaj, and V. Grover, Shaping Agility through Digital Options: Reconceptualizing the Role of Information Technology in Contemporary Firms. *MIS Quarterly*, 2003. 27(2): pp. 237–263.
85. Yoo, Y., O. Henfridsson, and K. Lyytinen, Research Commentary—The New Organizing Logic of Digital Innovation: An Agenda for Information Systems Research. *Information Systems Research*, 2010. 21(4): pp. 724–735.
86. Grover, V. and R. Kohli, Revealing Your Hand: Caveats in Implementing Digital Business Strategy. *MIS Quarterly*, 2013. 37(2): pp. 655–662.
87. Tiwana, A., B. Konsynski, and A.A. Bush, Research Commentary-Platform Evolution: Coevolution of Platform Architecture, Governance, and Environmental Dynamics. *Information Systems Research*, 2010. 21(4): pp. 675–687.
88. Yang, H. and M. Tate, A Descriptive Literature Review and Classification of Cloud Computing Research. *Communications of the Association for Information Systems*, 2012. 31(2): pp. 35–60.
89. Lyytinen, K. and G.M. Rose, Information System Development Agility as Organizational Learning. *European Journal of Information Systems*, 2006. 15(2): pp. 183–199.

90. Yoo, Y., et al., Organizing for Innovation in the Digitized World. *Organization Science*, 2012. 23(5): pp. 1398–1408.

91. Martin, J.A. and K.M. Eisenhardt, Rewiring: Cross-Business-Unit Collaborations in Multibusiness Organizations. *Academy of Management Journal*, 2010. 53(2): pp. 265–301.

92. Krancher, O. and P. Luther, Software Development in the Cloud: Exploring the Affordances of Platform-as-a-Service. In *The 36rd International Conference on Information Systems*. Fort Worth, TX, 2015.

93. Mell, P. and T. Grance. The NIST Definition of Cloud Computing. 2011 Feb 27th, 2018; Available from: http://nvlpubs.nist.gov/nistpubs/Legacy/SP/nistspecialpublication800-145.pdf.

94. Krancher, O., P. Luther, and M. Jost, Key Affordances of Platform-as-a-Service: Self-Organization and Continuous Feedback. *Journal of Management Information Systems*, 2018. 35(3): pp. 776–812. doi:10.1080/07421222.2018.1481636.

95. Balalaie, A., A. Heydarnoori, and P. Jamshidi, Microservices Architecture Enables Devops: Migration to a Cloud-Native Architecture. *IEEE Software*, 2016. 33(3): pp. 42–52.

96. Baldwin, C.Y. and K.B. Clark, *Design Rules: The Power of Modularity*. MIT Press, Cambridge, Vol. 1, 2000.

12

TACKLING THE CHALLENGE OF TRANSITION PHASES WITH KAIWA

How to steer the critical success factors of human interaction

Erik Wende and André Mertel

12.1 Overview – the transition as a pivotal phase of IT outsourcing

Every project manager has been in this situation: You are about to kick off an important new project involving two companies, and right from the start, there is this itch: Something doesn't feel right. The atmosphere between the key people involved does not fit; there is an inequality between the partners, and they don't seem to speak the same language, although on paper, every aspect should be ok.

Mere facts and figures are not everything. There is a layer in projects that is difficult to seize or quantify: it is the qualification and also the personality of the involved people – and their implicit knowledge. This layer becomes all the more important in *outsourcing* projects, as they tend to emphasize the existing frictions between the provider and the client company in the teams.

In the following chapter, we want to focus on the *challenges of the transition phase of IT outsourcing projects*, and then illustrate a method to manage and improve the communication of key people including their transfer of implicit knowledge, showing you a way to support you in upcoming outsourcing projects. Before we dive into the details, let us first have a closer look at the working context and wordings.

12.1.1 The context: outsourcing in a nutshell

Outsourcing is a process consisting of several phases. Overall, the process of outsourcing describes the transfer of a partial activity of a given company to a service provider [1]. The key goal of this transition: carry out a service (potentially more efficiently) by another party while maintaining or optimizing its quality. During some pivotal moments in the transition itself, e.g. the change of control, the services may be interrupted for a very short moment.

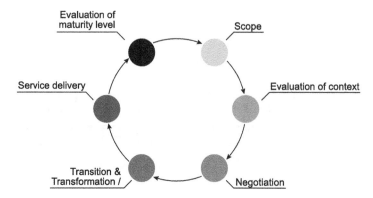

Figure 12.1   Outsourcing lifecycle

Looking at the bigger picture, we consider the phases of outsourcing being a lifecycle, as the context evolves along the line as well. The phases are as follows (Figure 12.1):

- definition of scope,
- evaluation of context, e.g. application landscape,
- negotiation of a framework contract,
- transition and transformation,
- service delivery,
- evaluation of maturity levels,
- closing and, if need be,
- renewal.

The reasons for outsourcing an activity are multifold: financial aspects, mitigate risks, efficiency and improved service can be a driver; often however, the goal is to unburden the internal teams of the company from rather simple operational tasks in order to gain resources for more strategic work and thus focus on company core business [2].

12.1.2 Transition and transformation: what does it mean?

Before we approach the phases and the challenges of the transition phase, we need to define the meaning of the notions itself. *Transition* is the transfer of a given activity from company A to company B – it is a *horizontal* move of the infrastructure and the activity without changing its configuration. In more simple words, it is the act of making an outsourcing activity happen. *Transformation* however, a word often used in the context of outsourcing, describes the change of the model of activity, so a modification of the infrastructure itself. It is a *vertical* change.

Both transition and transformation can be combined – and often are – during IT outsourcing projects. A combination of both aspects offers potential for optimization, and it is often one of the drivers of outsourcing projects: through partial or complete reconstruction, adaption, completion or reduction of infrastructure, operation can get more efficient for end users within the company, as well as more manageable for the service provider. However, it is important not to mix up the meanings of both aspects in this chapter.

T&T Phase Model

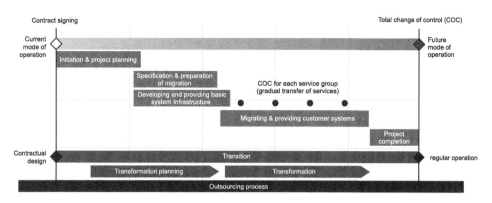

Figure 12.2   Transition and transformation phase model

12.1.3 *The transition phase: this is what we are talking about*

The transition phase itself, as the transfer of activity from the client company to the service provider, is the focus of this chapter. It consists of several sub-phases in which the transition is initiated, defined, prepared, executed step by step and system by system, and finally closed (see Figure 12.2).

The core goal of the phase is the transfer of the *current mode of operation* (carrying out the activity by the client company) to the *future mode of operation* – which is in the end achieved by an overall *change of control*. This change of control does usually not happen in one single step, but in several change of controls per service groups, e.g. by systems.

Hand in hand with the change of control, a *transfer of knowledge* happens alongside the transition phase. This transfer of knowledge is a key condition for a successful transition phase, and is often reduced to a simple handover of documentation. However, there are implicit levels of knowledge happening through human interaction that need to be included as well – this will be focused in the third part of this chapter.

12.1.3 *The target model*

Looking at the *future mode of operation*, a crisp clear *target model* is the key to tackle a transition well – without creating a never-ending story. Two elements are decisive:

*   A clear definition of *interfaces* before and after the transition, in order to know the starting point and the final image you want to achieve through the transition phase.
*   A clear definition of *processes* before and after, and especially during the transition, in order to know how you want to achieve the goal you have set, and without lacking accountability of crucial tasks during the transition phase.

12.1.4 *A first look at success factors*

Before we will focus on challenges, and then come to the main aspect in the third part of this chapter, let us have a quick look at the most important general ingredients for success in transition phases.

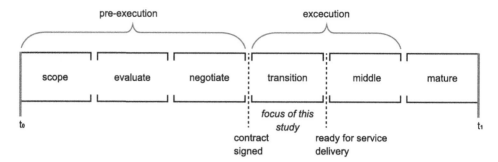

Figure 12.3 Outsourcing relationship lifecycle

- First, there is the question of *resources*. They can be financial – in order to invest into infrastructure – or human. In the latter case, it is of utmost importance to dispose of enough people of both ends of the outsourcing project, as well as having the people with the right qualifications.
- Then, as already mentioned regarding the target model, a clear view of systems involved, tasks, timelines and accountability including the moments of change of control. Having a *good plan* before starting the skirmish will help you to stay on track during rough times of any project (and every project has them).
- Third, and this is what this chapter will focus on, is an excellent use of *communication skills and channels*. As said in the introduction: while projects tend to be measured in facts and figures, there is always a human dimension that mostly will rise or fall with the quality of the communication between the key people of the project.

12.1.5 Borders of this chapter

The transition phase in outsourcing relations is considered to be the most critical phase for overall success. Transition includes the first joint operational steps amid the uncertainty that follows pre-execution and contract signing and involves the critical, but time-constrained knowledge transfer, as illustrated in Figure 12.3. The purpose of knowledge transfer in outsourcing situations is the conveyance of information from client to service provider that the service provider needs in order to deliver its services. Ineffective or failed knowledge transfer early in projects is frequently the main reason that outsourcing projects experience difficulties, delays or failure. In this chapter, we seek to *build a solution for implementing the transition phase* in order to address the problem of ineffective and failed knowledge transfer in IT outsourcing project work. This chapter will limit its focus to the transition phase, leaving out the pre-execution and post-transition phases.

12.2 The challenges and design requirements – when do transitions tend to fail?

Once I came to a multi-country kickoff meeting for a transition project.

We arrived the night before and came in early in the morning for the first meeting. However, the hosts completely ignored our presence – even when ordering coffee for the meeting. It was only years later, well after finishing the project, that I realized I had committed major mistakes in my communication: They would have appreciated a personal contact well before the meeting; and the meeting wasn't the time and space of decision making. It was the coffee corner.

12.2.1 *Typical risks, problems and challenges*

There are countless strategical, operational and technical risks during the transition phase. We want to outline the biggest ones here – which mainly deal with focus, resources and project communication. All of these challenges can be foreseen and remedied by anticipatory project management.

1   Changing priorities and parallel projects

The process of outsourcing an IT activity isn't done overnight. During this lengthy time period, priorities – be it strategical or operational – may shift, even for some days. Resources and people involved in the project may be needed urgently elsewhere. This will always impact the carefully crafted plans and timetables and will lead to freeze periods or congestions.

This challenge may be overcome by analyzing the entire project landscape of the key stakeholders of the client company, involving not only the people but also the context they are working in: their departments. Workshops can be a suitable instrument for harvesting information and building awareness. Backup plans are a must.

2   Resources not provided, not sufficiently provided or not soon enough provided

It may occur that the client company isn't able to provide the resources initially foreseen. In this case, the service provider should be the proactive party and solve the problem by supplying more personnel to the project, especially on project management side. Temporary congestions can be overcome this way. However, this may create new challenges regarding the transfer of knowledge at some point in the project (see next paragraph).

3   Insufficient transfer of knowledge

Especially during the transition phase, there is a risk that crucial knowledge of the client company is not or only insufficiently transferred to the service provider. A typical example: a client's employee assumes that the counterpart at the service provider knows about a given system or process without checking back, communicating or even thinking about it. This may lead to increased workload or even gaps in the activity with potential risks of interruption of services.

This is why the service provider's project management should impose regular workshops and physical meetings between the respective operational stakeholders. The importance of personal exchange for harmonizing definitions, goals, plans, even contract details and their measurability should not be underestimated.

4   Loss of knowledge through loss of resources

The orderly and documented transfer of previously not-documented knowledge of former people in charge is a prerequisite of any successful service transfer. Personal fluctuations and fading availability of experts (including of other external service partners) are a real threat to IT outsourcing projects. A possible solution is an open communication strategy involving these key people, and providing a clear (and possibly motivating) personal perspective. Managing expectations and synchronizing goals while keeping people in the loop for further cooperation is necessary and challenging.

12.2.2 Why we need to analyze problems first: methods and challenges don't always match

We focus on typical challenges because they have certain aspects in common: a *lack of communication, insufficient resources* or *sub-par planning*. Researchers and consulting companies have lots of different approaches on how to overcome these obstacles. However, we think that there is no such thing as one single solution on how to tackle IT outsourcing projects successfully.

This is why analysis of the situation at hand is the first step of any (outsourcing) project. Otherwise companies will apply general approaches to specific situations which will not support – or even harm – the process. We therefore rather want to focus on one pillar of transformation phases: the *challenge of communication*, especially regarding the transfer of knowledge.

Knowledge transfer difficulties often stem from clients failing to adequately plan for the influence of experiential differences between the team members. Clients often fail to identify what knowledge is critical to the project, in particular not recognizing the importance of implicit as well as explicit knowledge. Implicit knowledge is generally more difficult to articulate and more challenging to transfer than explicit knowledge, requiring interactivity and face-to-face communication between partners to support an ongoing process of sense making [3]. The success of implicit knowledge transfer is moderated by the quality of the relationship between group members [4]. If knowledge recipient and source do not have a trusting relationship [5], the willingness to transfer background information and implicit knowledge is inhibited [6].

Establishing effective team relationships and successful communication can be challenging in the context of IT outsourcing, since it typically involves ad hoc project teams that do not share a corporate culture nor an intrinsic motivation to cooperate. Distributed teams often face difficulties in developing systems that support the transfer of contextual and implicit knowledge [7]. Establishing cohesiveness among operational staff is challenging since interaction via communication media is known to slow the development of relationships [8].

Existing research into the causes of knowledge transfer problems has established a conceptual model of knowledge transfer in outsourcing projects (Figure 12.4). This conceptual model breaks down knowledge transfer into key constituents, thereby delineating aspects that should be taken into consideration when seeking to design a solution to failed knowledge transfer. In the conceptual model, the *project environment* comprises all aspects of the project context that influence communication within the team, including project scope and the communication capabilities of team members. *Communication inception* comprises the first engagement of operational team members with the project and the initial interaction between client and service provider operational team members. *Knowledge discourse* describes the process by which the interpretation of explicit knowledge is checked and implicit knowledge is transferred from client to service provider in a two-way interactive process. Successful knowledge transfer is dependent on effective knowledge discourse.

12.2.3 Excursus: language and behavior profiles as key to understanding and configuring a team

One of the key questions of successful project management and project communication is: how do we build successful relationships to and between the people in order to assure seamless workflows? This becomes especially relevant in the preparation of the kick-off

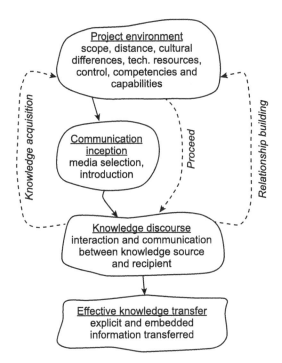

Figure 12.4   Conceptual model of a transition phase

meeting. It requires the project/transition manager to get in touch with all participants on the client as well as on the service provider side. So-called LAB and Reiss profiles can be accurate tools to get to know the functioning and the main stimuli of the people involved in the project.

The *Language and Behavior, or LAB, profile* is a way to analyze language style – and not the content – that allows us to understand how people get motivated, how they process information and how they make decisions [9]. It is composed of a set of questions that anyone can use as a formal survey. Its goal pays attention to how people talk when they answer, rather than what they talk about. Even if a person answers the question indirectly, or not at all, he/she will reveal a pattern. People communicate with their particular patterns naturally as they speak, both in words and in their body language. You can use these tools to establish a deeper level of rapport, to take the pain out of organizational change or to create high-performance teams by managing peoples' strengths.

The *Reiss Profile* was developed by psychologist Steven Reiss in the 1990s. He found that performance motivation and actions are permanently determined by 16 fundamental values and needs [10]. Reiss defines these 16 motives as elementary "ultimate motives" or "final causes" of action that we experience as core values and even as the sense of life – they therefore motivate us intrinsically. Although everyone is affected by all of the life motives, each person has an individual motive structure: it shows how strong the impact of every single motive is on a person's life. According to the Reiss Profile, we strive to satisfy and fulfill the strongest found motives. These commonly determine our life in a much more significant and permanent way than the motives that are of a lower importance.

12.2.4 *The quest for a method to manage human interaction: what are the design requirements to overcome communication challenges in implicit knowledge transfer?*

Our motivation in this research is to build a solution to the problem of ineffective knowledge transfer in offshore outsourcing. To approach this, we first seek to propose the requirements for a solution, based on our understanding of the problem. Design requirements (DRs) seek to answer the question, *what should the artifact afford to overcome the problem?*

As we have seen, a major cause of communication problems in IT outsourcing projects is the implementation of communication tasks, interaction patterns or modes of interaction that are beyond the communication skills of participants. Implementing communication choices that are beyond the capabilities of the service provider risks causing information overload or communication breakdown. We propose the first DR, *DR1: choose communication settings that match the communication capabilities of the team.*

As noted, significant cultural difference between client and service provider can make knowledge transfer challenging. Differences in communication norms, attitudes, values and working practices are all culturally embedded and can impede the establishment of communication and understanding among team members. A defining aspect of knowledge transfer in distributed work settings is the distance (organizational, physical, knowledge and norm) between knowledge source and recipient. Bridging such distances is of key importance to establishing the communication capability in the team to support the transfer of implicit knowledge particularly. We propose the second DR, *DR2: bridge distance between team members.*

IT outsourcing has complex knowledge demands, and although implicit knowledge may be as important, or more important than explicit knowledge, clients often fail to adequately attend to implicit knowledge requirements. Furthermore, transferring explicit knowledge in distributed work settings is challenging since even explicit knowledge is context specific. In other words, information that has been codified by the knowledge source may be incompatible with the recipient's understanding, leading to misinterpretation. We propose the third DR, *DR3: address implicit knowledge needs and interpretation of messages.*

The final DR reflects the understanding that monitoring and intervention by a project manager in the communication among operational team members can improve knowledge transfer outcomes. It is recognized that a project manager can have a positive influence on establishing effective communication through adopting instruments of control and motivation. We propose the fourth design principle, *DR4: find effective mechanisms for monitoring communication and knowledge transfer.*

Guided by the four DRs, and the conceptual model of the transition phase (Figure 12.5), we now seek to infer a basic method structure for knowledge transfer in IT outsourcing. The purpose of the method structure is to delineate key actions to be undertaken in the transition phase, in response to the DRs, and represent them in a logical sequence. The basic method structure is the starting point from which to develop the design framework.

Considering DR1 (*Choose communication settings that match the communication capabilities of the team*), we infer two method phases. The purpose of these is to *gather information about project and team* and *plan communication accordingly*. In order for the client to be able to match communication choices to communication capabilities, it follows that the client must be aware of these capabilities. With reference to the conceptual model, the first method phase can be understood as an information gathering phase with the purpose of gaining a sufficient understanding of the *project environment* in order to plan a communication approach which enables successful communication. This informed communication planning comprises the *second* method phase.

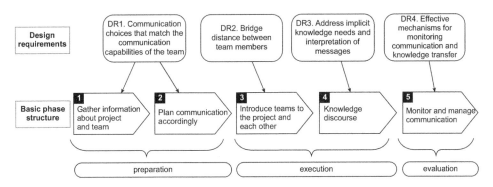

Figure 12.5   Basic phase structure for knowledge transfer in IT outsourcing projects

In response to DR2 (*Bridge distance between team members*), we infer a method phase with the purpose of *introducing team members to the project and each other*, based on communication plans devised in the previous phase. This phase reflects the concept of *communication inception*, which is influenced by the idea that the first involvement of operational team members in a project and the first interaction with remote colleagues can set the tone for relationships. For instance, interaction patterns during the first contact could serve to either reinforce or challenge established hierarchies.

An appropriate communication inception may be valuable in getting team relationships off to a good start, but DR3 (*Address implicit knowledge needs and interpretation of messages*) implies that a *knowledge discourse* and strong communication ties between team members are needed.

The final method phase responds to DR4 (*Find effective mechanisms for monitoring communication and knowledge transfer*) and reflects the understanding that intervention by a project manager in the communication between operational team members can improve knowledge transfer outcomes. The purpose of the fifth method phase is to monitor communication and manage communication.

Figure 12.5 depicts the derivation of the basic method structure from DRs.

To make the phase structure more memorable, and for ease of reference, we apply a name to it. We term the structure KAIWA, standing for the five phases: *Kaleidoscope, Adapt, Initiate, Weave* and *Analyze*. In the following part of the chapter, we will focus on KAIWA, the methods that come with it and some examples of how KAIWA can be applied best.

12.3 KAIWA, the conversation – the human factor as one of the keys to successful transition and transformation

Communication between human beings consists of facts and emotions.

Research has found that emotions make up the major part of communication – and not the facts.

Face-to-face interaction is therefore crucial for successful human knowledge transfer.

12.3.1 KAIWA: a model based on conversation

By now we have emphasized the importance of human interaction for the success of transition phases. The developed method's name is no coincidence: KAIWA is a Japanese word which means "to meet and talk," which is intended as a metaphor for the transition phase and seeks to emphasize the importance of successful communication in effective knowledge transfer. The purpose of KAIWA is to provide a logical sequence for knowledge transfer and a structure within which roles and responsibilities can be assigned, outputs can be defined and communication actions can be grouped.

12.3.2 Roles – the setting for KAIWA in IT outsourcing projects

In a first step, we want to set the stage for a typical transition situation in which KAIWA shall be used. Therefore, we need to identify and define roles, or functions, that are needed in IT outsourcing projects that fulfill different tasks. They can vary depending on the project – we will only provide a few typical roles hereunder.

The *project manager* is the driver of the project and therefore has a pivotal role – also regarding the implementation and application of KAIWA. He/she is the preparator, the organisator the steerer and the analyzer of the different steps not only of KAIWA but of the overall project. Therefore, the project manager needs two skills: excellent assessment of people, and outstanding communication capabilities. He needs to bridge the communication gaps between the team members, the different roles, and also in the client-provider relationship.

The same applies for the *sub-project manager*. He is responsible for managing a group of people for one key milestone of the overall project. He needs to respect the priority of the overall KAIWA process, but can also use KAIWA in order to structurize and improve the sub-project communication.

The *system engineer* is a structured thinker and overwatch. He must be able to understand, design and maintain a system. He can be focused on details while being able to understand the implications of one change to the entire construction. Team play is not necessarily his strength.

The *application manager* is a caretaker. He is responsible of managing the operation, maintenance, versioning and upgrading of an application throughout its lifecycle. During this process, the application becomes his main concern. While his focus on the application is useful for assuring a given functionality, he sometimes misses the overall context of a project.

There are, of course, many further roles. This is just to show that different roles in transition phases of IT outsourcing projects need different types of people with different types of knowledge and qualifications. Equally important is their ability to work within the team – that they are able to communicate with their counterparties and speak the same language. Therefore, let us have a look at the people themselves.

12.3.3 People – the actors of KAIWA

After looking at the roles, their tasks and what they need to bring along, we fill this "stage" with life – through the people involved in the project. We see people mainly as a bundle – a social construction – of the following four elements:

- *Personality* is the inherent core of an individual – the native basis of a person that cannot be changed.
- *Behavior* is the learned and trained interaction with family, friends and colleagues. It is the part defined by the social environment of a person – e.g. the company the person is working in – and can be reshaped and widened.

- *Knowledge* is the result of individual experience gained throughout life, education and job. It can be updated and enlarged.
- *Qualification* is formalized and quantified knowledge through tests, certificates and graduations. It can be updated and enlarged as well.

Through thorough research and analysis of the involved people, the project manager can create profiles of each of the team members, using publicly available information such as social media profiles, CVs, and by interviewing colleagues. Now, we can apply two dimensions of matching:

- Allocating the *right people to the right roles* in order to fulfill the tasks, depending not only, but preferably from their *knowledge* and their *qualification*;
- Matching the *right people with the right people* for effective teamwork, based not only, but preferably on their *personality* and *behavior*.

Based on these matchings, the project manager can also start to define a first set of rules of co-operation. These rules are dependent on the personalities involved and provide a framework for how the team shall communicate. This can involve wordings and tonalities, but also media and tools of communication. The rules of cooperation are there to enlarge and redefine the trained *behavior*, setting a social framework for the transition phase (see also the sequence on *working techniques* at the end of this chapter).

Furthermore, it is important for the project manager to start reflecting about the resources, the people, the (mental) locations and the impacts of *implicit and explicit knowledge* that is needed to achieve the transition – based on the findings about the involved people. This is extremely important as the transfer of knowledge is key to any outsourcing process.

12.3.4 Phases – the dramatugy of KAIWA

To develop the simple framework into a method, we build on it (in accordance with method engineering principles), through assigning roles, and defining key information outputs and communication activities, which respond to the phase requirements. In relation to the *kaleidoscope* phase, we propose that the project manager is responsible for achieving the phase requirement through collecting background information about team members, assessing their competencies (especially in relation to communication and collaboration), assessing knowledge levels and defining the level of cultural difference in the team. A further activity for the kaleidoscope phase is to assess the technical resources available to support communication between team members, since the project manager must be able to take this into account when planning interaction.

The *adapt* phase is also the responsibility of the project manager. In order to fulfill this phase, he needs to fulfill the following tasks: setting up technical resources, defining a media mix for the communication matrix which takes into account the team profile, planning actions to stimulate knowledge discourse, identify what knowledge is critical to the success of the project and seeking to identify likely knowledge gaps, and defining project objectives.

In relation to the *initiate* phase, we propose that the project manager has the main responsibility in achieving the phase requirement through introducing team members and ensuring that team members have some background information about each other as a basis for establishing familiarity and relationships. The project manager should also transfer explicit knowledge, introduce project goals and describe project context, explain expectations (especially about knowledge discourse) and explain the communication matrix by describing who should communicate with whom and by which media.

The *weave* phase is the responsibility of operational team members themselves. Activities for fulfilling the phase requirement are the execution of the interaction plan, engaging in knowledge discourse to fill knowledge gaps, confirmation and practice of gained knowledge, logging communication and knowledge gain in order that it can be tracked by the project manager, and informal dialogue to build relationships.

The project manager is responsible for the *analyze* phase, which runs concurrently with the weave phase and involves tracking knowledge discourse, checking for signs that communication is being inhibited (such as bias in communication) and intervening in knowledge discourse if necessary (Figure 12.6).

The KAIWA process can either be stopped at this point, prolonged to the operation phase, or, if need be, possibly restarted in order to recalibrate the interaction within the team. Important changes in staff within the team can also trigger the need for another KAIWA process. It is also possible to deduce just certain outcomes from the *analyze* phase which then lead to just a few recalibrations in team meetings, usage of communication media or matching of capabilities.

The most critical moment is the kick-off. It is important to keep in mind that the manner in which projects and teams are initiated is critical to knowledge transfer in projects. The establishment of relationships and communication may depend on how processes develop at initial meetings. The way in which technology-mediated team processes unfold in the beginning may create or avert persistent deficiencies as the team matures.

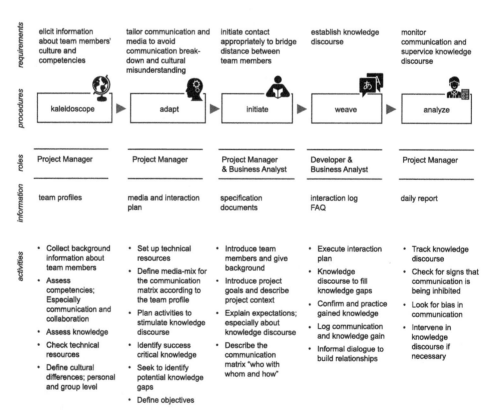

Figure 12.6 Overview of KAIWA method

All in all, we see KAIWA as a method to *strategically plan, build and maintain human inter- action and capabilities in critical projects.* It suits perfectly the needs of the transition phase of IT outsourcing projects, as it provides a clear *framework for implicit and explicit knowledge transfer* from the client company to the service provider.

12.3.5 Two greenfield examples: how KAIWA can ease transition phases

In the following sections, we will now be looking at two greenfield examples – both have happened, yet they are anonymized. As you will see, both have taken place in highly reg- ulated environments which put further external pressure on the transition. Indeed, due to increasing regulation, you will rarely encounter projects without impact from regulatory authorities. We chose these two cases in order to cover a maximum of possible aspects that you may encounter; hence, they are opposite in many ways.

Example 1: The optimization case

The following example may be the most common case you may encounter in IT outsourc- ing projects. Its core task consists of overtaking of the IT services of a rather large company infrastructure, while analyzing potential, yet smaller possibilities of consolidation and opti- mization of IT systems.

Landscape and starting point: While the company itself disposes of a multitude of highly interconnected and interdependent solutions, the application landscape is already well organized. This may also be due to the highly regulated environment the company is work- ing in – a lot of external pressure is weighing not only on the company, but also on its IT infrastructure. However, work on investment backlog is needed.

Target model: The client wants to transfer the totality of its IT systems to the service provider in order to release internal potentials for strategic IT projects. The ultimate goal of the IT outsourcing process is not so much driven by financial reasoning. Over the years, the client's staff has been stuck in operational hell, although the in-house IT experts would be better suited for more strategic work in order to develop the company's assets. Further optimization during or shortly after the transition phase is highly welcome in order to reduce pressure on the investment backlog.

Challenges during transition: There can be encountered several challenges in this case. First, the client and the service provider have to deal with an important *geographical distance* be- tween client and service provider of more than 100 kilometers. As a result, spontaneous physical meetings and short-term on-site work meetings are not possible. Therefore, there is a real risk of a *potential gap in implicit knowledge transfer* due to a lack of personal interaction. The geographical dis- tance also has an impact on the quality of human relationships within the project, as the involved people have no or very restricted possibilities of getting to know each other outside the working context. Then, the *pressure of regulation* on the transition itself and also on the further optimization of systems should not be underestimated: in this regime, there is a very small margin of error tol- erance which needs to be respected by both sides of the transition team; mutual trust, reliable and reactive communication channels are a must. Last but not least, there is a challenge in planning the *transition of responsibility* and organizing the internal and external competence. In such complex IT infrastructure landscapes, a transition does neither happen at once, nor at an easily determin- able moment in time. In other words: who is able to take decisions at which point of time?

How applying KAIWA can ease these challenges: As a framework for organizing human interaction, KAIWA can indeed help with some of the challenges above. Concerning

215

the *geographical distance*, the strategical approach of analyzing, matching and providing a constant communication guideline between key roles and key personnel will automatically lead to a more persistent and planned framework of physical meetings as well as a crisp clear establishment of communication channels. Through the application of KAIWA, the project manager will be able to narrow the gaps in personal and organizational interaction between the sides. In so doing, the *transfer of implicit knowledge* will be facilitated through a managed and monitored framework explicitly targeted at this topic. Monitoring the communication through KAIWA will also sharpen the awareness for the *pressure of regulation* and the subsequent narrow error margin. Also, the *transition of responsibility* from client company to service provider will be easier to manage, as KAIWA focuses on a constant and explicit visibility and transparency of roles and responsibilities, as well as functioning backup communication channels in case of emergency.

Example 2: The complexity reduction case

The second case is in many ways the opposite: this greenfield example consists of a rather complex application landscape which urgently needs to be reduced and consolidated, while, again, freeing up workforce for strategic projects. The case encountered several issues during its execution, especially regarding the transition phase.

Landscape and starting point: Just as in the first case, this second example takes place in a highly regulated market environment. Furthermore, the IT infrastructure of the client is a custom high-performance solution, which, at the same time, needs to run 24/7 on extremely high reliability, as the systems have an impact on international supply chains. The client, one of the oldest companies in a relatively young business, has been growing quickly over the past years. This has led to a multitude of interdependent, very customized systems with high potential for optimization. As a consequence, the in-house experts hold a knowledge monopoly on the architecture, the infrastructure and the processes.

Target model: The target model here is a rather simple one – at least at first sight. The IT service provider is asked to take over one historically grown core functionality of the client company. At the same time, the service provider needs not only to optimize this very system but also to reduce overall complexity of the interdependences with neighboring systems. This is done by isolating the core functionality and re-organizing all communication interfaces of this specific solution.

Challenges during transition: The project starts already with expectations that do not match the reality: in their negotiations, both the client and the service provider focus not enough on the application landscape surrounding the core system. Both parties highly *underestimate the complexity* of both the system itself and the task of unbundling, outsourcing and optimizing this very solution. In addition, ambitious expectations and wishes on client side concerning the optimization of infrastructure lead to a much *higher pressure* on the entire project than expected. But there are also challenges within the team.

Isolated knowledge within key people multiplies the dependencies, aggravates the risks of missing knowledge transfer and endangers again the overall timeline of the transition. Furthermore, *key people are not properly briefed* about the importance and the target model of the project, and they miss a clear personal perspective.

How applying KAIWA can ease these challenges: We now operate on the borders of KAIWA. The method cannot absorb the dangers of over-ambitious timelines and narrow resource planning. Also, KAIWA cannot create new resources: people need to be available for the transition which has to be planned by the company and project management.

In practice, applying KAIWA can help easing the pain in rough transition phases. Regarding the wrong estimations of complexity, KAIWA can quickly *reveal these imbalances between high-level planning and operational reality*. Furthermore, applying practices with the goal of team building can re-balance the team spirit in order to *prepare a group of people for rough times with high pressure*. The strategical approach to competences and qualifications – and asking key people for assistance in anticipation instead of in urgency – can also help getting people onboard. Especially during outsourcing situations, the client's staff may have no inherent motivation (e.g. because their personal development within the company is completely independent from the IT outsourcing project), or they may have shifted their focus already toward other tasks. By identifying the importance of certain peoples' qualifications beforehand, potential risks in resource planning can be made visible. In other words, KAIWA will not help to overcome the problems of bad planning, but it will *make congestions and challenges in knowledge transfer visible* before they appear. Finally, the KAIWA process is very explicit in *providing essential information on the context and the goals* of a project. This can heavily improve the motivation of staff that may not be properly briefed beforehand.

These two greenfield examples provide a brief glimpse on the upsides of implementing KAIWA. All in all, KAIWA prepares the ground for critical project phases. Next, we will have a look at some supporting techniques for the different phases of KAIWA.

12.3.6 A Handful of methods: some supports for implementing KAIWA successfully

KAIWA is highly dependent on the human framework. Any person applying the method may find varying results depending especially on the personalities, the mixture of the team and also external factors such as financial pressure or time constraints. However, there are several tools that are necessary for implementing KAIWA and that may help ease the process of getting people to work closer together and to experience a personal level of cooperation.

Below we describe several potential techniques, social practices and tools, but for the purposes of evaluation (in the following section), we do not specify details nor make their use prescriptive. Instead, we merely introduce the tools to project managers and leave them free to adapt and adjust them, or choose different tools entirely, which fulfill the phase goals.

12.3.6.1 Working techniques

Storytelling is a possible tool for the initiate phase. It could comprise short narratives about the project context, end users for the product or other notable aspects of the work. It could be transmitted via almost any media: text, video/audio recording, real-time video/audio. Storytelling is a recognized mechanism for conveying project information in "bite-size chunks."

Storyboard is a tool that a project manager could establish in the *adapt* phase. It involves plotting out the possible paths of interaction between both teams to foster collaboration and plan media usage accordingly. A project manager should define measurement and milestones for interaction, while taking into account that different paths are likely and plan alternatives.

Daily log is a tool that a project manager could implement in order to track key aspects of the project development on a daily basis. It comprises operational team members recording information about their activities and interactions as defined by the project manager, allowing him/her to monitor the project in order to inform about possible interventions.

A project manager could implement a *co-working* session in the *weave* phase, in which operational team members work jointly on a problem that needs to be solved. It requires an environment and media selection which fosters collaboration, since success is dependent on effective communication.

Monitor and filter is a tool that the project manager could adopt in the *analyze* phase. It could involve checking the operational communication (assuming that it is in a trackable format) for repeated misunderstandings, or signs that interaction is being inhibited (for example, if questions or requests are going unanswered or if certain team members are absent from communication). A project manager may define a list of critical terms and filter the conversation with this word list.

Furthermore, not only language itself may be an issue of analysis – also the way of using language is worth looking at. Every company develops a specific communication culture. People might be offended by the way a colleague may ask for assistance, as they may feel they have been given an order. *Communication guidelines* on how to approach a colleague and asking him for support may be needed. In international working situations – an even more extreme situation than just the clash of cultures between two companies – experience has shown that a rather defensive and personal communication that underlines the importance of the counterpart (e.g. asking for help) is much more effective than an administrative approach that underlines function and formal responsibility (e.g. giving orders).

12.3.6.2 Social practices

During the *initiate* phase and beyond, the project manager will need to apply some social practices: tools for classical teambuilding. Their key goal should be to reduce the – often humanly inherent – "we against them" feelings, which can often be achieved through forcing people to work together in gaming situations. This will almost automatically lead to a joint team identity in which the company-provider relationship fades into the background. We suggest three different axes:

* The relaxing atmosphere of joint *dinner and drinks* is a must in preparation of large-scale projects – not only within a given company but also across a client-service provider relationship. In other words, exchanging the normed context of an office for an informal setting will help people to open up and reveal other facettes of their personality.
* *Practicing team sports* such as football or, more in a more inclusive way, foosball or table tennis tournaments are a massive support in building human relationships. Be aware to mix teams across client and service provider to use the positive effect of creating joint memories. It might be useful especially during the *initiate* phase as it reinforces existing relationships.
* Diving into the *counterparty's hobbies* can be very personal, and, by this, become a strong bonding experience that can forge resilient and successful pairs and teams.

12.3.6.3 Digital tools

Human interaction can also be reinforced through the right usage of digital tools and media channels. Please find below some suggestions we have successfully used during KAIWA processes. They have proven useful especially regarding the *initiate* and *weave* phases.

* First and foremost, KAIWA is about opening communication possibilities. Therefore, applications for both formal and informal, *individual and group chat* are a must. Furthermore, they need to be independent from operating system platforms, and should cover

mobile devices as well. HipChat and Slack are two excellent solutions for such team and one-to-one communication. Plus, they have options to add customized emoticons – which will lead to increased group identification (e.g. through inside jokes) when used.

- *Task and responsibility management* is a pillar of successful transition projects. This can be carried out using a tool such as Trello. Tools like Trello reduce the pressure on meetings, and shrink the number of phone calls and e-mails, by creating a constant and transparent level playing field regarding the status of the overall project and its tasks.

- For the sake of *documentation* as well as team-wide *documented discussion* of contents, we have made good experiences with Confluence, a wiki-like tool. Its broad functionality and customization options make it a Swiss army knife for the accumulation of explicit knowledge. Furthermore, the tool is powerful yet easy to use and therefore inclusive regarding potential non-technical staff. In so doing, it can become a sort of digital workspace for remote teams and reduce the feeling of physical distance.

12.3.7 Risks and limits of KAIWA – where the "conversation" can fail

Although we now have clearly carved out the advantages and the potentials of KAIWA, there are of course limits and risks associated with the method:

- First and foremost, KAIWA needs time and therefore resources, especially in *adapt* and in the *analyze* phase. These resources must be agreed beforehand between both the client company and the service provider.

- Second, KAIWA does not cover nor cope with cost pressure aspects. The method is solely focused on the issue of communication quality between team members. As a result, KAIWA cannot resolve challenges by reason of lack of resources.

- Third, KAIWA does not resolve challenges caused by differences between high-level decisions and operational reality. However, it can support revealing and identifying such issues, e.g. by opening new, more informal communication channels for operational staff.

- Fourth, KAIWA cannot make up for bad planning. What KAIWA can do in this kind of situation: it can help to prepare a team for difficult times.

12.3.8 Résumé: KAIWA in transition phases of IT outsourcing projects – the takeaways

Let us summarize what we learned in this chapter. First, we had a look on the definition of a transition. We boiled it down to the "transfer of a given activity from company A to company B" – so a horizontal move of infrastructure and activity without changing its configuration.

In a second step, we focused on critical success factors of transition projects, and came to the conclusion that there are three main factors: sufficient resources, a clear plan and excellent communication skills.

We then discussed and derived logical DRs, and concluded four of them: choose communication channels, bridge distances, address implicit knowledge needs and define monitoring mechanisms.

We then dived into the core topic, discussed KAIWA itself, the method's phases and how to apply them to the roles and qualifications of the people. The main outcome here was: it's not about pure knowledge management, but about the act of communication that

Table 12.1 Techniques, practices and tools in the course of KAIWA implementation

	Phase (in particular)	Tool or method	Explanation
Working technique	Initiate	Storytelling	• Telling a story about a specific topic with a specific target (group) and its communication • Important to consider special characteristics like a narrative technique, key characters like heroes, motives, appearance of conflicts, drama/suspense, development of solutions, emotional appeal, etc. • Possible story types: fiction, reference reports, company histories, success stories, experience reports, etc. • Pay attention to the type of media (digital, text, speech, etc.), the setting, post-production, etc.
	Adapt	Storyboard	• Illustration of a story for the project at hand, which contains several "scenes" • Contents can be as different as in storytelling • Absolutely no constraints in the type of visualization methods
	Anytime	Daily log	• Daily record of significant activities • Different possibilities of tracking digitally or conventionally
	Weave	Co-working session	• Organization of a shared workplace, which allows freedom and creativity (best would be a place out of the enterprise) • Combination of different people, locations, working environments leads to new impulses and fruitful outcomes
	Analyze	Monitor and filter	• Getting an overview of the status quo by monitoring communication, results, etc. • A useful approach could be to filter the data by specific criteria
	Anytime	Communication guidelines	• Discussion about current communication behavior with all employees as a first step (to identify problems but also positive aspects) • Setting communication rules at the basis of the findings gained in the previous discussion
Social practices	Initiate	Dinner and drinks	• In the course of these teambuilding, communication-improving and relationship-strengthening activities always pay attention to the frameworks in which you come together
		Practicing team sports	
		Counterparty's hobbies	
Digital tools	Initiate weave	Chat tools	• There is a wide range of chat tools – keep in mind the aspects which are important to you when choosing a tool
		Task and responsibility management	• To organize tasks and responsibilities also check for tools that meet your requirements
		Documentation	• Wiki-tools and other intranet solutions can be very helpful

can heavily improve the transfer of all sorts of knowledge types – including the challenging implicit knowledge. KAIWA supports the transition phase by strategically researching, planning, matching, executing and analyzing the communication between people depending on their capabilities.

Furthermore, we had a look at practical tools and supports for the implementation of KAIWA. We presented working techniques, social practices and digital tools.

Finally, we briefly discussed the limits of KAIWA and constated that the method is supporting and improving the transition phase, but cannot replace or make up for resources themselves, project planning or management.

The knowledge transfer during the transition phase is a critical success factor for the overall IT outsourcing process. All in all, if we would need to reduce this chapter to one central finding, it would be that the knowledge transfer depends heavily on the skills of the project manager – especially regarding his communication and analysis capabilities. Also, a look at the bigger picture may help you to lower the pressure: knowing about and accepting pain points and intercultural preferences – and differences! – is an important step toward a successful inter-company cooperation.

We wish you good luck for your upcoming projects – and may your future transition phases be fueled by successful communication!

References

1. Blumenberg, S., Wagner, H.-T., Beimborn, D.: Knowledge Transfer Processes in IT Outsourcing Relationships and Their Impact on Shared Knowledge and Outsourcing Performance. *International Journal of Information Management* 29/5, pp. 342–352 (2009).
2. Charvet, S. R.: *Words that Change Minds: Mastering the Language of Influence.* Author's Choice Publishing (1997).
3. Chow, W.S., Chan, L.S.: Social Network, Social Trust and Shared Goals in Organizational Knowledge Sharing. *Information and Management* 45/7, pp. 458–465 (2008).
4. Gonzalez, R., Gasco, J., Llopis, J.: Information Systems Outsourcing Reasons and Risks: A New Assessment. *Industrial Management & Data Systems* 110/2, pp. 284–303 (2010).
5. Olson, J., and Olson, L.: Virtual Team Effectiveness and Sequence of Conditions. *International Journal of Management & Information Systems*, 17/1, pp. 1–12 (2013). doi:10.19030/ijmis.v17i1.7584.
6. Oshri, I., Van Fenema, P., Kotlarsky, J.: Knowledge Transfer in Globally Distributed Teams: The Role of Transactive Memory. *Information Systems Journal* 18/6, pp. 593–616 (2008).
7. Reiss, S.: *The Reiss Profile of Fundamental Goals and Motivational Sensitivities.* IDS Publishing Corporation, Columbus (2004).
8. Robert, L.P., Dennis, A.R., and Hung, Y.-T.C.: Individual Swift Trust and Knowledge-Based Trust in Face-to-Face and Virtual Team Members. *Journal of Management Information Systems* 26/2, pp. 241–279 (2009).
9. Rohde, F.H.: IS/IT Outsourcing Practices of Small- and Medium-Sized Manufacturers. *International Journal of Accounting Information Systems* 5, pp. 429–451 (2004).
10. Vlaar, P., van Fenema, P.C., Tiwari, V.: Cocreating Understanding and Value in Distributed Work: How Members of Onsite and Offshore Vendor Teams Give, Make, Demand, and Break Sense. *MIS Quarterly* 32/2, pp. 227–255 (2008).

13

PARTIES, PARTNERS AND THE LAW. SOME CONTRACTUAL AND COMPLIANCE ISSUES IN DIGITAL OUTSOURCING

Kees (C.) Stuurman

13.1 Introduction

In this chapter, we will focus on a number of trends that need attention when designing and implementing contracting structures to successfully support digital outsourcing transactions. Specifically, we will focus on: (1) partnerships requiring a shift of focus on relationships rather than delivery per se, (2) the consequences of the proliferation of parties involved (networks vs. single suppliers) and finally (3) the impact of growing compliance pressure on the chain of parties involved in the delivery of outsourcing services.

"Partnership" has been a buzzword in the IT scene long before an actual realization thereof was seemingly aimed at. Nowadays, the approach to successful technology-driven cooperation has become more mature. This however has consequences for outsourcing contracts[1] as well; real partnerships require a significant focus on the actual process of communication and cooperation, including dealing with disputes, rather than "only" KPI-driven service delivery.

Outsourcing as a tool for transforming organizations usually requires input from a range of capabilities. In the IT industry, the process of specialization has been ongoing for a long time already. In practice, this implies a growing range of subcontractors is being involved in the delivery of outsourcing services. In the contractual architecture, this is however often not reflected as the customer usually only enters into a contract with a single (main) supplier. Typically, the main contractor is responsible for its subcontractors. The main contractor is hence the single entry point. In this approach, the customer is fully dependent on the extent to which the main contractor effectively enforces the performance of its subcontractors since the customer has in general no legal basis for directly safeguarding his interests in relation to subcontractors providing vital services. Multi-party arrangements can provide a solution for these vulnerabilities.

Digital driven organizations have become subject to an increasing compliance pressure over the last few years. Data protection and cyber security are leading themes in this respect. Other, more sectoral driven legislation adds to the picture. Cooperation with a network of suppliers/partners implies that compliance becomes a multi-party issues in which the suppliers/partners have to work very closely with their customer in order to allow the customer to meet increasingly strict legal obligations. Very significant penalties, such as those applicable under the recent EU General Data Protection Regulation (GDPR) and increased reputation risks, are strong incentives for drafting adequately protective contractual arrangements supporting advanced compliance procedures (including auditing down the chain).

In the next paragraphs, we will first focus on the contractual basis for communication duties and then turn to multi-party contracting followed by a paragraph on the impact of compliance issues on the content of outsourcing contracts.

13.2 Partnerships: the contractual approach to communication

13.2.1 Introduction

Creating a "partnership" is often depicted as the holy grail for successful technology projects. As the word "partnership" is (very) multi-interpretable, everybody can have its own take, as can be seen often in marketing-driven communications involving complex technology transactions, like outsourcing. Both rather one-sided supply relationships as well true risk and benefit sharing forms of cooperation are labeled as "partnerships."

The legal side of partnerships potentially covers a wide array of issues, including the form in which the partnership operates (contractual, legal entity, etc.), the division of risks and responsibilities, potential competition law issues, etc.

In this paragraph, we will focus on a very specific aspect of partnerships: communication. In our view and experience from legal practice, this is one of the key factors setting (true) partnerships apart from more traditional customer-supplier relationships and the single most important factor for achieving success in complex outsourcing relationships.

In the next paragraph(s), we will discuss the way communication is structured as part of the contract, the potential supplementary effects of applicable statutes and some specific requirements that might apply.

13.2.2 Communication clauses

When analyzing outsourcing contracts from a communication perspective, it can be observed that usually the parties include a specific "communication clause" in their contract.

In such clause, various aspects are being covered, including:

- the obligation to inform each other, e.g. on "matters or circumstances that preclude proper performance"[2] or, even broader, "(…) keep each other informed of developments and changes that are or may be of importance to the performance of the Contract";[3]
- the channels or levels of communication, e.g. strategic, tactical operational, including a matrix linking types of issues and levels of communication;
- the format for communication, e.g. written reports, email, meetings, etc.;
- the language for communication;
- the process flow for the communication, in particular timelines for submission, decision-making (adoption, rejection, amendments), feedback and (other forms of) follow-up.

Commonly, this type of clauses is supported by one or more schedules setting out further procedural details, persons or functions involved, contact details and other operational aspects.

The incorporation of a specific communication clause might, when analyzing a contract, easily detract from the fact that such usually more "sweeping statements" are supplementing more specific communication duties that are "written all over" an outsourcing contract. Key examples include clauses on governance, service level evaluation, change procedures, acceptance procedures, contract management, reporting, audits, benchmarking as well as dispute resolution. All these clauses describe a certain process with an important communication component.

When analyzing the overall effect of commercial contracts in terms of communication obligations, one can in general distinguish several sources for such duties. In relation to outsourcing contracts, the following sources for communication duties are most relevant: (1) the text of the relevant clauses in the contract, (2) statutory obligations, (3) legal principles (e.g. good faith) and (4) the interpretation of the contract. The latter being in practice, although clearly relevant, often of somewhat less significance than the other sources. We will discuss the first three sources in more detail below.

13.2.2.1 *The text of the contract*

Above we gave a number of examples of key contract clauses with a major communication component, such as clauses on governance, service level evaluation, change procedures, acceptance procedures, contract management, reporting, audits, benchmarking and dispute resolution. These types of clauses can be categorized in several ways including:

- pre-defined reporting duties, like on KPI's, test results (…), etc. Basically, this concerns communications of which the content is delineated on forehand with "tangible" parameters. With providing the report, the party involved (usually the supplier) shows complying with a specific contractual obligation;
- open reporting duties, like these focusing on signaling risks or other (potentially) adverse consequences. The content of this type of clauses ("provide all relevant information," etc.; see for other examples above) often approaches the content of the supplementary obligations stemming from general contract law principles (see below);
- formal notifications, including those aimed at:
  - establishing elements of non-performance, including late payments, late approval/ discharge, non-compliance with specifications, etc.;
  - compliance with a specific obligation, like sending an audit report, proof of acceptance or proof of approval;
  - formally establishing the existence of a dispute;
  - establishing/conforming a specific legal effect, including notifications relating to audits, notices of default, etc.;
- cooperation clauses obliging the parties to actively exchange information, such as dispute-related clauses reaching beyond the mere exchange of information between the parties by imposing them to cooperate in finding an amicable solution;
- clauses reflecting commercial or technological choices and clauses mandatorily incorporated on the basis of statutes (e.g. imposing security obligations on suppliers or subcontractors as is mandatory under the European GDPR; see below) or on the basis of contracts (e.g. in software distribution related contracts).

When drafting communication-related clauses parties have to deal with various aspects thereof including the means of communication, the content thereof, sender(s), receiver(s), identification and security. In general, a more formal approach will be chosen when the stakes get higher. It is important to realize that for various reasons, including risk management, this has a fundamental and significant value. It intends to ensure that the safeguards underlying internal hierarchy/authorizations are being applied for careful decision-making on the right level of the organization, being the level on which the impact of the decision for the organization can be weighed taking all relevant information and interests into account. Experience from conflict resolution practice shows that choosing the right communication level and format is of crucial importance for preventing and solving (potential) disputes.

As regards the category of formal communications, it is furthermore important to keep in mind that binding statutory communication requirements will apply in some cases. Often, this will include especially notices of default and notices relating to data protection legislation. Non-compliance with such statutory requirements can have severe consequences. When in the context of termination no prior notice of default is given (which is often mandatory), the court might conclude that the statement aimed at terminating the contract is void and the contractual obligations can still be enforced.

The latter could be the basis for a supplier to claim payment of service fees and damages.

Notwithstanding excellent drafting skills, a contract can never detail all communication that is relevant for giving a partnership in the fundamental sense (risk and benefit sharing). From a legal perspective, such endeavor would also not be advisable as it would (1) render the text of the contract inaccessible and (2) it might give rise to the argument that parties have intended to be exhaustive which might block flexibility being a key requirement in modern outsourcing relations

13.2.3 *Statutory communication obligations*

13.2.3.1 *Statutory obligations to inform*

Depending on the type of business process that is being outsourced and the market sector in which the customer operates, various statutory communication duties can be applicable. In principle, these concern the customer but still impact the contract as it will reflect the derived obligation for the supplier to cooperate in enabling the customer to be compliant. A current example of the above is the notification duties relating to data breaches or other cyber security-related incidents. Relevant legislation in the European Union includes the GDPR (in case of breaches in processing of personal data; see below) and the EU Network Information Security Directive (in case of cyber incidents relating to critical infrastructure). Recently, the EU Cyber Security Act[4] has been added to this European framework for cyber security legislation relating to handling of disputes generally contains mandatory reporting/notification duties.

In some cases, the outsourcing supplier will be under an independent statutory obligation to report to the customer. This obligation will supplement the contractual obligations and will hence even apply if the contract does not provide for such duty. An example is the notification obligation for the supplier in case of a data breach when processing personal data under the GDPR for a customer qualifying as controller.

13.2.3.2 *Communication duties following from legal principles*

Duties to inform do not only arise from explicit contractual provisions but can also be derived from legal principles underlying contract law. A key example in the context of technology projects is the set of information duties based on principles such as "reasonableness and fairness" or "good faith." In civil law jurisdictions (continental Europe), these principles can act as a basis for supplementing contractual provisions with (unwritten) information duties. These information duties generally encompass (1) the duty to provide relevant information to the other party (on the basis of the knowledge and experience the relevant party has or should have), (2) the duty to investigate (including requesting information from the other party) and – in exceptional circumstances – (3) a duty to warn against damages or other seriously adverse effects. In the context of outsourcing, an example of the latter could for instance be that the supplier warns against the risk of planning a transition in a critical business period. In countries such as France and the Netherlands, these principles have already been applied in IT-related cases as early as the beginning of the 1980s[5] and are still an important tool for judges and arbitrators in dealing with IT disputes.

In key common law jurisdictions, such as the US and the UK, the role of these principles as a source for unwritten obligations is (far) less prominent.[6] In practice, outsourcing agreements across jurisdictions often contain explicit information duties since the parties rather rely on[7] express information duties spelled out in the contract than on the court deriving similar implicit obligations from the contract in case of a dispute.

13.3 Multi-party contracting: challenges and options

13.3.1 Introduction

Specialization is an ongoing process in the technology industry. Projected on outsourcing it implies that the outsourcing ecosystem has become more complex over time, hosting more and specialized companies. To support the growingly complex business process of customers, a range of different skills and competences needs to brought together, supported by an adequate contractual framework.

Interestingly, the legal structure of outsourcing deals seems to lag behind the developments in the industry more and more. However, complex the outsourcing solution is, and notwithstanding involvement of a range of specialized parties, ultimately the deal – with exceptions for a select group of highly complex top-level deals – usually results in a bilateral contract. On the basis thereof, the lead supplier subsequently subcontracts with the other parties involved on the supplier side.

In some cases, multivendor deals result in a "hub and spoke" structure with a series of bilateral contracts between the customer and each of the suppliers involved individually. In some cases, the contract structure is enriched with a type of "coordination agreement" between the various suppliers involved, usually in the form of an Operating Level Agreement (OLA).[8] This kind of agreement is in principle only effective between the supplier and subcontractors involved and does not constitute a binding agreement the customer can enforce when necessary.

The use of bilateral contracts in a multi-party context reduces the complex reality to a straightforward, traditional "customer"-"supplier" structure. This does not mean that the multi-party reality is not taken into account at all; subcontracting relationships are applied to connect other partners in the deal to this bilateral structure. So far, so good or not? In our view, it is time to reflect on the value of more advanced contracting models that better support the business reality and reduce risks involved in the traditional bilateral approach.

13.3.2 Why bilateral contracts are suboptimal

For several reasons, the current standard contracting model is suboptimal. First, the mismatch between the dominantly bilateral contract structure and the business reality impacts the focus of the partners (subcontractor) especially in the supplier ecosystem. Ultimately, their focus is on the supplier and not primarily – as it should be – on the other partners in the ecosystem and the customer, being the ultimate beneficiary of their services. Their contract with – only – the supplier steers them toward meeting the targets agreed with the supplier (and not the customer).[9]

Second, and even more important, the traditional bilateral contracting model introduces a significant risk for the customer. In principle, the supplier is responsible, and liable, for the selection and performance of subcontractors. However in most legal systems, the customer does not have any right of its own to secure enforcement by the subcontractors engaged by the (main) supplier. The latter implies that the customer, in case of supplier default, cannot directly secure his interest toward the relevant subcontractor on the basis of the main outsourcing contract (privity of contract). Let us take the example of a supplier that has engaged an external hosting party. In case an issue arises in their mutual cooperation (e.g. late or non-payment) on the basis whereof the hosting party suspends its performance, the customer can only exert pressure on the supplier but has in no title to act in its own legal right against the hosting party. The latter is vital for securing continuity, access to his data, access to information for meeting notification obligations toward supervisory authorities, etc. Obviously, this can have very severe consequences for the customer.

In the next paragraph, we will explore several potential solutions to deal with the challenges set out above.

13.3.3 Alternative legal frameworks supporting multi-party outsourcing relations

Bilateral contracts in principle only bind the signatories and do not have an effect on third parties. In customer-supplier-subcontractor relationships, this implies that in principle the customer cannot independently act against the subcontractor on the basis of his outsourcing contract with the supplier to ensure compliance. It should be noted that we focus on a common denominator over a range of legal systems and hence some exceptions to this rule could apply in specific jurisdictions or cases. In considering alternative approaches, we will also consider ways of improving the cooperation between the partners in the ecosystem (in terms of enhancing continuity, flexibility, etc.) and not focus on merely claiming damages when things went wrong. As discussed in the previous paragraph, we see an upside in creating a legal framework that not only provides more support for aligning the efforts of the network partners but also provides more safeguards especially for the customers in protecting his interests served by the supplier's subcontractors.

Various options can be considered to improve the quality of the contractual framework for outsourcing from the perspective set out above. In exploring these options, we will distinguish between:

1   solutions that can be qualified as "add-ons" to the current, predominantly bilateral contract structures;
2   multi-party contract solutions;
3   legal entity-based approaches.

13.3.4 *Add-on solutions to bilateral contract structures*

As we described above, one of the key issues in modern outsourcing relationships is that reducing network relationships to a set of bilateral contracts implies that (even) strong dependencies cannot be securely managed by (in particular) the customer without the active cooperation of the (main) supplier. This creates significant risks especially when subcontractors deliver critical services components for which the supplier cannot deliver backup solutions in case of their non-compliance. The latter is more and more common due to ongoing specialization in the IT industry as we discussed above.

Not only is the customer fully dependent on the supplier for securing his rights, the same holds for other subcontractors as they (usually) only contract with the supplier. The governance of their mutual cooperation hence always requires a triangle relationship: subcontractor 1-supplier-subcontractor 2, creating a potential burden, and hence inefficiencies for an optimal cooperation on the level of the subcontractors.[10] An effective remedy to reduce the risks for the customer is to conclude "safety net" contracts with the individual key subcontractors that contain obligations that can be relied on by the customer in case the supplier does not perform adequately or timely. It is hence to be considered as a "back-up" solution in case of (threatening) non-performance of the supplier.

Such contracts can include clauses aimed at:

- securing adequate direct communication channels between the customer and the subcontractor for specific cases;
- securing payment for the subcontractor when the supplier falls short of (timely) payments, preventing suspension of his obligations by the subcontractor;
- the obligation for the subcontractor to escalate any issues that could threaten the continuity of his service delivery timely to customer directly as well;
- the obligation for the subcontractor to act directly upon instruction of the customer in critical situations;
- the obligation for the subcontractor to cooperate with audits initiated by the customer or supervisory authorities.

Above we gave as an example of this approach a case in which a customer has concluded an independent contract with the hosting partner of his supplier to prevent suspension of performance in case of late or non-payment by the supplier. Depending on the relevant jurisdiction, different legal techniques could be used to create the "safety net" approach set out above, including – next to straightforward bilateral contracts – conditional contracts (kicking in only in specific cases) and conditional third-party beneficiary clauses inserted in the contract between the supplier and the subcontractor, etc.

Obviously, the application of such instrument requires a proper understanding of its scope and application as it might otherwise lead to an ongoing interference by the customer of the supplier's subcontractor management. The latter also not being in the interest of the customer. Clearly, suppliers will not always be comfortable with such approach as this could interfere with their way of managing the relationship with the subcontractor and it could weaken their position toward the customer, e.g. due to the improved information position of the customer.

13.3.5 *Multi-party contracting solutions*

Bilateral contracts also fall short in adequately supporting multi-party cooperations[11] for other reasons, including:

- A lack of provisions for joining or exiting a contract by a third party, thereby creating legal uncertainty;
- Change provisions are often inadequate to support flexibility in differentiation in roles and responsibilities between the various contracting parties;
- When using a set of individual, bilateral contracts to support multi-party cooperation, the number of contracts rapidly grows with the number of parties. Covering a cooperation between each and every of N parties requires $N \times ((N-1)/2)$ individual bilateral contracts. So for example, cooperation of 9 parties requires 36 individual bilateral contracts. This creates complexity and a significant administrative burden.

The use of multi-party contracts (hence contracts with more than two signatories[12]) can provide a solution to these and other issues. Most importantly, it can (1) provide a basis for ensuring compliance with a common set of obligations forming the basis of each and very interaction between the contracting parties but also (2) cater for distinct arrangements between a subset of the parties. As this is all encompassed in one single instrument, it can also – provided that it is adequately drafted and managed – support the entry or exit of parties and efficiently support flexibility across all arrangements. When this approach is successfully deployed, changes in the ecosystem do not require a burdensome amendment of all affected bilateral contracts.

While this is a major upside of this instrument, there are obviously also some concerns. The extent to which multi-party contracts are being addressed explicitly in contract law varies across jurisdictions. In the Netherlands, an example of a civil law jurisdiction (as most other European countries), the Civil Code enables creating multi-party contracts but does not provide detailed arrangements and to a large extent the relevant statutory provisions are not mandatory. This implies that the parties have on the one hand a significant liberty to create multi-party contract structures but on the other hand it also leaves uncertainty as to critical issues like the interpretation of the contract, suspension of obligations or dissolution of the contract. This challenge can be managed in the drafting process but requires additional skills. Some level of uncertainty will however remain since, as multi-party contracts are an exception rather than the rule, case law and jurisprudence regarding this type contracts are hence generally less developed than for traditional, bilateral contracts. On forehand this can however not be labeled as a blocking issue for exploring this approach.[13]

13.3.6 *Legal entity-based approaches*

More explorative might be the application of a legal entity (often referred to as a "joint venture"[14]) as a vehicle for creating rights and obligations across a spectrum of parties.

Let us explain by using the example of a sport association. In most cases, the association will be a legal entity with which individuals can enter into a membership relation. By the mere accession to the association (membership contract), the individual members are bound to all regulations declared applicable by the association. Also this could, next to the vertical relationship between the association and the individual member, result in horizontal relationships (rights and obligations) between the members mutually.[15] Now, outsourcing is a fascinating topic but not a sport with (in principle) equal participants. How could this approach nevertheless be relevant?

First of all, the use of e.g. an association could be a relatively easy way to impose the previously described "general requirements" to each and every party involved in the outsourcing, including ensuring mutual obligations. This has as an upside that the involvement of the (main) customer and supplier is not conditional for ensuring compliance with these requirements. This can strengthen the (quality of) mutual cooperation between the subcontractors involved. Second, the diversity of the parties involved can be catered for by creating various types (categories) of membership, catering for the individual or bilateral needs of subsets of the ecosystem. It should also be noted that flexibility, in terms of accession/exit of parties or changes in general or party-specific arrangements, can in principle be accommodated efficiently in this structure.

Notwithstanding these advantages, there are obviously also some challenges that would need further exploration. These include issues like the exact consequences of default of key members, the design of a detailed governance structure, potential tax issues and maybe even competition law issues. The choice for a specific type of legal entity will have to be considered carefully taking into account local characteristics of the solutions at hand and the extent to which they can effectively serve the parties interest in creating a suitable legal framework for facilitating a successful outsourcing. Despite these challenges, there seems to be an adequate amount of upside justifying the further exploration of this option in specific cases.

13.4 Compliance pressure: the impact on contracts

13.4.1 *Digitization as driver for upward compliance force*

The digitization of our society has impacted the governance pressure on outsourcing suppliers along two lines: the digitization of their internal processes as well as the digitization of their customer's business. This has resulted in a string of new compliance obligations. The sources for these obligations are manifold. Independent of their business focus, organizations have been confronted with new obligations concerning data security, data protection and electronic communication in general. Additionally, sector-specific rules have become applicable depending on the sector in which they operate. Important examples include finance, retail and healthcare.[16] The increased volume of applicable rules also resulted in more supervisory focus, especially in the fields of cyber security, data protection, finance and consumer protection. Additionally, the stakes have gone up as this new legislation in some cases also came with increased supervisory capacity and more stringent sanctions (like in case of the European GDPR; see below) and, sometimes even more important, a sharply risen risk of reputational damage. Obviously, this process is still ongoing with new rules for e.g. platforms, artificial intelligence and blockchain currently being debated in circles of policy makers and supervisory authorities.

Achieving compliance in this setting is no longer something an organization can do on its own or in cooperation with single supplier. As a consequence of the shift from basic bilateral relations to coupled ecosystems (as we discussed earlier in this chapter), compliance has become a "team effort" and requires intense cooperation within the technology and business ecosystem(s) in which an organization operates.

This has become even more complex due to the time-sensitive nature of various notification duties (relating to data breaches) that have been introduced, the stringent sanctions on non-compliance and the fact that – especially in the field of data protection – independent statutory obligations have been imposed on outsourcing suppliers (next to the obligations of their customers).

In view of the interests at stake, ensuring compliance requires a solid legal basis in terms of adequate contracts. More specifically, it requires in particular contractual provisions (1) setting out adequately the duty to cooperate in achieving compliance, (2) proper auditing clauses, (3) proper sanctions to ensure effectiveness of these arrangements and (4) ensuring passing on of the relevant clauses to third parties (subcontractors). Given the interests at stake (stringent sanctions, customer claims and reputational damage) especially outsourcing customers should carefully consider whether reliance on – merely – their outsourcing partner, instead of securing a direct contractual relationship with the supplier's key subcontractors, is in the given circumstances an acceptable risk. As discussed above, we see compliance pressure, in addition to continuity-related arguments, as an important driver for deciding to enter into "safety net" contracts complementing the main outsourcing contract with the supplier.

In the next paragraph, we will illustrate the above by focusing on the developments in the field of data protection regulation and in particular on the impact of the recent European GDPR. Due to its broad geographical scope, the GDPR not only impacts outsourcing relationships in Europe but is potentially relevant for customers and suppliers around the globe.

13.4.2 Case study data protection. The impact of the GDPR

13.4.2.1 Background and scope

As of 25 May 2018, the GDPR (Regulation 2016/679) constitutes the center piece of the European approach to data protection.[17] The GDPR replaces the EU Directive 95/46 (the "Data Protection Directive").[18] By its nature, the GDPR – being an EU Regulation – equally applies in all EU Member States. The GDPR also applies in a number of countries outside the EU (Norway, Iceland and Lichtenstein), together with the EU constituting the European Economic Area (EEA).

Although the introduction of the GDPR was partially driven by the desire to create a level playing field throughout the EU, national legislation remains of importance. This on the one hand since the GDPR leaves some room for national interpretations regarding some topics but also since the full EU data protection package includes a number of directives requiring national implementation. The latter includes EU Directive 2016/680 (Law Enforcement Directive)[19] effective as of 6 May 2018 and the e-Privacy Directive (2002/58/EC)[20] which in the near future[21] will be replaced by the EU e-Privacy Regulation.[22] The latter instrument will particularize and complement (as a "lex specialis") the general rules on the protection of personal data laid down in the GDPR for electronic communications data qualifying as personal data.

From an outsourcing point of view, it is particularly important to note that the GDPR seeks to extend the reach of EU data protection law compared to Directive 95/46/EC. In many cases, the GDPR will be relevant, and likely even directly applicable, for outsourcing partners from outside the EU when entering into contracts with customers having a business focus on Europe. The establishment of the customer or outsourcing supplier in the EEA or processing of data in the EEA is not mandatory per se for the applicability of the GDPR. The territorial scope of the GDPR extends even beyond the EEA as the Regulation applies:

1   to the processing of personal data in the context of the activities of an establishment of a controller or a processor in the Union, regardless of whether the processing takes place in the Union or not (art. 3 par. 1 GDPR);

2   to the processing of personal data of data subjects who are in the Union by a controller
     or processor not established in the Union, where the processing activities are related to
     offering goods or services to such data subjects in the Union or the monitoring of their
     behavior within the Union (art. 3 par. 2 GDPR).

Materially, the scope of the GDPR extends to almost all forms of processing of data since
the definition of "personal data" is very broad. Under Article 4 (1) GDPR "personal data"
include any information relating to an identified or identifiable natural person ("data subject") being a person who

> "can be identified, directly or indirectly, in particular by reference to an identifier such
> as a name, an identification number, location data, an online identifier or to one or more
> factors specific to the physical, physiological, genetic, mental, economic, cultural or
> social identity of that natural person."

13.4.2.2 GDPR principles, roles and responsibilities for data processors

The GDPR is based on a number of principles/rights, mainly:[23]

- fair, lawful and transparent processing (processed lawfully, fairly and in a transparent
  manner in relation to the data subject);
- purpose specification and purpose limitation (collected for specified, explicit and legitimate
  purposes and not further processed in a manner that is incompatible with those purposes);
- data minimization/proportionality (adequate, relevant and limited to what is necessary
  in relation to the purposes for which they are processed);
- data quality (accurate and, where necessary, kept up to date);
- storage limitation (kept in a form which permits identification of data subjects for no
  longer than is necessary for the purposes for which the personal data are processed);
- data integrity and confidentiality (processed in a manner that ensures appropriate security of the personal data).

Furthermore, the principles of lawful processing,[24] data portability[25] and "data protection by
design and default" are important elements in the GDPR. The "by design" principle refers
to the obligation of the controller to, both at the time of the determination of the means
for processing and at the time of the processing itself, implement appropriate technical and
organizational measures (such as pseudonymization) that are designed to effectively implement data-protection principles and to integrate the necessary safeguards for meeting the
requirements of the regulation.[26] Data protection "by default" encompasses the obligation of
the controller to implement appropriate technical and organizational measures to ensure, by
default, only personal data which are necessary for each specific purpose of the processing are
processed (in terms of amount of the personal data collected, the extent of their processing,
the period of their storage and their accessibility).[27]

The very broad scope of the GDPR in terms of both types of data covered and geographically is particularly relevant for outsourcing providers as they generally qualify as
"processors" under the GDPR. The qualification "processors" refers to an entity which
processes personal data on behalf of the "controller" – the latter being the entity responsible
for determining the purposes and means of the processing of personal data.[28] In the context
of outsourcing involving processing of personal data, basically the customer will qualify as

"controller" and the supplier as "processor." When the supplier also processes (parts of) the data for its own purposes, like some Cloud providers do, they will also qualify as "controller" for the relevant data processing activities.[29] On the side of the supplier, other parties involved (subcontractors) could qualify as "sub-processors."

The extension of the applicability of the data protection framework to processors constitutes a novelty in the EU approach to data protection and creates a basis for independent obligations pertaining to processors.

Art. 28 GDPR further clarifies the obligations of the processor and its relation to the controller and other parties involved. Without prejudice to the independent obligations of the processor, the controller is obliged to engage only processors providing "sufficient guarantees to implement appropriate technical and organizational measures in such a manner that processing will meet the requirements of this Regulation and ensure the protection of the rights of the data subject."

For outsourcing suppliers, it is important to realize that the GDPR does introduce some direct responsibilities for processors and non-compliance might result in severe fines or other sanctions.

Under the GDPR penalties can even amount to 4% of the total global annual turnover or €20 million (whichever is higher).[30] The UK Data protection Supervisory authority (ICO) has summarized the direct responsibilities obligations for data processors under the GDPR as follows:

- not to use a sub-processor without the prior written authorization of the data controller;
- to co-operate with supervisory authorities (such as the ICO);
- to ensure the security of its processing;
- to keep records of processing activities; or to notify any personal data breaches to the data controller;
- to employ a data protection officer;
- to appoint (in writing) a representative within the European Union if needed.[31]

13.4.2.3 Contractual aspects

Processing of personal data shall only take place by a processor on the basis of a contract[32] that is binding and sets out the subject matter and duration of the processing, the nature and purpose of the processing, the type of personal data and categories of data subjects and the obligations and rights of the controller.[33]

The mandatory elements of such contract include:[34]

- processing of personal data only on documented instructions from the controller;
- confidentiality obligations for staff authorized to process the personal data;
- the obligation to take all measures required to ensure the security of processing according to art. 32 GDPR;
- providing assistance to the controller for fulfilling his obligation to respond to requests for exercising the data subject's rights including providing information, access to information, erasure ("right to be forgotten" and correction) and the controller's obligations in case of data breach (including notification to the supervisory authority and communication of a personal data breach to the data subject);
- assisting the controller in performing data protection impact assessments;
- the obligation to cooperate with audits and inspections conducted by the controller or mandated auditors.

In practice, the data processing contract is often drafted in the form of a separate contract that is added as an annex to the main outsourcing contract. The upside of such approach is that the negotiations regarding the data processing contract can be entrusted to a dedicated data protection working group with experts from both sides. The potential downside of such approach is however that the terminology and content of the data processing contract significantly deviates from the approach taken in drafting the main outsourcing contract by the commercial/legal working group. In the latter case, this can in principle be balanced by priority and interpretation clauses in the main outsourcing contract.

Subcontracting by the processor (hence engaging sub-processors) is only allowed on the basis of prior specific or general written authorization of the controller.[35] Engaging sub-processors does not relieve the processor of its obligations toward the controller.[36]

Under the GDPR, the establishment of data protection certification mechanisms (as well as data protection seals and marks) is encouraged for the purpose of demonstrating compliance by controllers and processors (art. 42 GDPR).[37] Currently, there are already a significant number of potentially relevant schemes on the market. These schemes however differ in terms of sources (legislation, standards or combined), scope (geographical, sectoral, process), single issue (e.g. privacy by design or data security[38]) or comprehensiveness (all GDPR provisions covered). Additional complications include:

- A variety of different controls. Schemes operated by public authorities/privately owned schemes and schemes accredited/monitored by public authorities vs. national accreditation bodies, DPAs;
- Uncertainty as to the legal effect of certification. Certification does not reduce the responsibility of the controller or the processor (art. 42(3)). Under art. 83 (Fines), when a fine is being issued, "due regard shall be given to the (...) adherence to (...) approved certification mechanisms pursuant to Article 42";[39]
- No clarity as to the mutual recognition of certificates between Member States (a certificate has – so far – in principle only validity in one Member State) unless it concerns a certificate issued by the EDPB.[40] This implies that the controller might, worst case will, have to obtain a range of certificates in order to cover its activities across Europe.
- Uncertainty regarding the way effective certifications can be realized in relations to non-EU-based controllers or processors.[41]

It is not unlikely that customers will put pressure on their outsourcing suppliers to obtain the relevant certificates.[42] In the near future, next to GDPR-related certifications, additional certificates might be required under the European Cybersecurity Act[43] providing for product and process-related cyber-security certifications. Although the bringing about of the Regulation was in part driven by the aim of countering the rise of local certifications (and hence barriers to trade), the current framework still contains a serious risk of substantial complications for especially cross-sectoral operating providers.

13.5 Concluding remarks

Digitization is heavily impacting the way organizations operate, innovate and connect to customers and partners. Outsourcing supporting these processes can only be successful if adapted accordingly. This not only requires innovative ways of operating and connecting with customers but also requires adaptation to the changing landscape of the tech industry in terms of ongoing specialization, entrants and technological focus (Cloud computing, big data, cyber security, block chain, artificial intelligence, etc.).

From a contracting point of view, the increasing demand for flexibility and speed requires a strong focus on process rather than on merely fixed KPIs. However, also the contractual architecture underlying the outsourcing process needs to be adapted, calling for moving away from only deploying traditional bilateral contracts.

Bringing responsibilities close to the relevant partners can significantly enhance the customer's ability to monitor, guide and control their key delivery partners. The growing compliance pressure facing many customers of the outsourcing industry is, next to the drive for innovation, a strong second argument for substantiating such approach. Effectively realizing such approach requires the ability to consider alternative contracting structures as well.

Notes

1. In relation to outsourcing in practice both the terms "agreement" and "contract" are being used to reflect the document in which the main legal understanding between the parties is laid down. Although we consider both terms equivalent in this context, we will for the sake of clarity refer to "contract" or "contracts" unless the use of the phrase "agreement" is more common in the market, like in "service level agreement."
2. See e.g. Pon Template Sourcing Agreement v1.0, Clause 12.1 available through an internet search at: PON+outsourcing+agreement+template. For (other) notification duties, see for instance as well the recent Model Services Contract of the UK Government (see: https://www.gov.uk/government/publications/model-services-contract).
3. Art. 4.4. General Government Terms and Conditions for IT Contracts 2018 (Arbit 2018) as adopted by order of the Dutch Prime Minister, Minister of General Affairs, of 3 May 2018, no. 3219106 available at: https://www.pianoo.nl/nl/regelgeving/voorwaarden/rijksoverheid/algemene-rijksvoorwaarden-bij-it-overeenkomsten-2018-arbit-0.
4. Regulation (EU) 2019/881 of the European Parliament and of the Council of 17 April 2019 on ENISA (the European Union Agency for Cybersecurity) and on information and communications technology cyber-security certification and repealing Regulation (EU) No 526/2013 (Cybersecurity Act) (text with EEA relevance) PE/86/2018/REV/1 OJ L 151, 7.6.2019, p. 15–69.
5. Vandenberghe, G., *Partijenaansprakelijkheid bij softwareovereenkomsten. Een rechtsvergelijkend onderzoek.* Reeks Informatica en Recht Deel 2, Antwerpen/Deventer: Kluwer 1984 and De Lamberterie, I., *Les Contrats en informatique*, Litec, Paris, 1983.
6. Historically, there has been no established general concept of good faith in English law. In specific cases, like partnership agreements, the principle may however be considered relevant be it (considerably) less than in the European approach. In recent years, the English courts however seem more willing to consider express contractual good faith provisions to be enforceable. See: Sinanan, Andre, Good Faith in English Contract Law: A 'Contagious Disease of Alien Origin' (December 2, 2014). Available at SSRN: https://ssrn.com/abstract=2654752.
7. The level of enforceability may vary across jurisdictions.
8. In most cases OLAs are only used within the organization of the supplier to facilitate cooperation between the various internal departments involved in service delivery to the customer.
9. A similar reasoning could be developed for partners operating on the customer side of the ecosystem but this seems in general less relevant in practice.
10. Technically speaking, this could be solved by making a subcontractor a party to the customer-supplier contract. This "cure" might however be worse than the "disease" since – without major changes – such contract would not basically solve the issue of cooperation between subcontractors but does give rise to a wide range of issues (including governance, termination, liability, etc.) in the relation between (all) parties involved.
11. Stuurman, C., Wijnands, H. S. A., & Drion, C. E. (1998). *Electronic Commerce. Een privaatrechtelijk kader voor multilaterale EDI.* (ITeR; No. 12). Deventer: Kluwer, p. 10–11.
12. Or other forms of adherence, like acceptance of third-party clauses.

13. The way multilateral treaties and connected institutions function (like in the field of international trade) could also provide inspiration for further exploring multi-party approaches.
14. Although a joint venture could be purely contractual as well.
15. For instance by inserting third-party clauses in the membership contract.
16. See for an overview of the European legal framework for electronic communication in general: Lodder, A. R., & Murray, A. D. (Eds.) (2017). *EU Regulation of E-Commerce A Commentary*. Cheltenham Glos: Edward Elgar Publishing.
17. For electronic communications, additional rules will be set out in the forthcoming ePrivcay Regulation (proposal for a regulation of the European parliament and of the council concerning the respect for private life and the protection of personal data in electronic communications and repealing Directive 2002/58/EC (Regulation on Privacy and Electronic Communications), COM/2017/010 final – 2017/03 (COD)). This Regulation will (probably) take effect in the course of 2019.
18. Directive 95/46/EC of the European Parliament and of the Council of 24 October 1995 on the protection of individuals with regard to the processing of personal data and on the free movement of such data, Official Journal L 281 , 23/11/1995 P. 31–50.
19. Directive (EU) 2016/680 of the European Parliament and of the Council of 27 April 2016 on the protection of natural persons with regard to the processing of personal data by competent authorities for the purposes of the prevention, investigation, detection or prosecution of criminal offences or the execution of criminal penalties, and on the free movement of such data, and repealing Council Framework Decision 2008/977/JHA, OJ L 119, 4/5/2016, pp. 89–131.
20. Directive 2002/58/EC of the European Parliament and of the Council of 12 July 2002 concerning the processing of personal data and the protection of privacy in the electronic communications sector (Directive on privacy and electronic communications), OJ L 201, 31/7/2002, pp. 37–47.
21. Probably in late 2020.
22. Proposal for a Regulation of the European Parliament and of the Council concerning the respect for private life and the protection of personal data in electronic communications and repealing Directive 2002/58/EC (Regulation on Privacy and Electronic Communications), COM/2017/010 final – 2017/03 (COD).
23. Art. 5 GDPR.
24. Art. 6 GDPR.
25. The right to receive the personal data in a structured, commonly used and machine-readable format with the right to transmit those data to another controller without hindrance (art. 20 GDPR).
26. Art. 25 par. 1 GDPR.
27. Art. 25 par. 2 GDPR.
28. Art. 4 GDPR.
29. See as well art. 28 par. 10 GDPR: "(…), if a processor infringes this Regulation by determining the purposes and means of processing, the processor shall be considered to be a controller in respect of that processing."
30. Art. 83 par. 6 GDPR.
31. ICO GDPR guidance: contracts and liabilities between controllers and processors, v 1.0 draft for consultation, 2017, p. 21.
32. Or other legal act (e.g. a permit or (other) government decision) under Union or Member State law that is binding on the processor (Art. 28 par. 3 GDPR).
33. Art. 28 par. 3 GDPR.
34. Art. 28 par. 3 GDPR.
35. Art. 28 par. 2 GDPR.
36. Art. 28 par. 4 GDPR.
37. See also Consideration 81 ("The adherence of the processor to an approved code of conduct or an approved certification mechanism may be used as an element to demonstrate compliance with the obligations of the controller.").
38. For instance covering (only) ISO/IEC 27001.
39. It should be noted that this not necessarily implies that a fine will be mitigated when a certificate has been obtained. The fact that, even where a certificate was obtained, the GDPR was violated might also be considered an aggravating circumstance. See Article 29 Data Protection Working Party, Guidelines on the application and setting of administrative fines for the purposes of the Regulation 2016/679 (3 October 2017), p. 16: "Non-compliance with self-regulatory measures could also reveal the controller's/processor's negligence or intentional behavior of non-compliance."

40. Art. 42 par. 5 GDPR.
41. Art. 42 par. 2 GDPR provides the framework for these certifications. Implementing this provision gives rise to various questions regarding the organization and substance of these certifications (pending research of the Tilburg Institute for Law, Technology and Society, see: https://www.tilburguniversity.edu/research/institutes-and-research-groups/tilt/research/current-major-research-projects).
42. The recently introduced ISO 27701 standard (see: https://www.iso.org/standard/71670.html) could be an effective instrument in the process of achieving compliance and readiness for GDPR certification in this context.
43. Regulation (EU) 2019/881 of the European Parliament and of the Council of 17 April 2019 on ENISA (the European Union Agency for Cybersecurity) and on information and communications technology cybersecurity certification and repealing Regulation (EU) No 526/2013 (Cybersecurity Act), OJ L 151, 7.6.2019, p. 15–69.

PART 3

From on-site to Cloud

The Cloud is more demanding than ever. This requires full dedication of both service recipients and providers. In Chapter 14, Schuberg Philis, a Cloud provider, describes its journey towards a Mission Critical Cloud. Arjan Eriks describes the need to increase speed, improve release cycles and encourage change in the Cloud orchestration software. He also addresses the trend towards public Cloud.

In Chapter 15, Halckenhaeusser, Heinzl and Spohrer discuss SaaS-centric Cloud platforms, in particular platforms that provide marketplaces to trade and execute SaaS solutions. By creating marketplaces, platform providers open new sales opportunities for third-party developers of Cloud-based software. Distribution channels constitute a crucial element in the business model of SaaS-centric Cloud platforms. This study examines how and why SaaS-centric Cloud platforms gravitate, i.e. which factors help them attract and retain participants. Their findings based on four case studies of different SaaS-centric Cloud platforms suggest the existence of two sets of catalyzing and inhibiting factors for platform gravitation which are contingent upon the platform type.

The use of Cloud services entails specific risks, in particular technical risks, operational risks, organizational risks and compliance risks. Proper risk management and Cloud governance are necessary to mitigate those risks. To realize a successful Cloud implementation, the current IT governance mechanisms will have to be adapted and new mechanisms will have to be implemented.

In Chapter 16, Mertens, De Haes and Huygh discuss the required structures, processes and relational mechanisms to realize a clear governance approach which ensures the value creation and minimizes the associated risks of Cloud solutions.

In Chapter, 17 Ravindram, Gonzalez and Van den Bergh discuss how organizations handle ending an engagement with a Cloud service provider. Adopting a Cloud computing strategy typically involves a one-way migration of IT skills and capabilities out of the organization. Based on a survey of Spanish firms, some key insights on software as a service (SaaS) contracts in comparison to contracts containing application development and maintenance and others containing hardware services are identified.

14

WELCOME MISSION CRITICAL CLOUD

Arjan Eriks

14.1 Introduction

January 2016, it's time for a change. After years of satisfaction with the CloudStack community, we have today reached the point that our vision of the future is essentially different from some of our partners. We as a company need to increase speed, improve release cycles and encourage change in the Cloud orchestration software. After almost a year of deliberation, Schuberg Philis has reached the decision to fork CloudStack and start in a new direction: Mission Critical Cloud all the way.

Since the start of the company in 2003, Schuberg Philis has grown by managing dedicated infrastructures and application landscapes for its customers. In 2008, when Cloud technology started to take-off we started to develop the desire to enter the Cloud and Infrastructure as a Service (IaaS) space as part of our Mission Critical services. Our enthusiasm in CloudStack and the Apache Software Foundation began in 2011, when we started working with CloudStack. Citrix had acquired cloud.com, followed by the very exciting decision to donate the software as open source to Apache. Although being open source was not unique to CloudStack, we did like the intimacy of the community and its vision on Cloud orchestration developments for Mission Critical and enterprise level applications. As an experienced integrator we dislike vendor lock in, and this bold move by Citrix gave us the extra option we needed: an alternative to OpenStack that would allow us to enter this new time in an agnostic and open-source way.

In late 2011, a team of four engineers from Schuberg Philis began building the first stage of what would become our dedicated Mission Critical Cloud. At first, as with all new technology, we started with a proof of concept, and we built both an OpenStack and CloudStack orchestration layer to test and explore the features each could provide. As with many before us, and as many after discovered, CloudStack provided a reliability and simplicity that OpenStack simply could not match, and while OpenStack offered more features, it could not deliver the quality or reliability we desired in our IaaS software. Our goal was to build a Cloud environment for both our engineers and our customers, one controlled with a standard API that would use new and exciting technology and would help steer us towards the future, while empowering us to deliver our 100% goal in everything we do. To be really certain we made a technology shift, we promised ourselves to not use any tool or brand we had ever used before. This promise to ourselves assured that we could explore the real potential of Cloud technology. It avoided the use of historically developed design principles that may very well become obsolete in a Cloud-based world.

After the decision had been made, we rapidly began developing. From easy implementations of Nicira networking (now known as VMWare NSX) to hours of pain coaxing storage to work, we learned how to bring a Cloud-based architecture into Mission Critical environments. Some key points that we proved included:

1   Enterprise application workloads can run in a Cloud.
2   Being agnostic and using OSS means, we can drive the feature roadmap because we develop it ourselves.
3   Running open source at scale requires dedicated software engineers devoting their time to improving Cloudstack.
4   Our customers operate in sectors varying from online retail, financial services, utilities and public services. All our customers require rapid and frequent change to their applications and systems. Many of our customers operate in highly regulated markets resulting in strong (data) compliancy and security requirements. Our customers trusted us to take care of both their functional and nonfunctional requirements, ensuring that moving into the Cloud was not a blocker for them.

Our first development job we took on was to integrate Nicira into CloudStack. One of our engineers, Hugo Trippaers, boarded a plane to San Francisco to visit Citrix and Nicira, and following months of coding we delivered Software Defined Networking into CloudStack. This was the second major step of our journey to IaaS, not waiting for vendors and their roadmaps, but defining a feature, building it and delivering it ourselves.

Over time, our influence grew. Citrix bought Cloud.com which was rebranded to Cloudstack and open sourced by Citrix. We started by working closely with two senior technical executives (Shannon: VP Market Development & Cloud Platforms and Sameer: Group VP and GM Cloud Platforms Group) from Citrix on the core positioning strategy of Cloudstack in the market and within Citrix. Citrix offered a commercial version of Cloudstack (Cloudplatform) including enterprise support in bugs and features. As we valued our partnership with Citrix and we saw benefits in the enterprise support levels, we decided to buy CloudPlatform.

We actively participated in the open-source community. We were invited to talk at the CloudStack events in Las Vegas in December of 2012. A group of Schuberg Philis engineers attended the conference, including Hugo Trippaers, Harm Boertien, our Chief Community Officer and Jeroen de Korte, one of our Mission Critical Engineers. The stars of the party though were Funs Kessen and Roeland Kuipers, who delivered an entertaining talk on stage. A later performance in Budapest earned them the nicknames of Cloud Pinky and Perky. We used this opportunity to meet the original founders of cloud.com and users and developers from the greater community, which was a fantastic feeling for us.

This was not only a turning point in our usage and vision of Cloud technology, but also the start of our involvement in multiple open-source communities. We started becoming more connected with the DevOps community, the Lisa conference in North America, and we delivered a speech at the CloudExpo in Santa Clara too, a bridge not just to orchestration but also a discussion of enterprise level challenges, the security implications of a Cloud and how this can be integrated into CloudStack. But for the CloudStack community, we made the conscious decision to give back to the project.

We hired developers to document our own contributions and invested in conferences and events supporting the community. This increased our impact in the community and we were able to make a significant contribution. We started, in collaboration with Citrix, running "Build Your Cloud" days, designed to make CloudPlatform and CloudStack more visible in the market. The largest event we organized with our friends from the community was the epic CloudStack Collaboration Conference Amsterdam in November 2013, where almost 500 users and developers attended to discuss and plan for the future, although we still have to give the record of best beer and pizza event to ShapeBlue conference in 2014 near London West End.

The position of CloudStack at the Apache Software Foundation (ASF) itself developed rapidly as well. While it was first an incubator project, it very excitingly evolved into a full ASF project. Chip Childers became the first ASF CloudStack VP, later followed by our own Hugo Trippaers and after that being looked after by Sebastien Goasguen. We continued to commit more code, expanding our Cloud, our development team and progressed to being the release managers for multiple releases. It was in this final stage that we experienced, for the first time, friction between the community and ourselves on priorities on new functionalities and related non-functional requirements such as security and "deployability" of applications and systems.

In Spring 2015, several of the key collaborators in the project gathered together in London to discuss a roadmap for CloudStack, and agree on a new way of working. Following that, we all agreed to work more closely together going forwards. From a personal perspective, we wanted to increase test coverage, and at the CloudStack Collaboration Conference in Tokyo in June 2015 all of the key players in the community agreed that we needed to work on changing the release process to a weekly cycle instead of the nine months cycle used up to then.

We took on the role of release manager started from release 4.6, wrote documentation about our view of the release process and encouraged debate and discussion on the mailing list, followed by stabilizing the master branch of github. This was a big change from the previous method of creating a release branch and forming different QA teams to stabilize and release it, while development continued on master. This had two major benefits: first we could release a new version at any time, and now that releases were built on top of each other, we could guarantee that a fix would always be present in later releases of the software – if it was in 4.6, it would be in 4.7. This new way of working allowed a monthly release cycle, with increased code review and more automated integration tests. Over 500 changes were tested, reviewed and included into the source code between November 2015 and January 2016. The new way of working provided shorter release cycles, major improvements in overall stability, quality and backward compatibility of the releases. We broke the monolith down into smaller pieces and enhanced the maintainability of the code.

Acting as the release manager with so many volunteers, developers and company goals is a task that requires both tact and stamina. We had two key engineers who attempt the task: first Daan Hoogland (release 4.4) and then Remi Bergsma (4.6 till 4.8) attempted to not only organize and complete a release, but at the same time improve the speed, reliability and quality of the software. At the same time as we pushed for this change, we continued to run our Mission Critical customers on CloudStack. Our customers and colleagues depended on the bug fixes and quality assurance we were trying to deliver, and we had to develop while maintaining our service.

In the Fall of 2015, during this process, we were hit by a nasty bug. Without diving too deep, a code snippet in the HyperV module of CloudStack started reporting non-HyperV hypervisors as down, resulting in the CloudStack management server trying to shut down and migrate the VMs running on them. Thanks to a high-availability design at a layer above the Cloud we had no downtime, but it was a reminder of unused and untested code could cause outages. In retrospect, it became clear that these risks needed to be eliminated. We rely on CloudStack for our Mission Critical workloads. We required the Cloud to behave and perform on the same level or better as dedicated environments. It turned out that our minimum requirements for stability, performance and reliability were not being met. It was a wakeup call for us: pushing for quality in an open-source fashion is key, and we needed to redouble our efforts to insist upon it to prevent a recurrence of critical bugs.

It became clear to us that things had to change. We devoted more of our time with the community to make sure that new commits were properly tested, and encouraged stability and testing in the master branch, and a faster pace of developing bug fixes and feature releases. For us, this was almost the optimal way of working and we wanted to push it even further. But it became apparent that this was not so for others. We received push back from the community, from both users and developers, and after spending considerable time, considering multiple options the way forward for us became clear. We decided to fork CloudStack.

This was not a decision we made lightly, and we are keenly aware that this move has a number of implications not only for us as a company but also for the existing CloudStack community:

- We faced the risk that the community would not follow us. We should be prepared that we needed to be fully self-supporting.
- The total size of the community would become split; this would potentially lead to a reduced number of contributions. Slowing down the pace and volume of new functional developments.
- Our existing customers were asked to trust that the fork would not negatively affect their operations or future plans.

Over time, both versions may start to deviate from each other. We have decided that our fork will remain open source to allow for as much collaboration as possible. We are aware that others in the past have chosen to close forks of CloudStack and develop internally, but we believe in the power of sharing. Being open, inclusive and transparent are values we see as a key driver in making the IT world a little better. An open fork, with the tools and procedures we feel needed to ensure higher velocity, greater reliability and better quality, is, in our opinion, the best option at this point in time.

Our future roadmap is mainly focused on our customer requirements. We are a Mission Critical company, and have a need to cater for high performance computing, support for containers and integrate with other new technologies such as Kubernetes, Mesos and Nomad. Our customers' requirements change rapidly, and we need to be agile in creating new components while also guaranteeing quality. Besides customer requirements, we will start working on improving the architecture of CloudStack. Items that spring to mind are the plug-in model, removing dead code and refactoring of important items.

So there you have it. We have decided to create a fork. It will be open for all to use and contribute to, with new governance, procedures and tools all designed to deliver quality and velocity to the project. We would like to stress our dedication to being open and inclusive, and would like to welcome anyone who has ideas about our move, or is interested in joining us on this journey, or perhaps if anyone would like additional information about our decision, please do not hesitate to contact us.

We truly hope you understand what we are doing, and that this is not an attempt to hurt the current community.

I would like to personally thank everyone in the community for the opportunity to participate and contribute to this project over the past years, without you all we would not be where we are today, and I'm incredibly grateful for that. We will blog more in the coming weeks about how we foresee our community functioning, and hope to publish more information about the project governance and bylaws very soon. For now, I welcome any comments and pull requests!

May 2018

Since 2016 the need for new functionalities in the Mission Critical Cloud has reduced gradually. The focus is on optimization. Alongside, public Cloud is developing at a very high pace. Big Cloud providers such as Amazon Web Services, Microsoft Azure and Google Cloud are heavily investing in new computing and networking technologies, (micro)services integration platforms. The risk appetite of customers to embrace public Cloud is changing and new opportunities utilizing the potential of Cloud technology are emerging. Our company is rapidly adapting to these changes to be able to support and lead our customers in this journey.

15

GRAVITATION OF SAAS-CENTRIC CLOUD PLATFORMS

André Halckenhaeusser, Armin Heinzl and Kai Spohrer

15.1 Introduction

In the digital age, innovations in cloud computing are the impetus for the continuing trend to outsource IT resources. This contemporary computing paradigm is considered to be highly promising for sustaining economic and technological advantage due to benefits like reduced upfront investments and high scalability [1,2]. In particular, Software as a Service (SaaS) enjoys constantly growing interest and adoption among enterprise clients [3]. Coupled with a shift from internal to external innovation, currently emerging cloud platforms specifically provide support for the development and distribution of software [4]. Cloud platforms increasingly provide marketplaces to trade and manage SaaS solutions and, thus, become more and more relevant for supporting developers and consumers to connect and to transact with each other [5]. Such cloud platforms create two-sided markets, embracing developers and consumers of SaaS in one ecosystem [4]. We use the term *SaaS-centric cloud platform* to refer to such platforms that focus on the generation, provision and distribution of software services provided by multiple vendors. Providers of such SaaS-centric cloud platforms generate distribution channels, open new sales and marketing opportunities for third-party developers of SaaS solutions and promote collaboration as well as competition among the different ecosystem participants [2,6,7]. Thus, we refer to cloud platforms that provide marketplaces as an integral part of their business model.

Maintaining a flourishing ecosystem of developers and customers is non-trivial [8]. In fact, cloud platforms are constantly exposed to the risk of developers' discontinuing affiliation [9] and customers abandoning the platform due to the dynamics of multi-sided platforms (e.g., [10]). Consequently, some platforms thrive, whereas others remain unsuccessful as they fail to attract or retain developers and customers of SaaS offerings [11]. It is therefore crucial for providers of SaaS-centric cloud platforms to understand what makes platforms gravitate, i.e., what defines a cloud platforms' capability to grow an ecosystem by attracting and retaining developers and customers [12].

Although a considerable body of research has investigated platform ecosystems in the context of software platforms [13–15], research on SaaS-centric cloud platforms is still nascent [4,16]. In particular, it is still unclear which factors determine if SaaS-centric cloud platforms become successful. Prior research on cloud platforms focused primarily on their ecosystem-based development capabilities and gave only little consideration to the distribution and transaction facilitation capabilities of the business network [17]. The distribution channel, however, constitutes a highly important element of SaaS-centric cloud platforms' business models [6]. Therefore, in line with a call for more context involvement in research [18], we suggest that existing explanations of platform success in general may not suffice to understand why specifically cloud platforms that provide marketplaces to distribute SaaS solutions gravitate.

Extant literature has predominantly adopted two perspectives on platform ecosystems in general [19]. On the one hand, an economics perspective highlights the transaction facilitation capabilities of a platform and focuses on the attraction of participants on both sides of the market (i.e., developers and customers) in order to leverage network effects [20]. This perspective suggests that platforms gravitate if they connect those two sides and thereby overcome an existing transaction problem [19]. On the other hand, a technology-related perspective highlights the innovative capacity of a platform and underlines the importance of its technological architecture [21,22]. This perspective suggests that platforms gravitate if they are technically designed in a way that facilitates third-party innovation and thereby value co-creation [19].

Therefore, platform providers need to manage a shift from developing applications in-house to providing resources that support external innovation [12] and must ensure that participation is beneficial for the external third-party developers [23]. Although these perspectives provide valuable insights into gravitation of platforms in general, they do not sufficiently account for the specifics of SaaS-centric cloud platforms. A more holistic view on SaaS-centric cloud platforms may be necessary to explain why specifically they gravitate.

Against this backdrop, we follow various authors' calls for more research on platform-specific topics (e.g., [24,25]) and examine the factors that drive the gravitation of SaaS-centric cloud platforms. In particular, we aim to answer the question: *How and why do SaaS-centric cloud platforms gravitate?*

To do so, we follow an exploratory qualitative research design and conduct four case studies of SaaS-centric cloud platforms. We employ two theoretical perspectives on platform ecosystems that help us explore factors influencing the gravitation of SaaS-centric cloud platforms [19]. Overall, our study contributes to research on platform ecosystems by identifying catalyzing and inhibiting factors of platform gravitation. In this way, this study provides a starting point for future research on the drivers of gravitation of such platforms. Furthermore, the findings of this study have practical implications for platform providers that aim to maintain a flourishing ecosystem.

15.2 Background and conceptual foundations

cloud computing constitutes a change in IT delivery and in the IT business model [2] by transforming the traditional IT artifact from resources into services [26]. Since its recent emergence, cloud computing is increasingly gaining attention from both researchers and practitioners [26,27]. This recent computing paradigm can be defined as "a model for enabling ubiquitous, convenient, on-demand network access to a shared pool of configurable computing resources (e.g., networks, servers, storage, applications, and services) that can be rapidly provisioned and released with minimal management effort or service provider interaction" [28, p. 2].

In cloud computing, there are three service models that differ in their level of abstraction of the provided IT capability and help to categorize service offerings [28,29]: First, *Infrastructure as a Service (IaaS)* focuses on the provision of elementary, on-demand IT-infrastructural resources like storage or processing capabilities. Second, *Platform as a Service*

(PaaS) provides a platform that facilitates deployment and development of cloud-based applications. Third, *SaaS* refers to the provision of complete applications that run on cloud infrastructure and that are accessible through thin interfaces via a network.

In our study, we understand platforms as technologies, products or services which provide a common basis third-party firms can use in order to develop complementary products [30]. These third-party firms that are affiliated to a platform are referred to as complementors and expand the platform's market by providing subsidiary components [30,31]. A platform ecosystem constitutes a loosely coupled inter-firm network that embraces platform provider, complementors and consumers [32,33]. An important characteristic of platforms is the potential existence of network effects [34]. Network effects refer to the phenomenon that a platform's perceived value is contingent upon the number of users adopting it [35].

In the context of cloud computing, the term "PaaS" often highlights the technical aspects of a cloud-based development platform and does not extraordinarily prioritize the idea of business networks and connecting customer segments [17]. We suggest that the elaboration on SaaS-centric cloud platforms requires a more holistic view on the platform and the software services offered. A cloud platform can be defined as a "development and execution environment in which external developers deploy and run their complementary [components and applications]" [4, p. 553]. As stated by Giessmann and Stanoevska [36], cloud platforms are increasingly complemented with marketplace functionality in order to facilitate the trade of services. SaaS-centric cloud platforms offer distribution-channel capabilities, which third parties can leverage to promote and sell SaaS solutions to consumers. These platforms potentially increase market transparency of cloud computing, mitigate risks associated with this computing paradigm and in this way may spur adoption of cloud services especially by small and medium-sized enterprises [1,37].

The existence of a distribution channel that supports developers in transacting with users of SaaS solutions is therefore a central element of SaaS-centric cloud platforms. Distribution channels for SaaS solutions may exhibit distinct foundational specificities and are increasingly emerging in the context of all cloud service models (e.g., SaaS, PaaS, IaaS) [6]. Although the traditional distinction of SaaS, PaaS and IaaS is highly useful, it also has shortcomings. As such, it does not capture the differences in distribution channels but focuses on the service model that is provided. For this reason, we abstract from the traditional categorization of SaaS vs. PaaS vs. IaaS in our investigation of SaaS-centric cloud platforms.

In this way, we hope to be better able to capture the particularities of the different distribution channels regarding the provision and distribution of SaaS solutions. Thus, we choose a conceptualization of SaaS-centric cloud platforms that encompasses platforms focusing on SaaS, PaaS, as well as IaaS. Extant SaaS-centric cloud platforms differ considerably regarding the existence of a core product and the provided development capabilities. We use the categorization provided by Giessmann and Legner [4] who distinguish cloud platforms according to the main value proposition provided to technical users (i.e., developers): First, the conceptualization encompasses *application-based* SaaS-centric cloud platforms. These cloud platforms focus on the integration of software components, such as add-ons, into a core SaaS-solution. Providers of this core SaaS solution leverage external innovation by opening their core product to third-party developers and in this way allow for co-creation of value [22]. On this premise, the SaaS product functions as platform for countless extensions developed by third parties which extend the core product's functionality and adjustability. Second, we distinguish *development-focused* SaaS-centric cloud platforms, which focus on the provision of development and deployment capabilities. Platforms of this type, in contrast to the first category, lack an extensible core product and strongly support the application development process of comprehensive

SaaS solutions, which are then distributed via the platforms' marketplace. Third, *distribution-focused* SaaS-centric cloud platforms provide distribution channels and open marketing and sales opportunities to their users as a main value proposition. These cloud platforms exhibit strong user communities and facilitate sharing and trading of ready-to-use cloud software. In this category, cloud services are typically deployed to an external or internal infrastructure and do not require extensive development functionality.

Summarizing, SaaS-centric cloud platforms include distribution-focused, development-focused and application-based cloud platforms that offer distribution-channel functionality and focus on SaaS solutions. Table 15.1 provides an overview of typical SaaS-centric cloud platforms.

Table 15.1 Typical SaaS-centric cloud platforms and respective marketplaces (links accessed August 15, 2017)

Application-based SaaS-centric cloud platforms	
cloud platforms focusing on the provision of a core SaaS product that is open to external developers and that extends its functionality by add-ons	
Atlassian (Marketplace)	https://marketplace.atlassian.com
Intuit QuickBooks (Apps.com)	https://www.apps.com
NetSuite (SuiteApp.com)	http://suiteapp.com
Salesforce Force.com (AppExchange)	https://appexchange.salesforce.com
SAP cloud Platform (SAP AppCenter)	https://www.sapappcenter.com
SugarCRM (SugarExchange)	https://sugarexchange.sugarcrm.com
Zendesk (Apps Marketplace)	https://www.zendesk.com/apps/
Zoho (Zoho Marketplace)	https://marketplace.zoho.com
Development-Focused SaaS-Centric cloud Platforms	
cloud platforms focusing on the provision of a development and execution environment supporting the entire application development process	
Amazon Web Services (AWS Marketplace)	https://aws.amazon.com/marketplace
Google App Engine (G Suite Marketplace)	https://gsuite.google.com/marketplace/
Microsoft Azure (Azure Marketplace)	https://azuremarketplace.microsoft.com/
SoftwareAG (Digital Marketplace)	https://marketplace.softwareag.com/
Distribution-Focused SaaS-Centric cloud Platforms	
cloud platforms focusing on the provision of a distribution channel to offer and trade SaaS solutions to a larger community as main value proposition.	
1und1 cloud Apps	https://hosting.1und1.de/cloud-app-center/cloud-apps
AppDirect Marketplace	https://www.appdirect.com
Bitnami	https://www.bitnami.com
Comcast Business Marketplace	https://cloudsolutions.comcast.com/
Ingram Micro cloud Marketplace	https://de.cloud.im/
Interoute cloudStore	https://cloudstore.interoute.com
Nubocloud	https://www.nubocloud.de
Rackspace Marketplace	https://marketplace.rackspace.com
Singtel myBusiness	https://mybusiness.singtel.com/
Swisscom Business Marketplace	https://businessapps.swisscom.ch
Telekom cloud	https://cloud.telekom.de

We define gravitation of a SaaS-centric cloud platform inspired by the physical notion of gravity as their capability to attract and retain customers on both sides, i.e., developers and users of SaaS services. Being one of the four fundamental forces of physics, gravitation is defined as the mutual attraction of two forces. In astronomy, gravitational interaction is responsible for the fact that planets circulate around the sun and stay in their orbits [38]. Considering what is mentioned above, success of a cloud platform can be measured by its growth, and, thus, highly depends upon the degree to which the potential participants from affiliated sides gravitate toward the platform. This concept therefore alludes to a platform's attractiveness.

15.3 Method

In this study, we follow an exploratory qualitative research approach in order to identify factors influencing platform gravitation. Due to the recency of the object of investigation and consequently the scarcity of studies on the selected cloud platform concept, an exploratory approach was deemed appropriate [39]. In particular, we conducted four case studies of specific SaaS-centric cloud platforms [40]. According to Benbasat et al. [39], case study research is especially helpful for answering "how" and "why" research questions like ours. After having identified a variety of cloud platforms based on a web search and insights from research articles, a framework proposed by Giessmann and Legner [4] helped to categorize the cases (see Table 15.1). In case study research, only a limited number of examples can be examined effectively [40]. Therefore, we selected leading SaaS-centric cloud platforms in order to include only high performing platforms with mature ecosystems in our analysis. We included representative cases from all three categories of SaaS-centric cloud platforms outlined above. The selection of cases across the three categories allowed us to consider distinct platform types and mitigated the risk of setting a narrow focus. While the selected cases Alpha, Beta, Gamma and Delta differ considerably, they all focus on the provision and management of SaaS solutions. We chose representatives of the platform owners as interview partners. Table 15.2 presents the selected SaaS-centric cloud platforms and briefly describes each case.

15.3.1 Data collection

We base our analyses on semi-structured expert interviews with knowledgeable representatives and managers of the platform ecosystems as well as public and internal information from websites, presentations and e-mail conversations. We conducted five semi-structured interviews with these key informants that included questions regarding software, governance, infrastructure criteria as well as the evolution of the platform. The interviews were conducted via telephone and internet calls and lasted between 30 and 70 minutes. Each interview was recorded and transcribed subsequently. We triangulated and extended the qualitative data gained from the interviews by reviewing additional public and internal documents from websites (e.g., company presentation, developer documentation, learning centers), internal presentations and follow-up e-mail conversations with interviewees. The consideration of both interview data and additional documents helped increase data triangulation and validity [41]. Table 15.3 outlines the interview details.

15.3.2 Data analysis

Following Eisenhardt [40], we conducted within-case analyses of all cases individually. These helped us cope with the elevated complexity of the collected data and allowed us to

Table 15.2 Presentation of cases

Case company	Type [4]	Short description
Alpha	Application-based integration	Alpha is a leading provider of cloud-based enterprise software. Alpha offers a SaaS-solution that has been opened up to facilitate customizability and extensibility by add-ons. These add-ons are built on the cloud platform and are provided by the platform owner and third-party vendors. The platform offers a proprietary marketplace on which add-ons are offered to Alpha's customers.
Beta	Development focused	Beta is a leading software and service provider. The cloud platform offering comprises IaaS, PaaS and SaaS solutions and embraces various integrated services that support the development, deployment and management of cloud applications. The distribution channel connects software vendors and Beta's customers and offers cloud services that run on Beta's infrastructure.
Gamma	Distribution focused	Based on its expertise in software packaging, Gamma focuses on the provision of pre-packaged software services which are easily deployable in the cloud. These services are offered on the proprietary marketplace and on distribution channels of prominent cloud platforms. For application deployment and execution, Gamma developed an automated packaging system.
Delta	Distribution focused	Delta provides a leading platform to support distribution and management of cloud-based services. Besides operating an own distribution channel, Delta offers white-label marketplace platforms. Delta's distribution ecosystem embraces third parties operating a white-label platform as well as developers and customers. The distribution approach of Delta allows developers to reach a high number of potential customers.

Table 15.3 Interview details

Case company	Interviewee position	Date	Length of interview	Additional material
Alpha	Vice President of Customer Success (A#1)	07/2017	70 minutes	Internal marketing presentation, online documentation
Beta	Program Manager (B#1)	08/2017	55 minutes	Website, documentation
Gamma	Sales Representative (C#1)	08/2017	30 minutes	Website, online documentation, e-mail, business overview, white paper
Delta	cloud Expert (D#1)	08/2017	35 minutes	Website, online documentation, e-mails
	Key Account Manager (D#2)	08/2017	50 minutes	

Table 15.4 Taxonomy and selected coding examples

Taxonomy

Dimension	Concepts	Coding examples
Cloud Platform Main Value Proposition	Distinction between application-based integration, development focus and distribution focus	"Every app is integrated into the core product. The ISV cannot run independently, the core product and platform is essentially required." (A#1)
Software Criteria	Modularity	
	• App-decoupling	"[Add-ons] are highly decoupled. [...] Everything that has been built upon the platform [...] has to be robust for this process." (A#1)
	• Interface standardization	
	Integration	"[Cross-application integration] is possible. It depends upon the channels that the respective ISV opens. Software can be provided completely encapsulated or open to other solutions." (D#2)
	• Platform-app integration (e.g., Single-Sign-On)	
	• Cross-app integration	
	Development support	"We offer our customers SDKs that support the development of applications on Java, Python, Ruby, PHP [...] It is very diverse." (B#2)
	• Boundary resources (e.g., SDK, API, app reviews)	
	Technical openness of platform technology and SaaS (e.g., open-source)	"We are increasingly offering open-source and strongly evolving into an open platform. I think this is one of Delta's most significant." (D#2)
Underlying Infrastructure	Infrastructure Transparency	"You can freely choose the data-center region [your software will be deployed on]." (D#2)
	• Selection (fixed/selectable)	"We partly operate the infrastructure, but we also build on external data-centers [depending on the region]." (A#1)
	• Location Distribution	
	• Ownership (proprietary/external)	
Governance Criteria	Control mechanisms	"We have a [...] security review every application placed on our marketplace has to pass [.] It is important for us that they conform to our security standards [...]" (A#1)
Pricing Policies/ Revenue Model	Access/usage pricing Revenue sharing model	"these software providers have actually paid us to put their applications in our library." (B#1)
Marketplace Functionality	Portfolio	"The apps that we onboard to our platform are very selected, [...] we are working with around 300 different applications. [...] they are very specific." (C#1)
	• Number of applications	
	• Specificity of offerings	
	Domain Specificity	"We want to offer a high spectrum of applications to our customers [.] I can't even tell you how many apps we are offering on our marketplace right now, but it is a very high number." (D#2)
	Support of transaction phases	"We do not carry out billing on the platform. The ISV is responsible for that." (A#1) "The contract is closed directly over the platform and also embraces important elements like support." (D#2)

understand the specifics of the different cases. Subsequently, we employed a between-case analysis in order to identify commonalities and differences and to derive factors that influence the gravitation of SaaS-centric cloud platforms.

Interview transcripts were coded using the qualitative data analysis software NVivo 10, which helped to reduce complexity. In order to effectively conduct the data analysis, we synthesized relevant concepts from the extant literature on platform ecosystems, cloud platforms and marketplaces and derived a taxonomy that served as our analytical structure. In total, we included six dimensions in the taxonomy. This taxonomy allowed us to compare the selected cases and helped avoiding shortcomings in case study research approaches [40]. We relied on a priori codes on the basis of the dimensions and concepts proposed in our taxonomy. The taxonomy is presented in Table 15.4. Selected coding examples are added in order to facilitate the understanding of the concepts and the coding process.

15.4 Results

15.4 1 Within-case analysis

Alpha. The proprietary distribution channel embraces more than 3,000 applications that complement Alpha's core SaaS, which is a leading enterprise software system. Applications are highly decoupled from the platform. Both end consumers and developers appreciate and require the platform's rigor as far as stability and compatibility of the platform is concerned. Although the platform owner conducts several updates of the platform and its functionality, third-party solutions are broadly independent upon these changes. Furthermore, add-ons do not require specific interfaces in order to communicate with standard objects provided by the platform. This is due to the fact that extensions run in the application base of the platform and use the platform's functionality directly. The extensions are decoupled from the platform, yet rely on it due to their thorough integration with the platform and a lack of internal interfaces. The software services run natively on the platform and are generally integrated into the core product, avoiding any technical integration efforts between platform and add-ons. The platform thereby facilitates automatic deployment and provides Single Sign-On (SSO) of add-ons offered on the marketplace. Due to the fact that the communication between software services and the platform is realized via sharing one data model, no integration effort is necessary to facilitate the communication between different extensions.

Alpha is currently introducing a new component-model service, allowing customers to assemble components offered on the marketplace and thereby to create new combined services. Alpha attaches the developer community a high strategic importance (A#1: "Around 70% of the platform's load is Custom-Development while only 30% can be associated with the standard objects we provide with our SaaS offerings"). Developers appreciate the ease of getting started and the support and learning opportunities the platform provides. To this end, Alpha also provides comprehensive information and educational documentation and further conducts various programs and competitions with complementors. Alpha operates own infrastructure and leverages external infrastructure in smaller markets due to scalability reasons. Users are able to select a specific data center region that best fits their performance and compliance requirements.

The platform owner frequently conducts updates, and potentially integrates new functionality that was formerly exclusively provided by the solution of an independent software vendor (ISV). Furthermore, the platform owner occasionally offers own add-ons that are similar to the scope of application of ISVs' solutions and extend the functionality and attractiveness of the core product to end user. Alpha therefore possibly enters into a complementor's market by publishing a proprietary solution providing the same functionality of an existing ISV's offering or by integrating existing functionality into the platform. Especially in the latter case, the platform owner entry threatens the ISV's position.

As far as control mechanisms are concerned, Alpha is not very restrictive regarding content and functionality. However, security and reliability of the platform is highly important to Alpha. Therefore, a formal application is obligatory prior to participating in the marketplace. Alpha further conducts comprehensive security reviews on a recurring basis.

Alpha charges customers for using the SaaS product and developers for using its development platform. Moreover, developers are charged a fee for placing their applications on the marketplace and they share a certain percentage of their net revenues with Alpha.

The lacking focus on a specific business size regarding the services on the marketplace is criticized by Alpha since larger customers might not trust the reliability and support capabilities of products of small ISVs. As stated by the interviewee, the global orientation of the marketplace requires ISVs to provide a sufficient scaling of their solutions. Besides, Alpha aims at providing a comprehensive portfolio across industries and actively attracts significant developers that cater important business processes not supported hitherto by the ecosystem. In the past, the active attraction of significant software vendors has been an important factor for growth. While the marketplace supports contracting and deployment of services, Alpha does not carry out billing in order to concede ISVs certain autonomy. After having deployed an add-on, which is usually provided as a trial version first, the ISV asks customers for their payment details to gain full access. According to the interviewee, the easy deployment and integration of add-ons into the core product leads to high uncertainties regarding support and maintenance responsibilities of providers. "If they [customers] have installed 10 ISV applications, they also have to maintain them, enter into contracts with vendors and train skills" (A#1).

Beta. Beta attaches high importance to the robustness of its platform and the services offered. Services placed on the marketplace predominantly run in virtual machines and include a pre-configured environment for application execution. In this way, the dependencies between the platform and applications as well as across applications are minimized. Beta provides various components to facilitate integration of software services with the platform and provides SSO. Furthermore, the marketplace supports automated provision and deployment of software services. Cross-application integration is feasible and depends upon the way an ISV opens the respective software service. Third-party contributions on the marketplace are regarded as highly important for Beta. The platform provides strong and manifold development services that simplify access to the platform and the development of services, e.g., specific software development kits (SDK) focusing on various programming languages. Furthermore, Beta provides considerable educational resources. Beta operates a variety of own data centers worldwide. Customers may select a specific region for the deployment of software services in order to meet compliance and legal requirements or performance needs. Although data centers are proprietarily owned, Beta reacted on regulatory requirements in specific regions by implementing innovative models that exhibit different data-ownership structures. Beta controls its distribution channel and the offerings placed by ISVs. The input control embraces a formal application process. Furthermore, software services are reviewed thoroughly prior to publication. Regarding the revenue model, Beta keeps a percentage of revenues generated on the marketplace. Beta's portfolio provides a variety of different software services. While some applications clearly address developers, many pre-packaged images of software services cater specific business needs. Furthermore, Beta selects software services purposefully according to their relevance in order to provide a widespread portfolio. The marketplace thereby exhibits a low domain specificity. The trend of increasingly focusing on open-source offerings is regarded as one of Beta's "most significant factors of success" (B#2). As far as transaction on the marketplace is concerned, customers may adjust the selected service to own requirements and budget limitations. A formal contract is closed between the ISV and the customer. Payment and billing is then handled by the platform owner in case this is desired by the respective ISV. Finally, contracted software services are automatically deployed, a virtual machine is created and standard or custom configurations are set.

Gamma. The software services that are offered on Gamma's marketplace can be deployed to various infrastructure providers who are partnering with the case company. Once an infrastructure provider has been selected, the chosen SaaS services from the marketplace are deployed automatically. Afterward, services run highly decoupled from Gamma's platform. Nevertheless, the software services are not integrated with the platform after setup. Gamma counts on external applications and provides an easy-to-use process in order to onboard applications to its platform. This process of easily accessing and deploying services was explicitly demanded by Gamma's customers. The application selection is principally conducted by Gamma albeit partnering infrastructure providers and commercial ISVs may also influence it. Regarding technical openness, a focus on open-source software is apparent. Gamma offers an unprecedented flexibility regarding infrastructure. While Gamma does not operate own data centers, the services offered can be deployed to the partnering infrastructure providers immediately. The company realizes input control and examines applications with respect to their fit with the packaging and deployment technology and regarding additional components necessary for deployment. The onboarding process takes between one and two months and includes an extensive feasibility study. Gamma intents to keep it as simple as possible. Software services are selected purposefully based on the perceived value they bring to Gamma and partnering infrastructure providers. Due to the packaging process, Gamma controls the cloud images and the update process in order to ensure provision of secure applications. Gamma does not charge consumers for using its platform. In contrast, it charges developers for using its packaging services to prepare services for deployment and imposes a fee for placing an application on the marketplace. Furthermore, infrastructure providers pay Gamma commission fees for facilitating simple deployment of the offered services on their respective infrastructure. Thus, billing and payment handling is neither supported nor necessary. Fees related to the necessary infrastructure are handled by the respective IaaS provider. Gamma's portfolio embraces less than 200 offerings. In its portfolio, various offerings covering the same scope of application exist. For example, in the category of CRM, the marketplace lists more than ten different CRM solutions. Apart from its focus on open-source software, Gamma's portfolio exhibits low specificity regarding domain and applications.

Delta. Delta's approach facilitates high distribution channel capabilities. On the one hand, developers may publish applications on Delta's marketplace. On the other hand, once integrated with Delta, developers have the opportunity of placing their solution on a variety of third-party marketplaces associated with Delta. Delta provides open API in order to integrate external software services with the platform. The software services that Delta manages are decoupled from the platform. Due to the fact that the communication between platform and applications is clearly defined and kept simple, the platform and subsystems are fairly independent. The platform further supports SSO via OpenID as well as automated deployment for integrated applications. Delta provides a service for searching application-specific data and finding information stored in different cloud applications. However, the platform does not explicitly realize cross-application integration. "It is a future desire for anyone in the cloud space. That is definitely something that we will be able to offer [in the future]" (D#1). In order to support ISVs during the processes of onboarding and integrating applications, Delta provides a development environment. Besides providing integration assistance, the developers may manage product offerings (e.g., pricing and discounts), marketing and promotional activities, payments, orders, invoices and customers. Delta exerts input and output control by requesting a formal application and conducting an application review. Applications are thereby comprehensively evaluated regarding usability and service standards. A distribution agreement contract precedes the application review process.

Furthermore, once approved, each change made on an application necessarily needs to be approved before coming into effect. The onboarding process is conducted free of charge. Prior to the application integration and the publication of a software service, a revenue sharing model is negotiated and stipulated in a formal contract between Delta and ISVs. Besides, third-party marketplace operators are charged for using Delta's white-label marketplace platform. While Delta's portfolio embraces purposefully selected free and commercial applications, a focus on open-source software is not evident. Free offerings usually refer to trial versions that exhibit certain limitations, e.g., regarding the number of users, transactions or storage. Delta focuses neither on specific industries nor on a specific business size, albeit a slight focus on small and medium-sized enterprises becomes prevalent. Integrated applications can be contracted from the software vendor and are provisioned immediately. Besides the placement and distribution of software services, Delta manages payment and billing.

15.4.2 Between-case analysis

Based on the within-case analysis, a comparison of the single cases led us to understand factors that catalyze or inhibit gravitation of SaaS-centric cloud platforms. First, we report on the catalyzing factors. Subsequently, the identified inhibiting factors will be presented. Table 15.5 contrasts the results of the individual case analyses.

15.4.2.1 Catalyzing factors

Ease of Access and Use (1). It is noticeable that all cases aim at providing a high ease of access and use for both developers and customers. While ease of use predominantly refers to the way a user may interact with the platform, ease of access addresses the degree to which developers are supported and promoted in participating in the platform ecosystem and respectively the obstacles they might experience.

Integration, regarded as an important concept in the proposed taxonomy, applies to communication between platform and applications as well as across applications [13]. All cases provide SSO, which enable customers to access software services from different complementors easily. A tight integration of applications with the platform further facilitates management of contracted services in a central place. For instance, Delta provides a dashboard where users may contract and access services as well as modify subscriptions. Furthermore, all cases support various phases of a market transaction on the marketplaces. We use the phases defined in Menychtas et al. [42] and distinguish negotiation, contracting and settlement of a market transaction in our study. In the negotiation phase, service customization and price building take place. The contracting phase comprises the closing of a legally binding contract between provider and consumer. During the settlement phase, the services are delivered (delivery) and

Table 15.5 Comparison of cases

Dimension	Concept	Cases			
		Alpha	Beta	Gamma	Delta
MVP	Main value proposition	Application-based integration	Development focus	Distribution focus	Distribution focus
Software Criteria	Modularity	Medium (coupled with platform, no use of interfaces)	High (executed in sandboxes/virtual machines, highly decoupled)	High (apps are encapsulated, highly decoupled)	High (highly decoupled, standardized interfaces)
	Platform-app integration	Fully integrated	Apps run on or deploy to Beta, automated deployment, single sign-on	Deployment, server-management (reboot, shutdown, delete), single sign-on	Deployment, single sign-on, management and distribution of applications
	Cross-app integration	Fully integrated	Feasible, implementation necessary, supported by integration services.	Not feasible	Not feasible (albeit cross-application data searching service)
	Development Support	High. Development portal, various programs and competitions, learning center	High. Developer community, developer tools (IDE, SDKs), online documentation and resources	Medium. App packaging, online community, onboarding support	Medium. Onboarding, application review, development environment
	Technical openness	Closed, private marketplace available. Offerings: mainly closed source	Closed, private marketplace available. Offerings: open and closed source	Technology: closed source offerings: mainly open source	White-label marketplace platforms. Offerings: mainly closed source

Underlying Infrastructure	Infrastructure Transparency	User-selectable (region, hardware) worldwide distributed proprietary and external data centers	User-selectable (region, hardware) worldwide distributed proprietary data centers	User selectable (provider, region, hardware) worldwide distributed external data centers	Fixed (handled by SaaS vendor) external data centers
Governance	Control	Input: formal application Output: security reviews	Input: formal application Output: app nomination, app review	Input: formal application Output: feasibility study, application review and packaging	Input: formal application, contract Output: application review
Pricing / Revenue Policies	Pricing	Customer: license needed Developer: review fee (setup and annual)	Customer: no fee Developer: no onboarding fee	Customer: no fee Developer: publication fee (commercial software)	Customer: no fee Developer: no fee
	Revenue model	Revenue share: certain percentage	Revenue share: certain percentage	Revenue model: IaaS commission	Revenue share: upon negotiation
Marketplace Functionality	Portfolio	> 3,000 add-ons and components low app specificity	> 5,000 offerings low app specificity	> 150 pre-packaged offerings low app specificity	> 300 integrated apps low app specificity
	Domain specificity	Low (generic focus)	Low (generic focus)	Low (generic focus)	Low (generic, slightly SME focused)
	Support of transaction phases	No payment handling	All transaction phases supported	No payment handling	All transaction phases supported

charged (payment). In the analyzed cases, software services are easily executable in a cloud environment due to the abstraction of the service setup and deployment process. This clearly eases the settlement phase, due to reduced complexity regarding deployment and delivery on the marketplace and is suggested to promote a high user acceptance and satisfaction. Besides, all cases support third parties in their development work. Development support refers to the provision of resources and assistance to complementors that facilitate platform-specific development and therefore includes the concept of boundary resources [12]. For instance, SDKs, application programming interfaces (APIs) and onboarding processes may be part of a platform owner's support strategy [43].

Simplifying the access of developers may foster third-party participation on the platform. First, a straightforward onboarding and integration was found to be catalyzing. All examined cases exhibit and highlight their onboarding and platform-application integration support. Gamma, for instance, reduces the efforts of external developers to place solutions on the marketplace by carrying out software packaging and onboarding. Second, Alpha and Beta clearly focus on support of external contribution and innovation and clearly highlight their strategic significance for success. Both platforms provide considerable educational support like learning opportunities and comprehensive documentations. Alpha further conducts programs and competitions in order to spur innovation. Thus, the way a platform provider treats the developer community highly influences developers' participation decision and thereby the success of the platform. Consequently, simplifying the processes of provisioning, deployment and execution of software services and also supporting third parties in developing and distributing their solutions has been identified to catalyze a platform's gravitation.

Security (2). All examined cases highlight the importance of security regarding both the offered services and the underlying technology. In our work, security refers to the appropriateness and trustworthiness of software services as well as to the reliability and robustness of the platform technology. On the one hand, the analyzed cases exert control on third-party contributors and their software services. We distinguish input control, which makes reference to vertical openness to external developers and respectively to existing entrance barriers [44]. Output control refers to the proposal of favorable and necessary criteria concerning complementors' outputs and scrutinizing complementors' solutions prior to publication by implementing review processes [13]. All cases restrict access to their ecosystem by requesting a formal application of third-party firms. The implementation of output control mechanisms ensures the fit of applications regarding security and quality standards. Gamma automated the update process of both software and additional components and thereby guarantees that offered software services are permanently up-to-date and secure.

On the other hand, reliability and robustness of the underlying platform technology are found to be highly important to maintain developers' and customers' trust in the respective platform. The concept of modularity refers to the extent to which a platform's ecosystem depends upon changes. It can be accomplished by reducing interdependencies (app-decoupling) and defining the way the platform and applications interact (interfaces) [13]. In all cases, the software services are highly decoupled, which minimizes the risk of necessary investments in software updates due to possible changes on the platform. Especially for Alpha and Beta, the robustness and continuity of the platform are considered to be highly important success factors. Consequently, customers rely on the security regarding both the underlying platform technology and software services, thus representing a catalyzing factor.

Portfolio Significance (3). The analysis revealed that all cases explicitly curate a significant portfolio. We understand portfolio significance as the degree to which offerings have been purposefully selected. A significant portfolio thereby refers to a catalogue of service offerings on the platform's marketplace that is appropriate and relevant to the focused customer segments. Thus, this concept may allude to the quantity, quality and specificity of the offerings and further relates to control mechanisms. On the one hand, high portfolio significance may be achieved by purposefully selecting and actively searching for suitable software services with regard to core processes of addressed industries, as in the case of Alpha. Similarly, Gamma selects the applications according to their highest perceived value. By exerting input and output control, all cases limit the existing portfolio at least to a certain degree. Moreover, offering open-source software services has been found to be especially beneficial due to their usefulness and cost-effectiveness, as the case of Gamma illustrates. Gamma explicitly focuses on open-source software and highlights the elevated demand for such solutions. Similarly, Beta increasingly focuses on offering significant open-source solutions as well. Thus, this factor further addresses the concept of technical openness of the software services. On the other hand, the participation of large and significant ISVs can highly impact the platform's appeal on both software vendors and customers. In the case of Alpha, the attraction of significant software vendors profoundly affected the evolutionary trajectory of the platform. Due to their prominence, many other participants joined the ecosystem as well. Consequently, the provision and maintenance of a significant portfolio has been identified as a catalyzing factor of gravitation.

Infrastructural Flexibility and Transparency (4). It is conspicuous that the majority of examined cases grant customers high degrees of flexibility regarding the underlying infrastructure on which the software services run. Major issues influencing the adoption of cloud computing are related to security, trust, privacy as well as legal aspects. These issues are highly interdependent with the cloud infrastructure [45]. Due to the layered architecture of cloud computing, the underlying network structure is usually abstracted from the user of a specific service model, which may lead to a lack of transparency. Gamma provides an elevated flexibility across significant providers due to the maintenance of partnerships with a variety of IaaS providers. A customer may choose between various IaaS providers and may further select concrete data center regions. In the cases of Alpha and Beta, customers and developers may select the desired region of the assigned data centers. In the special case of Beta, tailored regional offerings address extraordinary regulatory requirements (e.g., legal issues, compliance). Enabling customers to select certain elements of the underlying infrastructure may further increase service transparency. Due to this selection, a user is potentially aware of the provider and location of the underlying infrastructure. Consequently, the facilitation of infrastructural flexibility and correspondingly transparency has been found to be an important factor regarding the platform's gravitation (Table 15.6).

Table 15.6 Catalyzing factors and exemplary characteristics

Catalyzing factors	
Ease of access and use	• Simplifying provisioning, deployment and execution of services • Support of development and onboarding processes
Security	• Selection and trustworthiness of complementors and services • Reliability and continuity of the platform
Portfolio significance	• Appropriate selection of services (growing relevance of open source) • Attraction of large developers
Infrastructural flexibility and transparency	• Addressing regulatory requirements • Enabling customers to select elements of the infrastructure (e.g., location)

15.4.2.2. Inhibiting factors

Intra-Platform Competition (1). This factor focuses on the degree to which developers compete with other ecosystem participants, including the platform owner. On the one hand, all examined cases provide various services that cover similar scopes of application. Although all cases control both the input and the output, developers and platform owners are allowed to publish software services that are similar to those which already exist. The openness regarding the scope of application leads to an increase in the quantity of the application portfolio and a possible decrease in the specificity of the offered services. This, in turn, might have an impact on the mode of competition prevailing in the platform ecosystem [15]. For example, Gamma's application catalogue embraces 12 different CRM solutions. Similarly, Delta lists 138 results in the category of CRM. On the other hand, especially in application-based SaaS-centric cloud platforms, a potential threat of the platform owner entering a complementor's market is evident. Especially for Alpha, this represents an inhibiting factor since third-party developers might be put in a disadvantage. Consequently, based on the findings we suggest that an increased intra-platform competition represents an inhibiting factor.

Contractual Complexity (2). Contractual complexity refers to the degree of complexity of the contractual commitment negotiated between ecosystem participants. In some settings, customers may be exposed to an increased contractual complexity as a result of having purchased various applications on the marketplace. The majority of the examined cases support the immediate contracting and deployment of software services. Thereby, customers usually enter into a contract with the respective software vendor who publishes a solution on the platform's marketplace. Furthermore, platform owners engage in rather arm's length relationships with third-party developers, and these complementors therefore often manage their own contracts with customers. Especially in the case of Alpha, an uncertainty regarding support responsibilities arises. This is due to the degree of integration of the offered add-ons into the core product, which is characteristic of application-based SaaS-centric cloud platforms. In the event of errors or failures, customers struggle to determine the cause and the ISV in charge of the problem. Alpha reports that the resulting complexity presents a considerable challenge for its customers. While in the other examples the origin of an error is likely to be more easily identifiable, customers still have to deal with a variety of different contracts. Our analysis reveals that the contractual complexity could be confronted by maintaining overall agreements embracing all developers who provide software services to a specific customer. In such settings, platform owners would engage in high-level relationships with developers, i.e., they would provide the customer with one specific contract that envelops all service providers related to that customer.

This would require different contractual constructs that govern responsibilities, duties and error handling. Consequently, the potentially complex contractual situation a customer is confronted with on a platform's marketplace represents an inhibiting factor.

Lack of Customer Centricity (3). The concept of customer centricity is based on the idea of positioning customers at the center of focus of a company and assumes that an organization needs to focus on and especially listen to the needs of the customers it directly addresses [46]. In this context, the degree to which a platform addresses specific industries can be understood as domain specificity. All examined cases exhibit a low domain specificity since they do not focus on selected industry branches in particular. Furthermore, all cases exhibit a global orientation and embrace participants of all business sizes in their ecosystems. Therefore, the customer focus of the analyzed platforms seems to be rather unspecific. In the case of Alpha, the lack of a regional focus as well as a lack of a focus on a specific business size might produce

Table 15.7 Inhibiting factors and exemplary characteristics

Inhibiting factors	
Intra-platform competition	• High number of competing services covering a similar scope of application • Threat of a platform owner entering the market
Contractual complexity	• Customers enter in a variety of contracts due to immediate provisioning • Uncertain support responsibilities in the case of errors
Lack of customer centricity	• Support deficiencies due to a lacking focus on specific domains or regions • Reduced trust in scaling capabilities due to differences in business size

a reluctant behavior of customers. Similarly, considerable differences in business sizes be-tween vendor and customer might further reduce the trust in a vendor's capability to provide global support. As the interview with Alpha reveals, especially larger companies might be influenced in their decision to contract services from smaller ISVs. For example, a larger com-pany might lack trust in the ISV's capabilities to provide sufficient scaling and support of its service. A customer-centric orientation regarding developers has been therefore identified to be beneficial. According to the interviewee from Alpha, specific addressed industries might benefit from a closer collaboration between platform owner and developers. Consequently, an insufficient customer centricity represents an inhibiting factor (Table 15.7).

15.4.2.3 Platform type as a moderating factor

Although our exploration yielded catalyzing and inhibiting factors that affect platform grav-itation, not all of these effects were equally strong in all cases. A closer examination of the differences showed that several effects differed in strength depending on the platform type on which they were observed. Our analysis showed no differences regarding the factors "ease of access and use," "security and robustness" (catalyzing factors) and "lack of customer centricity" (inhibiting factor) across the cases. In the following, we elaborate on the rest. Figure 15.1 summarizes the moderating effects.

Portfolio Significance. The distribution channels of all examined cases limit the portfolio to a certain degree and in this way ascribe certain importance to a selected portfolio. Neverthe-less, in the cases of application-based and distribution-focused platforms, providers especially emphasized the strategic importance of a highly curated service portfolio for success. The curation of a significant portfolio allows these platforms to provide a relevant and high-quality service catalogue that specifically caters to the platforms' customers and addresses all relevant business processes. In contrast, development-focused platforms, such as Beta, do not extraordinarily focus on the provision of a tailored portfolio. This platform type puts less emphasis on portfolio curation because its customers are more widespread and it strongly tar-gets developers. Particularly, developers may prefer a wide and diverse repository of services which they can orchestrate and use within their development work. Besides, the marketplace facilitates them to easily distribute their specific services to users. The comprehensive cov-erage of a single domain with few specific services may be less relevant to them. Therefore, we argue that the impact of portfolio significance is especially high in application-based and distribution-focused platforms but less pronounced in development-focused platforms.

Infrastructural Flexibility and Transparency. As outlined, development- and distribution-focused platforms highlight the infrastructural flexibility granted to customers. Although

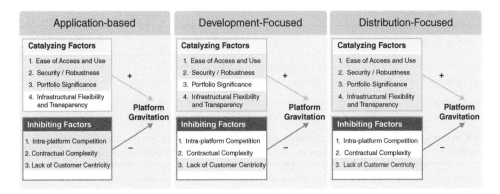

Figure 15.1 Moderating effects of platform type (highlighted factors have a high impact on platform gravitation in the respective type)

application-based platforms also list their services transparently, our analysis suggests that the impact of this factor is lower in application-based platforms. While customers of application-based platforms may select the data-center region the core application is deployed to, additionally contracted services directly run in the customer's application base. Thus, no further specification of the infrastructure is necessary. Customers of application-based platforms may be more interested in a neat integration of contracted services with the core application rather than their physical location. Decisions about infrastructural aspects are therefore more readily delegated to the provider of this core application, who abstracts the underlying infrastructure from customers in order to provide a more integrated experience with the core application. Thus, we argue that this factor is particularly relevant in development- and distribution-focused platforms but less so in application-based platforms.

Intra-Platform Competition. We further identify that the impact of intra-platform competition is contingent upon the service integration. Our results show that the threat of a platform owner entering the market is especially strong if services are highly integrated with the platform's core. In application-based platforms such as Alpha, external developers are exposed to challenging situations if the platform owner integrates functionality into its core application that was formerly exclusively provided by third parties. Competing complementors must therefore constantly fear that the platform includes the service of one of the competitors in the core application thereby making the complementors' service effectively unnecessary. Consequently, third-party service providers on such platforms tend to refrain from making large investments or access many such competitive settings at the same time if the platform owner does not mitigate this fear. Therefore, we argue that this factor has an especially high impact in application-based platforms.

Contractual Complexity. As mentioned earlier, customers engage in a variety of individual contracts with the service providers on SaaS-centric cloud platforms. Due to the straightforward transaction-phase support of the marketplaces, such contracts are quickly negotiated and closed. In the event of errors, however, customers are unable to easily identify the responsible service provider if the contracted service is highly integrated with a platform's core, as it is the case in application-based platforms. When a tightly integrated complementary service causes errors, customers may actually be unable to identify which service is faulty. Consequently, they face problems in finding the right contracted service provider to address with a maintenance request or compensation claims. What is more, contractually agreed service levels may differ across the core application and complementary services and therefore pose a major challenge for customers in enforcing a satisfactory overall service level of the integrated set of platform core and complementary services. Owners of application-based platforms can therefore highly increase their platform's attractiveness to customers if they can reduce this contractual complexity and offer customers a sole interface and contract for maintenance requests and related issues across all services, not only regarding the platform core. In distribution-focused and development-focused platforms, services run more isolated from each other and from the platform. Consequently, such problems occur less frequently. Contractual complexity therefore has a particularly strong impact on platform gravitation in application-based platforms.

15.5 Discussion

The overarching objective of this study is to explore the factors that influence gravitation in SaaS-centric cloud platforms, a specific type of cloud platform that exhibits capabilities to distribute and manage SaaS solutions. Gravitation refers to a platform's capability to attract and retain participants in its ecosystem. Our study therefore identified important factors that influence the success of SaaS-centric cloud platforms. Specifically, we have elaborated four catalyzing factors, which are (1) ease of access and use, (2) portfolio significance, (3) security and (4) infrastructural flexibility and transparency. Furthermore, we discovered three inhibiting effects to the gravitation of SaaS-centric cloud platforms, namely (1) intra-platform competition, (2) contractual complexity and (3) lack of customer centricity. Moreover, we show that the factors are contingent upon the respective platform type.

15.5.1 *Implications for research*

The identification of catalyzing and inhibiting factors of platform gravitation provides insights into beneficial settings of SaaS-centric cloud platforms. Our research contributes to the emergent literature on cloud platform ecosystems in several ways.

First, this study identifies a need to focus on alternative contractual configurations that may be beneficial for all ecosystem participants to reduce contractual complexity. As stated by Wareham et al. [15], platform ecosystems are exposed to the risk that direct responsibilities of complementors might be difficult to determine. Contractual agreements of ecosystem participants have been taken into consideration in the extant literature, highlighting their potential to facilitate value co-creation in platform ecosystems [22]. This study contributes to this existing research by suggesting that maintaining rather high-level relationships might be a viable means to counter the contractual complexity customers are exposed to. Our results suggest that high-level contracts between complementors and platform owners that provide a single, unified contract to customers may be beneficial for customers especially in the case of application-based SaaS-centric cloud platforms. This could clarify responsibilities and duties of complementors. Future research should elaborate on concrete contractual configurations and possible arrangements. However, this would mean a relationship-specific investment for platform owners. Prior work suggests that platform owners seek to balance arm's length coordination that reduces investments in single relationships and allows for leveraging synergies with the freedom they provide to ecosystem participants that allows them to co-create value [14]. Future work may therefore need to investigate how platform owners can achieve a balance between reducing the contractual complexity for customers and still keeping relationship-specific investments moderate.

Second, our findings suggest that the benefits of narrow customer foci need to be illuminated for SaaS-centric cloud platform ecosystems, especially from an economics perspective. By drawing on the concept of customer centricity, we identify a lack of a specific customer focus on specific industries, regions and business sizes as inhibiting gravitation. This finding is in line with the recommendation of a vertical focus that could provide domain-specific knowledge necessary for certain industries [5,47]. Our findings are thereby also consistent with research that identifies inequalities with respect to business size to be considerably inhibiting the co-creation of value in inter-organizational settings [22,23]. Specifically, this study reveals that differences in business size further affect the relationship between complementors and consumers.

Research on platform ecosystems argues from an economics perspective that platforms should refrain from a narrow focus in order to leverage strong network effects [48]. Research that is in favor of a limited focus mainly elaborates on the tension between quality and quantity of offered services (e.g., [20,49]). However, another perspective suggests that a narrow focus could provide domain-specific knowledge necessary for certain industries [5,47]. Especially in the context of SaaS-centric cloud platforms, the examination of such domain-specific settings has received little attention in research so far [50]. In this study, we provide support for the perspective arguing that a narrower focus on specific customer groups can mitigate restraining reactions of consumers. Future research should therefore investigate how to balance these two strategies and identify contingency factors to understand the effectiveness of these strategies in different circumstances.

Third, the elaboration on the factor ease of access and use unveils promising contemporary themes considering developments regarding integration and onboarding. Our findings suggest that cross-application integration represents a promising concept affecting ease of use and thereby platform gravitation. This is in line with related work that predicts that the demand for cloud-based integration is likely to increase due to the ongoing IT outsourcing (e.g., [51]). With regard to the case examples, avoiding isolated software services might become increasingly relevant. As stated by [52], this type of integration is likely to play an important role in the trajectory of cloud computing. As our findings show, the emergence of mashup tools might further increase in relevance. As such, mashup tools facilitate modeling of software services on the platform without programming and thereby increase ease of access and use [6]. This may represent a considerable means in order to promote innovation on the platform allowing users to develop add-ons specifically tailored to their business needs without coding. This field may therefore constitute a promising area for future design science research.

Fourth, we identify moderating effects of the platform type on the impact of the catalyzing and inhibiting factors. In this context, our study contributes to research on intra-platform competition. This phenomenon has been examined from different theoretical perspectives suggesting positive (e.g., [53]) and negative effects (e.g., [10]) on a platform ecosystem. Although platform settings are increasingly characterized by competition [21], especially the literature on multi-sided markets suggests that excessive competition represents a source of market failure [10]. Extant literature proposes secondary beneficial mechanisms of a platform owner's entry that may foster innovation activities [53]. The findings of our study suggest an inhibiting effect that is contingent upon the integration of competing software services into the platform core, e.g., if the platform owner integrates functionality of complementors' services into the platform core. Future research is needed to shed light on these dynamics and elaborate on potential contingencies.

15.5.2 Implications for practice

Since the success of a platform ecosystem strongly depends on its size [11], gravitation of a platform is highly important. Our findings may therefore provide several valuable implications for practice. First, it seems to be beneficial to increase the ease of access and use of a SaaS-centric cloud platform and thereby to consider all sides. In this context, the integration of software solutions plays an important role. Due to the importance of developers and customers in platform ecosystems, facilitating their access to and improving their experience on the platform may sustain competitive advantage. Second, this study highlights the importance of side-specific requirements of both developers (e.g., degree of development support required) and customers (e.g., desired portfolio, infrastructural transparency, compliance and legal issues). We recommend that practice takes this into consideration. Third, the degree of intra-platform competition might allude to an inherent challenge. As outlined above, a tension between control and diversity is existent in platform settings. Therefore, the situation of developers and the strategic focus of the platform owner should be continuously scrutinized. Fourth, we identify an inhibiting effect of contractual complexity, which underlines the need to focus on ownership structures and contractual configurations that may be beneficial for all ecosystem participants. Finally, by ensuring security and reliability regarding the technological foundation and the software services, platform owners might increase the participants' trust in their platform. Taking into account these recommendations may be beneficial for platform owners and may help SaaS-centric cloud platforms to gravitate.

15.5.3 Limitations

This study offers a few limitations. The first limitation concerns the applied sampling strategy. The selection of cases according to category resulted in relatively divergent cases. Although this allowed us to analyze very different strategies and to thereby learn from extremes, it may also limit the generalizability of our findings. In future studies, the focus might be set on specific categories in order to better understand within-group commonalities and differences. A second limitation is the number of interviews conducted per case. The selected interview partners were highly suitable for our study due to their sophisticated knowledge regarding both operational and strategic platform decisions. Nevertheless, the involvement of more than one representative of each platform could allow data triangulation. Integrating the perspectives of customers and complementors in the case analysis could further increase data validity and provide a more comprehensive view. Thus, the consideration of other ecosystem participants in future studies might reveal further valuable insights. Last, especially development-focused cloud platforms sometimes provide marketplaces for reusable components to support the development on the respective platforms. Examples of these distribution channels, which exhibit a focus on developers, are Engine Yard Add-Ons (https://addons.engineyard.com, accessed on August 15, 2017) and Heroku Elements (https://elements.heroku.com, accessed on August 15, 2017). Due to our focus on platforms that facilitate distribution and management of SaaS solutions, these examples have been neglected. Focusing on the specificities of these distribution channels might provide a fruitful avenue for future studies.

15.6 Conclusion

In today's digital age, the outsourcing of IT resources in the context of cloud computing is considered to be highly promising and has seen a strong proliferation. In this study, we examined factors influencing the gravitation of SaaS-centric cloud platforms, i.e., their capability to attract and retain ecosystem participants. Based on four case studies, we identified four catalyzing factors (ease of access and use, security, portfolio significance, infrastructural flexibility and transparency) as well as three inhibiting factors (intra-platform competition, contractual complexity, lack of customer centricity) for SaaS-centric cloud platform gravitation. Our findings represent a starting point to support the academic conversation on cloud platforms, which are subject to constant change and development. Due to the ongoing trend of implementing domain-specific individual solutions instead of adopting one holistic software system, SaaS-centric cloud platforms might offer viable avenues to confront the increasing complexity of heterogeneous IT landscapes [54]. The demand of integration in such a heterogeneous software environment poses a significant contemporary challenge that still needs to be overcome. In fact, it is likely to constitute the key challenge for cloud platforms in our digital age.

References

1. KPMG and Bitkom. (2015). https://www.bitkom.org/sites/default/files/file/import/cloud-Monitor-2015-KPMG-Bitkom-Research.pdf
2. Yang, H., Tate, M.: A Descriptive Literature Review and Classification of cloud Computing Research. Communications of the Association of Information Systems. 31, 2, 35–60 (2012).
3. Ma, D., Seidemann, A.: Analyzing Software as a Service with Per-Transaction Charges. Information Systems Research. 26, 2, 360–378 (2015).
4. Giessmann, A., Legner, C.: Designing Business Models for cloud Platforms. Information Systems Journal. 26, 5, 551–579 (2016).
5. Hahn, C., Röhrer, D., Zarnekow, R.: A Value Proposition Oriented Typology of Electronic Marketplaces for B2B SaaS Applications. In: AMCIS 2015 Proceedings (2015).
6. Giessmann, A., Stanoevska-Slabeva, K.: Business Models of Platform as a Service (PaaS) Providers: Current State and Future Directions. Journal of Information Technology Theory and Application. 13, 4, 31–55 (2012).
7. Aydin, M.N., Perdahci, N.Z., Odevci, B.: cloud-Based Development Environments: PaaS. In: Murugesan, S., Bojanova, I. (eds.) Encyclopedia of cloud Computing, pp. 62–69. John Wiley & Sons. Ltd. Publishing, Chichester (2016).
8. Dellermann, D., Jud, C., Reck, F.: Understanding Platform Loyalty in the cloud: A Configurational View on ISV's Costs and Benefits. In: Proceedings der 13. Internationale Tagung Wirtschaftsinformatik (WI), pp. 514–528, Siegen (2017).
9. Tiwana, A.: Evolutionary Competition in Platform Ecosystems. Information Systems Research, 26, 2, 266–281 (2015).
10. Hagiu, A.: Strategic Decisions for Multisided Platforms. MIT Sloan Management Review, 55, 2, 71–80 (2014).
11. Schreieck, M., Wiesche, M., Krcmar, H.: Design and Governance of Platform Ecosystems – Key Concepts and Issues for Future Research. In: ECIS 2016 Research Papers (2016).
12. Ghazawneh, A., Henfridsson, O.: Balancing Platform Control and External Contribution in Third-Party Development: The Boundary Resources Model. Information Systems Journal. 23, 2, 173–192 (2013).
13. Tiwana, A., Konsynski, B., Bush, A.A.: Platform Evolution: Coevolution of Platform Architecture, Governance, and Environmental Dynamics. Information Systems Research. 21, 4, 675–-687 (2010).
14. Huber, T.L., Kude, T., Dibbern, J.: Governance Practices in Platform Ecosystems: Navigating Tensions between Cocreated Value and Governance Costs. Information Systems Research. 28, 3, 563–584 (2017).
15. Wareham, J., Fox, P.B., Cano Giner, J.L.: Technology Ecosystem Governance. Organization Science. 25, 4, 1195–1215 (2014).
16. Hahn, C., Huntgeburth, J., Winkler, T.J., Zarnekow, R.: Business and IT Capabilities for cloud Platform Success. In: Proceedings of the 37th International Conference on Information Systems, pp. 1–20 (2016).

17. Hahn, C.: Digitalisierung der IT-Industrie mit cloud Plattformen – Implikationen für Entwickler und Anwender. HMD Praxis der Wirtschaftsinformatik. 53, 594–606 (2016).
18. Johns, G.: The Essential Impact of Context on Organizational Behavior. Academy of Management Review. 31, 2, 386–408 (2006).
19. Gawer, A.: Bridging Differing Perspectives on Technological Platforms: Toward an Integrative Framework. Research Policy. 43, 1239–1249 (2014).
20. Boudreau, K.J.: Let a Thousand Flowers Bloom? An Earlier Look at Large Numbers of Software App Developers and Patterns of Innovation. Organization Science. 23, 5, 1409–1427 (2012).
21. Ceccagnoli, M., Forman, C., Huang, P., Wu, D.J.: Cocreation of Value in a Platform Ecosystem: The Case of Enterprise Software. MIS Quarterly. 36, 1, 263–290 (2012).
22. Sarker, S., Sarker, S., Sahaym, A., Bjørn-Andersen, N.: Exploring Value Cocreation in Relationship Between an ERP Vendor and Its Partners: A Revelatory Case Study. MIS Quarterly. 36, 1, 317–338 (2012).
23. Kude, T., Dibbern, J., Heinzl, A.: Why Do Complementors Participate? An Analysis of Partnership Networks in the Enterprise Software Industry. IEEE Transactions on Engineering Management. 59, 2, 250–265 (2012).
24. Ghazawneh, A., Henfridsson, O.: A Paradigmatic Analysis of Digital Application Marketplaces. Journal of Information Technology. 30, 3, 198–208 (2015).
25. Yoo, Y., Henfridsson, O., Lyytinen, K.: The New Organizing Logic of Digital Innovation: An Agenda for Information Systems Research. Information Systems Research. 21, 4, 724–735 (2010).
26. Wang, N., Liang, H., Jia, Y., Ge, S., Xue, Y., Wang, Z.: cloud Computing Research in the IS Discipline: A Citation/Co-Citation Analysis. Decision Support Systems. 86, 35–47 (2016).
27. Kappelman, L., Nguyen, Q., McLean, E., Maurer, C., Johnson, V., Snyder, M., Torres, R.: The 2016 SIM IT Issues and Trends Study. MIS Quarterly Executive. 16, 1, 47–80 (2017).
28. Mell, P., T. Grance, T.: The NIST Definition of cloud Computing. Special Publication 800-145. National Institute of Standards and Technology, Gaithersburg, MD (2011).
29. Voorsluys, W., Broberg, J., Buyya, R.: Introduction to cloud Computing. In: Buyya, R., Broberg, J., Goscinski, A.M. (eds.) Hoboken. Cloud Computing Principles and Paradigms, pp. 3–42. John Wiley & Sons, Hoboken, NJ (2011).
30. Gawer, A., Cusumano, M.A.: Industry Platforms and Ecosystem Innovation. Journal of Product Innovation Management. 31, 3, 417–433 (2014).
31. Cusumano, M.A., Gawer A.: The Elements of Platform Leadership. MIT Sloan Management Review. 43, 3, 50–58 (2002).
32. Hilkert, D., Benlian, A., Hess, T.: Perceived Software Platform Openness: The Scale and Its Impact on Developer Satisfaction. In: Proceedings of the 32th International Conference on Information Systems, pp. 1–20 (2011).
33. Hurni, T., Huber, T.L.: The Interplay of Power and Trust in Platform Ecosystems of the Enterprise Application Software Industry. In: ECIS 2014 Proceedings, pp. 1–15 (2014).
34. Katz, M.L., Shapiro, C.: Systems Competition and Network Effects. Journal of Economic Perspectives. 8, 2, 93–115 (1994).
35. Evans, P.C., Gawer, A.: The Rise of the Platform Enterprise: A Global Survey. The Emerging Platform Economy Series No. 1. The Center for Global Enterprise. (2016). https://www.thecge.net/app/uploads/2016/01/PDF-WEB-Platform-Survey_01_12.pdf
36. Giessmann, A., Stanoevska, K.: Platform as a Service – A Conjoint Study on Consumer's Preferences. In: Proceedings of the 33th International Conference on Information Systems, pp. 1–20 (2012).
37. Floerecke, S., Lehner, F.: cloud Computing Ecosystem Model: Refinement and Evaluation. In ECIS 2016 Proceedings, pp. 1–14 (2016).
38. Tipler, P.A., Mosca, G., Wagner, J.: Physik: für Wissenschaftler und Ingenieure. Springer Spektrum, Heidelberg (2015).
39. Benbasat, I., Goldstein, D.K., Mead, M.: The Case Research Strategy in Studies of Information Systems. MIS Quarterly. 11, 3, 369–386 (1987).
40. Eisenhardt, K.M.: Building Theories from Case Study Research. The Academy of Management Review. 14, 4, 532–550 (1989).
41. Yin, R.K.: Case Study Research: Design and Methods. Sage, Thousand Oaks, CA (2003).
42. Menychtas, A., García-Gómez, S., Giessmann, A., Gatzioura, A., Stanoevska, K., Vogel, J., Moulos, V.: A Marketplace Framework for Trading cloud-Based Services. In: Vanmechelen, K.,

Altmann, J., Rana, O.F. (eds.) Economics of Grids, clouds, Systems, and Services. GECON 2011. Lecture Notes in Computer Science, vol. 7150, pp. 76–89. Springer, Heidelberg (2012).

43. Eaton, B., Elaluf-Calderwood, S., Sørensen, C., Yoo, Y.: Distributed Tuning of Boundary Resources: The Case of Apple's iOS Service System. MIS Quarterly. 39, 1, 217–243 (2015).

44. Benlian, A., Hilkert, D., Hess, T.: How Open Is This Platform? The Meaning and Measurement of Platform Openness from the Complementors' Perspective. Journal of Information Technology. 30, 3, 209–228 (2015).

45. Buyya, R., Pandey, S., Vecchiola, C.: cloudbus Toolkit for Market-Oriented cloud Computing. In: cloudCom 2009: Proceedings of the 1st International Conference on cloud Computing (2009).

46. Parniangtong, S.: Competitive Advantage of Customer Centricity. Springer Nature, Singapore (2017).

47. Hompel, M. ten, Rehof, J., Wolf, O.: cloud Computing for Logistics. Springer International Publishing, Basel (2015).

48. Rochet, J.C., Tirole, J.: Platform Competition in Two-Sided Markets. Journal of the European Economic Association. 1, 4, 990–1029 (2003).

49. Hagiu, A.: Quantity vs. Quality and Exclusion by Two-Sided Platforms. Harvard Business School Strategy Unit Working Paper No. 09-094, pp. 1–26 (2009).

50. Daniluk, D., Holtkamp, B.: Logistics Mall – A cloud Platform for Logistics. In: Hompel, M. ten, Rehof, J., Wolf, O. (eds.) cloud Computing for Logistics, pp. 13–27. Springer International Publishing, Cham (2015).

51. Ebert, N., Schlatter, U.: cloud-basierte Integration. Informatik-Spektrum. 40, 3, 278–282 (2017).

52. Fortiş, T.F., Munteanu, V.I., Negru, V.: Towards a Service Friendly cloud Ecosystem. In: 11th International Symposium on Parallel and Distributed Computing (ISPDC), pp. 172–179 (2012).

53. Foerderer, J., Kude, T., Mithas, S., Heinzl, A.: Does Platform Owner's Entry Crowd Out Innovation? Evidence from Google Photos. Information Systems Research. 29, 2, 444–460 (2018).

54. Hentschel, R., Leyh, C.: cloud Computing: Gestern, heute, morgen. HMD Praxis der Wirtschaftsinformatik. 53, 5, 563–579 (2016).

16

GOVERNING CLOUD COMPUTING SERVICES

Risks and mitigating controls

Mathew Mertens, Steven De Haes and Tim Huygh

16.1 Introduction

The increasing shift towards agile enterprises has led to the augmented application of IT outsourcing. To realize this, several options can be applied. Cloud services can be considered as one of the most applied options and has therefore led to a fundamental change in the IT landscape throughout the last decade. Despite that the use of Cloud services is often perceived as an IT-driven choice, it should be seen as an IT-based business model realizing the agile business strategy [1].

The adaptation of the new IT operating model will continue to increase as evident from recent Gartner research, stating that within the next five years a total of approximately one trillion dollars will be spent on the implementation and use of Cloud services [2]. Although the use of Cloud services will continue to be key to realize organizational agility, several organizations remain reluctant to the adoption of Cloud services, due to the risks such adoption might entail [3]. To mitigate or minimize these risks, a formal Cloud governance approach needs to be defined.

This chapter will contribute to these aspects by elaborating upon the potential risks and the corresponding mitigation controls. Before deep-diving into the required governance mechanisms, an overview of the associated risks and benefits will be provided. Based on a risk analysis, the required IT governance mechanisms (i.e. structures, processes and relational mechanisms) to enable risk mitigation will be identified and discussed.

16.2 An overview of Cloud computing services

As defined by NIST (2011), Cloud computing services enable simple and on-demand network access to a shared pool of configurable computer resources, such as servers, applications and services [4]. These resources can be utilized with minimal effort and management involvement and minimal interaction with the service provider. In the following sections, the benefits and risks associated with Cloud services adoption are discussed.

16.2.1 *The benefits of using Cloud services*

As defined by the 'Technology Business Management methodology', transparency and cost performance are two core elements for realizing business value [5]. Even though technology innovations have led to increasing capabilities and lower costs of IT infrastructures, the increasing complexity of organizations has resulted in increasing costs of information management [6].

Shifting internal control towards an external service provider can therefore reduce IT complexity. This change will realize a transfer from required capital investments towards operational expenditures and will enable cost transparency due to the predefined costs per use [3,7].

Cloud computing can therefore be considered as a next step, realizing scalability and availability by decoupling the performed business services and the required IT infrastructure to support the services by using distributed resources [6,8,9].

Outsourcing datacentre management will moreover significantly impact the required IT staff and other resources and will moreover enable a substantial effect on the cost structure and internal operations of the organization. The adoption of Cloud services should therefore be initiated as a strategic choice enabling the value realization of the business units by reducing complexity, enabling flexibility and reducing time-to-market for new innovative initiatives [6,10].

As illustrated, the adoption of Cloud services can lead to several (IT-related and organizational) benefits. It is however required to identify all potential risks and take them into account.

16.2.2 *The associated risks of using Cloud services*

Despite the increasing adoption rate of Cloud services, several organizations remain resistant to the use of Cloud services due to the existence of several risks. As defined in COBIT 5, an enterprise governance and management of IT framework developed by ISACA (2012), both the internal context, including management and IT-related capabilities, and the external context need to be considered to evaluate risk [11].

The risks associated with Cloud services can be divided into four categories, namely technical risks, operational risks, organizational risks and compliance risks. The impact and nature of these risks depends on the organization, the used Cloud service model (IAAS, PAAS, SAAS) and the applied deployment model (private, public, community, hybrid) [12].

As illustrated in Figure 16.1, the Cloud service model defines the nature of control and therefore directly impacts the risk level.

16.2.2.1 *Technical risks*

Recurring scepticism on Cloud services is mainly related to data security and privacy. Privacy is a part of security and solely relates to the content and communication of personal information. To fully cover *data security*, the CIA (confidentiality, integrity, availability) principles need to be managed and controlled efficiently and effectively.

Confidentiality is ensured when the data is only accessible to those who are authorized to access the data. When using Cloud services, data can be made accessible through the Internet everywhere around the world. Therefore, the risk of unauthorized access increases significantly. Moreover, the application of a multi-tenancy model, leading to shared data storage facilities, can result in an increased risk in unauthorized access to data and could also result

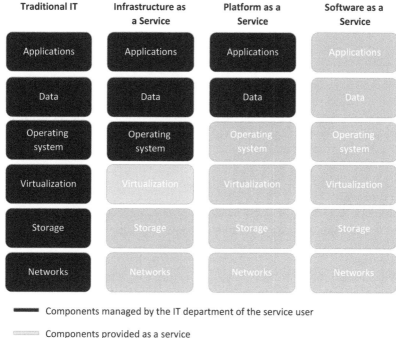

Traditional IT	Infrastructure as a Service	Platform as a Service	Software as a Service
Applications	Applications	Applications	Applications
Data	Data	Data	Data
Operating system	Operating system	Operating system	Operating system
Virtualization	Virtualization	Virtualization	Virtualization
Storage	Storage	Storage	Storage
Networks	Networks	Networks	Networks

━━━ Components managed by the IT department of the service user

▭▭▭ Components provided as a service

Figure 16.1   Components of Cloud services [13]

in data remanence when the data is not properly deleted [14, 15]. *Integrity* refers to the secure state of the data, meaning that no unauthorized users should be able to change and delete the stored data. The data must comply with all states of the ACID characteristics and therefore needs to be atomic, consistent, isolated and durable. When requesting and transferring the data, these states should remain unchanged [14]. Cloud computing services should have a positive impact on the *availability* of the stored data and applications. Cloud services enable worldwide availability of data and applications on all supported devices connected to the Internet. The increased accessibility could however result to unauthorized network attacks, such as DDOS, spoofing and snipping.

The efficiency of the Cloud service is dependent on the *architecture and networks* provided by the service provider. The scalability and processing requirements should be assessed to ensure all required CPU power is available at all time. Due to the dependency on a steady Internet connection, the risk of an unstable or inaccessible network connection could lead to latency, resulting in major operational impact [16, 17].

Due to outsourcing of responsibilities, the Cloud user will become dependent on the Cloud service provider. Therefore, the lack of efficient *datacentre management* by the provider will have a direct impact. These inefficiencies could relate to lack of updates and patch management, an inefficient service desk and inefficient or non-existing disaster recovery procedures. The service provider can also be dependent on a third party, such as an infrastructure provider. Therefore, a lack of contractual transparency could lead to a turmoil of accountabilities [14, 18].

Investing in Cloud services to enable flexibility can have a positive impact on the strategy execution of the organization. The success will however be dependent on the *compatibility* between the Cloud service and the existent legacy systems. Lack of integration can lead to duplication and a lack of data transparency, leading to increased data management costs [19].

16.2.2.2 Operational risks

Several risks can have an immediate impact on the operational processes of the organization, resulting in increased operational costs. Business processes are dependent on information, which should be managed by the business units in cooperation with the IT department. *Information management* should focus on data in use, in transport and at rest. To fully cope with all risks regarding information management, the information lifecycle model can be used, which illustrates all five phases of data management.

1 Data collection
   Although Cloud services can enable new data collection techniques (e.g. using internet of things), the use of Cloud services as such will not impact the collection of data [20].
2 Data storage
   When using infrastructure as a service, the user will remain in charge of the content of the data, but will outsource the physical storage of the data. This could lead to fragmentation and lack of transparency about the location of the data. The use of distributed databases will moreover lead to increased complexity and increased risk of data redundancy. When the user is subject to data privacy regulations, the lack of data location transparency could lead to non-compliance [21, 22, 23, 24, 25].
3 Data usage
   The use of the data is dependent on the performance and accessibility of the Cloud service. Direct operational impact will be realized whenever the data is crucial for the continuity of the business processes.
4 Data retention
   Because data under retention requirements will not be accessed frequently, data fragmentation will arise. The data will moreover relate to sensitive information for which no flexible capacity is required [26].
5 Data deletion
   Whenever data does not have to be retained, it needs to be either deleted or anonymized. Because data is stored on hardware, which is being managed by a third party and is shared with other organizations, the risk of improper deletion could lead to the recovery of data using forensic techniques [20, 26, 27, 28].

Because the availability of the data, which is stored in a Cloud environment, is dependent on the actions performed by the service provider, the risk of *data lock-in* occurs. As discussed, technical issues regarding the network and hardware can lead to inaccessibility of data. More risks regarding inaccessibility can occur whenever the service provider suddenly stops the support of the service or whenever discussions occur and the service provider blocks the access to the data servers [21].

Using Cloud services can enforce cost transparency due to the pay per use model. The use of this service can however lead to an increase in users and therefore usage, leading to an increase in the required data transfer capacity, which will be reflected in augmented costs. When using platform as a service, lack of control could lead to the installation of illegal software or the violation of license agreements, which could result in financial penalties.

The use of Cloud services can then lead to a lack of *use transparency*. Therefore, it is required to define the distinction between core and non-core data and define which elements can safely be stored in a Cloud environment [12, 29]. This lack of transparency could moreover result in a *lack of control*, relating to the relationship between the service user and the service provider [12].

16.2.2.3 Organizational risks

Lack of control can have an impact on the governance mechanisms throughout the organization. Specifically, the lack of transparency and control on the physical storage of the data will complicate the risk analysis, which can lead to inefficient *decision-making*, resulting in inefficient governance [8]. While the service provider is responsible for ensuring appropriate security measures, the service user will remain owner of the data stored in a Cloud environment and will therefore be accountable for security breaches. To cope with the risk and impact of security breaches, the service user is therefore required to implement efficient *incident management* procedures. The dependency on the service provider could lead to improper follow-up and escalation of incidents leading to inefficient incident management, which could result in reputational damage of the organization [30].

Organizations might opt for a Cloud service to realize cost reductions. These cost reductions could be achieved by reducing the IT staff, due to the outsourcing of IT responsibilities. When reducing the number of FTEs of the IT department, the organization needs to take all required *knowledge and skills* into account to ensure business continuity. Furthermore, the selection, implementation and follow-up of the Cloud service will require new expertise [12].

Although Cloud services enable flexibility, each service provider will provide a specific service, which can be incompatible with other services. Switching services and service providers can therefore become very complex and lead to *vendor lock-in* [22].

16.2.2.4 Compliance risks

Even though not all organizations are entirely data driven, each organization is dependent on data. To regulate the use of this data, organizations are subject to national, international and industry-specific data regulations. Because the physical location of the stored data is subject to *data privacy and security regulations*, using Cloud computing services has a major impact for the user of these services. Organizations need to comply with these regulations to ensure the confidentiality and integrity of personal, medical and financial data. Several regulations already exist that regulate the communication, storage, access and confiscation of data [6].

Due to the differences in data privacy regulations worldwide, remaining compliant to all specific regulations is a challenge for organizations that operate globally. To provide an overview of these differences, three geographic areas are discussed, namely Europe, the USA and Asia.

The European data privacy regulation (EU Directive 95/46/EC) has, in comparison to the USA and Asia, a specific focus on personal data, because privacy is perceived as a fundamental right. The American privacy regulation only focuses on personal data regarding medical information (HIPAA). The European privacy law moreover defines the user of the data as responsible to ensure data privacy, which implicates the accountability of the Cloud service user. Because the above-mentioned EU Directive focuses on the internal communication of data between two parties, this regulation is no longer sufficient to regulate the use and privacy of data stored and shared in Cloud environments. Therefore, the 'General Data Protection Regulation' was defined by the European Union in 2015 with 25 May 2018 as enforcement date. This new regulation fully regulates the use and storage of personal data to assure data privacy.

The new GDPR harmonizes all existing European privacy regulations and focuses on the responsibilities of the data controllers and data processors and incorporates financial sanctions for non-compliance up to 4% of the global yearly income of the organization [31, 32, 33].

When inspecting the American privacy regulation, three main acts can be defined to which the contractual agreements between the service user and the service provider need to comply. First, the USA PATRIOT Act (UPA) incorporates the potential access and confiscation of the data by the FBI, based on a court order. Second, certain domain-specific acts, such as the Electronic Communications Privacy Act (ECPA) and the Fair Credit Reporting Act (FCRA), regulate the potential involvement of the Government. Lastly, the well-known Sarbanes-Oxley Act (SOX) is implemented to protect the data of investors and regulate the storage and communication of financial data. All American public companies and public companies listed in the USA need to be compliant to SOX [34].

The 'Asia Pacific Economic Corporation (APEC) Privacy Framework' is built based on best practices to ensure flexibility regarding the transition towards Cloud environments. In comparison with the GDPR, the Asian framework is defined as a guideline rather than a mandatory regulation [35]. Next to the international privacy regulations, several industry-specific regulations are defined, for instance relating to health (HIPAA, HITECH) and finance (GLBA).

The risks that can be associated with compliancy are not limited to privacy and security regulations. The involvement of intellectual property, related to data stored in a Cloud environment, and the discontinuation of contractual agreements can be identified as compliancy risks as well. Cloud services should be used for the storage of non-critical data. Whenever the organization opts to store data relating to intellectual property in the Cloud environment, discussions could occur regarding the ownership of the *intellectual property*. The increased availability could moreover potentially lead to violations of copyright or the loss of competitive advantage. When using a platform as a service Cloud environment, several licence-based applications can be installed. The lack of use transparency, due to the increase in users, could lead to the use of this software by unauthorized users, which could result in substantial fines.

Both the service user and the service provider are responsible for maintaining security and compliancy. Since the service provider has no insight on the nature of the data and the service user does not know the physical location of the data, discussions regarding the accountability could occur. Therefore, it is required to define clear *contractual agreements* to predefine the responsibilities and accountabilities. The lack of follow-up of the service level agreements could moreover lead to insufficient datacentre management and the failure to comply with the agreed upon contractual agreements throughout the contractual lifecycle. The discontinuation of the contract could also have an operational impact whenever the termination procedures are not clearly defined [35, 36].

16.2.3 *The impact of the identified risks*

Risk analyses need to be performed to select the appropriate service and service provider and monitor the service throughout the lifecycle. Note that the impact of these risks is dependent on the service model and therefore impacts the required management practices [37].

Although the selection of the service type impacts the risk level, all mechanisms listed underneath need to be considered for all services types. The degree and implementation of specific controls, to optimize the limited control over the data and resources, will however be dependent on the chosen service type.

To perform a risk analysis, the organization needs to outline its risk appetite, which illustrates the risks the organization is willing to take to realize its strategy. The risks can be defined based on the standardized ISO 27005 method and 'COBIT 5 For Risk' including the focus on probability and the business impact [28]. Based on the risk analysis, one of the four risk measures (i.e. accept, transfer, avoid, mitigate) needs to be selected.

Because responsibility and accountability regarding Cloud services are contractually defined, it is not possible to shift the risk to the service provider. Moreover, several risks are inherent to the storage and use of data. Choosing or neglecting a Cloud service will therefore not entirely enable the avoidance of the risk. Mitigating the risks by implementing control measures will consequentially be the optimal solution. The effectiveness of these control measures will be dependent on the governance mechanisms as defined and implemented by the organization.

16.3 IT governance mechanisms for Cloud computing services

Governance relates to the decision rights, the accountability and the responsibilities that need to be fulfilled by the management team and the board of directors to realize the strategic goals and optimize the risk profile [17]. Efficient and effective IT governance is required to realize business-IT alignment and can be realized by focusing on three types of mechanisms [19]. These IT governance mechanisms relate to the structures, processes and relational mechanisms and are therefore part of the Governance enablers as defined by ISACA in COBIT 5.

Because the use of Cloud services can be perceived as the implementation of a new IT provisioning model, it will have a direct impact on the organizational governance, due to the outsourcing of control. To realize a successful Cloud implementation and realize agility, the current IT governance mechanisms will have to be adapted and new mechanisms will have to be implemented.

The focus on the required structures, processes and relational mechanisms to realize a clear governance approach is therefore obligatory to optimize the value creation and minimize the associated risks [3, 39].

16.3.1 Structures

It is crucial to have effective Cloud leadership to govern and manage the selection, implementation and follow-up of the Cloud service. Outsourcing responsibilities also leads to a decentralization of the decision-making and control. Therefore, several structures or roles with the required expertise need to be allocated to manage the Cloud service in order to realize the desired agility and achieve the anticipated business goals [17, 40, 41].

COBIT 5 clearly states the need for the *involvement of the board of directors* to clarify the difference between governance and management. Because the use of Cloud services should be based upon strategic initiatives, the board of directors needs to be involved in the selection procedure and the definition of the risk appetite.

To define centralized Cloud leadership, a *Chief Cloud Officer (CCO)* needs to be appointed, who has the required expertise to manage the Cloud service. Note that the CIO can fulfil this role, if he/she has the necessary expertise [40, 42].

Because the decisions regarding the implementation and follow-up of the Cloud service should not be made by one individual, a *Cloud management committee (CMC)* needs to be established, which will consist of members of both the top management team and the middle management team so that the service can be comprehensively managed. To fully manage the follow-up of the Cloud service, the service provider should also be represented in this committee, which separates this committee from the IT steering committee. This committee needs to define what the Cloud service needs to realize and is therefore accountable for creating alignment between the service and the strategic goals as defined by the board of directors [6, 40].

To properly manage the operational follow-up of the Cloud service, a *Cloud service facilitation centre (CSF)*, which could be headed by a *Cloud service manager*, should be established as an internal single point of contact. The operational follow-up involves the monitoring of required data capacity and the execution of the decisions taken by the CMC and therefore entails how the implementation and use of the service will take place.

Due to the dependency on the service user, a transparent and trustworthy relationship will be the key to a successful Cloud implementation. A *Cloud relationship centre (CRC)* should therefore operate as a single point of contact with the service provider and should be responsible for the follow-up of internal policies and the service level agreements [40]. For small- and medium-sized organizations, these roles could be aggregated into a single role, known as the *Cloud service broker*. This internal broker is appointed as single point of contact and is responsible for the entire coordination and support of the Cloud service [43].

The implementation of a Cloud service does not only require new structures, but also impacts the current organizational structures. As discussed, the *Chief Information Officer (CIO)* can occupy the role of CCO, when he/she has the required knowledge and expertise. Otherwise a new CIO/CTO or CCO should be appointed. Due to the regulatory impact of Cloud services, the *Data Protection Officer (DPO)* should be involved in the selection and follow-up of the Cloud service regarding the regulatory impact.

The presence of a DPO is moreover required when the organization is subject to the GDPR [44]. The implementation of a Cloud service moreover impacts the responsibilities of the Security Officer, Risk Officer, Legal Advisor, Portfolio Manager and Infrastructure Architect. These individuals all need to be involved in the Cloud service selection process to ensure an optimal organizational fit [45].

16.3.2 Processes

IT governance processes relate to the formalization of strategic decisions and the follow-up of the predefined procedures. To identify the required IT governance processes, 'COBIT 5 Enabling processes' as part of ISACA's COBIT 5 framework can be used, which provides 37 IT governance and management processes [11, 46].

Within the COBIT 5 framework, the process enabler is further structured in process categories. This also enables a clear separation between IT governance and IT management processes. The first process category, 'Evaluate, direct and monitor' (EDM), bundles the IT governance processes and therefore illustrates the need for appropriate selection and monitoring of the Cloud service to achieve benefits realization. The remaining four COBIT 5 process categories all contain IT management processes. The management team needs to be involved in the planning and monitoring processes, as defined in the process category 'Align, plan and organize' (APO). The categories 'Build, acquire and implement' (BAI) and 'Deliver, service and support' (DSS) illustrate the need for defining and implementing clear requirements and the need for continuous operational support of the service to ensure

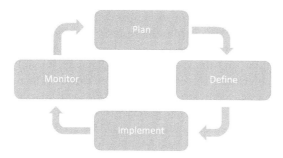

Figure 16.2   Governance lifecycle [47]

business continuity. Monitoring procedures need to be in place to prevent incidents and assess whether the anticipated goals are achieved. COBIT 5 therefore defines the need for the process category 'Monitor, evaluate and assess' (MEA) to indicate the need for clear measures to evaluate the success and effectiveness of the Cloud service [11].

The four COBIT 5 management process categories are required to realize effective and efficient IT Governance and can be allocated to the four phases of the Cloud governance lifecycle [47, 48] (Figure 16.2).

First, the strategic goals and requirements need to be identified during a planning phase. Based on these strategic goals, the specific functional and technological requirements can be defined, resulting in the selection of a specific Cloud service and service provider. After that, the service needs to be integrated with the systems in use. Before initiating a go-live, several test stages need to be conducted to assure the correct implementation of the Cloud service regarding usage, security and compliancy. After the successful implementation of the service, these elements and the accompanied risks need to be evaluated on a continuous basis.

16.3.3 *Relational mechanisms*

Relational mechanisms relate to the need for participation and communication between all stakeholders involved. The organizational culture and ethics have a severe impact on the effectiveness of the organizational governance. To assure that employees comply with the defined policies and standards, internal communication and transparency is required to generate insight on the need and impact of these requirements. When implementing a Cloud service, users need to be aware of the license agreements and potential security harms by clarifying the potential impact of these incidents. Training and awareness campaigns focused on security and compliancy should be organized to create awareness and assure the optimal behaviour of all users [48, 49, 50, 51].

16.3.4 *Mitigating controls for the identified risk categories*

When mapping the COBIT 5 processes to the governance and management of a Cloud environment, it is clear that all processes are crucial to realize the anticipated benefits of the Cloud service. It is however not possible to assign each process to a specific risk, since several processes have an organization-wide impact and will therefore impact the entire selection and monitoring process of Cloud services.

The COBIT 5 process '*Manage strategy*' is one of the essential starting points of a Cloud implementation and has an organization-wide impact. Organizations choose to implement a Cloud service to realize flexibility or minimize costs. This choice is therefore based on the anticipated optimizations that need to be realized to achieve the strategic goals of the organization. Choosing for a Cloud service could also depend on the external environment, including the competition and the client portfolio. Benchmarks and SWOT analyses can be used to identify and evaluate the opportunities and threats. The selection of the Cloud service model and the service provider will be based on a portfolio analysis and the service level agreements as defined by the service provider [11].

The impact of the organizational change realized by a Cloud implementation will be dependent on the implemented service model. Effective *change management* will however be required to make sure that stakeholders are aware of the risks and benefits that can be realized by this change so that change resistance can be minimized.

Risk management is a process with an organization-wide impact, as it relates to both the identification and follow-up of the risk profile. Risk assessments need to be performed by the Risk Officer on a periodic basis to evaluate the current impact of the Cloud service on the risk appetite [34, 52]. The risk management framework for Cloud computing [53] defines five phases that need to be executed to structurally perform risk management based on the predefined risk appetite:

- Assessment of user requirements
- Assessment of the Cloud service provider
- Risk evaluation
- Independent assessment by an external party
- Continuous monitoring.

By applying the CSA, NIST, ENISA and ISACA frameworks, the remaining governance and management processes can be directly assigned as mitigating controls to specific risk categories.

16.3.4.1 *Mitigating technical risks*

16.3.4.1.1 ENSURING DATA SECURITY AND PRIVACY

The required measures to assure security can be identified using the NIST Cyber Security Framework [54]. This framework identifies five functions that need to be managed to mitigate potential security risks, by referring to the related COBIT 5 management processes.

1 Identification of security threats
   The first function relates to the identification of security threats by performing asset management and risk management processes. The effectiveness of the performed measures will be dependent on the service provider. A careful selection based on CSA and ISO certificates and the use of SOC 2 reporting mechanisms will therefore be elementary selection criteria.

2 Realize protection by implementing the required security measures and controls
   To realize data integrity and confidentiality, encryption, firewalls, authentication and authorization mechanisms need to be integrated by both the service user and the service provider. Data encryption should be applied to data at rest, data in use and data in transport, to assure data confidentiality and integrity in a multi-tenancy environment. The encryption standard 'Transport Layer Security' (TLS) can be applied to ensure a secured

bilateral connection between two parties. Single sign on procedures can be integrated to increase the ease of use.

To assure a successful implementation of these security measures, one of the following best practices could be used [22]:

- Security Assertion Markup Language (SAML)
- Open Authentication (OAuth)
- OpenID.

Next to data encryption, several identity and access management controls need to be implemented to assure data integrity. A login procedure needs to be implemented to assure authorized access. The service user moreover needs to define authorities for each user or user type based on certificates and attributes. Only when the user possesses the required authority, access will be granted and decryption of the data will be performed [14, 22].

The service user moreover needs to apply end-point security measures in case of single sign-on and could opt for the implementation of a remote access and lockdown mechanism to block unauthorized access. Because no physical isolation can be achieved in a multi-tenant environment and public networks, implementing local networks and firewalls can achieve virtual isolation [55]. The service provider or infrastructure provider will be responsible for the physical security of the infrastructure and needs to ensure efficient patch management to monitor and test code changes and realize data integrity.

Availability of the data will be dependent on the used infrastructure and networks. Continuity can therefore be realized by applying duplication and geographical fragmentation of the data, by taking the regulatory requirements into account. Next to these technical implementations, awareness needs to be created to assure appropriate use of the Cloud service.

3   Perform continuous monitoring to detect security breaches

Although security breaches cannot be completely prevented, service providers and users should implement intrusion detection and prevention systems. These systems will register the used IP address and ports and will block those if required [56, 57]. The service user could moreover opt for additional firewalls to prevent unauthorized access or key loggers. Next to the implementation of technical solutions, the service user needs to create awareness on the use policies to prevent negligence.

4   Perform incident management to timely resolve and mitigate incidents

The effectiveness of these detection systems is crucial to timely escalate occurred incidents and undertake the appropriate actions to minimize the impact of the incident. Clear communication between the service provider and the Cloud relationship centre is therefore essential to achieve efficient incident management.

5   Recover and realize continuity

Finally, to ensure incidents do not develop into long-term problems of discontinuity, appropriate monitoring procedures need to be established. To optimize continuity, the organization should moreover opt for duplication and geographical fragmentation of the data, for which the regulatory requirements need to be taken into account [55]. The organization could moreover opt for a public network rather than a VPN connection to reduce the single-point-of failures, for which the organization should consider the required security measures [30, 58].

16.3.4.1.2 ENSURING SYSTEM PERFORMANCE

The service provider will perform the maintenance and monitoring of the Cloud infrastructure for a public Cloud service. The selection procedure, including test phases, and the establishment of clear contractual agreements are therefore essential for the assurance of continuity. The service user could opt for internal backup servers for the stored data to assure continuity. This will however negatively impact the anticipated scalability benefits. The service user needs to monitor the agreed upon performance levels based upon predefined benchmarks [56].

16.3.4.1.3 MONITORING DATACENTRE MANAGEMENT

The service provider is responsible for managing the virtual machines, physical security and service requests through a service desk. The service user therefore needs to be able to rely on external audit validations and the disaster recovery procedure, as defined by the service provider. The service user needs to assign the Cloud relationship centre to clearly communicate and follow up the service requests [59].

16.3.4.1.4 ENSURING COMPATIBILITY

The use of a Cloud service will incur the outsourcing of data storage and maintenance to achieve scalable IT resources. The selected service model will therefore impact the complexity of the compatibility with the internal IT resources. The implementation of a private or hybrid Cloud solution will require the adaption of the current configurations and IT architecture. To avoid unanticipated costs, the Cloud user needs to estimate the required adjustments that need to be performed to integrate the Cloud service and provide a cost buffer. When using a public or hybrid Cloud solution for application management, the implemented architecture model needs to be integrated into the existing architecture of the service user to realize compatibility.

16.3.4.2 Mitigating operational risks

16.3.4.2.1 MANAGING THE INFORMATION LIFECYCLE

To mitigate the risks regarding the control on data use and storage, full transparency is required. The Cloud user therefore needs to focus on the three phases of data usage, namely data at rest, data in use and data in transport. To assure security, encryption of data needs to be applied to all three data phases. Because data in use directly impacts the continuity of the operational processes, backup and data recovery procedures need to be in place to ensure business continuity. These procedures need to be contractually defined in the service level agreements. Because the business units are owner of the data stored, the appropriate business representatives need to be involved in the determination and follow-up of these service level agreements [21].

All organizations are dependent on certain legal requirements, including data retention policies. When this data needs to be kept for several years, without further use, cost calculations might prefer internal storage. When opting for a Cloud storage solution for retention data, fragmentation will be applied due to the lack of usage and will result in complexity and the lack of transparency. Further contractual agreements regarding the storage location will therefore be required for the data that is bound to legal requirements. Whenever the required capacity will be time-based, the Cloud user needs to timely estimate the required capacity in cooperation with all business process owners to ensure continuity. Clear manuals and procedures need to be defined to ensure data in a Cloud environment is properly deleted and to avoid that other users of the shared infrastructure can retrieve the data by applying forensic techniques.

16.3.4.2.2 PREVENTING DATA LOCK-IN

To ensure business continuity, the discontinuation of the service provider needs to be anticipated to prevent data lock-in. Lack of anticipation might moreover lead to increased migration costs and augmented complexity regarding configurations. Selecting a service provider with a strong market position and strict compliancy procedures regarding privacy regulations and license agreements is therefore essential. To prevent access to the data being blocked by the service provider due to mutual disputes, complete and consistent service level agreements need to be defined.

16.3.4.2.3 ENSURING USE TRANSPARENCY

The scalability and availability features realized by a Cloud environment will result in an increase of users. Insufficient estimations regarding the required data capacity will therefore result in unforeseen costs and will negatively impact the perceptions on the Cloud benefits. The initial budgeting process, which will impact the Cloud decision, therefore needs to contain a certain budget buffer to anticipate the potential increase of data usage.

To ensure use transparency and prevent the exponential increase of data usage, the number of users needs to be limited. Afterwards, the number of users can be gradually increased under strict supervision. Because the number of users needs to be defined by the business units, effective business-IT alignment is required to appropriately estimate and anticipate the required data transfer capacity [17].

The violation of license agreements can result in substantial fines. Defining clear use policies and creating awareness regarding these policies is therefore crucial to ensure appropriate use of the service and licensed applications.

16.3.4.2.4 ENSURING CONTROL

The success of outsourcing responsibilities is dependent on the mutual trust relationship between the two parties involved. Because the service provider only disposes of partial control, reasonable assurance on security and compliancy needs to be obtained by performing external audits. Since every Cloud user wants to obtain assurance on those topics, Cloud providers can obtain audit certifications to prevent a specific internal audit for each individual client [60].

When selecting a service provider, the organization therefore needs to base its decision on the possession of one of the following audit standards for Cloud security and data privacy:

- CSA Star certificate: Cloud security assurance
- ISO/IEC27018: ISO standard for Cloud privacy
- ISAE 3402: IT Outsourcing standard as an update of the SAS70 standard
- SOC 2 and SOC 3: Data security and privacy.

SOC 1 reporting should also be implemented to create transparency on the impact of the implemented control measures on the financial reporting [61].

Audits can be performed in two specific areas, namely security and compliancy. Whenever a security-based audit is performed, events, logs and monitoring procedures need to be evaluated [55, 62].

The 'Cloud computing management Audit/Assurance program' of ISACA can be applied to ensure a standardized approach.

The service user needs to monitor the effectiveness of the implemented controls on a continuous basis so that the quality of the service can be assessed, shortcomings of the predefined service level agreements can be identified and the risk appetite can be monitored [63].

16.3.4.3 *Mitigating organizational risks*

16.3.4.3.1 OPTIMIZING DECISION-MAKING

Ensuring transparency and control on the used Cloud service is required to realize the benefits. But to realize and govern this control, the listed governance structures and processes need to be implemented. First, clear use policies need to be defined based on the organizational processes. The identified inefficiencies and shortcomings need to be identified by the business process owners and need to be reported to the CIO and/or the CCO. This cooperation between the business end users and the IT department will positively impact the mutual alignment and cooperation [11]. The effectiveness of the decisions taken by the executive management and the board of directors is dependent on the adequacy and quality of the delivered data. The data therefore needs to be available for internal and external audits, which should be based on the COBIT and ISO frameworks [64].

Implementing a Cloud service will severely impact the investment portfolio due to the required implementation costs and the shift towards periodic variable costs. The portfolio therefore needs to be evaluated on a periodic basis by business and IT representatives to identify potential synergies. The implementation of a private Cloud solution will result in optimized transparency regarding costs, but will increase the variation of the costs whenever the infrastructure is managed internally [3].

Because there are no capital investments regarding IT infrastructure, no sunk costs will have to be considered for the implementation of a public Cloud service. To define an overview of the return on investment, the organization needs to take all future cash flows into account. To compare the cash flows for Cloud services with the current IT model, the net present value method needs to be applied [30, 57]. Shifting towards a Cloud environment can realize quick wins and will therefore positively impact the change process, if the project is effectively managed.

16.3.4.3.2 ENSURING INCIDENT MANAGEMENT

As the service user remains accountable for the data-related risks, the service user needs to implement incident management procedures and define an incident response plan to ensure timely and effective resolution management based on the predefined risk appetite [63]. Because the service user is dependent on the service provider, the incident management process needs to be adapted to incorporate the cooperation with the service provider into the escalation and resolution process. The Cloud relationship centre and service facilitation centre therefore need to be involved to realize efficient escalation [63].

16.3.4.3.3 ENSURING THE REQUIRED KNOWLEDGE AND SKILLS

Outsourcing IT responsibilities will lead to a potential reduction of the required FTEs for IT maintenance and support. When reducing the IT staff, the organization needs to consider all required skills and knowledge to ensure business continuity. The implementation of a new service will moreover lead to the need for additional knowledge and skills, which can be realized by hiring new experts or providing training to the current IT staff and IT management team. Shifts in responsibilities could therefore be realized to implement a Cloud relationship centre and service facilitation centre with the appropriate number of experts.

16.3.4.3.4 PREVENTING VENDOR LOCK-IN

Next to the compatibility between the Cloud service and the internal systems, the service user needs to evaluate the potential compatibility between several Cloud services. Whenever an organization opts for a Cloud solution that is not compatible with other services provided by other service providers, vendor lock-in could occur. Switching from provider could then lead to substantial migration costs. The organization therefore needs to take the compatibility with other services into account when selecting a provider. The service user moreover needs to define an exit strategy to assure a smooth Cloud migration if required [63]. The complexity regarding the migration of data will however be limited when using an infrastructure as a Cloud service based on standardized virtual machines [65].

16.3.4.4 *Mitigating compliance risks*

16.3.4.4.1 COMPLYING TO DATA PRIVACY AND SECURITY REGULATIONS

Even though both the service provider and the service user are responsible for complying with the data security and privacy regulations, the service user will remain accountable for the data stored in a Cloud environment. The selection procedure of the service provider should therefore incorporate the evaluation of ISO and SOC reports. To ensure continuity regarding compliancy, the organization needs to monitor national, international and industry-specific requirements on a continuous basis. To be compliant with the GDPR, the organization needs to assign a Data Protection Officer who will be responsible for the privacy assessments. To appropriately comply with the GDPR, organizations can invoke the assistance of third parties with juridical, technological and audit expertise [17, 21, 31].

Whenever the data is bound to national borders, the storage location of the data needs to be contractually defined and agreed upon in the service level agreements. To prevent inappropriate usage of the data leading to compliancy violations, the organization needs to create awareness on the use policies and the impact of these violations.

The government is authorized to seize the data whenever an organization violates certain regulations. When the data of a co-tenant of the Cloud infrastructure is seized due to compliancy violations, the government might seize the entire server infrastructure. Data backups will therefore prevent data lock-in.

16.3.4.4.2 SAFEGUARDING INTELLECTUAL PROPERTY

Cloud data storage should only be used for non-critical data to ensure business continuity, prevent data breaches and avoid the loss of intellectual property. Whenever the organization opts to store sensitive data in a Cloud environment, the contractual agreement clearly needs to state the ownership and accountability regarding the content of the data to avoid mutual disputes and maintain intellectual property and knowhow. The contractual agreement should furthermore incorporate clauses regarding compensations for agreement violations. Safeguarding intellectual property moreover relates to the monitoring of the license agreements. These agreements need to be followed up to prevent unauthorized use and avoid financial penalties [65].

16.3.4.4.3 MANAGING THE CONTRACT LIFECYCLE

To ensure clear and complete contractual agreements, all stakeholders with legal, financial and IT expertise need to be involved in the development process. These agreements should incorporate the required resources, configurations, network requirements, data security and privacy measures, the location of the data storage and compensations for violating the agreements. The complete contractual lifecycle needs to be monitored on a continuous basis to timely anticipate violations and potential contractual terminations. Therefore, a clear exit strategy needs to be defined, which incorporates the backup and migration of data.

The main Cloud service providers (e.g. Microsoft, Amazon and Google) do however contain a strong market position and will therefore shift several responsibilities towards the service user. The defined SLAs need to be specific, measurable, assignable, realistic and time-related (SMART). To ensure the completeness of the defined service level agreements, the WSLA framework for web services can be used. This framework defines three requirement categories that need to be incorporated in the service level agreements, namely [66]:

- The roles and responsibilities of all parties involved need to be clearly defined.
- Guaranties need to be defined based on clear SLA parameters, based on specific measurable metrics.
- Next to the goals of the service, the contract needs to entail financial parameters relating to compensation whenever the SLA parameters are not realized.

16.4 Conclusion

A Cloud migration can enable the strategic goals of an organization by facilitating scalability and cost transparency whenever the service is appropriately selected and managed. To ensure proper Cloud governance and management, the organization needs to implement the required structures, processes and relational mechanisms to mitigate the following risks:

- **Technical risks**, incorporating data security and data privacy, technical shortcomings and failures of the used IT infrastructure and networks, inefficient datacentre management and the lack of compatibility between the service and the legacy systems.
- **Operational risks**, relating to data lock-in and the lack of control and transparency.
- **Organizational risks**, incorporating vendor lock-in, ineffective incident management, lack of skills and expertise and inefficient decision-making.
- **Legal risks**, relating to the lack of compliancy on data privacy regulations, violations of intellectual property and contractual shortcomings.

Both new structures (CCO, CMC, CSF, CRC) and changes to current structures will have to be implemented to achieve effective Cloud governance. The required processes can be identified using the COBIT 5 framework, which includes governance and management processes related to the planning phase, the definition phase, the implementation phase and the monitoring phase. As illustrated, additional frameworks (CSA, NIST, ENISA) will have to be applied to achieve the required control measures to mitigate and monitor the identified risks.

References

1. Madhavaiah, C., Bashir, I., Shafi, S. I. (2012). Defining Cloud Computing in Business Perspective: A Review of Research. *The Journal of Business Perspective*, 16(3), 163–173.
2. Gartner. (2016). *Gartner Says by 2020 "Cloud Shift" Will Affect More Than $1 Trillion in IT Spending.* Consulted from http://www.gartner.com/newsroom/id/3384720
3. Zhang, Q., Cheng, L., Boutaba, R. (2010). Cloud Computing: State of the Art and Research Challenges. *Journal of Internet Services and Applications,* 1, 7–18.
4. NIST. (2011). *NIST Cloud Computing Standards Roadmap.*
5. Tucker, T. (2016). *Technology Business Management: The Four Value Conversations CIO's must have with their Businesses.* Washington, DC: TBM Council.
6. Marston, S., Li, Z., Bandyopadhyay, S., Zhang, J., Ghalsasi, A. (2011). Cloud Computing – The Business Perspective. *Decision Support Systems*, 51, 176–189.
7. Peiris, C., Balachandran, B., Sharma, D. (2010). Governance Framework for Cloud Computing. *International Journal on Computing*, 1 (1), 88–93.
8. Rimal, B. P., Choi, E., Lumb, I. (2009). A Taxonomy and Survey of Cloud Computing Systems. *Proceedings of the Fifth International Joint Conference on INC, IMS and IDC* (pp. 44–51). IEEE Computer Society, Washington, DC.
9. Bhardwaj, S., Jain, L., Jain, S. (2010). Cloud Computing: A Study of Infrastructure as a Service (IAAS). *International Journal of Information Technology and Web Engineering*, 2 (1), 60–63.
10. Son, I., Lee, D. (2011). Assessing a New IT Service Model: Cloud Computing. In *Proceedings of Pacific Asia Conference on Information Systems*, Queensland, Australia.
11. ISACA. (2012). *COBIT 5 Enabling Processes.*
12. Dutta, A., Peng, G. C. A., Choudhary, A. (2013). Risks in Enterprise Cloud Computing the Perspective of It Experts. *Journal of Computer Information Systems*, 53 (4), 39–48.
13. Wang, C., Wood, L. C., Abdul-Rahman, H., Lee, Y. T. (2016). When Traditional Information Technology Project Managers Encounter the Cloud: Opportunities and Dilemmas in the Transition to Cloud Services. *International Journal of Project Management*, 33, 371–388.
14. Zissis, D., Lekkas, D. (2012). Addressing Cloud Computing Security Issues. *Future Generation Computer Systems,* 28, 583–592.
15. Kesavaraj, G., Anitha K., Divya, R. (2016). Addressing Cloud Computing Security Issues. *International Journal of Innovative Research in Computer and Communication Engineering*, 4 (6), 11478–11483.
16. Aich, A., Sen, A. (2015). Study on Cloud Security Risk and Remedy. *International Journal of Grid Distribution Computing*, 8 (2), 155–166.
17. Bannerman, P.L. (2010). Cloud Computing Adoption Risks: State of Play. In *Proceedings of the 17th Asia Pacific Software Engineering Conference*. Sydney, Australia, 30 November–03 December.
18. Soundararajan, V., Anderson, J. M. (2010). The Impact of Management Operations on the Virtualized Datacenter. *ISCA'10*, Saint-Malo, France, 19–23 June.
19. ISACA. (2011). *IT Control Objectives for Cloud Computing: Controls and Assurance in the Cloud.*
20. Shin, Y. N., Chun, W. B., Jung, H. S., Chun, M. G. (2011). Privacy Reference Architecture for Personal Information Life Cycle. *Advanced Communication and Networking: International Conference,* Brno, Czech Republic, 15–17 August.
21. Caroll, M., van der Merwe, A., Kotzé, P. (2011). Secure Cloud Computing: Benefits, Risks and Controls. *Information Security South Africa Conference*, IEEE Computer Society, Johannesburg, South Africa, 15–17 August.
22. Ertaul, L., Singhal, S., Saldamli, G. (2010). *Security Challenges in Cloud Computing.* California State University, East Bay.
23. Goyal, P. (2010). Enterprise Usability of Cloud Computing Environments: Issues and Challenges. *Workshops on Enabling Technologies: Infrastructure for Collaborative Enterprises* (pp. 54–59). IEEE Computer Society, London.

24. Reddy, S. R., Mohan, Y. R., Naik, J. S. (2015). An Overview of Cloud Computing and Security Issues. *International Journal of Scientific Engineering and Applied Science*, 1 (3), 159–161.

25. Yang, H., Tate, M. (2012). A Descriptive Literature Review and Classification of Cloud Computing Research. *Communications of the Association for Information Systems*, 31 (2), 35–60.

26. Swire, P., Ahmad, K. (2012). *Foundations of Information Privacy and Data Protection.* International Association of Privacy Professionals, Portsmouth, NH.

27. ISACA. (2013). *COBIT 5 Enabling Information.*

28. ISACA. (2013). *COBIT 5 for Risk.*

29. Armbrust, A., Fox, A., Griffith, R., Joseph, A. D., Katz, R. H., Konwinski, A., … Zaharia, M. (2009). *Above the Clouds: A Berkeley View of Cloud Computing.* Electrical Engineering and Computer Sciences University of California, Berkeley.

30. Enslin, Z. (2012). *Cloud Computing: COBIT-Mapped Benefits, Risks and Controls for Consumer Enterprises* (Master Thesis). Consulted from Stellenbosch University Library, Stellenbosch.

31. Bartolini, C., Gheorghe, G., Giurgiu, A., Sabetzadeh, M., Sannier, N. (2015). *Assessing IT Security Standards against the Upcoming GDPR for Cloud Systems.*

32. Kuner, C. (2012). *The European Commission's Proposed Data Protection Regulation: A Copernican Revolution in European Data Protection Law.* Privacy and Security Law Report, Bloomberg, New York.

33. O'Donovan, C. (2016). On *Security Intelligence.* GDPR Compliance Regulations: The New Challenge for the Cloud Operations Manager. Consulted from https://securityintelligence.com/gdpr-compliance-regulations-the-new-challenge-for-the-cloud-operations-manager

34. Ahmad, R., Janczewski, L. (2011). Governance Life Cycle framework for Managing Security in Public Cloud: From User Perspective. In *4th International Conference on Cloud Computing*, IEEE Computer Society, Washington, DC.

35. Mather, T., Kumaraswamy, S., Latif, S. (2009). *Cloud Security and Privacy: An Enterprise Perspective on Risks and Compliance.* O'Reilly, Sebastopol.

36. Hon, W. K., Millard, C., Walden, I. (2012). Negotiating Cloud Contracts: Looking at Clouds from Both Sides Now. *Stanford Technology Law Review*, 16 (1), 79–129.

37. Zhang, X., Wuwong, N., Li, H., Zhang, X. (2010). Information Security Risk Management Framework for the Cloud Computing Environments. In *International Conference on Computer and Information Technology* (pp. 1328–1334). IEEE, Washington, DC.

38. De Haes, S., Van Grembergen, W. (2015). *Enterprise Governance of Information Technology; Achieving Alignment and Value, featuring COBIT 5.* Springer, Switzerland.

39. De Haes, S., Van Grembergen, W. (2013). COBIT 5 and Enterprise Governance of Information Technology: Building Blocks and Research Opportunities. *Journal of Information Systems*, 27 (1), 307–324.

40. Prasad, A., Green, J., Heales, P. (2014). On Governance Structures for the Cloud Computing Services and Assessing their Effectiveness. *International Journal of Accounting Information Systems*, 15 (4), 335–356.

41. Prasad, A., Green, J. (2015). Governing Cloud computing services: Reconsideration of IT governance structures. *International Journal of Accounting Information Systems*, 19, 45–58.

42. Block D. (2012). *Governing the Cloud as Cloud-based services evolve, so must today's governance functions.* KPMG, Amstelveen.

43. Grivas, S. G., Kumar, T. U., Wache, H. (2010). Cloud Broker: Bringing Intelligence into the Cloud. In *3rd International Conference on Cloud Computing*, Miami, 5–10 July.

44. IAPP. (2016). *Top 10 Operational Impacts of the GDPR: Part 2 – The Mandatory DPO.* Consulted from https://iapp.org/news/a/top-10-operational-impacts-of-the-gdpr-part-2-

45. Joha, A., Janssen, M. (2012). Transformation to Cloud Services Sourcing: Required IT Governance Capabilities. *ICST Transactions on e-Business*, 12 (7–9), 1–12.

46. Mohapatra, S., Lokhande, L. (2014). *Cloud Computing and ROI a New Framework for IT Strategy.* Springer, New York.

47. Bounagui, Y., Hafiddi, H., Mezrioui, A. (2016). COBIT Evaluation as a Framework for Cloud Computing Governance. *International Journal of Cloud Applications and Computing*, 6 (4), 1–18.

48. Karkoskova, S., Feuerlicht, G. (2016). Cloud Computing Governance Lifecycle. *Acta Informatica Pragensia*, 5 (1), 56–71.

49. De Haes, S., Van Grembergen, W. (2009). An Exploratory Study into IT Governance Implementations and Its Impact on Business/IT Alignment. *Information Systems Management*, 26, 123–137.

50. Peterson, R. R. (2003). Information Strategies and Tactics for Information Technology Governance. In W. Van Grembergen (Ed.), *Strategies for Information Technology Governance*. Idea Group Publishing, Hershey, PA.

51. Weill, P., Ross, J. W. (2005). A Matrixed Approach to Designing IT Governance. *MIT Sloan Management Review*, 46 (2), 26–34.

52. Khrisna, A., Harlili. (2014). Risk Management Framework With COBIT 5 And Risk Management Framework for Cloud Computing Integration. *International Conference of Advanced Informatics: Concept, Theory and Application* (pp. 103–108). IEEE, Washington, DC, 20–21 August.

53. Xie, F., Peng, Y., Zhao, W. Chen, D., Wang, X., Huo, X. (2012). Risk Management Framework for Cloud Computing. In *Proceedings of 2nd International Conference on Cloud Computing and Intelligent Systems*, IEEE, Hangzhou, 30 October–1 November.

54. NIST. (2017). *Framework for Improving Critical Infrastructure Cybersecurity (Update)*.

55. Zhou, M., Zhang, R., Xie, W., Qian, W., Zhou, A. (2010). Security and Privacy in Cloud Computing: A Survey. *Sixth International Conference on Semantics, Knowledge and Grids* (pp. 105–112). IEEE Computer Society, Washington, DC.

56. Ardagna, C. A., Asal, R., Damiani, E., VU, Q. H. (2015). From Security to Assurance in the Cloud: A Survey. *ACM Computing Surveys*, 48 (1), 2.

57. Benali, F., Bennani, N., Gabriele, G., Cimato, S. (2010). A Distributed and Privacy-Preserving Method for Network Intrusion Detection. *Lecture Notes in Computer Science book series*, 6427, 861–875.

58. Enslin, Z. (2012). Cloud Computing Adoption: Control Objectives for Information and Related Technology (COBIT) – Mapped Risks and Risk Mitigating Controls. *African Journal of Business Management*, 6 (37), 10185–10194.

59. Srivastava, H., Kumar, S. A. (2015). Control Framework for Secure Cloud Computing. *Journal of Information Security*, 6, 12–23.

60. Ko, R. K. L., Jagadpramana, P., Mowbray, M., Pearson, S., Kirchberg, M., Liang, Q., Lee, B. S. (2011). TrustCloud: A Framework for Accountability and Trust in Cloud Computing. *2nd IEEE Cloud Forum for Practitioners*, Washington DC, 7–8 July.

61. ISACA. (2014). *Controls and Assurance in the Cloud*.

62. Mateescu, M., Sgârciu, V. (2015). Cloud Computing Audit. In *9th International Symposium on Applied Computational Intelligence and Informatics*, (pp. 31–42). IEEE Computer Society, Timisoara, Romania, 15–17 May.

63. Horwath, C., Chan, W., Leung, E., Pili, H. (2012). *Enterprise Risk Management for Cloud Computing*. Committee of Sponsoring Organizations of the Treadway Commission, Chicago, IL.

64. Brender, N., Markov, I. (2013). Risk Perception and Risk Management in Cloud Computing: Results from a Case Study of Swiss Companies. *International Journal of Information Management*, 33 (5), 726–733.

65. ENISA. (2009). *Cloud Computing: Benefits, Risks and Recommendations for Information Security*.

66. Patel, P., Ranabahu, A. R., Sheth, A. P. (2009). *Service Level Agreement in Cloud Computing*. 9e Ohio Center of Excellence in Knowledge – Enabled Computing, Dayton, OH.

17

WHEN THE CLOUD RUNS OUT OF ITS SILVER LINING

Kiron Ravindran, Juan Manuel Gonzalez Muñoz
and Alex van den Bergh

17.1 When the Cloud runs out of its silver lining

Firms have been steadily moving to the Cloud as the dominant source for procuring infrastructure and software. Gartner estimates the market size for this industry to be around $250 billion [1]. Moving IT infrastructure to the Cloud brings with it various advantages of scalability, reliability and better cash flow management [2]. However, as in any outsourcing arrangement transaction costs can undermine the value of outsourcing.

Transaction costs or friction in the outsourcing arrangement can manifest itself in creating hold-ups between vendors and clients that have made relation-specific investments. To counter such friction, contracts have evolved to include a fine balance of formal and informal controls [3]. Literature has also addressed how clients that have severed an outsourcing arrangement might opt for backsourcing, where the client takes back in-house work that was once outsourced [4].

The context of Cloud computing shares various similarities with traditional outsourcing but differs starkly in others. The concerns, drivers and values accrued from Cloud computing are often like those from traditional outsourcing [5].

17.1.1 Comparison of the drivers of adoption

Let us first consider the literature on IT outsourcing drivers:

the drivers of outsourcing tend to be cost reduction, the ability to focus on the core business while the vendor can specialize in the service being provided and access to scarce capabilities.

Comparing the drivers for outsourcing IT internationally, Apte et al. [6] find cost reduction to be the most important driver followed by access to capabilities that the firm did not possess. Ang and Cummings [7], McLellan et al. [8] and Smith et al. [9] highlight the focus on reducing the cost of the IT operations. Loh and Venkatraman [10] separate the cost argument further into the cost reduction potential in IT and the cost reduction potential of business operations.

Loh and Venkatraman [11] list the internal business cost structure, and internal IT cost structure as two key determinants. The paper also shows that low internal IT performance is an important driver to lead to externalizing IT.

The aspect of enhancing the performance of IT departments was also identified by McLellan et al. [8]. They also raised the issue of financial motives to outsource the functions of the IT department. Building on the literature on Resource-Based View [12], scholars of IT outsourcing have identified accessing scarce capabilities an important motivation to outsource IT capabilities [13]. The argument here being that IT service providers with superior capabilities and economies of scale can offer IT capabilities that the focal firm may not be able to possess even at a higher cost.

The third common explanation for why firms would outsource their IT capabilities is to focus on strategic core functions and assign their non-core IT functions to external providers. Slaughter and Ang [14] examine the labor side of IT capabilities. They identify that in uncertain times and dynamic economic times, firms seeking a competitive edge are likely to outsource IS jobs when IS is not core to their business. Further given that IS jobs are likely to face volatile demands, the job functions that have a surplus supply are likely to be kept in-house while the scarce skills are likely to be sourced from elsewhere.

Let us direct our attention to sourcing software from the Cloud:

the value offered by Cloud computing is fundamentally similar. Cloud services allow the firm to benefit from the providers' specialization to enjoy lower operation cost and better reliability, enjoy almost infinite access to capacity and capabilities [15]. The client firm can then focus on the value-generating part of the business while having access to better capabilities that the service providers offer.

Cloud computing aims to provide computing capability as a utility [15]. For individual firms, controlling every piece of IT infrastructure comes at a price. Installation, updating and planned obsolescence are critical to operations but rarely afford much strategic advantage. Outsourcing such applications to a third-party provider lowers some of the inconvenience but firms had to give up a certain extent of control to while entrusting a third party. Cloud computing allowed firms to maintain a larger level of control while freeing themselves from the constant cycle of installing and updating. Cloud computing as in the case of IT outsourcing allows firms to access individual applications, or complete solutions or even the hardware to host such solutions which were all hosted on the internet and managed by a service provider against service level guarantees.

17.1.2 *Terminating externalized services*

Contract termination for outsourcing typically involves at least some of the following: compensating the service provider if the termination is for convenience, an asset buy-back clause, employment offer provisions for transferred employees, hand-over protocols and transfer provisions for licenses and know-how [16]. In comparison, Cloud service providers are less likely to demand compensation for the termination of a Cloud service contract as hardly any transaction-specific investment is made by the service provider [17].

Terminating Cloud services offer yet another convenience over traditional outsourcing: the enforced standardization in the hardware, software, protocols and internal processes (at least in the migration to a public Cloud if not a private or hybrid Cloud) can help transition from one provider to another or back in-house if the need should arise. From a technical perspective, virtualization which is a key element in Cloud-based architecture is best exploited with standardized hardware [18] and standardized protocols [19]. On the organizational size, Cloud migration is often associated with a move toward service centricity. This tends to tilt the organization from processes limited by ad hoc internal IT constraints to a focus on centralized delivery of standardized services [20]. Taken together standardized processes hosted on the Cloud are, at least theoretically, easier to terminate and bring back in-house or to transfer to a new provider.

However, despite the theoretical ease of re-integrating or transitioning services between vendors, the failure of Cloud providers to adopt universal standards in data storage does pose a real challenge [21].

In addition, in both cases, a business process once outsourced to a service provider on a multi-year basis is likely to be accompanied with a reduction in the internal IT staff associated with those processes. Limited internal capability to perform this task later, should the client choose to bring back the task in-house, is what that makes such re-integration (also called backsourcing) especially challenging [4].

17.2 Survey findings

In this chapter, we report the findings from the annual survey conducted in 2017 jointly by Quint Wellington Redwood (https://www.quintgroup.com/en/) and Whitelane Research (https://whitelane.com/). Our focus in the analysis is on why firms terminated outsourcing arrangements especially Cloud services, how they subsequently proceeded and what the biggest challenges were.

17.2.1 Data description

In the first half of 2017, Quint Wellington Redwood and Whitelane Research conducted a survey that was to provide the data for their annual report on IT Services Outsourcing, Spain [22]. In this survey, 206 Spanish firms responded to a survey about various aspects of their technology sourcing arrangements. They reported 697 service contracts with over 27 service providers.

The services included in these contracted covered the typical gamut of infrastructure services such as Datacenters, Managed Infrastructure services, Hosting, Networks, Telecom and Helpdesk; application services such as software development, maintenance and testing; and Software-as-a-Service. Outsourcing represented 10–50% of the IT budget in about 50% of the respondents and over 50% for about 30% of the firms. The respondents represent a heterogeneous mix of industries. Overall, the sample is heterogeneous and representative (Table 17.1).

17.2.2 Overall satisfaction

Looking at the entire sample, we see that overall satisfaction is high. Ninety-three percent of the contracts in our sample have satisfactory outcomes. And almost 20% of these contracts

Table 17.1 Summary statistics of share of the IT budget dedicated to outsourcing

Percentage of total IT budget dedicated to IT outsourcing (%)	Number of firms	Percentage of firms (%)
<10	13	11.30
10–50	64	55.65
>50	38	33.04
Total	115	100

(124 of the 697 contracts) are reported to have very high satisfaction. Unlike the satisfaction levels for Cloud services, when the firm has outsourced infrastructure, satisfaction levels are likely to drop.

The survey captured to what extent vendor capabilities were the drivers of general satisfaction. Vendor capabilities were captured along four dimensions: Delivery Competencies, Relationship Competencies, Transformation Competencies and Commercial aspects. The first three correspond to the vendor capabilities in Feeny et al. (2005) [23].

Overall satisfaction is most highly associated with Delivery and Relationship management competencies and less with price levels. Competencies of transformation and innovation appear to play a less important role than Delivery in creating general satisfaction (Tables 17.2 and 17.3).

Table 17.2 Satisfaction levels in general and upon exit

	Mean	*Range^a*
General satisfaction	1.357	−3 to +3
Exit satisfaction	0.763	−3 to +3
Exit satisfaction (if prematurely terminated)	0.4	−3 to +3

a Very unsatisfied (−3), somewhat unsatisfied (−2), unsatisfied (−1), satisfied (+1), somewhat satisfied (+2), very satisfied (+3).

Table 17.3 Random-effects GLS regression of general satisfaction on vendor capabilities

Variables	*(1)*	*(2)*
	General satisfaction Coef	*Se*
Service delivery	0.334***	(0.0328)
Account management	0.137***	(0.0319)
Proactivity	0.0626**	(0.0293)
Trust	0.0987***	(0.0348)
Price level	0.0797***	(0.0298)
Contractual flexibility	−0.0133	(0.0256)
Innovation	0.0238	(0.0265)
Transformation	0.0499*	(0.0300)
Business understanding	0.0136	(0.0334)
Constant	0.199***	(0.0733)
Observations	652	
Number of ids	201	

Standard errors in parentheses ***$p < 0.01$, **$p < 0.05$, *$p < 0.1$.
R^2: overall = 0.3803 Prob > chi^2 = 0.0000. (Firms have reported multiple contracts. An unbalanced panel was set up and a random-effects model was chosen based on the Breusch-Pagan test.)

Table 17.4 Random-effects GLS regression of general satisfaction on vendor capabilities by contracted service types

Variables	(1) General satisfaction Coef (Apps)	(2) General satisfaction Coef (HW)	(3) General satisfaction Coef (SaaS)
Service delivery	0.391★★★	0.354★★★	0.434★★★
Account management	0.168★★★	0.0508	0.00613
Proactivity	0.121★★	0.00584	0.201★★
Trust	0.0793	0.128★★★	0.0307
Price level	0.144★★★	0.0445	−0.0751
Contractual flexibility	0.0196	−0.00671	0.0624
Innovation	−0.0278	0.0197	0.0880
Transformation	0.0639	0.109★★★	0.0259
Business understanding	−0.0373	0.114★★	−0.0168
Constant	−0.0805	0.151★	0.376★
Observations	302	370	102
Number of ids	136	177	71

Standard errors have not been reported in the interest of space ★★★$p < 0.01$, ★★$p < 0.05$, ★$p < 0.1$. (An unbalanced panel was set up and a random-effects model was chosen based on the Breusch-Pagan test. Each column represents a restricted sample of contracts that include Apps, HW or SaaS respectively.)

Comparing the drivers of overall satisfaction across the three kinds of service contracts, we see the following:

In the case of application maintenance and development contracts, satisfaction levels are significantly associated with Delivery competence and Relationship competence. In addition, vendors that can offer acceptable price levels are likely to generate a greater overall satisfaction when it comes to application services contracts. For infrastructure and hardware, while Delivery competence still matters, the variability seems to arise from Trust and the Transformation competence. Service providers that possess these competences are likely to benefit from greater overall satisfaction in the clients. Client satisfaction with Cloud computing service contracts appears to mainly be driven by Delivery competence. It is likely that given the largely homogenous set of offerings from Cloud service vendors, satisfaction levels are also driven by proactive solutions from service providers. The comparability among offerings from the different providers is likely the reason why vendor pricing does not seem to influence satisfaction in Cloud service contracts (Table 17.4).

17.2.3 Premature termination

The respondents were asked what their reasons for termination were. Approximately 60% of our responding firms (127 firms) had terminated a contract in the past year and of these, 53% (68 firms) had terminated a contract before the natural expiration of the contract. Despite the maturity of the outsourcing process and the general satisfaction with sourcing IT services and infrastructure, such *premature* termination of service contracts appears to be common. Further, there appears to be no systemic difference in the likelihood of premature terminations in application contracts, infrastructure contracts or SaaS contracts.

Table 17.5 Random-effects regressions of premature termination and exit satisfaction on vendor capabilities

Variables	(1) Premature termination	(2) Exit satisfaction
Service quality	7.450★★★	−0.822★★★
Account management	2.009★	−0.613★★
Proactivity	3.201★★	0.112
Price level	7.568★★★	0.249
Contractual flexibility	3.650	−0.221
Transformation	4.609★★★	−0.640★★
Business understanding	7.204★★	−0.615
Others	13.30★★★	0.00916
Constant	−6.463★★★	1.117★★★
Observations	419	419
Number of ids	127	127

Standard errors have not been reported in the interest of space ★★★$p < 0.01$, ★★$p < 0.05$, ★$p < 0.1$.

(An unbalanced panel was set up and random-effects estimation was chosen based on the Breusch-Pagan test: Logit model for column 1 and a GLS for column 2.)

However, the service provider capabilities associated with premature termination appear to vary with the services sourced. Premature termination tends to be highly correlated with Delivery competence, just as overall satisfaction is. Relationship management skills while not the most important factor in general satisfaction seemed to show an impact in reducing the likelihood of premature termination. Other reasons for termination are factors such as a lack of Delivery competence and Transformation competence and mismatched prices (Table 17.5).

17.2.4 Exit satisfaction

Firms that terminated contracts responded with their levels of satisfaction while exiting the contract. Seventy-nine percent stated that they were satisfied with the exit process with 15% being extremely satisfied. This is expectedly lower than general satisfaction (79% versus 93%) and further there is only a 15% correlation between the two. In fact, 56% of the responses indicated a greater general satisfaction than exit satisfaction. Quite naturally, premature terminations have significantly lower exit satisfactions. However, it is interesting that the satisfaction levels even at termination are relatively high. It is likely that the high satisfaction levels reflect a tendency toward standardized services and limited asset and process specificity.

When looking at the associations of service provider capabilities with exit satisfaction, we see a clear negative association with service delivery capability, change management and relationship management. Comparing the coefficients of regression, we see a clear pattern that exit satisfaction lowers with Delivery, Transformation and Relationship capabilities in that order. The hierarchy of service provider competencies stays consistent in determining overall satisfaction, premature termination or satisfaction with exiting a contract. The evidence

Table 17.6 Random-effects regressions comparing the effect on vendor capabilities on exit satisfaction in contracts with apps, HW or SaaS alone

Variables	(1) Exit satisfaction	(2) Exit satisfaction	(3) Exit satisfaction
Service quality	−0.754★★★	−0.731★★	−1.333★★
Account management	−0.780★★	−0.554	2★★★
Proactivity	−0.273	0.731	
Price level	0.541	−0.00595	−1.333★★
Contractual flexibility	−0.696	0.452	
Transformation	−0.323	−1.387★★★	
Business understanding	−0.0156	0.495	0.667
Others	0.351	0.148	0.667
Constant	0.959★★★	1.242★★★	2.333★★★
Observations	208	210	12
R-squared	0.1	0.07	0.655
Number of ids	89	98	

Standard errors have not been reported in the interest of space ★★★$p < 0.01$, ★★$p < 0.05$, ★$p < 0.1$.

(An unbalanced panel was set up and random-effects estimation was chosen based on the Breusch-Pagan test: Logit model for column 1 and a GLS for column 2. Column 3 reports an OLS regression as the smaller sample caused multicollinearity in the RE GLS model.)

seems to point toward the importance of Delivery over Transformation and least of all on Relationship management (Table 17.6).

It is interesting to examine the difference in exit satisfaction based on service types. Exit satisfaction is lower for application development and maintenance contracts. However, exit satisfaction in contracts with hardware is higher than in contracts with no hardware and higher still when contracts contain SaaS rather than not. The higher levels of satisfaction with the exit of SaaS contracts suggest an easier transition from one SaaS provider to another or back in-house compared to doing the same with traditional outsourcing of application development and maintenance or hardware (Table 17.7).

17.2.5 Exit strategy

Unlike outsourcing stand-alone software development projects, outsourcing application development or infrastructure or Cloud services is associated with a certain dependence on the service provider for continuity of service. As a result, when such an engagement is to be terminated firms need to identify an exit strategy for business continuity. The two options, should negotiations fail, are of backsourcing or finding a new provider to take over the provision of service.

Literature has highlighted the challenges in bringing back in-house outsourced application development and maintenance contracts in terms of knowledge re-integration [24], re-staffing and organizational disruption to re-integrate these processes [25]. Only 12% of our respondents who terminated a contract found it worthwhile to bring the task in-house.

Table 17.7 Comparing the mean exit satisfaction in contracts with apps, HW or SaaS alone

Variables	Apps		HW		SaaS	
	Mean (group0)	Mean (group1)	Mean (group0)	Mean (group1)	Mean (group0)	Mean (group1)
Exit satisfaction	1.071	0.62★★★	0.689	1.005★★	0.808	2.167★★★
Exit Strategy						
Internalized	0.090	0.144★	0.139	0.095	0.115	0.167
New known provider	0.190	0.168	0.182	0.176	0.177	0.250
New reputed provider	0.081	0.053	0.043	0.090★	0.064	0.167
New provider from competitive bids	0.716	0.649	0.627	0.738★★	0.688	0.500
Challenges						
Know–how transfer	0.592	0.779★★★	0.746	0.624★★★	0.695	0.333★★★
HW transfer	0.123	0.034★★★	0.038	0.119★★★	0.079	0.083
SW transfer	0.038	0.087★★	0.086	0.038★★	0.064	0.000
IP transfer	0.024	0.019	0.033	0.010★	0.022	0.000
People transfer	0.137	0.130	0.129	0.138	0.133	0.167

★★★$p < 0.01$, ★★$p < 0.05$, ★$p < 0.1$.

T-tests to compare the significant difference in means. Group1 is the group of contracts that contain the respective service and Group0 does not.

These challenges are likely less concerning when the services that have been outsourced require minimal customization as in the case of hardware compared to application maintenance and development. This likely explains why our survey suggests that firms are less likely to hesitate with terminating hardware or Cloud service contracts. While transitioning to a new vendor is theoretically easier in the case of Cloud computing compared to traditional outsourcing, a non-standard implementation of data structures limits easy transferability.

Literature is relatively silent on preparing for a transition post-Cloud computing. However, we can learn from the observations made on early IT outsourcing arrangements that were reintegrated back to the focal firm. Veltri et al. list that backsourcing IT is accompanied by challenges in re-staffing, bringing back IT assets and activities that were once outsourced.

In our sample, 88% chose to go with a new provider after termination. Reaching out to a new vendor poses another challenge. Does a firm seek a new vendor based on prior experience, reputation or through an open competitive bid process? Going with a service provider familiar with the business has been shown to be a standard risk mitigation technique as it can reduce adverse selection [26]. Among the 88% that seek a new provider, 68% went with a new provider selected through a competitive bid process. From a transaction cost perspective, when there is less relationship specificity, the market offers a more efficient source of capabilities [27]. That a significant portion chose a new unfamiliar provider suggests standardization and limited relationship specificity.

We see a small yet statistically significant difference in the behavior of application development and maintenance contracts from hardware contracts. As one could imagine, transferring application development to a new vendor is riskier and more complicated and we see a small preference toward transferring the task back in-house rather than to a new provider.

Backsourcing is the choice for 14% of the application contracts that have been terminated while only 9% would backsource in contracts that do not have application development and maintenance services. Not surprisingly we see the opposite behavior for hardware contracts. Services such as telecom and networking come with a lesser need for customization and not surprisingly we see terminated hardware contracts are more often taken to the market seeking a new provider. Further those seeking new providers chose to go with competitive bidding rather than relying on reputation or prior experience with bidders.

Considering the exit strategies along with the satisfaction levels of exiting, we see a pattern emerging of firms likely to consider a more transactional approach to sourcing for hardware or Cloud services but a more relationship-specific approach to application maintenance and development contracts.

17.2.6 Challenges with exit

As in any contract termination, terminating an IT services contract comes with its own challenges. These challenges arise because of the service-providing capabilities disappearing from within the organization. The issue of vendor lock-in is not trivial in both traditional outsourcing and Cloud computing services. Typically, the range of challenges includes transferring know-how, software, hardware, people and IP licenses. The greater the challenge the less likely that the contract would in fact be terminated.

One can expect that services such as application development and maintenance which comes with a greater expectation of customization would face greater challenges, while hardware services would be lower. Given the promise of SaaS of offering a more generic service on the Cloud, one would expect far lower levels of exit challenges with SaaS. However, earlier studies have shown that despite the existence of Cloud standards enforcements of such standards were not common resulting in limited portability between providers [21].

In our data, we see that in the case of application contracts, the challenges lie in the transfer of know-how and software transfer. The challenge with know-how transfer is heightened with a premature termination. As expected, hardware contracts typically face higher levels of challenge in transferring the hardware and lower levels of other challenges. Interestingly, contracts that have SaaS claim none of the listed challenges as increasing and in fact show a statistically significant drop in know-how transfer as a challenge. It is likely that Cloud service providers have moved toward more consistent adoption of standards in terms of storage and APIs.

17.3 Conclusion

We started out wanting to know what the end of a Cloud computing service contract looks like. The insights came from a self-reported survey with responses from senior IT staff from over 200 firms. The survey captured details of three classes of outsourced services: application development and maintenance, hardware and SaaS. Tracking these three services allows us to contrast the behavior of clients when it comes to SaaS as against more traditional services.

We see indications that overall, sourcing services externally is mature and established as a business process. While low levels of satisfaction and failed contracts were quite common in the early 2000s, we see here a high level of overall satisfaction. Premature termination lowers the satisfaction levels but exit satisfaction even when premature is still high. Vendor capabilities that are most sought after tend to be Delivery competence over Relationship management.

Our analysis seems to suggest that client firms seem to seek standardized services from external vendors which can explain both the satisfaction upon exit and the strategy adopted post-termination. Firms tend to go with a new provider rather than bringing the task in-house. Further, this new provider is chosen via competitive bidding in the open market.

A key restriction in terminating contracts has often been that of vendor lock-in. Studies in outsourcing and Cloud computing have pointed out this challenge in terminating contracts. We see such a challenge when applications and hardware are outsourced, yet we do not see such a challenge with SaaS contracts.

Taken together, the insights from our survey seem to point to maturity in sourcing Cloud services, higher levels of satisfaction, limited challenges in terminating such services and further an explicit effort to source new providers to exploit market efficiencies.

From a service provider's perspective, it is likely that we see far greater adoption. Given the low levels of perceived challenges with exit, it is likely that service providers will see greater churn in clientele. While this can be problematic for large incumbent providers, it creates opportunities for new entrants offering specialized Cloud computing offerings with consistent quality of service assurances and better relationship management capabilities.

References

1. http://www.gartner.com/newsroom/id/3616417 (accessed Aug 2018).
2. Armbrust, M., Fox, A., Griffith, R., Joseph, A. D., Katz, R., Konwinski, A., ... Zaharia, M. (2010). A View of Cloud Computing. *Communications of the ACM*, 53(4), 50–58.
3. Susarla, A., Subramanyam, R., & Karhade, P. (2010). Contractual Provisions to Mitigate Holdup: Evidence from Information Technology Outsourcing. *Information Systems Research*, 21(1), 37–55.
4. Veltri, N. F., Saunders, C. S., & Kavan, C. B. (2008). Information Systems Backsourcing: Correcting Problems and Responding to Opportunities. *California Management Review*, 51(1), 50–76.
5. Low, C., Chen, Y., & Wu, M. (2011). Understanding the Determinants of Cloud Computing Adoption. *Industrial Management & Data Systems*, 111(7), 1006–1023.
6. Apte, U. M., Sobol, M. G., Hanaoka, S., Shimada, T., Saarinen, T., Salmela, T., & Vepsalainen, A. P. J. (1997). Is Outsourcing Practices in the USA, Japan and Finland: A Comparative Study. *Journal of Information Technology*, 12(4), 289–304.
7. Ang, S., & Cummings, L. L. (1997, May–June). Strategic Response to Institutional Influences on Information Systems Outsourcing. *Organization Science*, 8(3), 235–256.
8. McLellan, K., Marcolin, B. L., & Beamish, P. W. (1995). Financial and Strategic Motivations Behind Is Outsourcing. *Journal of Information Technology*, 10(4), 299–321.
9. Smith, M. A., Mitra, S., & Narasimhan, S. (1998). Information Systems Outsourcing: A Study of Pre-Event Firm Characteristics. *Journal of Management Information Systems*, 15(2), 60–93.
10. Loh, L., & Venkatraman, N. (1995). An Empirical Study of Information Technology Outsourcing: Benefits, Risks, and Performance Implications. Proceedings of the *16th International Conference on Information Systems*, Amsterdam, The Netherlands.
11. Loh, L., & Venkatraman, N. (1992). Determinants of Information Technology Outsourcing: A Cross-Sectional Analysis. *Journal of Management Information Systems*, 9(1), 7–24.
12. Barney, J. (1991). Firm Resources and Sustained Competitive Advantage. *Journal of Management*, 17(1), 99–120.
13. Bharadwaj, A. S. (2000). A Resource-Based Perspective on Information Technology Capability and Firm Performance: An Empirical Investigation. *MIS Quarterly*, 24(1), 169–196.
14. Slaughter, S. A., & Ang, S. (1996). Employment Outsourcing in Information Systems. *Communications of the ACM*, 39(7), 47–54.
15. Zhang, Q., Cheng, L., & Boutaba, R. (2010). Cloud Computing: State-of-the-Art and Research Challenges. *Journal of Internet Services and Applications*, 1(1), 7–18.
16. Bahli, B., & Rivard, S. (2003). The Information Technology Outsourcing Risk: A Transaction Cost and Agency Theory-Based Perspective. *Journal of Information Technology*, 18(3), 211–221.

17. Newcombe, L., Heppenstall, D., & Clarke, N. (2016). Moving to the Cloud – Key Considerations, KPMG, February 2016. https://home.kpmg.com/content/dam/kpmg/pdf/2016/04/moving-to-the-cloud-key-risk-considerations.pdf (accessed Aug 2018).

18. Cáceres, J., Vaquero, L. M., Rodero-Merino, L., Polo, Á., & Hierro, J. J. (2010). Service Scalability Over the Cloud. In *Handbook of Cloud Computing* (pp. 357–377). Springer, Boston, MA.

19. Voorsluys, W., Broberg, J., & Buyya, R. (2011). Introduction to Cloud Computing. In Buyya, R., Broberg, J., & Goscinski, A. (eds.), *Cloud Computing: Principles and Paradigms* (pp. 1–41). Wiley, New Jersey.

20. Lin, G., & Devine, M. (2010). The Role of Networks in Cloud Computing in Handbook of Cloud Computing. In *Handbook of Cloud Computing.* Springer, Boston, MA.

21. Leavitt, N. (2009). Is Cloud Computing Really Ready for Prime Time? *Computer*, 1, 15–20.

22. https://whitelane.com/2017/11/2017-spanish-it-outsourcing-study-results-published/ (accessed Aug 2018).

23. Feeny, D., Lacity, M., & Willcocks, L.P. (2005). Taking the Measure of Outsourcing Providers. *Sloan Management Review*, Spring. https://sloanreview.mit.edu/article/taking-the-measure-of-outsourcing-providers/

24. Ejodame, K., & Oshri, I. (2018). Understanding Knowledge Re-Integration in Backsourcing. *Journal of Information Technology*, 33(2), 136–150.

25. Veltri, N. F., Saunders, C. S., & Kavan, C. B. (2008). Information Systems Backsourcing: Correcting Problems and Responding to Opportunities. *California Management Review*, 51(1), 50–76.

26. Gefen, D., Wyss, S., & Lichtenstein, Y. (2008). Business Familiarity as Risk Mitigation in Software Development Outsourcing Contracts. *MIS Quarterly*, 32, 531–551.

27. Williamson, O. E. (1981). The Economics of Organization: The Transaction Cost Approach. *American Journal of Sociology*, 87(3), 548–577.

PART 4

Developments to come

In this final part, we conclude with a discussion on two emerging technologies and how they may impact a digital outsourcing strategy.

In Chapter 18, Vaassen discusses blockchain and other distributed ledgers. Blockchain is a *distributed database* that contains sequentially interlinked ('chained') clusters of transactions ('blocks') with *tokens* that follow the rules of a specific *trust protocol*. Blockchain is the underlying technology of bitcoin; being extremely well thought out, it has served as an example for most of the blockchain applications as we currently know them. The chapter reviews the importance of public and private keys for digital signatures, the use of digital signatures in tokens, and data sources outside blockchains for blockchain applications. Along with the discussion of a classification of distributed ledgers, also smart contracts and alternative consensus mechanisms are discussed since the type of distributed ledger, the type of smart contract (if any), and the consensus mechanism are not independent. This overview ends with a discussion of examples of distributed ledger technology use cases. The chapter concludes with some guidance for deciding whether or not to engage in a distributed ledger project or remain confined to legacy centralized databases.

In Chapter 19, Baron discusses the internet of things (IoT) and exemplifies IBM's view on the development, application, and implementation of this technology. After defining the phenomenon, prediction of its use, and the business value of IoT, the review closes with a business perspective on implementing and managing IoT. Furthermore, this chapter concludes that in future quantum computing capabilities will remove the current constraints of IoT processing power. Finally, this chapter includes a review of examples of applications of IoT and explains that the real value of IoT comes when insights and concrete actions are generated through Artificial Intelligence (AI).

18

BLOCKCHAIN AND OTHER DISTRIBUTED LEDGERS

Eddy H.J. Vaassen

18.1 Introduction

A blockchain is a *distributed database* that contains sequentially interlinked ('chained') clusters of transactions ('blocks') with *tokens* that follow the rules of a specific *trust protocol*. In this description, three concepts stand out. First, a distributed database, as opposed to a centralized database, is an organized collection of data that is integrally held at physically or logically separated storage devices. This implies that each of these storage devices contains a full copy – not a subset – of the database in question. Second, in essence, a token may either be a hardware device (for example, a chip card) or a piece of data (for example, a string of characters), although there are more sophisticated taxonomies that apply multiple criteria to classify tokens in blockchains [1]. A token as a piece of data is the type of token that lives on a blockchain. Specifically, in the realm of blockchain a token is a chain of digital signatures that represents (tangible or intangible) assets that are exchanged in transactions. The cryptocurrency Bitcoin can be considered a token. Third, the software that manages the exchange of assets via tokens on a blockchain is dubbed the trust protocol to indicate that in a blockchain world trusted third parties are replaced by this software.

Blockchain as the technology underlying the Bitcoin was first described by the yet unknown Satoshi Nakamoto [2] but has gained traction ever since resulting in many more tokens and variants thereof, including Ether, Bitcoin Cash, Litecoin, and other (over 3,000) cryptocurrencies.[1] There is not just one blockchain, each cryptocurrency has its own blockchain or has its own part of a certain blockchain. Blockchain can also be used for other tokens than cryptocurrencies. As a matter of fact, this chapter argues that applications in other tokens than cryptocurrencies will gain momentum in the forthcoming years because they enable more efficient and effective ways of transacting (by, for example, improved business processes and business process interoperability across supply chains), as well as more efficient and effective accounting, controlling, auditing, and oversight practices (by, for example, linking a continuous monitoring system in a blockchain, or making additional journal entries in a blockchain to enhance the verifiability of local databases).

Although blockchain often is called a new technology, strictly speaking this is not entirely correct. Because blockchain is a combination of various existing technologies, theories, and algorithms such as public and private key cryptography [3], hashing and digital signatures [4], smart contracts [5,6], game theory [7], and triple-entry accounting [8], the innovation of blockchain lies in the smart combination of these.

Currently blockchain is at the top of the hype [9] and there is a reason for that. It has some inherent features that are said to disrupt the way transactions are managed and accounted for, including:

1   It eliminates the need for trusted third parties and replaces these by trust protocols. By means of disintermediation processes become more efficient and substantially less prone to human manipulation.
2   It is built upon a distributed consensus model. A transaction can only be recorded in the blockchain if it has been validated by a majority of the nodes that participate in the network of that blockchain.
3   Once a transaction is recorded in the blockchain, it cannot be removed or altered. Because of its design, blockchain is the shared single source of truth.

Along with the said blockchain hype goes the vast number of publications on blockchain's use cases and its underlying technology. Many of these publications are just adaptations of other publications. This may not be a problem that should interest us as such. However, due to the innovative nature of blockchain a *common body of knowledge* with agreed upon syntactical and semantical tenets is still lacking. Hence, any text on blockchain currently still makes many more arbitrary choices with respect to the syntax and semantics to be used than more mature fields. While trying to explicate the blockchain language as clearly as possible and making use of the scarce literature on blockchain ontological issues (for example, [10]), this chapter is no exception since the very same arbitrary choices are made.

The remainder of this chapter first discusses Bitcoin 'under the hood'. The reason for giving an in-depth discussion of Bitcoin is that its underlying blockchain technology is extremely well thought out and has served as an example or at least as the main source of inspiration for most of the blockchain applications as we currently know them. It then continues with a section on the importance of public and private keys for digital signatures, the use of digital signatures in tokens, and data sources outside blockchains for blockchain applications. Extending our discussion from blockchain to distributed ledger technology, the subsequent section then discusses some more versatile applications that go beyond the exchange of cryptocurrencies as in the Bitcoin blockchain. By exploring new types of application inevitably blockchain technology may prove itself to be not the right term. Therefore, while maintaining many of the basic principles of blockchain, this section broadens the notion of blockchain to the more generic term *distributed ledger technologies* (DLT). Along with the discussion of a classification of distributed ledgers, also smart contracts and alternative consensus mechanisms are discussed since the type of distributed ledger, the type of smart contract (if any), and the consensus mechanism are not independent. Having acquired a good sense of the language of distributed ledger technologies and to illustrate the richness of potential applications, a wide variety of examples of distributed ledger technology use cases is then discussed. The chapter concludes with some guidance for deciding whether or not to engage in a distributed ledger project or remain confined to legacy centralized databases.

18.2 Bitcoin

Fiat money such as the Euro and US Dollar, although intrinsically just worth the price of the paper or metal used for printing or minting it, has value because it is scarce and people can use it for purchasing goods and services. Money is made scarce by a central authority (the central bank) that in return guarantees to transactors that it is always backed. Because of this backing people trust it. If there were no central authority trust would be difficult to build and maintain because one cheating transactor could undermine the entire system. The Bitcoin blockchain provides a mechanism for creating electronic money that can be trusted and for that reason used without having a central authority in place. The obvious question then arises who creates new Bitcoins if there is no central authority. The Bitcoin trust protocol, dubbed the Bitcoin core to distinguish it from the cryptocurrency Bitcoin, uses a mechanism called proof-of-work to create new Bitcoins out of thin air.

18.2.1 Proof-of-work

Imagine a gold mine where miners spend hours of hard work to once in a while find a nugget of gold. Nakamoto [2] applied this notion of having to put a lot of hard work into something with a low rate of success to the creation of new Bitcoins. Whereas fiat money is created by banks giving out loans to their clients and central banks in the realm of monetary policy by buying government bonds and occasionally printing new banknotes or minting new coins, Bitcoins (and currently most other cryptocurrencies) are created by computers working hard to mine these cryptocurrencies. In the blockchain, the concept of computers working hard boils down to expending CPU power to solve a cryptographic puzzle by trial and error. So, the fact that Bitcoins have been created means that the CPU power indeed has been expended, hence the term *proof-of-work*. Mining is done by so-called mining nodes, or briefly miners. Although the metaphor of mining gold being quite intuitive, it is not completely accurate. In the Bitcoin blockchain, mining refers to the creation of new blocks of transactions, so mining new blocks, which goes in parallel with creating new Bitcoins. So, creating new Bitcoins, thus providing an incentive to miners to expend CPU power, is not the only goal of mining. The proof-of-work serves the following two overarching goals:

1   It accomplishes that a block, after the cryptographic puzzle has been solved, gets written to the blockchain.
2   It accomplishes that it becomes extremely difficult to make other changes to the blockchain than those that are based on consensus among the nodes in the blockchain.

Since there must be consensus among the nodes in the blockchain network about which node will be allowed to write a block, the proof-of-work requirement is called a consensus mechanism. Of all the features of a blockchain as mentioned at the beginning of this chapter the immutability of the blockchain database stands out, making it the shared single source of truth. Figure 18.1 depicts the chain of blocks that is being held together by a series of hashes in the Bitcoin database. Note that these blocks are sequentially recorded, hence the importance of a timestamp in each block.

A hash (also referred to as a digest) is the outcome of a hash function. Typically input data that is fed into a hash function leads to a fixed-length hash. The type of hash that is used in a blockchain is a so-called *cryptographic* hash. Such an algorithm allows easy verification that the input data after hashing equals a known hash, but if the input data is unknown, it is deliberately made difficult to reconstruct the input data by knowing the stored hash value. That is why such a hash is also called a mathematical trapdoor. In the Bitcoin blockchain, the Secure Hashing Algorithm 256 (SHA-256) is used. Given some specified input data and

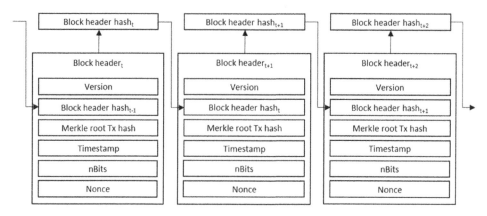

Figure 18.1   Hashing in the Bitcoin blockchain

consistent use of the SHA-256, this input will always lead to the same hash. Only if the input changes, the hash will change. The SHA-256 produces a 256-bit hash (32 bytes) in hexadecimal notation, so 64 digits in the range 0–9 and A–F.[2]

The Merkle root Tx hash is the digest of all the transactions in the block. By calculating the hashes of all pairs of transactions in the block (in case of an odd number the last transaction is hashed with a copy of itself) and doing the same with the resulting pairs of hashes, ultimately the Merkle root hash that fully describes all the transactions in a block is calculated as one 32 bytes hexadecimal number. If one transaction is modified, the Merkle root hash changes too.

Now consider the following. In the Bitcoin blockchain, a fraudster wants to change a transaction in a block that has already been recorded in that blockchain. This means that the Merkle root hash needs to be changed, and as a result also the block header hash of the block the transaction is part of. But if a new block has already been recorded after the block with the fraudulent alteration, the block header hash of that new block also has to be changed. And if that block is followed by another newly recorded block, then the block header hash of that block has to be changed too. Given that calculating a hash from input data is easy, it would not be difficult for the fraudster to change all the subsequent block header hashes until the block header hash of the most recent block is changed and hence the blockchain from the block with the fraudulent transaction onward. To avoid tampering with the database and hence make changing all the subsequent block header hashes difficult, the Bitcoin blockchain uses proof-of-work.

As indicated before, proof-of-work is expending CPU power to solve a cryptographic puzzle by trial and error. Nakamoto [2] wanted a system in which on average every ten minutes a block of transactions could be recorded in the blockchain. To accomplish this, the Bitcoin core software sets a target hash with a challenge. The challenge for a miner is to find such a number (a nonce: number used once) that after hashing with the other data from the block header produces a hash that is smaller than or equal to the target hash. If a miner finds such a number then the miner broadcasts this number to the blockchain network so that all nodes can verify that the miner has found a solution. Different from finding the nonce, verification is easy since this merely encompasses filling in the nonce and other data from the block header into the SHA-256 hashing algorithm and check if the outcome indeed is smaller than the target hash. If the other nodes agree that the nonce indeed produces a hash that is smaller than the target hash, then the miner records the block he has been

Block #536201		
Block header component	**Notation in blockchain**	**Notation for block header string**
Version	0x3fff0000	0000ff3f
Previous block header hash	00000000000000000000289652dbe08d40 d3a7ce52561981b564fb98ff062b8bdc	dc8b2b06ff98fb64b581195652cea7d340 8de0db52962800000000000000000000
Merkle root hash	fbb64c2cc1d4826afbddea1230995d632 5eac8ecc7722ccc1ff7647054c64a9c	9c4ac6547064f71fcc2c72c7ecc8ea2563 5d993012eaddfb6a82d4c12c4cb6fb
Timestamp	11 Aug 2018, 04:17:13	39556e5b
nBits	172f4f7b	7b4f2f17
Nonce	2,120,628,932	c43a667e
Block header string	0000ff3fdc8b2b06ff98fb64b581195652cea7d3408de0db52962800000000000000000 009c4ac6547064f71fcc2c72c7ecc8ea25635d993012eaddfb6a82d4c12c4cb6fb395 56e5b7b4f2f17c43a667e	
Block header hash	000000000000000002b281e847addb6ee94f0019524922bff6cc960fd41d1be	

Figure 18.2   Block header hash composition for a block in the Bitcoin blockchain

working on in the blockchain. At this point all the transactions in that block are recorded in the blockchain database and the miner receives a reward of (currently) 12.5 Bitcoins plus the sum of the transaction fees that the initiators of the transactions in that block have paid.[3] The transaction that pays out the block reward is called the coinbase transaction, and the reward the coinbase. This is a transaction without an input and this is why this transaction creates new Bitcoins 'out of thin air'.

After every 2016th block, the target hash is calculated from the nBits field in the block header. This field sets the difficulty for solving the cryptographic puzzle. The number 2016 is the outcome of the required ten minutes to record a block, and a period of two weeks to evaluate the difficulty of solving the cryptographic puzzle (=6 blocks per hour ⋆ 24 hours ⋆ 14 days). The Bitcoin core automatically increases (decreases) the difficulty if the time that was needed to find a nonce that led to a hash smaller than the target hash is shorter (longer) than two weeks. The value of the nBits field is calculated as follows:

1   Only re-calculate the nBits field if the current block is a multiple of 2016.
2   Take the timestamp of the current block and that of the block that is 2015 blocks before the current block.[4]
3   Calculate the difference between these two timestamps.
4   Multiply the difference by the current nBits converted from compact form to the target it represents and divide the result by two weeks.[5]
5   Convert the result to compact form[6] and use that as the new nBits value.

This boils down to a lower target hash when the puzzle was too easy and a higher target hash when the puzzle was too difficult.

The block header string is the concatenated form of the version, previous block header hash[7], timestamp, nBits, and nonce. Figure 18.2 gives the block header composition for block 536201 in the Bitcoin blockchain, including the block header hash.

18.2.2 Nodes

Bitcoins are stored in electronic wallets. A Bitcoin wallet can take various forms – one more secure than the other – but the principle for safeguarding one's Bitcoins is always the same. A Bitcoin wallet has an identification code, the wallet ID that acts as a username for any logical access control. For example, a Bitcoin wallet ID may look like: 8a15ne4d-3d6c-6745-d282-da885h64pqf9. To log into this wallet, the user needs to know this wallet ID, a password, and any other code(s) she has enabled for multi-factor authentication. A wallet ID is only used for the login process and cannot be used as an address to send Bitcoins from (an output transaction) or to (an input transaction). It is different from a Bitcoin address, which is a single-use token that is used as the send-from and send-to address in a Bitcoin transaction. A Bitcoin transaction may be compared to sending an email with the message that the sender wants to transfer a certain amount of Bitcoins to a recipient. However, unlike e-mail addresses, people may have many different Bitcoin addresses whereas a unique Bitcoin address should be used for each transaction. An example of a Bitcoin address is: 1B2S4Nf8jD3fshHodzuY-hframoQsQaZEcZ. By logging on to a Bitcoin wallet the user has access to one or more Bitcoin addresses that she can use to transfer Bitcoins from or receive Bitcoins to.

It is important to notice that a Bitcoin is a token that can be moved in the blockchain. A wallet does not contain the number of Bitcoins the owner of the wallet has at a certain moment in time, it rather calculates this position from all the input and output transactions that were done with the Bitcoins that are linked to the Bitcoin addresses the wallet owner uses. For that purpose, the wallet only needs to store that part of the blockchain that contains the bitcoin addresses that are used by the wallet owner.

Wallets can run on any computer, from an app on a smartphone to a database, with all the transactions that were ever done on the blockchain in a full node or a miner. Wallets do not verify, validate nor relay transactions, which miners do. Full nodes are between wallets and miners: they relay valid transactions to other nodes so that miners can find the pending transactions to incorporate in a block, and they relay blocks that are created by the miners thus helping to synchronize the blockchain. In the original Bitcoin whitepaper, Nakamoto [2] did not distinguish between full nodes and miners, considering both to be nodes that could validate and relay transactions, as well as create new blocks of transactions.

Gradually, creating new blocks of transactions became a specialist operation that required heavy investments in computer hardware and involved large amounts of electricity usage.[8] As a result, full nodes and miners became separate groups of nodes on the Bitcoin blockchain. So, whereas full nodes only relay transactions and blocks to other nodes, miners also validate and create new blocks of transactions to append to the blockchain.

Nakamoto [2, p. 3] lists the steps to run the Bitcoin blockchain network without making a distinction between full nodes and miners. Adjusting these steps to our contemporary world with separate full nodes and miners, and using the terminology as discussed in this section yields the following steps:

1   Wallets broadcast new transactions to all nodes.
2   The miners, after verification of each individual transaction, collect the new transactions into a block.
3   Each miner works on finding the nonce for the block the miner in question is working on.
4   When a miner finds a proof-of-work, it broadcasts the block to all nodes (the other mining nodes and the full nodes).
5   Nodes only accept a block if all transactions in it are valid and the nonce yields a block header hash that is smaller than the target hash.
6   Full nodes express their acceptance of a block by relaying it to the other nodes; miners express their acceptance of a block by working on the next block in the chain, using the hash of the accepted block as the previous hash.

From this it should be clear that recording a block can only take place by a miner that has acquired the right to write that block through proof-of-work. This also implies that a fraudulent alteration to a previously written block requires the fraudster to redo the proof-of-work of the block he is changing but also of all the blocks after the block with the alteration. For example, suppose currently the miners are working on block #533064. A fraudster wants to change a transaction in block #533061 so that he can double-spend the bitcoins in that transaction. He then has to redo the proof-of-work for all the blocks that have been mined so far, so blocks #533061 till 533063, which will take on average 30 minutes (3 blocks ★ 10 minutes). However, the other miners keep on trying to mine new blocks with valid transactions from block #533064 onward. Two important rules in the Bitcoin core are that new valid blocks are always appended to the longest chain of blocks (and after this has been done the entire blockchain accepts this chain as the shared single source of truth) and that a new block can only be mined if the previous block has been mined (as a result of the hash of the previous block being part of the cryptographic puzzle to solve for the current block). So, in case a fraudster – who can only be a miner – is trying to redo the proof-of-work of the block he wants to change and all the following blocks that have already been written to the blockchain, he has to do this faster than the other miners who are already ahead of him since they are working on block #533064, and continue with the subsequent blocks at an average pace of ten minutes per block. Given that the other miners, just like the fraudster, have fast CPUs to deliver the proof-of-work, it is extremely difficult, if not impossible, for the fraudster to catch up with the other miners and create his own version of the blockchain that becomes the longest chain. It can easily be seen that the more blocks have been written after a block that contains an invalid alteration the more difficult it becomes to make such an alteration. After six new blocks have been mined and hence written (these are called confirmations), it is impossible to make changes to an older block, but in practice this is already the case after three newly mined blocks (Figure 18.3).

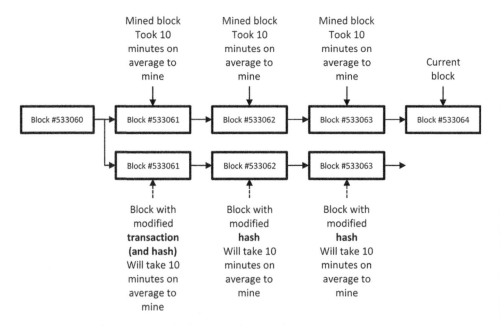

Figure 18.3 Proof-of-work to redo if a previously mined block is modified

In the Bitcoin blockchain proof-of-work or a majority of 51% of the hashing power is needed to validate blocks. This means that if a fraudster wants to change a block, thus creating his own version of the blockchain, he can only accomplish this with a majority of the hashing power to provide the necessary proof-of-work. If he has 51% of the hashing power or more, he can make any changes to the blockchain (in practice this turns out to be a slightly higher percentage since acquiring permission to write is still a random process). Hence, it is crucial for the trust in the blockchain that no single miner has 51% or more of the hashing power. Currently, the largest miner (Poolin) has an estimated 18% of the hashing power with the largest five miners all being located in China and together having an estimated 70% of the hashing power [11]. Therefore, the term 'China risk' is used to indicate that there is a risk that the Chinese miners join forces and take over the Bitcoin blockchain. However, these miners most likely do not have any intention to do a 51% attack on the network since this ould be extremely costly but moreover would completely undermine the trust in the network and render Bitcoins (including theirs) and the mining rigs[9] that they heavily invested in worthless. Yet, on the other hand it would be naive to think that a concentration of hashing power in just a few miners that moreover are located in one single country is not at odds with Satoshi Nakamoto's original idea of a completely democratic currency.

18.2.3 Open source

The Bitcoin core is open-source software. By downloading and installing it on her computer, a user can unilaterally decide that she wants to make her computer a node in the Bitcoin network. Such a node does not require exceptional computing power nor an enormous amount of disk space since the software only serves to support full nodes and not mining nodes, and transactions only consist of an input address, an output address, and the amount to be transferred, which consumes only limited memory space.

The Bitcoin core, as most other distributed ledger software, is not managed on-chain but on an open-source software platform. This creates a conventional form of transparency that generally is considered safer than privately developed software.

18.3 Digital signatures, tokenization, and oracles

In a distributed ledger, each transaction must have a cryptographic digital signature that unlocks the funds from that transaction. Only the person who has the appropriate private key can create a valid digital signature and only a person who has his own appropriate private key can verify that the digital signature is valid [3]. This ensures that funds can only be spent by their owners. A system of digital signatures is based on public and private keys. Since an electronic coin is a chain of digital signatures, a brief explication of private and public keys and how these relate to digital signatures is needed.

Imagine that Alice and Bob use a Bitcoin wallet service (for example by downloading an app to their smartphone). As they download the wallet, they are assigned a private and a public key by the wallet, which are stored in the wallet software on their behalf. Alice and Bob can use their private and public keys to exchange information secretly, even over the public internet provided that the public keys that they exchange and that are completely visible for the outside world are derived from the same encryption algorithm. Note that encryption with keys is different from hashing, since the encrypted data can be converted back to the original information (decrypting) through the use of the keys. As such encryption is an application of hashing. Alice and Bob choose a hashing algorithm and agree on the parameters of that algorithm, say 3x mod 17, where x is a private key or a combination of a private key and a public key.[10] Suppose Alice has private key 7 and Bob has private key 6. Since these are private keys, they don't show these to anybody. Using the chosen algorithm Alice arrives at a public key of 11 (=3^7 mod 17) that she can publicly send to Bob, and Bob of 15 (=3^6 mod 17) that he can publicly send to Alice. Filling in the values of the public (11 and 15) and private keys (7 and 6) leads to a shared secret of 8 (=11^6 mod 17, which equals 15^7 mod 17) that both Alice and Bob know because it was communicated via the internet. Note that nobody else was able to intercept and read this shared secret because it was communicated using public keys that were hashed from private keys. So, by creating a public key out of a private key an ingenious system emerges whereby encryption is done with the private key of the sender and decryption with the private key of the recipient. This system can be tweaked for creating digital signatures to be sent along with a message. A valid digital signature gives a recipient reason to believe that the message was created by a known sender (authentication), that the sender cannot deny having sent the message (non-repudiation), and that the message was not altered in transit (integrity).

This works as follows:

1 Alice sends a message in non-encrypted form to Bob.
2 Alice also calculates a hash from that document and encrypts it with her private key, resulting in a digital signature.
3 Alice sends the digital signature to Bob.
4 Bob calculates the hash from the document that he received from Alice.
5 Bob decrypts the digital signature using Alice's public key.
6 Bob can now verify that the received hash from the document equals the decrypted digital signature.

In a distributed ledger verification is programmed in the protocol that manages the ledger.

As indicated a coin, as an instantiation of a token, is a chain of digital signatures. In many distributed ledgers, tokens are needed to make the system tick, whether it be as an incentive for nodes to maintain the ledger, as a digital representation of virtual or physical assets, or both. When a token serves as a digital representation of assets, tokenization becomes an important part of the functioning of the distributed ledger, which creates its own dynamics regarding the interaction between the real world and the ledger.

Tokenization is a method that converts rights to an asset into a digital token. With digital assets, tokenization is fairly easy since the only thing that needs to be done is linking the digital assets also to the digital token. This can be as simple as creating a digital signature from the digital asset in combination with some private key. When the digital assets change ownership, the token also moves from the old to the new owner with only a limited risk that the assets and the token become decoupled. With physical assets this is different since the link between the physical asset and the token must be continuously safeguarded and in many instances it is extremely difficult to uniquely identify a physical asset with a tag that is inseparably connected to the asset. For example, Everledger provides a platform for recording expensive diamonds in a blockchain [12]. To tokenize each diamond, the unique characteristics of the diamond must be determined and attached to the diamond. A code that is attached to the diamond in the form of a laser inscription on the girdle will generally not be sufficient to guarantee that it is the right diamond and not a falsification or an otherwise cheaper piece. In addition to a laser inscription on the girdle, physical characteristics of the diamond must be measured to arrive at a digital thumbprint for each diamond. Such a thumbprint consists of 40 metadata points, including the laser inscription and the stone's color, clarity, cut, and carat weight. These digital thumbprints are then written to the blockchain.

There are various classifications of cryptographic tokens varying from a simple dichotomy (cryptocurrencies and other tokens) to a whole multidimensional typology as presented by Euler [1]. At this point, this chapter will not discuss the entire richness of cryptographic tokens in theory but will in the following sections on use cases refer to certain types of token that may be suitable in the designated distributed ledgers.

Oracles are the measurement systems that collect data from real life to feed these into a distributed ledger and that receive data from distributed ledgers to initiate pre-defined actions in real life. As such oracles are closely related to the IoT. Oracles can be classified into inbound and outbound, and into software and hardware devices.

Examples of inbound software oracles are temperature, inventory level, cash receipt, price change, and a train delay. Examples of inbound hardware oracles are RFID/NFC chips, GPS, WiFi, drones, and movement sensors. Examples of outbound software oracles are sending an order confirmation, placing an order, making a journal entry, transferring money, and populating picking list. Examples of outbound hardware oracles are switching on a heating, opening a lock, moving a robot, launching a drone, and picking goods from the warehouse. Since oracles live in a world outside of the distributed ledger, they introduce failure points. Currently, it is being investigated if and how trustless computation oracles can mitigate this issue [13].

18.4 Extending blockchain to distributed ledger technology

Although blockchain is the most widely known term, it is more accurate to speak of the more generic term distributed ledger technology (DLT). DLT includes blockchain but there are many blockchain variations that make use of DLT without having all the characteristics a typical blockchain has. This section discusses the potential of smart contracts for DLT applications, alternative consensus mechanisms in other distributed ledgers than the blockchain, and ultimately arrives at a classification of distributed ledgers.

18.4.1 Smart contracts

Unlike the name might imply a smart contract is not a legal contract but rather a piece of program code that initiates at least one action if the conditions in that contract are met. An example of a smart contract is the execution of a payment after ordered goods have been received and a certain period of time has elapsed. A smart contract is not necessarily built upon a blockchain. As a matter of fact the concept of smart contracts was proposed by Szabo [5,6], long before the idea of decentralized cryptocurrencies on a blockchain was launched by Nakamoto [2]. However, by building a smart contract on a blockchain its execution becomes guaranteed without having the need for calling upon a trusted third party or a judiciary system to enforce compliance with the contract. Hence, a smart contract running on a blockchain can execute business logic using tamper-proof technology that is upfront compliant and unstoppable.

The Bitcoin blockchain can be used for smart contracts, but since Bitcoin was not developed for other applications than secure transactions between parties without having the need for a trusted third party Bitcoin-based smart contracts are quite conservative and don't allow for smart contracts that account for the richness of most real-life business transactions. Ethereum is a blockchain that was specifically designed for running smart contracts that go beyond the applications the Bitcoin blockchain originally was designed for. In the Ethereum blockchain, any smart contract is possible, including an investment fund, a land registry, an accounting system with cross-organization transaction validation, a voting system, an exchange for energy, a tracking and tracing system for products within their supply chains, and a token that can only be spent to acquire designated assets. Given the versatility of the Ethereum blockchain, the question arises why Ethereum has not become the main blockchain platform at the expense of Bitcoin. The simple answer is that versatility comes with a price: by being conservative in its applications Bitcoin is extremely secure whereas Ethereum has sacrificed some security to become more versatile and flexible. Smart contracts may have bugs in them that make them vulnerable to all kinds of attacks and fraud schemes. For that reason smart contracts, unlike the Ethereum blockchain itself, need to be subject to regular audits.

Although, as indicated, smart contracts are not legal contracts, they are based on legal code. Because smart contracts are program code, the more standardized and rule-based the legal code, the greater the potential for high-quality program code in smart contracts [14].

18.4.2 *Alternative consensus mechanisms*

A consensus mechanism is needed to secure that only nodes that have received the right to write (blocks of) transactions to a distributed ledger can do so and to keep the ledgers synchronized. Distributed ledger technology makes use of either a proof model such as proof-of-work or some variant of Byzantine fault tolerance (BFT) as its consensus mechanism. BFT is the ability of a distributed ledger to function as desired and correctly reach sufficient consensus despite some malicious nodes defaulting or relaying incorrect information to other nodes. Its objective is to minimize the influence these malicious nodes have on the correct functioning of the distributed ledger and on the desired consensus that should be reached by the honest nodes. As explicated, in the Bitcoin blockchain the consensus mechanism is proof-of-work. Since this mechanism requires an enormous amount of electricity that is used to solve, utterly pointless, cryptographic puzzles, it is not considered sustainable by many. For that reason alternative consensus mechanisms that still produce sufficient proof or fault tolerance to grant a node the right to write to the distributed ledger are being developed, including proof-of-stake (POS), practical Byzantine fault tolerance (PBFT), and federated Byzantine agreement (FBA).

In proof-of-stake, the right to write to the blockchain is given on the basis of a random allocation process that weighs the stake a node has in the total number of native tokens (for example, Ethers) of that blockchain. In this variant the money that normally would be expended on capital investments (mining rigs for proof-of-work) is now expended on the purchase of the tokens whereas no additional money is spent on energy as in proof-of-work.

In practical Byzantine fault tolerance, the assumption is that the number of malicious nodes in the network cannot simultaneously equal to or exceed one-third of the overall nodes in the system in a given time window. The more nodes there are in the network, the more unlikely it becomes that one-third of the nodes are malicious [15]. In essence, all of the nodes in the PBFT model are ordered in a sequence with one node being the leader and the others the backup nodes. The role of the leader switches per consensus round. Nodes need to prove that a message came from a specific peer node, but also need to verify that the message was not modified during transmission, hence the importance of digital signatures.

In federated Byzantine agreement, the nodes do not have to be known and verified in advance, participation in the distributed ledger is open, and control is decentralized. Nodes can choose what other nodes to trust. System-wide quorums (the required minimum number of nodes) emerge from choices made by individual nodes.

Depending on the desired type of distributed ledger one consensus mechanism may be more suitable than the other. Consensus models used by distributed ledgers are largely driven by the type of application the ledger expects to support and the threats it envisages to the integrity of the ledger.

Typically, the permissionless ledgers such as Ethereum and Bitcoin achieve robust consensus among very high numbers of unknown, and hence untrusted peers using computational or memory complexity while sacrificing transaction finality and throughput [16]. However, the permissioned, consortium ledgers such as R3 for banking are less scalable but have a much higher throughput that ensures faster transaction finality. When looking at distributed ledger technology to solve business problems, the scale of the intended network, the trust between participants, performance, confidentiality, and the required disintermediation are important criteria for determining the platform and the consensus model to use.

18.4.3 *Classification of distributed ledgers*

Due to the immaturity of the research field, consensus on blockchain semantics is still lacking (de Kruijff & Weigand 2017). There is a lot of discussion, mainly in blogposts, on the dimensions along which to compare various types of distributed ledger. A much debated issue is the distinction between private and public distributed ledgers on the one hand, and permissioned and permissionless distributed ledgers on the other hand (for example, [17,18,19]). Trying to find common semantics regarding this distinction appears to be quite an onerous task. However, since the transitions between the various types of distributed ledger are mostly not discrete but rather continuous, and moreover many applications take hybrid forms that combine distributed ledgers with traditional centralized databases, understanding the distinction between private and public on the one hand, and permissioned and permissionless on the other hand merely serves as a starting point for the design of distributed ledgers that match the specific problem that needs to be solved.

Ethereum and Bitcoin are permissionless public distributed ledgers. Here, permissionless means that there is no designated party that assigns certain nodes the right to validate and write transactions or blocks of transactions to the ledger. In a permissionless distributed ledger, the right to validate and write transactions or blocks of transactions is acquired through the consensus mechanism that the distributed ledger uses. In a permissionless system, any node can validate and write transactions or blocks of transactions as long as the rules of the distributed ledger's consensus mechanism are followed. It should be noted that just acquiring the right to validate and write transactions is not the incentive for nodes to make substantial CPU capacity available and expending substantial amounts of energy. The real incentive is that nodes can earn native tokens[11], for example Bitcoins or Ethers, by doing so. If in a distributed ledger any node that runs the right software (for example the Bitcoin core software) can broadcast a transaction, i.e., initiate a transaction in the distributed ledger network, then that ledger is considered a public ledger. As represented in Figure 18.4, there are more types of digital ledger than permissionless public distributed ledgers.

Some general characteristics distinguish permissionless from permissioned distributed ledgers and private from public ones. First, in a permissionless distributed ledger the needed consensus mechanism is either proof-of-work, proof-of-stake, or federated Byzantine agreement because a central authority that determines which node is going to write (blocks of) transactions to the blockchain is not needed. Second, in a public distributed ledger a token is needed because such a ledger is secured through cryptography (note that a token is a chain of digital signatures that make use of public and private keys) and the token is needed as an

Broadcasting transactions (private/public)

		Broadcasting transactions is limited to a pre-defined set of nodes (private)	Any node that runs the right software can broadcast transactions (public)
Validating and writing (permissioned/permissionless)	Validating and writing (blocks of) transactions is granted by a central authority to a pre-defined set of nodes (permissioned)	(2) Permissioned private distributed ledgers	(1) Permissioned public distributed ledgers
	Any node can validate and write (blocks of) transactions within the used consensus mechanism (permissionless)	(3) Permissionless private distributed ledgers	(4) Permissionless public distributed ledgers

Figure 18.4   Classification of distributed ledgers

incentive for the nodes to maintain the ledger. Third, in a permissionless distributed ledger transactions are clustered into blocks to solve the double-spend problem. In that sense, permissionless distributed ledgers are the only true blockchains whereas permissioned ledgers do not necessarily need to make use of blocks since the double-spend problem is solved by a central authority. For that reason the term 'blockchain' should only be used for distributed ledgers that indeed cluster transactions in blocks to be appended to the blockchain. In all other cases, the generic term distributed ledger should be used. Corda as used by R3 is an example of a permissioned private distributed ledger that is inspired on blockchain but does not record blocks of transactions but just individual transactions and moreover does not completely synchronize the entire ledger but just the subset that is relevant for the nodes that were involved in the transactions in question. As such Corda is closer to traditional centralized databases than to permissionless public distributed ledgers. Yet, through its partial decentralized set-up it belongs to the family of distributed ledgers.

18.5 Distributed ledger technologies for managerial purposes

Distributed ledger technology has many managerial applications that are yet unknown. Through experimentation and bold ventures, new potential applications are still being discovered. However, there are some promising use cases, such as the already mentioned Everledger, that may serve as anchors for further experimentation and discovery. Moreover, there are also major fields where distributed ledger technology is still unexplored, including accounting, control, audit, and oversight. This section discusses some use cases thereby also giving direction to interesting strands for further exploration.

18.5.1 Identity

The Dutch Ministry of Internal Affairs has commissioned research into the combination of digital identity and digital ledger technology. With digital identity so-called zero-knowledge proof can be given about otherwise personal information, including age, health history, fines, income, other legal sentences, and payment history. For example, one of the projects was age control while purchasing age-restricted goods, such as cigarettes or alcohol. The owner of a shop only needs to know that the person trying to buy cigarettes or alcohol is older than 18 years, but currently has to ask for a passport or identity card containing much more personal data. Another example is the personal information a healthcare professional needs to know about a patient, such as allergies, prescribed medication, reanimation desired, blood type, person to contact in case of emergency, and health history in general, so that the healthcare professional can provide the right care. An obvious device to use that can replace the many proprietary ID cards (driver's license, insurance pass, bank card, library card, office pass, customer loyalty passes, and the like) is the person's smartphone. In a once-only action, an individual's smartphone is prepared for identity on mobile device by having her go to the city hall for linking her smartphone via an app to her citizen record at the municipality. By putting such a system in a distributed database, the ecosystem of participants can grow while the person involved can still determine who is able to see what personal data about her.

18.5.2 Land registry

Honduras (using the Factom platform) has experimented with a blockchain-based cadastral register but has stalled the project in 2015. Ghana is still experimenting with an on-chain cadastral register, as are Sweden, the Republic of Georgia, and some local governments such as Cook County in Chicago [20]. These countries explore the possibilities of DLT for land title registrations for various reasons. For example, Honduras and Ghana did not have proper cadastral records for real estate. As a result, there was never any assurance whether or not the transfer of ownership of land and buildings was recorded. With a cadaster, a trusted third party, this problem is solved. But with DLT emerging a more efficient solution might be to create a DLT-based cadastral register that serves as the shared single source of truth regarding who owns which piece of land or building.

18.5.3 Tickets (concerts, museums, football games)

Guts tickets provide an app that is built upon a blockchain for selling tickets directly from the performer to the visitor. In addition, it maximizes the price a reseller can charge to 120% of the official price. Guts has financed its business via an initial coin offering (ICO) with the Ethereum-based token GET. Payment of tickets does not need to be done in this token. As in most viable DLT use cases payment is done in fiat money, i.e. Euros.

18.5.4 Elections

A vote can be considered a token. If the double-spend problem with that token is solved, then a vote can only be casted once. This may be the future of democratic voting systems that have been experimenting with various IT applications but that often failed due to a lack of security. Distributed ledger technology in combination with identity on an electronic device (most likely a smartphone) provides the technical solution.

18.5.5 Track and trace supply chain

Startup Seal had developed a blockchain-based system for tracing branded products back to their origin. By scanning a built-in NFC chip with a smartphone app, the potential buyer can see whether or not the product is counterfeited. The same track and trace technology can be used for tracing back agricultural products that are on the shelves in our grocery stores to their origins. The potential buyer will then be able to find out whether there have been any links in the supply chain that are non-compliant with certain corporate social responsibility guidelines or regulations. For example, coffee can be traced back to the plantation where the beans were grown to find out about the labor circumstances and usage of pesticides.

18.5.6 Internet auctions

Internet auctions are organized by a trusted third party, but with blockchain it is possible to buy and sell directly via the internet without parties having to know and trust one another. When digital assets are traded a smart contract can manage the exchange of money and assets completely on chain. In case of physical goods, a solution to the trust issue is that the seller ships the goods prior to the payment by the buyer, with a clause (i.e., a programmed business rule) in the smart contract that the payment will automatically be made after the shipment has been delivered by the carrier to the buyer. As is inherent to smart contracts, the action of making the payment is unstoppable once delivery has taken place.

18.5.7 Registration and management of intellectual property

Renowned DJ Hardwell has experimented with putting the rights to his music into a distributed database. His aim was to bring more transparency and a more honest distribution of rights and funds in the music industry. Services such as Spotify, YouTube, and Facebook, via such an application, will exactly know how much they need to pay for each track. The same approach can be followed for any form of intellectual ownership, including books, videos, photos, articles, and art.

Hardwell sure isn't the only artist that puts a firm belief in distributed ledger technology. British award-winning singer Imogen Heap has been working on the Mycelia project for quite some time. Mycelia records the rights to her music in a blockchain and via a smart contract automatically settles payments she (and others in the chain) is legally entitled to.

18.5.8 Personal healthcare budget

When a personal healthcare budget is given to a patient that can only be spent on designated healthcare products, a whole system of checks and balances needs to be put in place for compliance purposes. Usually checking is done retrospectively. Putting the budget in a token on a distributed ledger that can only be spent on transactions the token is programmed for creates a system that leads to spending being compliant by default.

18.5.9 Healthcare files

The Dutch government has developed a working prototype of a distributed database that contains all the healthcare-related information per individual patient. The patient himself gives permission to various parties to access his information and the data are recorded in an immutable ledger. Since there are many different parties involved in healthcare applications, a shared (yet permissioned) database greatly enhances the efficiency of healthcare processes.

18.5.10 Micropayments via internet

Micropayments are made possible by third-party applications such as PayPal, Amazon Pay, and Stripe. The user is required to create an account in these platforms to be able to make a micropayment transaction. Such a system has several disadvantages, including high transaction fees, payment delays, intransparency, and complexity of user interfaces in combination with these being proprietary and hence unique for each producer. A distributed ledger that uses smart contract for fair distribution is a feasible solution to these problems. Bitcoin startup Blockstream has released a micropayment processing system that it claims makes it simpler to build bitcoin apps on top of its Lightning Network.[12]

18.5.11 Energy

The Brooklyn Microgrid project is an initiative of a small group of New Yorkers who have solar panels on their rooftops and who want to make as efficiently as possible use of the collected energy by moving surpluses from one participant to other participants who have shortages without having time-consuming and expensive middlemen to manage this process. For that purpose they had a technology partner (energy startup LO3) design and build a private distributed ledger application to exchange energy between the participants in this little ecosystem.

18.5.12 Accounting, audit, and control

Despite meaningful applications of distributed ledger technology in accounting, audit, and control being quite easy to imagine, the development of such systems is still lagging. However, given the immutability and hence a near 100% reliability of a DLT-based accounting system, auditors and other accountants are now becoming increasingly interested in a concept that has been labeled triple-entry accounting avant la lettre by Grigg [8]. It turns out that DLT is a great enabler of triple-entry accounting by creating a distributed database that is managed by each entity in the ecosystem and that serves as the shared single source of truth. By making journal entries not only locally in each entity's ERP system but also in the distributed database, a normative position is continuously maintained against which the local databases can be checked. This system aims to improve the quality of data to a near 100% reliability.

18.6 Discussion

Given the many (potential) use cases and the discussed DLT-related concepts, it is now possible to give some guidelines for evaluating if distributed ledger technology is a feasible solution for certain business problems. The overarching question should always be if DLT is taken into consideration because there is a real business problem or because there are political or publicity motives. The phrase 'we need to do something with blockchain' can be heard too often without the speaker really understanding what is meant by blockchain or related technologies. So, a thorough analysis of the problem, as always, is quintessential.

The conditions for DLT to be taken into consideration are:

1   There is a need for a shared database in which all the users are able to read or verify everything, but no single user controls who can write what.
2   There are multiple parties who write data to the shared database, verify, or read these data.
3   Those parties are members of different legal or economical entities. Because organizational boundaries are crossed, an in-house company solution with bilateral agreements between parties to share data is less efficient than a solution with one (albeit distributed) database.

4   There is no or limited trust between these parties because the parties don't know one another or they have reason to distrust one another.

5   It is not economically or technically feasible to put a trusted third party in place.

If all these conditions are met, a distributed ledger may be considered. The decision to actually make a DLT design also is moderated by various other factors, including complexity of regulations (regulations that can easily be transformed into business rules are better suited for DLT applications than more complicated regulations), desired reliability (when 100% reliability is not needed, DLT may not be needed either), and the degree of standardization (the more standardization in the process to model in the DLT application, the more viable a DLT solution may be).

Once the choice is made to enter into a DLT application, the choice for the type of distributed ledger must be made. This boils down to determining if the ledger should be public or private, permissionless or permissioned, and whether a (native) token is needed to make the application work.

It should thereby be kept in mind that the trade-off between confidentiality needs (private, permissioned is better at this than public, permissionless) and disintermediation needs (the more open, public and permissionless, the better disintermediation may work). It also should be noted that hybrid forms of distributed ledgers are much more likely to be successfully implemented than pure forms such as the Bitcoin blockchain. In that sense, the boundaries between the various types of distributed ledger are rather fuzzy than well-demarcated.

From the analysis in this chapter, some promising classes of use case emerge. In accordance with the designations Greenspan [21] distinguishes, these classes comprise lightweight financial systems, provenance tracking, inter-organizational record keeping, and multiparty aggregation. *Lightweight financial systems* are aimed at transactions with digital assets in which the economic stakes are relatively low. Putting this in a distributed ledger requires a token to be incorporated. Examples are loyalty points, local currencies (including gift cards), and crowdfunding. *Provenance tracking* also requires a digital token. Such a token is linked to the asset whose provenance must be tracked. The token then travels on the distributed ledger along with the travel of the asset in the real world. Examples include wine, diamonds, brand articles, agricultural products but also purchase contracts and ownership certificates of real estate. *Inter-organizational record keeping* on a distributed ledger does not require a token to be administered. Instead the ledger acts as a tool for administering any type of data (financial or non-financial, quantitative or non-quantitative). Examples include maintaining an audit trail, a contract register, and other control registers for checking purposes. Finally, *multi-party aggregation* is closely related to inter-organizational record keeping but whereas the latter is mainly aimed at maintaining a system of checks and balances, the former is merely aimed at making access to data more efficient. The idea is that multiple parties in a DLT ecosystem have designated rights to access the ledger and read, verify, or write data. Examples include a system that grants subsidies based on a wide variety of data sources, users having to submit multiple different forms with (almost) identical data to various different parties as in applications for permits, licenses, or exam results.

In the near future, as a result of the enormous attention that is given to blockchain and other distributed ledger technologies, many new and yet unknown applications will see the light. It will be a challenge for practitioners, educators, and researchers to join forces in design science, action research, grounded theory, and other practical problem-solving research paradigms to explore a great variety of DLT projects to move the domain forward.

Notes

1   See Armasu [22] for an overview of the top 25 cryptocurrencies by market cap as on June 1, 2018.
2   To distinguish a decimal number from a hexadecimal number, the code '0x' is prepended to the hexadecimal number.
3   The block reward for the miner who solves the cryptographic puzzle is halved every 210.000th block, which is roughly every four years. This means that the creation of Bitcoins will stop at a point far in the future: in the year 2140 a maximum total of 21 million Bitcoins will be created, leaving only the transaction fees as an incentive for the miners to provide proof-of-work.
4   The Timestamp is the Unix epoch notation of the time a block is recorded.
5   There are some more rules for exceptional cases to prevent the difficulty to decrease or increase by more than a factor 4 or to prevent having a target that exceeds the maximum target as set for the first ever mined 2016 blocks, including if the difference is greater than eight weeks then set it to eight weeks, if the difference is less than half a week then set it to half a week, and if the result is greater than the maximum target ($2^\wedge(256 - 32)-1$) then set it to the maximum target.
6   Compact form is a floating point notation with the first byte being the exponent e and the last three bytes the mantissa c in the formula: $c\star 2^\wedge(8\star(e-3))$.
7   The Block header hash is calculated by running the Block header through the SHA-256 algorithm twice.
8   The electricity consumption of the Bitcoin blockchain in 2017 was 61.4 billion kWh (=61.4 TWh), which is the total electricity consumption of countries like Austria and Switzerland.
9   A mining rig is hardware that contains application specific integrated circuits (ASICs) that will only do the mining for one specific native token. So, a Bitcoin mining rig cannot do the mining for Ether, and vice versa.
10 Hashing algorithms are mostly based on modulus (MOD) functions.
11 A native token is a cryptocurrency that is the sole medium of exchange on a specific blockchain, is tradeable on a market, and hence has value in the real world. Bitcoin and Ether are the most well-known examples of native tokens. Because of their value these tokens serve as the incentive for nodes to validate and write blocks of transactions to the blockchain.
12 Lightning adds an extra layer to the Bitcoin blockchain to enable cheaper and faster payments but with the same security backing of the Bitcoin blockchain.

References

1.   Euler, Th. (2018, January 18). The token classification framework: A multi-dimensional tool for understanding and classifying crypto tokens. Available online at: http://www.untitled-inc.com
2.   Nakamoto, S. (2008). Bitcoin: A peer-to-peer electronic cash system. Available online at: https://bitcoin.org/bitcoin.pdf
3.   Diffie, W., and M.E. Hellman (1976). New directions in cryptography. *IEEE Transactions on Information Theory*, IT-22 (6), pp. 644–654.
4.   Haber, S. and W. Stornetta (1991). How to time-stamp a digital document. *Journal of Cryptology*, 3(2), pp. 99–111.
5.   Szabo, N. (1994). Smart contracts. Available online at: http://www.fon.hum.uva.nl/rob/Courses/InformationInSpeech/CDROM/Literature/LOTwinterschool2006/szabo.best.vwh.net/smart.contracts.html
6.   Szabo, N. (1997). Formalizing and securing relationships on public networks. *First Monday*, 2(9), September 1. Available online at: http://journals.uic.edu/ojs/index.php/fm/article/view/548/469
7.   Lamport, L., R. Shostak, and M. Pease (1982). The Byzantine generals problem. *ACM Transactions on Programming Languages and Systems*, July, 4 (3), pp. 382–401.
8.   Grigg, I. (2005). *Triple entry accounting*. Systemics, Inc. Available online at: http://iang.org/papers/triple_entry.html
9.   Panetta, K. (2017, October 3). Gartner top 10 strategic technology trends for 2018. Available online at https://www.gartner.com/smarterwithgartner/gartner-top-10-strategic-technology-trends-for-2018/
10. Kruijff, J. de, and H. Weigand (2017). Understanding the blockchain using enterprise ontology. In: E. Dubois and K. Pohl (eds.), Proceedings of the *29th International Conference on Advanced Information Systems Engineering*, Essen (Germany), June 12–16, pp. 29–43.

11. Tuwiner, J. (2018, June 30). Bitcoin mining pools. Available online at: https://www.buybitcoinworldwide.com/mining/pools/

12. Kemp, L. (2017, January 25). Putting bling on the blockchain: the everledger story. Available online at: http://institute.swissre.com/research/library/Rdm_Blockchain_Leanne_Kemp.html

13. Teutsch, J. (2017). On decentralized oracles for data availability. TrueBit. Available online at: http://people.cs.uchicago.edu/~teutsch/papers/decentralized_oracles.pdf

14. McKinney, S. A., R. Landy, and R. Wilka (2018). Smart contracts, blockchain, and the next frontier of transactional law. *Washington Journal of Law, Technology & Arts*. 13(3), Spring. Available online at: https://digitalcommons.law.uw.edu/wjlta/vol13/iss3/5

15. Castro, M., and B. Liskov (1999). Practical Byzantine fault tolerance. In: Proceedings of the *Third Symposium on Operating Systems Design and Implementation*, USENIX, New Orleans.

16. Baliga, A. (2017, April). Understanding blockchain consensus models. *Whitepaper Persistent*. Available online at: https://pdfs.semanticscholar.org/da8a/37b10bc1521a4d3de925d7ebc44bb606d740.pdf

17. Kolisko, L. (2018, April 3). In-depth on differences between public, private and permissioned blockchains. Available online at: https://medium.com/@lkolisko/in-depth-on-differences-between-public-private-and-permissioned-blockchains-aff762f0ca24

18. Kravchenko, P. (2016, September 26). Ok, I need a blockchain, but which one? Available online at: https://medium.com/@pavelkravchenko/ok-i-need-a-blockchain-but-which-one-ca75c1e2100

19. BitFury Group (2015). Public versus Private Blockchains, Part 2: Permissionless Blockchains. Available online at: https://bitfury.com/content/downloads/public-vs-private-pt2-1.pdf, 20 October

20. Shin, L. (2016, April 21). Republic of Georgia to pilot land titling on blockchain with economist Hernando de Soto. *BitFury*. Available online at: https://www.forbes.com/sites/laurashin/2016/04/21/republic-of-georgia-to-pilot-land-titling-on-blockchain-with-economist-hernando-de-soto-bitfury/#5df3211544da

21. Greenspan, G. (2016, May 10). Four genuine blockchain use cases. Available online at: https://www.multichain.com/blog/2016/05/four-genuine-blockchain-use-cases

22. Armasu, L. (2018, June 1). Top 25 cryptocurrencies by market cap. Available online at: https://www.tomshardware.com/picturestory/778-biggest-cryptocurrencies.html#s2

19

INTERNET OF THINGS

Marcel Baron[1]

19.1 What is the Internet of Things or IoT?

What exactly is IoT? Before there were Internet-connected umbrellas and juicers, water bottles, and factories—before there was even a modern Internet—there was a Coke machine in Pittsburgh, Pennsylvania that could report its contents through a network. Though it was primitive by today's standards, it held a unique characteristic: it was, as far as anyone knows, the world's first IoT device. IoT was invented in the early 1980s by David Nichols, a graduate student in Carnegie Mellon University's computer science department. In his office on the campus at Wean Hall, he was regularly longing for a soda. However, his office was "a relatively long way" from the building's Coke machine, and considering his fellow students' substantial caffeine habits, Nichols knew there was a good chance it would be empty—or that, if the machine had recently been refilled, the sodas inside would be tragically warm. As happens often, necessity was the mother of invention. With a few students, he developed the idea to apply existing technology like sensors and the Arpanet, and to write a program for the gateway that would check the status of each column's light of the vending machine a few times per second, and the IoT was born. If a light transitioned from off to on but then went off again a few seconds later, the program knew that a Coke had been purchased. If the light stayed on more than five seconds, it assumed the column was empty. When the light went back off, the program knew that two cold Cokes—which were always held in the machine in reserve—were now available for purchase, while the rest of the bottles were still warm. The program tracked for how many minutes the bottles had been in the machine after restocking. After three hours, the bottles simply registered as "cold" [1]. This story shows that IoT is not something new but was already there in the 80s. Today however with cheaper technology, faster networks, and computers, we are now able to implement it on a much larger scale.

This example of the first IoT machine lays the foundation for the definition used by IBM:

> The network of physical devices, vehicles, buildings, equipment, applications and other "things"—embedded with electronics, software, sensors, actuators or something smart and network connectivity that enables these objects to collect and exchange data. Each device can be identified individually providing accurate monitoring and management possibilities.

For consumers, these devices include mobile phones, smart watches, sports wearables, home heating and air conditioning systems. For businesses, these are devices and sensors embedded in manufacturing equipment, the supply chain, and in-vehicle components.

Four different functions can be attributed to the use of IoT: Detection, Monitoring, Analytics, Artificial Intelligence. Below we provide the explanation of each of the functions in a manufacturing environment.

The detection of an event or a "limit breach." An "event" could be that a production line has stopped due to a "limit breach" that a temperature sensor is reading too high or too low.

Monitor Key Performance Indicators of a condition rather than an event. Examples might be that a production line is only producing 80% of the expected volume, or that the temperature has been gradually increasing, even though it has not gone past a limit yet.

Analytics built using the data from a sensor or a combination of sensors. Quality Early Warning Systems or Predictive Maintenance and Quality performance analytics toolsets fit here. Analytics goes past reacting to an event, or preventive actions due to monitoring, and begins to utilize predictive analytics. Analytics can tell "your machine is going to shut down in three hours unless you perform maintenance on it."

Artificial Intelligence tools that can go beyond even the algorithms used in analytics, and learn from watching the data over time. This requires that IoT data be available for an extended period so that it is possible to learn from it.

19.2 What domains are expected to be affected by IoT?

Many companies predict a future of a world that is instrumented, interconnected, and intelligent. IoT is expected to have a vital role in this development. Where does IoT play that role? IoT can indeed connect everything with everything. However, where will it bring most value for consumers and business is a matter of understanding the needs and is a matter of evolution. At the moment, there are many different possible use cases for IoT. The identified areas are, e.g., buildings, environment, factories, home, sports, stores, vehicles. Figure 19.1 gives a quick overview of what can be expected.

19.3 Predictions of IoT

Leading market research companies (i.e., IDC [2,3], Gartner, Forrester) foresee many opportunities for the application of IoT, especially for IT consulting services and System Integration services and those companies that build solutions in the coming three to five years. The expectation is that in the coming years IoT projects will move beyond pilot projects; the focus of mature applications will be to reduce project failures and improve ROI. Enterprises envisage the use of IoT platforms that provide comprehensive analytics and outcome-based focused functionality. The implementation of 5G wireless connectivity increases the use of real-time IoT data insights. Due to the privacy law GDPR in Europe, more investments will be made on edge computing to avoid data connectivity to devices related to homes and persons. IoT in combination with AI will support identification and prediction for products and new product development but also make the IoT more intelligent. Another technology that will be added to IoT is blockchain to ensure immutability and integrity.

Most companies predict high revenues and compound annual growth rates for IoT. IoT is clearly a fast-growing market. Bain predicts that by 2020 annual revenues could exceed $470 billion for the IoT vendors selling the hardware, software, and comprehensive solutions. McKinsey estimates the total IoT market size to grow from $900 million in 2015

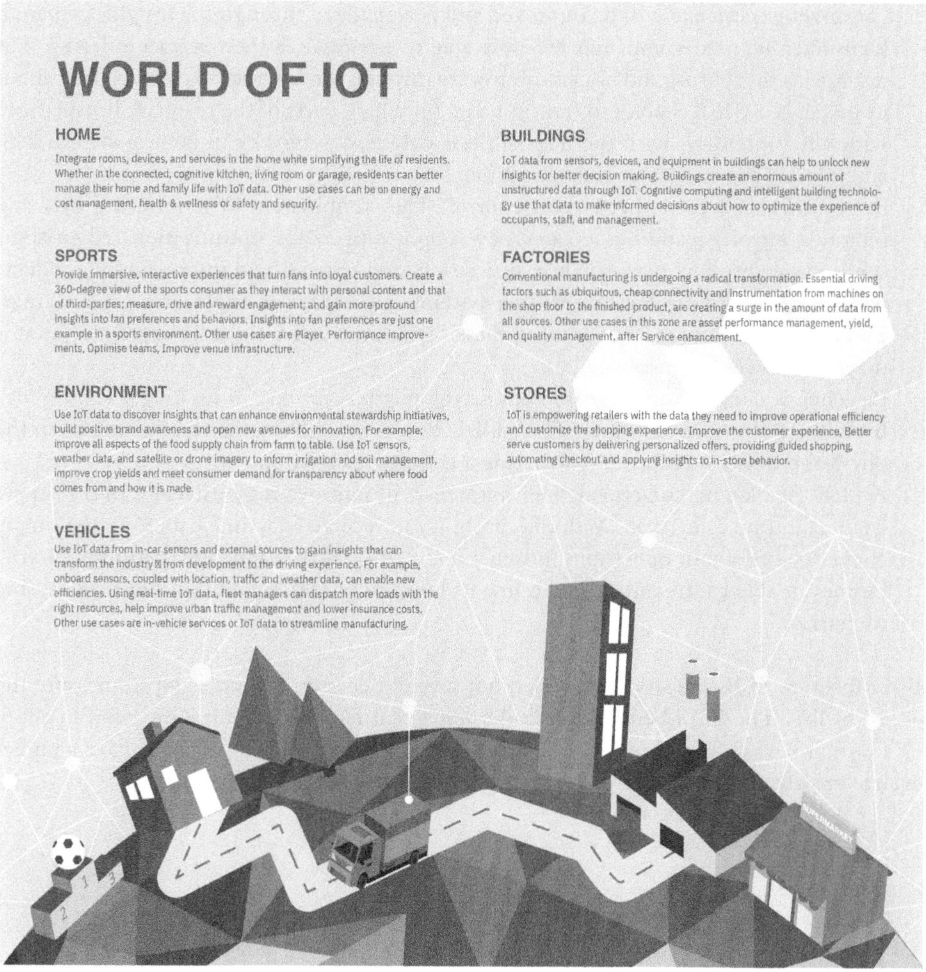

WORLD OF IOT

HOME

Integrate rooms, devices, and services in the home while simplifying the life of residents. Whether in the connected, cognitive kitchen, living room or garage, residents can better manage their home and family life with IoT data. Other use cases can be on energy and cost management, health & wellness or safety and security.

SPORTS

Provide immersive, interactive experiences that turn fans into loyal customers. Create a 360-degree view of the sports consumer as they interact with personal content and that of third-parties; measure, drive and reward engagement; and gain more profound insights into fan preferences and behaviors. Insights into fan preferences are just one example in a sports environment. Other use cases are Player Performance improvements, Optimise teams, Improve venue infrastructure.

ENVIRONMENT

Use IoT data to discover insights that can enhance environmental stewardship initiatives, build positive brand awareness and open new avenues for innovation. For example; improve all aspects of the food supply chain from farm to table. Use IoT sensors, weather data, and satellite or drone imagery to inform irrigation and soil management, improve crop yields and meet consumer demand for transparency about where food comes from and how it is made.

VEHICLES

Use IoT data from in-car sensors and external sources to gain insights that can transform the industry & from development to the driving experience. For example; onboard sensors, coupled with location, traffic and weather data, can enable new efficiencies. Using real-time IoT data, fleet managers can dispatch more loads with the right resources, help improve urban traffic management and lower insurance costs. Other use cases are in-vehicle services or IoT data to streamline manufacturing.

BUILDINGS

IoT data from sensors, devices, and equipment in buildings can help to unlock new insights for better decision making. Buildings create an enormous amount of unstructured data through IoT. Cognitive computing and intelligent building technology use that data to make informed decisions about how to optimize the experience of occupants, staff, and management.

FACTORIES

Conventional manufacturing is undergoing a radical transformation. Essential driving factors such as ubiquitous, cheap connectivity and instrumentation from machines on the shop floor to the finished product, are creating a surge in the amount of data from all sources. Other use cases in this zone are asset performance management, yield, and quality management, after Service enhancement.

STORES

IoT is empowering retailers with the data they need to improve operational efficiency and customize the shopping experience. Improve the customer experience, Better serve customers by delivering personalized offers, providing guided shopping, automating checkout and applying insights to in-store behavior.

Figure 19.1   The world of IoT – visual design: Femke van der Zande

to $3.7 billion in 2020, thus realizing a 32.6% CAGR. General Electric predicts investment in the Industrial Internet of Things (IIoT) to top $60 trillion during the next 15 years. IHS forecasts that the IoT market will grow from an installed base of 15.4 billion devices in 2015 to 30.7 billion devices in 2020 and 75.4 billion in 2025.

Summarizing, overall the expectations are high with significant transformation driven by IoT. However, the market (end users and vendors of IoT) will become more mature and eventually develop more realistic expectations based on use cases for IoT for industry operations and business functions. These mature views may flatten the overheated views of many market predictions.

19.4 Why are companies pressured to invest in IoT?

In general, companies are eager to invest in IoT because of the competitive opportunities that it offers. Data captured through IoT enables companies to increase their impact in four areas [7].

1   Customer experience will be improved and personalized through the insights gathered. Consumer-focused companies are now able to personalize their service offering. For example, a toothbrush did not communicate through the Internet to its originator about its usage. Now IoT enables to transmit data on which parts of the teeth are brushed and with what intensity; with the help of these data new services can be provided to help end users to improve their teeth brushing.

2   Better insights support better cost control. The combination of monitoring data and remote-control capabilities creates new opportunities for optimization. Algorithms can improve product performance, utilization, and uptime, and improve how products work with related products in broader systems, such as for example in smart buildings. Elevator manufacturer Kone is using these capabilities and insights to optimize elevator usage and lower maintenance cost.

3   Revenue is expected to increase because the physical product is no longer the key deliverable for the end customer. The added value is brought by the services in which the physical product is embedded, fostering a continuous relation.

4   An IoT-enabled manufacturing environment will improve responsiveness of the supply chain and time to market. With the capability to receive real-time data from the supply chain devices, about operations, production, quality, utilization, and consumption, the business is able to streamline and refine its business processes and thus improve its time to market.

IBM's Institute of Business Value carried out several benchmark studies [4] to measure the success of IoT. The 2018 benchmark study shows that leading organizations tend to adopt IoT for improved customer insight. The study shows these companies tend to have a higher revenue growth, higher profit, and a better market perception (Figure 19.2).

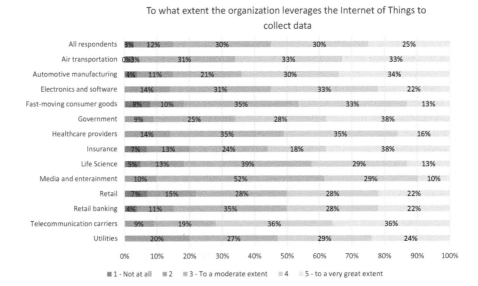

Figure 19.2   Source: "2018 marketing performance benchmarking study – marketing KPIs" IBV, 2018, https://w3.ibm.com/services/lighthouse/documents/108220

19.5 The roadmap for IoT

Because of the perceived opportunities, many organizations plan to start with IoT. Based on its design thinking and agile approach, IBM developed several methodologies that support companies in the selection and execution of IoT projects that promise a high added value, while mitigating the risks associated with large investments. If necessary these methodologies also help organizations to go back on earlier decisions, and thus avoid wasting resources. These roadmaps guide organizations through the steps of first prudently touching the water, and then moving forward, step by step, toward full implementation (Figure 19.3).

These methods are based on a standard four-stage procedure that goes from:

(a) Discover the value by identifying use cases and make a selection, to
(b) Prove the value where companies create a proof of concept, and
(c) Implement the value while testing the proof of concept in a production environment, which eventually (d) provides a go or no go decision.

Each step is strongly focused on the end-user customer experience and builds around the design thinking methodology.

Besides that the product is tested, the organization learns from the experience. It needs to re-assess its current processes and adjust the business model to support the IoT software development and releases into the market.

An important pitfall is that ideas are being pushed forward without proper end-user research, or when design thinking workshops have been executed without the involvement of the sponsor user (end user) or key team members. It is difficult for companies to accept to invest a little and then have to conclude that the idea will not bring enough value and hence the project has to stop. Failing fast or better learn fast is something not many companies adopt in their business operations, accepting that a wrong decision has been taken is not part of their culture.

The IoT Roadmap from Discovery to Implementation

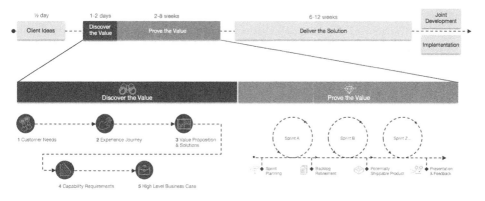

Figure 19.3   Source: Watson IoT Roadmap Lab Electronics – Marcel Baron

19.6 The IT and business perspective on implementing and managing IoT

Those companies that enable their devices with IoT capabilities have to manage many IoT devices. The expectation is that the number of IoT devices will grow at an incredible rate. As a consequence, what environment to choose that grabs the data from those IoT devices, puts the data somewhere, and processes them is a difficult decision in many respects. It is complicated to decide which environment to use, what would be the best technology to resolve the problem, and how long that technology will be developed and enhanced before the next wave will make it obsolete and not used anymore. The question arises to either create an infrastructure or make use of a platform. The difference between an OiT Infrastructure and an IoT platform is substantial. The former exposes its infrastructure components to the applications, the latter provides ways to abstract and normalize the technologies so that the applications will not have to be refactored when the world behind it changes and improves. As an example, take the smart parking lot sensors where at a particular moment the sensors break and need to be replaced. The problem arises that the same sensor devices with similar specs are no longer available. If in that case a company decided to create its infrastructure, it will have to rewrite the complete parking application to manage the new sensors devices type. With a platform, for each physical device one creates a logical device type with the same specs as a physical device. With that, all different sensors can be managed without changing the application as each device type is providing similar inputs for the application.

In, IoT platform for parking sensor and sensor tag devices shows the difference between an OiT Infrastructure and an IoT platform. The infrastructure processes flows of data, whereas the platform shapes and abstracts the environment to coherently transform flows of data into modeled information for the applications by using a declarative approach decoupled from the application itself.

The base components for an OiT Infrastructure contain the IoT sensors and devices, the storage and compute environment to collect all data, to facilitate communication, and to ensure connectivity. On top of that, we have IoT platforms and IoT applications. To make sure that the quality of data meets the country-specific data restrictions, a security layer is covering all parts of the OiT Infrastructure zones.

19.7 IBM Watson IoT [5]

The IBM Watson IoT business unit is explicitly focused on integrating IBM's security, Cloud, analytics, cognitive, and industry expertise to drive leadership in the IoT market. Based on the Watson IoT Platform, IBM is currently helping customers transform in three discrete areas:

1   improving operational performance and lowering costs,
2   creating new products and business models,
3   driving engagement and customer experience.

IBM's IoT platform is called Watson IoT Platform. The core Watson IoT Platform capabilities can be organized into four areas:

1   **Connectivity**: Secure connectivity, device management, and visualization;
2   **Risk management**: Proactive protection, security analytics, and anomaly detection;

3 **Information management**: Storage, data transformation/integration/augmentation, and weather;

4 **Analytics**: Predictive, cognitive (ML, NLP, video/image analytics, and text analytics), real time, and edge.

IBM's Watson IoT does include various capabilities within each of these areas; however, some capabilities, such as machine learning and security analytics, are add-on products. IBM offers a gateway SDK that can be pre-embedded into hardware for edge capabilities. IBM has also integrated Blockchain and payment processing capabilities (via a partnership with Visa) into the platform.

19.8 The case of a global appliance manufacturer and the use of Watson IoT

The company in this example is one of the world's leading appliance manufacturers. It is active in more than 170 countries worldwide; it produces and sells laundry appliances, refrigerators and freezers, cooking appliances, dishwashers, and compressors. Because the manufacturer sells its appliances through retail outlets and delegates its repair service to third-party contractors, it has little direct connection to its customers, unless they call the contact center for repairs. Further, the lack of customer relationship results in customer service representatives often spending valuable time ascertaining the customer's identity, appliance type, and model before they could address the repair issue. The appliance giant knew that its machines could provide the needed information through their embedded sensors and internal diagnostics, but it had no practical way to capture or gain insight from this data. In order to improve its service provisioning, reduce repair costs, and improve the design of appliances, the company wanted to engage with its customers more directly. For electronics companies, it is now possible to connect their appliances to the Watson IoT to create and support new relationships with their customers. The appliance company in this example plans to use a Cloud-based preventive maintenance and analytics solution. It captures and analyzes real-time appliance data that provide diagnostic information to call center agents and repair technicians, thus speeding repairs and reducing service-call costs. Using insights from data-driven customer-use analysis enables the company's research and development (R&D) and engineering departments to enhance and improve product design and quality. For example, if customers find machine feature choices overwhelming and only use 5 of 20 options, the company may choose to design simpler models or to only include the more complex options on higher-end machines. Analytical insight can also help the company spot product or component defects faster, sometimes even before shipping, helping to avoid costly repairs or recalls. By putting the analytics in the Cloud, the electronics company can quickly scale the solution to include more models and multiple appliance lines making use of Watson IoT [6].

19.9 The digital twin

Product development is a rapidly growing area in the use of IoT technologies. The digital twin is a virtual model of a product, process, physical asset, or service. It serves as a bridge between the physical and digital world. Via the IoT platform, this pairing of the physical and virtual world brings physical operational/performance data into the virtual digital twin simulation model. These data provide information on how a product is performing compared to its design intent, and closes the loop from the operations group back to the design group.

Without this closed-loop product simulation models used in design lack any knowledge of the physical product. With this closed loop, a product simulation model (part of its digital twin) allows analysis of real time product data and monitoring of product assets to improve product design and prevent development problems before they can even occur. It prevents development delays and downtime, exposes new opportunities, and even supports planning for the future.

Ultimately, the digital twin accelerates the product development timeline at reduced costs. As the digital counterpart of a physical product, the digital twin allows product developers to create, test, build, monitor, maintain, and service products in a virtual environment. In short, the digital twin empowers organizations to shift to an operations-centric view, where proactive and predictive maintenance enables front-line personnel to keep product development humming and to act before costly delays or failures occur.

19.9.1 Port of Rotterdam using a digital twin to become the smartest port in the world

Like in the automotive industry where IoT enables the driverless car, in the shipping industry, the connected ships through IoT operate autonomously and communicate with each other, thus avoiding the risk of a collision. The port of Rotterdam wants to support this capability by 2025 [8].

19.9.2 The digital twin port to test out scenarios

In order to build this digital twin capability, the port of Rotterdam actively enhances the entire 42-kilometer port area, from the City of Rotterdam all the way into the North Sea, with IoT technologies. With IoT the port will create a digital twin of the port—an exact digital replica of the operations that will mirror all resources at the port of Rotterdam, tracking ship movements, infrastructure, weather, geographical and water depth data with 100% accuracy. This part of the digitization initiative will help to test out scenarios and better understand how to improve efficiencies across operations while maintaining strict safety standards. With more than 140,000 ships processed every year, coordinating the berthing of each vessel is a complex task that involves multiple parties that need to cooperate safely and securely. This activity can take many hours. With a new digital dashboard, the port management can view the operations of all parties at the same time and increase volume and efficiency of shipped goods that pass through the port. Shipping companies and the port stand for saving up to one hour in berthing time, which can amount to about $80,000 dollars in savings for ship operators and enables the port to dock more ships each day.

19.9.3 Predicting capability using water and weather conditions

With the use of IoT sensors, Artificial Intelligence (AI), and weather data, the port can measure things like the availability of berths and other vital statistics. For example, specific water (hydro) and weather data will allow shipping companies to predict the best time to enter the port of Rotterdam by identifying the most favorable conditions. Having access to data about air temperature, wind speed, (relative) humidity, turbidity and salinity of the water plus water flow and levels, tides and currents enables the port to better predict visibility on a given day, thus helping to calculate clearance heights for ships. Additionally, by predicting water conditions, wind direction, and speed, the port will be able to determine how smooth a ship's entry into port is likely to be. Such data will also have a significant positive economic impact on shipping costs. Calm water and weather conditions allow for lower fuel consumption rates, facilitate cost-effective per-ship payloads, and help ensure the safe arrival of cargo [10].

19.10 IoT safety, privacy, and GDPR

Its simplicity, its ubiquitous nature, and its ability to digitalize the physical world is the beauty of IoT. However, the examples of the appliance manufacturer and digital twin show that it is also inevitable that IoT sensors are exposed to harsh conditions as they are embedded in a plethora of devices and locations. Connecting objects like cars, homes, ships, and machines exposes a lot of (privacy) sensitive data, such as the location of people in a building or medical records of patients. This data must be protected in accordance with the key information security principles, the CIA triad: *confidentiality*, *integrity*, and *availability*, and in the EU the General Data Protection Regulation (GDPR).

In contrast to a regular IT environment, IoT assets are not designed to incorporate security measures. It is imperative however that if natural elements or human intervention compromise a device, the compromise is prevented or detected as quickly as if it occurred inside a controlled environment. The variety of IoT devices and their use also present a larger surface to protect. Possible attacks include obtaining private or confidential data, manipulating or controlling devices, or confusing or denying service to applications that use and supply data within IoT systems. There is always a need to balance the level of security, the usability and value of the solution, and the potential risk or damage to the organization in the event of an incident.

Taking all of this into consideration, a simplified approach can be taken by focusing on three essential elements:

1   **Device and data protection:** Begin by securing the devices and data from the context within which they have been deployed. Ensuring secure connectivity to IoT platforms, payload encryption, device identity using certificates, and segregation and encryption of data in transit and at rest.

2   **Proactive threat intelligence:** Leverage tooling to visualize and prioritize threats aiding security and operations experts to focus their attention on the real-time issues. Have, where appropriate, automated responses to provide proactive protection while not impacting business operations.

3   **Artificial Intelligent risk management:** To proactively deal with threats as they adapt in the future, the use of artificial intelligence as a critical asset in the IoT security tool-kit is instrumental, to be able to learn from the security intelligence gathered within the IoT landscape, and to provide better insights. In sheer numbers alone, it will not be possible to rely on human response to deal with situations experienced by the plethora of connected devices deployed for IoT solutions. The vast number of devices demands that systems detect and respond to situations observed and is an area where we expect cognitive computing to assist in handling the complexity and scale of the challenge.

These elements should be considered as a journey requiring consistent attention and multiple iterations through a continuous lifecycle/delivery approach.

IoT Cloud operators can offer the above services but there is an area of difference between them. The GDPR (General Data Protection Regulation) in Europe ensures no connection is allowed between the person and the data generated unless this is a legal requirement like financial transaction data. There are IoT Cloud services that provide analytical services but it is important that all provided sources and the outcome of the analytics stay with the owner of the data provider [9].

19.11 References—use cases

Electra Group (http://www.electra.co.il/en/), Israel's leading manufacturer and distributor of consumer goods, is collaborating with IBM to create smart air conditioning solutions, which incorporate Watson IoT technology. IBM Watson IoT enables Electra's customers to connect to their air conditioning units and control them when at home or remotely, via a bespoke mobile app that was created and is maintained by IBM. Additionally, Watson IoT technology enables Electra to perform maintenance checks on its smart air conditioning solutions to both detect defects and predict potential malfunctions, which results in time savings and cost efficiencies for the consumer goods manufacturer.

Sole Co-operativa (http://www.solecooperativa.com/), an Italian elderly care provider and provider of assisted living facilities, has implemented IBM Watson IoT at Oasi Serena, its residence in Rimini, Emilia-Romagna on Italy's Adriatic Coast. In a pilot project, a variety of ambient and wearable sensors that detect the motion, location, and more of each resident have been installed throughout the facility, collecting and analyzing data that is turned into insights which are used to alert nursing staff in real time when residents' daily activity deviates from the norm. This way, nurses can easily prioritize visits to residents who are in urgent need of assistance, day and night. The IoT-based solution has already increased operational efficiencies by 15–20%, with caregivers increasingly more able to focus on core tasks. Besides, these new data insights enable Sole Co-operativa to reduce risk factors and improve personalized patients' assistance.

19.12 The world of IoT in ten years

We continue to progress in a world where all devices are instrumented with sensors. The connectivity between all these devices needs to be resolved with the ability to have cheap connections between the IoT devices but also with an infrastructure that transports the petabytes of data all these devices generate. The IoT platforms will be improved with enhanced services to manage all of these devices and ensure easy software updates for all of these devices are offered. The real value of IoT comes when insights and concrete actions are generated through Artificial Intelligence. New business models and ecosystems will arise with more intelligent industry-specific solutions like transport, health or segment specific personal, home, car, ships, planes, and factories. Possibly current emerging technologies like augmented reality and blockchain will be incorporated to enhance solutions. To come to real-time insights, connectivity and computing power is needed to improve and solve our day-to-day struggles like traffic jams. The quantum computing capabilities will resolve the processing power needed in the future world of IoT.

Note

1 Marcel Baron is a senior managing consultant at IBM Global Services and part of the Global Electronics Center of Competence. He is an expert in digital transformations regarding marketing and sales and new technologies.

References

1. The Little-Known Story of the First IoT Device, IBM Industrious on Medium, IBM Blog Jordan Teicher.
2. Worldwide Spending on IoT, Michael Shirer, Marcus Torchia, IDC IoT Forecast, 2017.
3. Worldwide IoT Platforms, Stacy Crook, Carrie MacGillivray, Vernon Turner, IDC MarketScape, 2017.
4. Institute of Business Value: Marketing Performance Benchmarking Study – Marketing KPIs, 2018.
5. Institute of Business Value: Correlation between IoT Adoption and Performance on KPIs, 2017.
6. Institute of Business Value: Who's Leading the Cognitive Pack in Digital Operations: Progress, Priorities and Profits, 2017.
7. Institute of Business Value: Why Cognitive Manufacturing Matters in Electronics: Activating the Next Generation of Production, 2017.
8. www.ibm.com/iot.
9. https://www.ibm.com/blogs/internet-of-things/iot-reshaping-electronics-industry/.
10. How leaders effectively building applications and services to succeed with the Internet of Things, Jim Rapoza, Aberdeen group, 2017.

INDEX

Note: **Bold** page numbers refer to tables and *italic* page numbers refer to figures.

For Product Safety Concerns and Information please contact our EU
representative GPSR@taylorandfrancis.com Taylor & Francis Verlag GmbH,
Kaufingerstraße 24, 80331 München, Germany

Printed and bound by CPI Group (UK) Ltd, Croydon, CR0 4YY
08/05/2025
01864511-0008